# GENEALOGICAL GLEANINGS FROM NEW YORK FRATERNAL ORGANIZATIONS

Volume 2

Sherida K. Eddlemon

HERITAGE BOOKS
2006

**HERITAGE BOOKS**
*AN IMPRINT OF HERITAGE BOOKS, INC.*

Books, CDs, and more—Worldwide

For our listing of thousands of titles see our website
at
www.HeritageBooks.com

Published 2006 by
HERITAGE BOOKS, INC.
Publishing Division
65 East Main Street
Westminster, Maryland 21157-5026

Copyright © 2005 Sherida K. Eddlemon

All rights reserved. No part of this book may be reproduced or transmitted in any form or by any means, electronic or mechanical, including photocopying, recording or by any information storage and retrieval system without written permission from the author, except for the inclusion of brief quotations in a review.

International Standard Book Number: 978-0-7884-3591-4

# PREFACE

Our ancestors joined many different fraternal organizations for a number of reasons such as social, service, trade or political. These organizations have been around for a long time, but they are private societies. One of the most well-known fraternal societies is the Freemasons. They have been active in our country from the colonial days.

Many of the records have not survived through the years. However those records that have survived are genealogical gems because they put an ancestor in an area at a particular point in time. They help to fill in the gaps left by missing census, burned records, etc. In later times, female companion organizations developed expanding the scope of individual information. A man belonging to a Lodge of Free Masons might have a wife joining the Order of the Eastern Star.

These are some interesting 1875 masonic decisions made by the Grand Lodge mentioned in the 1875 Masonic Directory and Almanac.

*"Thus by the five points of fellowship are we linked together in one indivisible chain of sincere affection, brotherly love, relief and truth. June, A. L., 5811."* *"Color is not one of the qualifications of a candidate, and each member of the Lodge has the right, and it is his duty, to vote upon every candidate of whatever color as in his conscience he may decide to be in the interest of his Lodge and of the Fraternity."*

*"It is the duty of a Masonic Lodge to defray the funeral expenses of one of its own members buried by another Lodge."*

*"A lodge of Masons, as such, should never attend a funeral unless they are permitted to perform the Masonic burial ceremonies."*

*"To hold membership in a lodge it is not necessary to be a resident in its jurisdiction."*

*"It is not proper to confer the degrees on one having a club foot. A candidate who has lost the first joint of his right thumb is not physically qualified to receive the degrees.*

*A petitioner who has lost one eye, but is otherwise perfect in his physical qualifications, is not thereby disqualified for the degrees of Masonry. An applicant who has a stiff knee which he can not place in the form of a square is, by such physical defect, disqualified for the degrees of Masonry."*

*"The candidate should not be rejected because he is Roman Catholic. He should be informed that the policy of his church is hostile to Masonry and that he would not be permitted to divulge Masonic secrets in the confessional."*

*"The loss of over one-half of the second joint of the index finger of the right hand, amounts to physical disqualification."*

*"A Lodge can not rely upon evidence given in court against a member, such testimony is not positive evidence of guilt."*

Good luck on your family research and hopefully your ancestor is within these pages.

## ABBREVIATIONS

| | |
|---|---|
| B | Born |
| D | Died |
| PRTS | Parents |
| MD | Marriage Date |
| CO | County |
| CMTS | Comments |
| C | Cemetery |
| ID | Issue Date |
| BP | Birth Place |
| DP | Place of Death |
| IDM | Issue date of Marriage License |
| RDM | Return date of Marriage License |
| CH | Children |
| MIL | Military Information |
| PMD | Place of Marriage |
| Race | Race |
| RES | Resident |
| F | Fraternal Order |
| CEN | Census |
| OC | Occupation |
| AKA | Also Known As |
| WPRTS | Wife's Parents |
| SIB | Siblings |

## MASONIC CALENDAR

The Masonic Rites have their own form of the calendar. When examining some older Masonic documents, these dates may appear. These dates are not used in this volume. However, I felt other genealogists might find this dating system of value. The 1875 Masonic Directory and Almanac contain a concise explanation of the different forms used.

*"Masons in all parts of the world working in the York or English Rites and in the French Rites, add 4,000 years to the Christian era, calling it Ann Lucis, which they abbreviate A.L. signifying In the Year of Light. Thus: A.D. 1874, would be A.L. 5874.*

*It is a practice with Masons of the Ancient and Accepted Scottish Rite, which adds 3,700 years to the Christian era, (the year beginning on the –th of September,) calling it Anno Muni, or A.M., Year of the World. Thus A.D. 1874 would be A.M. 5634.*

*Royal Arch Masons date from the year in which Zerubbabel began the second temple, 530 years before Christ, and style it Anno Inventionis, A.L. or A. Inv., In the Year of Discovery. Thus A.D. 1874 would be A. Inv. 2404.*

*The Royal and Select Masters, date from the completion of the first temple, styling it Anno Depositionis, A. Dep., In the Year of the Deposit. Thus A.D., 1874 would be A. Dep., 2874.*

*The Knight Templar date from the origin of the order in 1118, and style it Anno Ordinis, The Year of the Order. Thus A. D. 1874 would be A.O. 756."*

Aaron, Jesse M.: (F) Member Society of American Magicians,
   Apr., 1931, New York, (RES) New York City
Aaronson, Harry E.: (F) Member Arcana Lodge, No. 246,
   F. & A. M., 1934, New York, NY, (JD) May 7, 1923
Abbey, William N.: (F) Member Lowville Chapter No. 223, R. A. M.,
   1929, Lowville, NY, (CO) Lewis, (JD) Jan. 2, 1894, (AKA)
   William Nelson Abbey, (B) Mar. 21, 1854, (BP) Greig, Lewis Co.,
   NY, (MD) Feb. 26, 1881, (PMD) Port Leyden, NY, (PRTS)
   Rockwell Manning Abbey, (b. Sep. 26, 1815, bp. VT, d. Oct. 10,
   1891) and Elmira Smith, (b. Aug. 18, 1825), (Spouse) Ella Burley,
   (b. Sep. 15, 1862, bp. DeKalb NY), (CH) May Emogene, (CMTS)
   Parents of Elmira Smith are Elijah Smith and Calista Delano. Ella
   Burkley's parents are David Burkley and Margaret Gadis, (CEN)
   Greig, Lewis Co., NY, Rockwell Abbey, 65, VT, Saw and Grist
   Milling, Elmira, 55, George, 20, Frederick, 17, Hattie L., 15, (SIB)
   Rockwell Edward Manning, b. Apr. 17, 1857, md. Aug. 6, 1881,
   Spouse: Lizzie McMillan
Abbot, Rev. Lyman: (F) Member The Plymouth League, 1888, Brooklyn,
   (I ) *"Brooklyn Eagle,"* Dec. 12, 1888. Article regarding Societies
   aiding churches., (CMTS) Helping Plymouth Church, President,
   (CEN) 1880 Cornwell, Orange Co., NY, Lyman, 45, MA,
   Minister, Abbie F., 42, ME, Harriet F., 19, IN, Ernest, 10, NY,
   Theodore, 7, NY, Beatrice V., 5, NY
Abbott, George B.: (F) Member Sons of New England, New England
   Society of the City of Brooklyn, 1890, (CMTS) *"Brooklyn Eagle,"*
   Dec. 21, 1890, 11th Annual Dinner, Attendees, (CEN) 1880,
   Brooklyn, Kings Co., NY, Listed with Benj. F. Abbott, 58, Pres.
   Man. Co., Diancy P., 61, George B. 30, Lawyer, Eva T., 28
Abbott, Miss Alice D.: (F) Member The Young Women's Guild, 1888,
   Brooklyn, (I) *"Brooklyn Eagle,"* Dec. 12, 1888. Article regarding
   Societies aiding churches, (CMTS) Helping Plymouth Church,
   Treasurer, (AKA) Alice Dane Abbot, (B) Oct. 12, 1861, (PRTS)
   Benjamin V. Abbott and Elizabeth Titcomb
Abbott, Mrs. Lyman: (F) Member The Young Women's Guild, 1888,
   Brooklyn, (I) *"Brooklyn Eagle,"* Dec. 12, 1888. Article regarding
   Societies aiding churches., (CMTS) Helping Plymouth Church,
   President, (AKA) Abbie F. Abbott, (CEN) 1880, Cornwall,
   Orange Co., NY, Lyman, 45, MA, Minister, Abbie F., 42, Harriet,
   F., 19, IN, Ernest, 10, Theodore, 7, Beatrice V., 5.
Abrams, Myers: (F) Member Washington Lodge, No. 85, 1900, Albany,
   NY
Abramson, Saml.: (F) Member Arcana Lodge, No. 246, F. & A. M., 1934,
   New York, NY, (JD) Oct. 13, 1925
Acker, Conrad: (F) Member Grand Council of the Princes of Jerusalem,
   1882, Albany, NY, (OC) Currier, (RES) Albany, 1889, 1890,
   1891, (CMTS) Albany City Directory, 1889, 1890, 1891

Acker, Conrad: (F) Member Ineffable and Sublime Grand Lodge of
 Perfection, 1882, Albany, NY, (OC) Currier, (RES) Albany, 1889,
 1890, 1891, (CMTS) Albany City Directory, 1889, 1890, 1891,
 (CEN) 10thWard, Albany, Albany Co., NY, 47, Ger, Currier,
 Margaret, 40, Ire, Cattie, 16, Maggie, 15, Cora, 11, Lillie, 9,
 Jacob C., 3
Acker, John J.: (F) Member Temple Lodge, No. 14, 1900, Albany, NY,
 (CMTS) Life Member, (CEN) 1880 16th Ward, Albany, Albany
 Co., NY, 41, Lawyer, NY, Maggie, 31, Grace, 11, Ettie, 8, Jay, 6,
 Cora, 4, Avery, 1
Ackerman, Alfred H.: (F) Member Temple Lodge, No. 14, 1900, Albany,
 NY, (CEN) 1880 13th Ward, Albany, Albany Co., NY, 40,
 Hardware, Mary, 36, Elfride, 2, (B) Jan. 10, 1838, (PRTS) Gasret
 Ackerman
Ackerman, Jno. A. V.: (F) Member Arcana Lodge, No. 246, F. & A. M.,
 1934, New York, NY, (JD) Dec. 18, 1912
Acri, Anthony: (OBIT) *"Journal News,"* Anthony Acri, a lifelong resident
 of Mount Vernon, died on February 28, 2004 at the Dumont
 Masonic Home. He was 79. Anthony was born in Mount Vernon to
 Francisco and Louise Acri on January 13, 1925. He served our
 country in the United States Army from 1946-1947 and the New
 York National Guard from 1948-1954. He also served as Captain
 of the Mount Vernon Volunteer Fire Department, Engine 4, for
 many years. Anthony was employed by the City of Mount Vernon
 Department of Public Works for 35 years. He loved to watch
 wrestling and go fishing. He is survived by his wife of 52 years,
 Sylvia Acri; his son, Charles Acri and daughter, Frances DeFreitas
 and her husband D. Nick DeFreitas of White Plains as well as two
 grandsons, Anthony and Joseph DeFreitas. He also leaves behind
 his sisters, Florence (Jerry) Gagliardi and Alice Shaughnessey;
 sisters-in-law Irene Acri and Ann Acri; sister-in-law Laura Amadio
 and brother-in-law Louis Amadio. Anthony was the devoted uncle
 to many nephews and nieces. His brothers, John, Nicholas, Frank,
 Louis and Charles Acri and sister, Gloria Virrill died earlier.
 Friends may visit the funeral home on Monday evening from 7-
 9pm and Tuesday from 2-4 and 7-9pm. The Mass of Christian
 Burial will be held Wednesday 10am at Our Lady of Victory
 Church. Interment Holy Sepulchre Cemetery in New Rochelle.
Adams, Elmer J.: (F) Member Lowville Lodge No. 134, F. & A. M., 1929,
 Lowville, NY, (CO) Lewis, (JD) May 14, 1886
Adams, Ernest A.: (F) Member Lowville Lodge No. 134, F. & A. M.,
 1929, Lowville, NY, (CO) Lewis, (JD) Feb. 10, 1899, (CEN) 1880
 Lowville, Lewis Co., NY listed with Wm. R. Argens, 37, Ireland,
 Farmer, Emma, 24, wife, NY, Earnest A., 12, NY
Adams, George J.: (F) Member Mount Vernon Lodge, No. 3, 1900,
 Albany, NY

Adams, J. P.: (F) Member Sons of New England, New England Society of the City of Brooklyn, 1887, (CMTS) *"Brooklyn Eagle,"* Dec. 22, 1887, Annual Dinner, Attendees

Adams, John P.: (F) Member Sons of New England, New England Society of the City of Brooklyn, 1890, (CMTS) *"Brooklyn Eagle,"* Dec. 21, 1890, 11th Annual Dinner, Attendees

Adams, Joseph L.: (F) Member Arcana Lodge, No. 246, F. & A. M., 1934, New York, NY, (JD) Mar. 7, 1921

Adams, Michael T.: (F) Member Mount Vernon Lodge, No. 3, 1900, Albany, NY

Adams, William: (F) Member Sons of New England, New England Society of the City of Brooklyn, 1890, (CMTS) *"Brooklyn Eagle,"* Dec. 21, 1890, 11th Annual Dinner, Attendees, (CEN) 1880, Brooklyn, Kings Co., NY, 39, Publisher, Martha Adams, Mother, 64

Adams, William: (F) Member Brooklyn Revenue Reform Club, 1886, (I) *"Brooklyn Eagle,"* Jan. ,27 1886, Attendees at a dinner

Adams, Jr., Sandford: "(OBIT) ""Roman Citzen,"" Rome, Oneida Co., NY, June 13, 1884. By the death of Sanford Adams, Sr., which occurred Thursday evening of last week, (June 5, 1884) Rome loses one of her oldest and most respected citizens. He was in his 78th year, and for the past 49 years he had been in active business in this city. He was born in Litchfield, Herkimer Co., November 7, 1806. At the age of 18 years he began life for himself, learning the trade of machinist. Up to 1835 he worked at his trade in different places in this State and Canada. In July of that year Mr. Adams and Eri Seymour, also now deceased, came to this city from Utica and bought the small foundry and machine shop of Josiah Wood, then located on Dominick street, between George and Madison. In the Spring of 1851 they erected the large foundry and machine shop now standing at the corner of George street and the Erie Canal. On the death of Mr. Seymour in 1860, Mr. Adams assumed the entire business and took his son, Sanford Adams, Jr., in as partner, and from that time to the present the firm has been known far and wide as S. Adams & Son. For the last few years he has ceased to take active part in the business of the foundry, his increasing years and delicate health not permitting it. In early life he was a Whig in politics, and afterwards a staunch Republican. When Rome was a village he was one of its prominent officers. In 1848 he was elected County Treasurer, the late E. B. Armstrong being his opponent. Mr. Adams was a man greatly esteemed by all whoever had business or social relations with him. He was twice married, and his second wife still survives him, as do also two sons by his first wife, Sanford Adams, Jr., of Rome, and Willard Adams of Tuscadora, Nevada, and one by his second wife, Henry V. Adams, of this city. The funeral was largely attended from his late residence, Monday, at 2pm. The services were conducted with Masonic ceremonies, deceased having been a member of that order. Rev. Dr. Egar, of Zion Church, was the officiating clergyman. The pallbearers were Messrs. Jerome Graves, W.W. Williams, S. Millington, William H. Davies and John Groves of Rome, and Frank Vane of Oneida. The remains were interred in the Rome Cemetery. "

Addington, George: (F) Member Temple Lodge, No. 14, 1900, Albany, NY

Adler, Abram: (F) Member Arcana Lodge, No. 246, F. & A. M., 1934, New York, NY, (JD) Oct. 13, 1925

Adler, Daniel: (F) Member Washington Lodge, No. 85, 1900, Albany, NY

Adler, Louis: (F) Member Arcana Lodge, No. 246, F. & A. M., 1934, New York, NY, (JD) Nov. 18, 1918

Adler, Milton D.: (F) Member Society of American Magicians, Apr., 1931, New York, (RES) New York City

Adler, Oscar: (F) Member Arcana Lodge, No. 246, F. & A. M., 1934, New York, NY, (JD) Nov. 10, 1931

Agens, Ernest A.: (F) Member Lowville Lodge No. 134, F. & A. M., 1929, Lowville, NY, (CO) Lewis, (JD) Dec. 3, 1901

Ager, Jr., C. Leonard J.: (F) Member Lowville Chapter No. 223, R. A. M., 1929, Lowville, NY, (CO) Lewis, (JD) May 8, 1923

Aibel, Frederic L.: (OBIT) "Journal News'" Sunday, Jun. 13, 2004. Fredric L. Aibel, longtime Briarcliff Manor resident, died June 10, 2004 in Wellington, FL, at the age of 90. Mr. Aibel was born June 14, 1913 in Brooklyn, NY to Hyman and Minnie Aibel. He was graduated from Brooklyn College with a Bachelors degree in Chemistry. A member of Fraternity-Dunderberg Lodge, Mr. Aibel served as District Deputy Grand Master for the Grand Lodge of Free and Accepted Masons of New York, giving lectures throughout the Masonic District. He was a member and president of the Congregation Sons of Israel in Briarcliff Manor. Mr. Aibel's hobby as a sculptor kept him occupied during retirement after selling his knitting plant in Poughkeepsie, NY. He also acquired patents for his inventions. In addition to his wife Harriet, Mr. Aibel is survived by a son Steven and his wife Bethof El Cerrito, CA; a daughter Robin and her husband Andrew Harding of Devon, England; three grandchildren Sonja, Jasmine and Raima and his sister Mary Kaufman. Funeral service Sunday, June 13, 2004, 2 pm from Hellman-Garlick Memorial Chapels, 1300 Pleasantville Road, Briarcliff Manor, NY\

Akin, Isaac W.: (F) Member Masters Lodge, No. 5, 1900, Albany, NY

Albee, Harley C.: (F) Member Society of American Magicians, Apr., 1931, New York, (RES) New York City, (CMTS) Life

Member

Albert, L.: (F) Member Herber Lodge, No. 698,1898, F. & A. M., New York, NY, Greenpoint area, (RES) New York City

Alden, John: (F) Member Sons of New England, New England Society of the City of Brooklyn, 1890, (CMTS)*"Brooklyn Eagle,"* Dec. 21, 1890, 11th Annual Dinner, Attendees

Alder, W. D.: (F) Member Long Island Lodge, No. 382, F. &. A. M. 1874, NY

Alderman, Morris: (F) Member Arcana Lodge, No. 246, F. & A. M., 1934, New York, NY, (JD) Mar. 9, 1926

Alexander, Edna: (F) Member Hope Rebekah Lodge No. 10, 1949-1950, Brockport, NY, (CO) Monroe, (CMTS) Sitting P. N. G.

Alexander, Philip G.: (F) Member Arcana Lodge, No. 246, F. & A. M., 1934, New York, NY, (JD) Apr. 3, 1916

Alger, George W.: (F) Member Lowville Lodge No. 134, F. & A. M., 1929, Lowville, NY, (CO) Lewis, (JD) Apr. 5, 1912, (CEN) 1880 Lowville, Lewis Co., NY 35, Cheesemaker, NY, Mary, 34, Herbert, 5, Leapha, 3, (PRTS) Leonard Alger

Allain, Clement B.: (F) Member Lowville Chapter No. 223, R. A. M., 1929, Lowville, NY, (CO) Lewis, (JD) Nov. 13, 1923

Allain, Clement B.: (F) Member Lowville Lodge No. 134, F. & A. M., 1929, Lowville, NY, (CO) Lewis, (JD) Jun. 28, 1921

Allaire, Mrs.: (F) Member Nativity Sewing Society, 1900, Brooklyn, (I) *"Brooklyn Eagle,"* Feb. 3, 1900. Article regarding raising money to buy clothing for the poor.

Allaire, Mrs. William A.: (F) Member Nativity Sewing Society, 1900, Brooklyn, (I) *"Brooklyn Eagle,"* Feb. 3, 1900. Article regarding raising money to buy clothing for the poor.

Allan, B. Myron: (F) Member Arcana Lodge, No. 246, F. & A. M., 1934, New York, NY, (JD) Mar. 26, 1929

Allan, Benjamin : (F) Member Washington Lodge, No. 85, 1900, Albany, NY

Allanson, James E.: (F) Member Mount Vernon Lodge, No. 3, 1900, Albany, NY, (CMTS) Past Master 1880, (CEN) 1880 15th Ward, Albany, Albany Co., NY. Listed with his mother, Jane Allsanson, 66, widow, James, 33, carpenter, Susie, wife, 27, Janes, 1

Allen, Clarence E.: (F) Member Lowville Chapter No. 223, R. A. M., 1929, Lowville, NY, (CO) Lewis, (JD) May 9, 1922, (CEN) 1880 New Bremen, Lewis CO., NY listed with Joel E. Allen, 36, Engineer, Emma V., 30, Waters, 11, son, Clarence E., 2

Allen, Clarence E.: (F) Member Lowville Lodge No. 134, F. & A. M., 1929, Lowville, NY, (CO) Lewis, (JD) Apr. 16, 1920, (CEN) 1880 New Bremen, Lewis CO., NY listed with Joel E. Allen, 36, Engineer, Emma V., 30, Waters, 11, son, Clarence E., 2

Allen, Clark B.: (F) Member Society of American Magicians, Apr., 1931, New York, (RES) New Brighton, L. I., NY

Allen, E. Stanton: (F) Member Lowville Lodge No. 134, F. & A. M., 1929, Lowville, NY, (CO) Lewis, (JD) Apr. 7, 1893

Allen, Franklin: (F) Member Sons of New England, New England Society of the City of Brooklyn, 1887, (CMTS) *"Brooklyn Eagle,"* Dec. 22, 1887, Annual Dinner, Attendees

Allen, Harold T.: (F) Member Lowville Chapter No. 223, R. A. M., 1929, Lowville, NY, (CO) Lewis, (JD) Jun. 7, 1921

Allen, Henry J.: (F) Member Lowville Lodge No. 134, F. & A. M., 1929, Lowville, NY, (CO) Lewis, (JD) Jun. 3, 1904

Allen, Sr., Harrison: (OBIT) "The River Reporter," Jan. 11, 2001.
Allen, Sr. of Monticello, a maintenance worker for the Apollo Mall, a lifelong musician with the Allen Brothers Band and a longtime area resident, died Saturday, December 30, 2000 at the Seelig Division of Community General Hospital in Harris. He was 57. Son of James P. Allen and the late Sally Jetson Allen, he was born May 5, 1943 in Fairhope, AL. He was a member of the Bethlehem Temple Church in Fairhope, AL until moving to Monticello. He was member of the Masonic Lodge. Survivors include his father of Monticello; his companion, Annie McCoy, at home; two sons, Harrison, Jr. and Terry Hooks, both of Monticello; two daughters, Jackie Allen Powell of Monticello and Cheryl Jackson of Los Angeles, CA; three brothers, Oswald and Cecil, both of Monticello and Elder Wyan of Boston, MA; three sisters, Virginia Smith, Annie Bolden and Leona, all of Monticello; nine grandchildren; nieces and nephews. Services were held at the Bethlehem Temple Church in Monticello. The Rev. Mervin Armstead officiated. Burial was in the Rock Ridge Cemetery in Monticello.

Allis, Frank C.: (F) Member Murray Lodge, No. 380, F. & A. M., 1906, Holley, Orleans, Co., NY

Allshesky, Theodore F.: (F) Member Mount Vernon Lodge, No. 3, 1900, Albany, NY, (CEN) 1880, 7th Ward, Albany, Albany Co., NY, 40, NY, Fur Dresser, Ellenor, 45, NJ, (PRTS) Theodore Alsheksy and Jane ????, (PRTSCEN) 1880, New York, Manhattan, 73, Poland, Fur Dresser, Jane, 65, Lida, daughter, 25.

Alpert, Max: (F) Member Arcana Lodge, No. 246, F. & A. M., 1934, New York, NY, (JD) May 7, 1917, (BP) Russia, (MD) Jun. 7, 1889, (Spouse) Mary Davidson, (PRTS) Henach Alpert and Sarah Zudelson

Alsdorf, John J.: (F) Member Temple Lodge, No. 14, 1900, Albany, NY

Alter, Mark: (F) Member Arcana Lodge, No. 246, F. & A. M., 1934, New York, NY, (JD) Nov. 21, 1904, Life Member, (MD) Mar. 16, 1897, (Spouse) Fannie Brockman, (PRTS) Saloman Alter and Elizabeth Silver

Alterman, Morris: (F) Member Arcana Lodge, No. 246,

F. & A. M., 1934, New York, NY, (JC) Apr. 2, 1923

Altman, Isadore I.: (F) Member Society of American Magicians, Apr., 1931, New York, (RES) New York City, (B) May 6, 1897, (D) Sep., 1965

Alyea, W.: (F) Member Long Island Lodge, No. 382, F. &. A. M. 1874, NY , (CEN) 1880 Census, Brooklyn, Kings Co., NY, Listed with Geo. F. Covert, 67, NY, Union Ferry Time Keeper, Cornelia Covert, 56, William Alyea, 37, Son-in-law, Cornelia, Alyea, 33, daughter, Nellie Alyea, 6, Howard Alyea, 2, Thomas Covert, 29, son

Ambler, Dr. J. G.: (F) Member Brooklyn Dental Society, 1877, Brooklyn, NY, (CMTS) *"Brooklyn Eagle,"* Dec. 15, 1877. Celebration of 10th Anniversary. Society established Dec. 14, 1867, (CMTS) Present from New York, (CEN) 1880, New Utrecht, Brooklyn, Kings Co., NY, John G. Ambler, dentist, 25, NY, Ella A., 33

Amelunxen, L. V.: (F) Member Herber Lodge, No. 698,1898, F. & A. M., New York, NY, Greenpoint area, (RES) New York City, (AKA) Louis Von Amelunxen, (BP) Germany, (PRTS) Theodore Amelunxen, (MD) Jul. 31, 1869, (Spouse) Louis Reitsch, (PMD) Manhattan

Ames, Judson: (F) Member Mount Vernon Lodge, No. 3, 1900, Albany, NY

Amsdell, Theodore M.: (F) Member Temple Lodge, No. 14, 1900, Albany, NY, (CMTS) Life Member, (CEN) 1880, $13^{th}$ Ward, Albany, Albany Co., NY 51, Brewer, Ellen, 44, Dora M., 11

Anable, Samuel: (F) Member Masters Lodge, No. 5, 1900, Albany, NY

Anderson, Harry C.: (F) Member Society of American Magicians, Apr., 1931, New York, (RES) Cleveland, OH

Anderson, J. D.: (F) Member Long Island Lodge, No. 382, F. &. A. M. 1874, NY

Anderson, Peter: (F) Member Long Island Lodge, No. 382, F. &. A. M. 1874, NY

Andrew, Walter M.: (F) Member Society of American Magicians, Apr., 1931, New York, (RES) New York City

Andrews, Elmer W.: (F) Member Lowville Lodge No. 134, F. & A. M., 1929, Lowville, NY, (CO) Lewis, (JD) Jun. 11, 1926

Andrews, J.: (F) Member Long Island Lodge, No. 382, F. &. A. M. 1874, NY

Angell, M. H.: (F) Member Sons of New England, New England Society of the City of Brooklyn, 1890, (CMTS)*"Brooklyn Eagle,"* Dec. 21, 1890, 11th Annual Dinner, Attendees

Angus, Charles H.: (F) Member Temple Lodge, No. 14, 1900, Albany, NY, (CEN) 1880, $16^{th}$ Ward, Albany, Albany Co., NY Listed With Charles Angus, 36, NY, Bookkeeper, Mary S., 33, Charles H., 12, William W., 10, Arthur G., 8, Edith, 6, Grace, 3, Marian

W., 1

Angus, George C.: (F) Member Temple Lodge, No. 14, 1900, Albany, NY, (CEN) 1880, 16th Ward, Albany, Albany Co., NY, Listed With John G. Angus, 63, Segar Maker, Maryann, 53, George C., 11

Anketell, W. T.: (F) Member Long Island Lodge, No. 382, F. &. A. M. 1874, NY, (AKA) William Thomas Anketell, (Spouse) Mary Ann Wills

Annable, Mrs. R. D.: (F) Member Ladies Social and Benvolent Circle, 1888, Brooklyn, (I) *"Brooklyn Eagle,"* Dec. 12, 1888. Article regarding Societies aiding churches., (CMTS) Helping St. John's Methodist Episcopal Church, Secretary

Anson, J.: (F) Member Long Island Lodge, No. 382, F. &. A. M. 1874, NY

Anthony, Horace C.: (F) Member Temple Lodge, No. 14, 1900, Albany, NY, (AKA) Horace Chase Anthony, (B) Mar. 12, 1847, (BP) Utica, Oneida Co., NY, (PRTS) Jacob Anthony

Appleby, G. H.: (F) Member Long Island Lodge, No. 382, F. &. A. M. 1874, NY

Appleton, Henry D.: (F) Member Masters Lodge, No. 5, 1900, Albany, NY

Appleton, Joseph L.: (F) Member Temple Lodge, No. 14, 1900, Albany, NY

Aramour, Miss Lizzie: (F) Member Mispah Circle, 1888, Brooklyn, (I) *"Brooklyn Eagle,"* Dec. 12, 1888. Mentioned in an article about a fair raising funds for a Home for the Blind

Archer, Foster O.: (F) Member Lowville Chapter No. 223, R. A. M., 1929, Lowville, NY, (CO) Lewis, (JD) Feb. 14, 1922, (B) Jul. 30, 1896, (D) Jul., 1982, (DP) Lewis Co.

Archer, Foster O.: (F) Member Lowville Lodge No. 134, F. & A. M., 1929, Lowville, NY, (CO) Lewis, (JD) Apr. 19, 1918, (CMTS) Past Master

Archer, John K.: (F) Member Lowville Lodge No. 134, F. & A. M., 1929, Lowville, NY, (CO) Lewis

Archer, Leonard D.: (F) Member Lowville Lodge No. 134, F. & A. M., 1929, Lowville, NY, (CO) Lewis, (JD) Jan. 18, 1929

Archer, Louis C.: (F) Member Lowville Lodge No. 134, F. & A. M., 1929, Lowville, NY, (CO) Lewis, (JD) Mar. 18, 1910

Armington, Anthony R.: (F) Member Temple Lodge, No. 14, 1900, Albany, NY

Armor, Dr. S. G.: (F) Member Brooklyn Dental Society, 1877, Brooklyn, NY, (CMTS) *"Brooklyn Eagle,"* Dec. 15, 1877. Celebration of 10th Anniversary. Society established Dec. 14, 1867, (CMTS) Present, From Long Island College Hospital

Armstage, Charles H.: (F) Member Temple Lodge, No. 14, 1900, Albany, NY

Armstrong, Mrs. C. : (F) Member Nativity Sewing Society, 1900, Brooklyn, (I) *"Brooklyn Eagle,"* Feb. 3, 1900. Article regarding raising money to buy clothing for the poor.

Arnold, Chas. H.: (F) Member Murray Lodge, No. 380, F. & A. M., 1906, Holley, Orleans, Co., NY

Arnold, Freeman S.: (F) Member Temple Lodge, No. 14, 1900, Albany, NY, (CEN) 1880 Watervliet, Albany Co., NY, 20, Bookkeeper, MA

Arnold, Hugh A.: (F) Member Masters Lodge, No. 5, 1900, Albany, NY, (CEN) 1880 5th Ward, Albany, Albany Co., NY Listed with Joseph Arnold, 53, Eng, S. Engine Mfg., Jane, 35, William, 12, Charles, 10, Hugh, 6, Lillian, 1

Arnold, J.N.: (F) Member Clyde Lodge No. 341, F. A. M., 1905, Clyde, NY, (CO) Wayne, (CMTS) Past Master 1876, 1877

Arnold, William D.: (F) Member Masters Lodge, No. 5, 1900, Albany, NY, (CEN) 1880 5th Ward, Albany, Albany Co., NY Listed with Joseph Arnold, 53, Eng, S. Engine Mfg., Jane, 35, William, 12, Charles, 10, Hugh, 6, Lillian, 1

Aronofsky, Samuel: (F) Member Arcana Lodge, No. 246, F. & A. M., 1934, New York, NY, (JD) Nov. 16, 1914

Arthur, Charles H.: (F) Member Lowville Chapter No. 223, R. A. M., 1929, Lowville, NY, (CO) Lewis, (JD) Apr, 17, 1923, (CMTS) Past Master

Arthur, Charles H.: (F) Member Lowville Lodge No. 134, F. & A. M., 1929, Lowville, NY, (CO) Lewis, (JD) Jul. 2, 1909, (B) Dec. 3, 1874, (D) Feb. 27, 1939, (DP) Syracuse, NY, (PRTS) Edwin B. Arthur and Alice M. Weller, (MD) Jan. 24, 1900, (Spouse) Ella Star

Arthur, Eddie A.: (F) Member Lowville Lodge No. 134, F. & A. M., 1929, Lowville, NY, (CO) Lewis, (JD) Jun. 1, 1908, (CEN) 1880 Lowville, Lewis Co., NY, 19, NY, Farmer, Emogene, 22, wife, Olive Carter, 19, Sister in Law, (B) Jul. 8, 1860, (BP) Martinsburg, Lewis Co., NY, (PRTS) Augustus Arthur, (b. May 8, 1816, d. Sep. 29, 1892, md. Mar. 22, 1837) and Catherine Searle, (b. Jun. 26, 1819, d. Feb. 11, 1879), (SIB) Augusta, Maurice H., Henry Clay, Helen A., Julia, William W., Florence N., C. B., Lacholine

Arthur, Eugene: (F) Member Lowville Lodge No. 134, F. & A. M., 1929, Lowville, NY, (CO) Lewis, (JD) Jan. 25, 1884, (B) Nov. 22, 1858, (BP) Glenfield, Lewis Co., (PRTS) Alfred Arthur and Louisa Slater, (Spouse) Flora Adams, (MD) Dec. 2, 1879, (CEM) 1880 Lowville, Lewis Co., NY, 21, Merchant, NY, Flora A., 21, NY, wife

Arthur, F. Wayland: (F) Member Lowville Lodge No. 134, F. & A. M., 1929, Lowville, NY, (CO) Lewis, (JD) May 31, 1918

Arthur, Leroy W.: (F) Member Lowville Chapter No. 223, R. A. M., 1929, Lowville, NY, (CO) Lewis, (JD) Apr. 1, 1913

Arthur, Leroy W.: (F) Member Lowville Lodge No. 134, F. & A. M.,
    1929, Lowville, NY, (CO) Lewis, (JD) Dec. 6, 1907
Ascher, Herman: (F) Member Arcana Lodge, No. 246, F. & A. M., 1934,
    New York, NY, (JD) Dec. 3, 1917
Askins, Luther B.: (F) Member Lowville Lodge No. 134, F. & A. M.,
    1929, Lowville, NY, (CO) Lewis, (JD) Mar. 2, 1923,
    (B) Mar. 31, 1887, (D) Feb., 1966, (RES) Beaver River, Dadville,
    Harrisburg, Lowville, Montague, New Breman, Waston, West
    Lowville, Lewis Co.
Aspinall, J. H.: (F) Member Anglo Saxon Lodge No. 137, F. A. M.,
    1887, (CMTS) Meeting Notes, *"Brooklyn Eagle,"* Mar. 23, 1887,
    Stood as guardian at the meeting, (CEN) 1880 Brooklyn, Kings
    Co., NY Listed with William Aspinall, 49, Car Driver, Eng,
    Carolina, 46, Joseph 26, Lawyer, William F., 23, clerk, Francis L.,
    23, clerk, daughter-in-law, Estel V., 1, grandaughter, Geo. Clark,
    46, Wool Sorter
Aspinall, Joseph: (F) Member Anglo Saxon Lodge No. 137, F. A. M.,
    1887, (CMTS) Meeting Notes, *"Brooklyn Eagle,"* Mar. 13, 1887,
    (Raised) Feb. 7, Acted as Senior Deacon at the Meeting, (CEN)
    1880 Brooklyn, Kings Co., NY Listed with William Aspinall, 49,
    Car Driver, Eng, Carolina, 46, Joseph 26, Lawyer, William F., 23,
    clerk, Francis L., 23, clerk, daughter-in-law, Estel V., 1,
    grandaughter, Geo. Clark, 46, Wool Sorter
Atken, Miss Margaret: (F) Member First District Suffolk, Adah Chapter.
    No. 52, 1923, Northport, NY, (CMTS) Associate Matron, (RES)
    Northport
Atkins, B. B.: (F) Member Murray Lodge, No. 380, F. & A. M., 1906,
    Holley, Orleans, Co., NY
Atkins , A. B.: (F) Member Sons of New England, New England Society
    of the City of Brooklyn, 1890, (CMTS)*"Brooklyn Eagle,"* Dec. 21,
    1890, 11th Annual Dinner, Attendees
Atkinson, Dr. William H.: (F) Member Brooklyn Dental Society, 1877,
    Brooklyn, NY, (CMTS) *"Brooklyn Eagle,"* Dec. 15, 1877.
    Celebration of 10th Anniversary. Society established Dec. 14,
    1867, (CMTS) Present from New York, Corresponding Secretary,
    Clinics Committee
Atwood, Clinton H.: (F) Member Lowville Lodge No. 134, F. & A. M.,
    1929, Lowville, NY, (CO) Lewis, (JD) May 21, 1920
Auer, Louis C.: (F) Member Washington Lodge, No. 85, 1900, Albany,
    NY, (CEN) 1880 5th Ward, Albany,Albany Co., NY Listed with
    brother, David Auer, 31, Dealer in Gets Goods, Bohemia, Martha,
    24, Blanche, 3, Florence May, 3mo, Louis, 26, Brother, Dealer in
    Gents goods
Austin, Arthur C.: (F) Member Temple Lodge, No. 14, 1900, Albany, NY
Austin, Charles: (F) Member Lowville Lodge No. 134, F. & A. M., 1929,

Lowville, NY, (CO) Lewis, (JD) Apr. 18, 1909, (B) May 28, 1850, (BP) Denmark, Lewis Co., NY, (D) Jan. 19, 1931, (PRTS) Hiram Austin and Betsey Doig, (Spouse) Sarah Ponto

Austin, William L.: (F) Member Masters Lodge, No. 5, 1900, Albany, NY, (CEN) 1880, 5$^{th}$ Ward, Albany, Albany Co., NY, Listed with Frederick Austin, 31, Wales, Musician, Johanna, 29, William, 11, Freddie, 8, Martin, 4, Ellen Hennessey, Mother-in-law, 51, Ire.

Axt, Adam: (F) Member Long Island Lodge, No. 382, F. & A. M. 1874, NY, (CEN) 1880, Newark, Essex Co., NJ, 44, Shoe Manufacturer, Hellen, 45, Emma, 17, George, 15, Edward, 13, Flora, 8, Frederick, 3, Mena, 1

Babbott, F. I.: (F) Member Sons of New England, New England Society of the City of Brooklyn, 1887, (CMTS) *"Brooklyn Eagle,"* Dec. 22, 1887, Annual Dinner, Attendees

Babbott, F. I.: (F) Member Sons of New England, New England Society of the City of Brooklyn, 1890, (CMTS) *"Brooklyn Eagle,"* Dec. 21, 1890, 11th Annual Dinner, Attendees

Babcock, Cordtland S.: (F) Member Temple Lodge, No. 14, 1900, Albany, NY

Babcock, D. S.: (F) Member Sons of New England, New England Society of the City of Brooklyn, 1890, (CMTS) *"Brooklyn Eagle,"* Dec. 21, 1890, 11th Annual Dinner, Attendees

Babcock, Daniel: (F) Member Denmark Ecclesiastical Society, Sep. 21, 1810, (CO) Lewis, (CMTS) Trustee

Babcock, William L.: (F) Member Lowville Lodge No. 134, F. & A. M., 1929, Lowville, NY, (CO) Lewis, (CMTS) Past Master 1866, 1867, 1869, 1870, Lowville Business Directory, 1867-1868, W. L. Babcock, (OC) Hardware, Stoves, Tinware

Babcock, William L.: (F) Member Lowville Lodge No. 134, F. & A. M., 1929, Lowville, NY, (CO) Lewis, (JD) May 3, 1895, (OC) Hop Raiser and Farmer, Lowville, Gazetteer and Business Directory, Lewis Co., NY 1872-1873

Babilot, Emily Grace: (OBIT) *"News Journal,"* Wednesday, Jun. 2, 2004.
Emily Grace Babilot, a former longtime Montrose resident, died Monday at Sky View Health Care Center. She was 95. Emily was a retired operator for NY Telephone in the Bronx. She was born on May 2, 1909 in Hoboken, NJ to John and Katherine Rettig Collins. Mrs. Babilot was the widow of Edward Babilot, who died in 1981. She was a parishioner of the Reformed Church of Cortlandtown, a member of the Cortlandt Sr. Citizens, and a former member of the Order of the Eastern Star and the NY Telephone Pioneers.
Survivors include her son, Edward Babilot of Paramus, NJ; a daughter, Audrey Carathanasis of Southport, NC; a brother Glen Collins of Dayton, OH; a sister Dorothy McEvoy of Mobile, AL; eight grandchildren; and seven great-grandchildren. Besides her husband, she is predeceased by a sister Louise Delahanty.

Bachman, Louis: (F) Member Arcana Lodge, No. 246,
  F. & A. M., 1934, New York, NY, (JD) Oct. 20, 1919
Backer, James F.: (F) Member Temple Lodge, No. 14, 1900, Albany,
  NY
Backmore, H. C: (F) Member Long Island Lodge, No. 382, F. &. A. M.
  1874, NY
Bacon, G. R.: (F) Member Clyde Lodge No. 341, F. A. M., 1905, Clyde,
  NY, (CO) Wayne, (CMTS) Past Master 1892, 1893
Bader, E.: (F) Member Long Island Lodge, No. 382, F. &. A. M. 1874,
  NY
Badger, W. S.: (F) Member Sons of New England, New England Society
  of the City of Brooklyn, 1890, (CMTS) *"Brooklyn Eagle,"* Dec. 21,
  1890, 11th Annual Dinner, Attendees
Badgley, Claude M.: (F) Member Masters Lodge, No. 5, 1900, Albany,
  NY
Bagley, Roger: (OBIT) *"Journal News,"* Oct. 19, 2000. Roger Bagley a
  lifelong resident of Greenwich died October 18, 2000. He was 77
  and was born on October 10, 1923 in New York City to the late
  Harry E. and Marguerite McDonough Bagley. He was raised and
  educated in Greenwich and graduated from Greenwich High
  School in 1938. Mr. Bagley was married in Port Chester to
  Elizabeth "Betty" Babb on September 2, 1951. He was a train
  engineer with Metro North Railroad for 45 years until his
  retirement in 1987. He was a member of the All Souls Presbyterian
  Church in Port Chester, a member of the Port Chester Masonic
  Lodge, and a member of the Stamford Mineralogical Society. He is
  survived by his wife, Betty Bagley of Greenwich, CT, two
  daughters Janice Bagley of Norwalk, CT, Lynne Bagley of
  Greenwich, CT, and brother Walter Bagley of Stamford, CT.
Bailey, Charles A.: (F) Member Masters Lodge, No. 5, 1900, Albany,
  NY
Bailey, Frank: (F) Member Sons of New England, New England Society
  of the City of Brooklyn, 1890, (CMTS) *"Brooklyn Eagle,"* Dec. 21,
  1890, 11th Annual Dinner, Attendees
Bailey, James S.: (F) Member Sons of New England, New England
  Society of the City of Brooklyn, 1890, (CMTS) *"Brooklyn Eagle,"*
  Dec. 21, 1890, 11th Annual Dinner, Attendees
Bailey, Melvin M.: (F) Member Lowville Lodge No. 134, F. & A. M.,
  1929, Lowville, NY, (CO) Lewis, (JD) May 8, 1903, (B) 1874,
  (D) 1967, (C) Beeches Bridge, Watson, Lewis Co., NY
Bailey, Theodore P.: (F) Member Mount Vernon Lodge, No. 3, 1900,
  Albany, NY, (CEN) 1880, 5$^{th}$ Ward, Albany, Albany Co., NY,
  Listed with James S. Bailey, 50, NY, Physician, 50, NY, Fannie J.,
  48, CT, Estella K., 24, AL, daughter, Theadore, P, 22, AL,
  Physician, George I., 18, TX, son, Corrine, 16, TX, daughter
Bailly, John P.: (F) Member Mount Vernon Lodge, No. 3, 1900, Albany,

NY
Bain, William H.: (F) Member Temple Lodge, No. 14, 1900, Albany, NY, (CEN) 1880, 16th Ward, Albany, Albany Co., NY, 28, Bookkeeper, Gitty M., 28.
Baird, Andrew D.: (F) Member Sons of New England, New England Society of the City of Brooklyn, 1887, (CMTS) *"Brooklyn Eagle,"* Dec. 22, 1887, Annual Dinner, Attendees, (B) Oct., 1838, (PRTS) Andrew Beard and Ellen ????.
Baird, Lillian: (F) Member Hope Rebekah Lodge No. 10, 1949-1950, Brockport, NY, (CO) Monroe, (CMTS) Sick Committee
Baker, Al.: (F) Member Society of American Magicians, Apr., 1931, New York, (RES) Brooklyn, NY
Baker, Charles A.: (F) Member Masters Lodge, No. 5, 1900, Albany, NY
Baker, Charles N.: (F) Member Temple Lodge, No. 14, 1900, Albany, NY
Baker, David A.: (F) Member Lowville Lodge No. 134, F. & A. M., 1929, Lowville, NY, (CO) Lewis, (JD) Dec. 6, 1909, (CEN) 1880 West Turin, Lewis Co., NY, Listed with John C. Baker, 71, Farmer, France, Mena, 57, Germany, wife, David, cooper, 32, Frederick, 30, NY, Farm Laborer
Baker, Geo.: (F) Member Clyde Lodge No. 341, F. A. M., 1905, Clyde, NY, (CO) Wayne, (CMTS) Past Master 1865, 1866
Baker, George C.: (F) Member Masters Lodge, No. 5, 1900, Albany, NY
Baker, George O.: (F) Member Clyde Lodge No. 341, F. A. M., 1905, Clyde, NY, (CO) Wayne, (CMTS) Past Master 1878, 1879
Baker, James A.: (F) Member Masters Lodge, No. 5, 1900, Albany, NY
Baker, James F.: (F) Member Masters Lodge, No. 5, 1900, Albany, NY, (CMTS) Past Master
Bakie, Thomas J.: (F) Member Mount Vernon Lodge, No. 3, 1900, Albany, NY
Balcom, M. H.: (F) Member Murray Lodge, No. 380, F. & A. M., 1906, Holley, Orleans, Co., NY, (CMTS) Past Master
Baldridge, H.: (F) Member Mount Vernon Lodge, No. 3, 1900, Albany, NY
Baldwin, Chas. S.: (F) Member Long Island Lodge, No. 382, F. &. A. M. 1874, NY, (CMTS) Past Master
Ball, Charles A.: (F) Member Temple Lodge, No. 14, 1900, Albany, NY
Ball, Henry D.: (F) Member Temple Lodge, No. 14, 1900, Albany, NY
Ball, T. F.: (F) Member Long Island Lodge, No. 382, F. &. A. M. 1874, NY
Ball, William Henry: (F) Member Temple Lodge, No. 14, 1900, Albany,

Ballenburg, Wm.: (F) Member Arcana Lodge, No. 246, F. & A. M., 1934, New York, NY, (JD) May 18, 1908

Ballin, Sials: (F) Member Washington Lodge, No. 85, 1900, Albany, NY

Ballin, Simon L.: (F) Member Washington Lodge, No. 85, 1900, Albany, NY

Ballou, W. A.: (F) Member Long Island Lodge, No. 382, F. &. A. M. 1874, NY

Bamer, Jr., William: (F) Member Mount Vernon Lodge, No. 3, 1900, Albany, NY

Bank, Ph. V.: (F) Member Herber Lodge, No. 698,1898, F. & A. M., New York, NY, Greenpoint area, (RES) Brooklyn

Banks, A. Bleecker: (F) Member Grand Council of the Princes of Jerusalem, 1882, Albany, NY

Banks, A. Bleecker: (F) Member Ineffable and Sublime Grand Lodge of Perfection, 1882, Albany, NY

Banks, A. Bleecker: (F) Member Masters Lodge, No. 5, 1900, Albany, NY

Banks, Robert Lenox: (F) Member Grand Council of the Princes of Jerusalem, 1882, Albany, NY

Banks, Robert Lenox: (F) Member Ineffable and Sublime Grand Lodge of Perfection, 1882, Albany, NY

Banks, W. H.: (F) Member Long Island Lodge, No. 382, F. &. A. M. 1874, NY

Banks, Jr., Robert L.: (F) Member Masters Lodge, No. 5, 1900, Albany, NY

Bannon, Bryan B: (F) Member Lowville Lodge No. 134, F. & A. M., 1929, Lowville, NY, (CO) Lewis, (JD) Dec. 16, 1916

Bard, William H.: (F) Member Society of American Magicians, Apr., 1931, New York, (RES) Mt. Vernon, NY

Bardin, A. G.: (F) Member Brooklyn Choral Society, 1889, (CMTS) *"Brooklyn Eagle,"* Oct. 2, 1889, (CMTS) Chairman

Bardo, George M.: (F) Member Lowville Lodge No. 134, F. & A. M., 1929, Lowville, NY, (CO) Lewis, (JD) Nov. 26, 1926, (MD) Dec., 1895, (Spouse) Rose C. Maurer, (PRTS) Peter Bardo and Hannah Heimhilger, (CEN) 1880 Croghan, Lewis Co., NY listed with Peter Bardo, 29, Blacksmith, NY, Hannah, 27, George, 8, Carrie, 7, Frederick, 6mos

Barker, Miss Lida: (F) Member Mispah Circle, 1888, Brooklyn, (I) *"Brooklyn Eagle,"* Dec. 12, 1888. Mentioned in an article about a fair raising funds for a Home for the Blind

Barker, Walter J.: (F) Member Lowville Lodge No. 134, F. & A. M., 1929, Lowville, NY, (CO) Lewis, (JD) Mar. 21, 1920

Barnes, Alfred C.: (F) Member Sons of New England, New England

Society of the City of Brooklyn, 1890, (CMTS) *"Brooklyn Eagle,"* Dec. 21, 1890, 11th Annual Dinner, Attendees

Barnes, Clinton L.: (F) Member Lowville Lodge No. 134, F. & A. M., 1929, Lowville, NY, (CO) Lewis, (JD) Jul. 1, 1904

Barnes, Earl H.: (F) Member Lowville Lodge No. 134, F. & A. M., 1929, Lowville, NY, (CO) Lewis, (JD) Mar. 30, 1906

Barnes, Earle H.: (F) Member Lowville Chapter No. 223, R. A. M., 1929, Lowville, NY, (CO) Lewis, (JD) Apr. 2, 1907

Barnes, Harrison: (F) Member Educational Society of Lewis Co., NY, Nov. 14, 1845, (CMTS) Corresponding Secretary

Barnes, J. E.: (I) *"Brooklyn Eagle,"* Dec. 7, 1896. 12th Annual Memorial Services, Plymouth Church, Brooklyn Lodge No. 22, B. F. O. Elks, Roll Call of the dead. Address made by Maryland Senator George L. Wellington, (CMTS) Name called.

Barnes, Mrs. A. S.: (F) Member Society for the Relief of Respectable Indigent Females, Brooklyn, (I) Brooklyn Eagle, Nov. 13, 1879, (CMTS) Treasurer

Barnes, William D.: (F) Member Sons of New England, New England Society of the City of Brooklyn, 1890, (CMTS) *"Brooklyn Eagle,"* Dec. 21, 1890, 11th Annual Dinner, Attendees

Barnet, Jonas S.: (F) Member Mount Vernon Lodge, No. 3, 1900, Albany, NY

Barnet, William: (F) Member Washington Lodge, No. 85, 1900, Albany, NY

Barnett, David: (F) Member Sons of New England, New England Society of the City of Brooklyn, 1890, (CMTS) *"Brooklyn Eagle,"* Dec. 21, 1890, 11th Annual Dinner, Attendees

Barr, Jr., Joseph A.: (F) Member Sons of New England, New England Society of the City of Brooklyn, 1890, (CMTS) *"Brooklyn Eagle,"* Dec. 21, 1890, 11th Annual Dinner, Attendees

Barrett, Fred G.: (F) Member Lowville Chapter No. 223, R. A. M., 1929, Lowville, NY, (CO) Lewis, (JD) Jun. 12, 1923

Barrett, Fred G.: (F) Member Lowville Lodge No. 134, F. & A. M., 1929, Lowville, NY, (CO) Lewis, (JD) May 2, 1913, (CEN) 1880 Lowville, Lewis Co., NY Listed with George, 50, VT, Carpenter, Louisa M., 48, NY, wife, Robin H., 17, son, Fred G., 14, 20, Eugene Buxton, 26, carpenter, nephew

Barrett, G. D.: (F) Member Clyde Lodge No. 341, F. A. M., 1905, Clyde, NY, (CO) Wayne, (CMTS) Past Master 1904, 1905

Barrett, Isaac B.: (F) Member Masters Lodge, No. 5, 1900, Albany, NY

Barrie, A.: (F) Member Sons of New England, New England Society of the City of Brooklyn, 1890, (CMTS) *"Brooklyn Eagle,"* Dec. 21, 1890, 11th Annual Dinner, Attendees

Barter, Miss: (F) Member Nativity Sewing Society, 1900, Brooklyn, (I) *"Brooklyn Eagle,"* Feb. 3, 1900. Article regarding raising money to buy clothing for the poor.

Bartlett, C. H.: (F) Member Murray Lodge, No. 380, F. & A. M., 1906, Holley, Orleans, Co., NY

Bartlett, Franklin: (F) Member Sons of New England, New England Society of the City of Brooklyn, 1890, (CMTS) *"Brooklyn Eagle,"* Dec. 21, 1890, 11th Annual Dinner, Attendees

Bartlett, H. D.: (F) Member Murray Lodge, No. 380, F. & A. M., 1906, Holley, Orleans, Co., NY, (CMTS) Past Master

Bartlett, Willard: (F) Member Sons of New England, New England Society of the City of Brooklyn, 1890, (CMTS) *"Brooklyn Eagle,"* Dec. 21, 1890, 11th Annual Dinner, Attendees

Bassett, Richard O.: (F) Member Temple Lodge, No. 14, 1900, Albany, NY

Batchelder, Walter W.: (F) Member Masters Lodge, No. 5, 1900, Albany, NY, (CEN) 1880, 11$^{th}$ Ward, Albany, Albany CO., NY, Listed With N. W. Batchelder, 48, VT, Insurance, Elen, 42, Albert E., 20, WI, Walter W., 15, MI, (SIB) Albert Edward, b. Apr. 2, 1860, bp. Janesville, Rock Co., WI, (PRTS) Norman W. Batchelder, b. and Oct. 24, 1831, bp. Orange Co., VT, Ellen M. Whipple, md. Oct. 12, 1858, Rutland Co., VT (CMTS) Ellen M. Whipple's parents were Cyrus C. Whipple and Rebecca M. Fish. Norman W. Batchelder's parents were Jospeh Batchelder and Electa Barrett.

Bateman, Charles E.: (F) Member Lowville Lodge No. 134, F. & A. M., 1929, Lowville, NY, (CO) Lewis, (JD) Nov. 21, 1921

Bateman, Niles C.: (F) Member Lowville Lodge No. 134, F. & A. M., 1929, Lowville, NY, (CO) Lewis, (JD) Feb. 15, 1907

Battersby, John: (F) Member Temple Lodge, No. 14, 1900, Albany, NY, (CEN) 1880, 12$^{th}$ Ward, Albany, Albany Co., NY, 45, Ire, Butcher, Lucinda J., 37

Battin, Isaac: (F) Member Grand Council of the Princes of Jerusalem, 1882, Albany, NY, (CEN) 1880, 5$^{th}$ Ward, Albany, Albany Co., NY, 48, PA, Supt. Gas Works, Nancy W., 38,PA, Susan W., 21, CT, Henry W., 19, CT, Alice T., 14, NY, John W., 12, NY, Benjamin F., 7, NY, Thomas W., 5, NY, Nacy M. 4, NY, William J., 2, NY

Battin, Isaac: (F) Member Ineffable and Sublime Grand Lodge of Perfection, 1882, Albany, NY

Baulsir, Edward: (F) Member Long Island Lodge, No. 382, F. &. A. M. 1874, NY, (B) Aug. 7, 1840, (BP) Brooklyn, NY, (D) Nov. 25, 1879, (MD) Mar. 15, 1865, (Spouse) Annie Mason

Baumann, Arthur: (F) Member Arcana Lodge, No. 246, F. & A. M., 1934, New York, NY, (JD) May 29, 1911

Baumel, Max: (F) Member Arcana Lodge, No. 246, F. & A. M., 1934, New York, NY, (JD) May 17, 1915

Baxter, Duncan: (F) Member Temple Lodge, No. 14, 1900, Albany, NY,

(CEN) Listed with Duncan Baxter, 1880 13th Ward, Albany, Albany Co., NY, 41, Eng, Sexton of Church, Hannah, 34, George, Sindey, 8, Amelia, 3

Baxter, Miss: (F) Member Nativity Sewing Society, 1900, Brooklyn, (I) *"Brooklyn Eagle,"* Feb. 3, 1900. Article regarding raising money to buy clothing for the poor.

Baxter, Sidney F.: (F) Member Temple Lodge, No. 14, 1900, Albany, NY, (CEN) 1880 13th Ward, Albany, Albany Co., NY, 41, Eng, Sexton of Church, Hannah, 34, George, Sidney, 8, Amelia, 3

Bayley, Geo. H.: (F) Member Long Island Lodge, No. 382, F. &. A. M. 1874, NY

Baylis, Floyd E.: (F) Member First District Suffolk, Jepthah's Daughter, No. 187, 1923, Huntington, NY, (CMTS) Patron, (RES) Melville, Long Island

Beach, John L.: (F) Member Lowville Chapter No. 223, R. A. M., 1929, Lowville, NY, (CO) Lewis, (JD) Nov. 10, 1885, (CEN) 1880 Watson, Lewis Co., NY, 29, Farmer, NY, Emogene, 26, wife, Marcie, 8

Beach, John L.: (F) Member Lowville Lodge No. 134, F. & A. M., 1929, Lowville, NY, (CO) Lewis, (JD) Apr. 25, 1884, (CEN) 1880 Watson, Lewis Co., NY, 29, Farmer, NY, Emogene, 26, wife, Marcie, 8, (B) Aug. 7, 1850, (MD) Dec. 24, 1879, (Spouse) Emogene Flint, (PRTS) Ralph Beach and Phildelia Main John L., (B) 1850, (D) 1930, Emogene J., (B) 1852, (D) 1904, (C) Beeches Bridge Cemetery, Watson, Lewis Co., NY

Beach, W. H.: (F) Member Long Island Lodge, No. 382, F. &. A. M. 1874, NY

Beadle, H. H.: (F) Member Sons of New England, New England Society of the City of Brooklyn, 1890, (CMTS) *"Brooklyn Eagle,"* Dec. 21, 1890, 11th Annual Dinner, Attendees

Beadle, H. H.: (F) Member Sons of New England, New England Society of the City of Brooklyn, 1887, (CMTS) *"Brooklyn Eagle,"* Dec. 22, 1887, Annual Dinner, Attendees

Beadle, Harry W.: (I) *"Brooklyn Eagle,"* Feb. 19, 1902. Funeral Services at the Club House of the Brooklyn Lodge, No. 22, B. P. O. Elks for Wm. H. West. Elk services were first then masonic ervices by New York Lodge No. 330, F. A. & M., (CMTS) Royal Knight

Beagley, G. H.: (F) Member Long Island Lodge, No. 382, F. &. A. M. 1874, NY

Beam, H.: (F) Member Long Island Lodge, No. 382, F. &. A. M. 1874, NY

Beam, Miss M. Edna: (F) Member The Young Women's Guild, 1888, Brooklyn, (I) *"Brooklyn Eagle,"* Dec. 12, 1888. Article regarding Societies aiding churches, (CMTS) Helping Plymouth Church, Secretary

Beatty, John W.: (I) *"Brooklyn Eagle,"* Dec. 7, 1896. 12th Annual

Memorial Services, Plymouth Church, Brooklyn Lodge No. 22, B.
F. O. Elks, Roll Call of the dead. Address made by Maryland
Senator George L. Wellington. , (CMTS) Name called.
Bechtel, John: (F) Member Mount Vernon Lodge, No. 3, 1900, Albany,
NY
Beck, Miss: (F) Member Mispah Circle, 1888, Brooklyn, (I) *"Brooklyn
Eagle,"* Dec. 12, 1888. Mentioned in an article about a fair raising
funds for a Home for the Blind
Becker, Axel E.: (F) Member Arcana Lodge, No. 246, F. & A. M., 1934,
New York, NY, (JD) Jun. 7, 1920
Becker, John A.: (F) Member Masters Lodge, No. 5, 1900, Albany, NY
Becker, Julius: (F) Member Arcana Lodge, No. 246, F. & A. M., 1934,
New York, NY, (JD) May 29, 1911
Becker, Rev. Edwin A.: (F) Member Society of American Magicians,
Apr., 1931, New York, (CMTS) Life Member
Beckman, George F.: (F) Member Mount Vernon Lodge, No. 3, 1900,
Albany, NY
Beebe, George M.: (F) Member Monticello Lodge, No. 532, F. & A. M.,
(CO) Sullivan Co., NY, (CMTS) Past Master 1870, 1872
Beebe, William H.: (F) Member Washington Lodge, No. 85, 1900,
Albany, NY
Beecher, C. Y.: (F) Member Long Island Lodge, No. 382, F. &. A. M.
1874, NY
Beecher, Mrs. Heard Ward: (F) Member The Ladies Sewing Society,
1888, Brooklyn, (I) *"Brooklyn Eagle,"* Dec. 12, 1888. Article
regarding Societies aiding churches., (CMTS) Helping Plymouth
Church, President
Behrens, Henry J.: (F) Member Lowville Lodge No. 134, F. & A. M.,
1929, Lowville, NY, (CO) Lewis, (JD) Mar. 3, 1922
Beirds, T. H.: (F) Member Long Island Lodge, No. 382, F. &. A. M. 1874,
NY
Beker, Alexander R.: (F) Member Temple Lodge, No. 14, 1900, Albany,
NY, (CMTS) Life Member
Belais, Arnold: (F) Member Society of American Magicians, Apr., 1931,
New York, (RES) New York City
Belding, Samuel B.: (F) Member Mount Vernon Lodge, No. 3, 1900,
Albany, NY
Bell, James B.: (F) Member Sons of New England, New England
Society of the City of Brooklyn, 1890, (CMTS)*"Brooklyn Eagle,"*
Dec. 21, 1890, 11th Annual Dinner, Attendees
Bell, James C.: (F) Member Grand Council of the Princes of Jerusalem,
1882, Albany, NY
Bell, James C.: (F) Member Ineffable and Sublime Grand Lodge of
Perfection, 1882, Albany, NY
Bellows, Edgar: (F) Member Temple Lodge, No. 14, 1900, Albany, NY
Bendell, Herman: (F) Member Washington Lodge, No. 85, 1900, Albany,

NY, (CMTS) Past Members
Bendell, Moses: (F) Member Washington Lodge, No. 85, 1900, Albany, NY, (CMTS) Past Members
Bender, Matthew: (F) Member Masters Lodge, No. 5, 1900, Albany, NY
Bendict, Robert D.: (F) Member Sons of New England, New England Society of the City of Brooklyn, 1890, (CMTS)*"Brooklyn Eagle,"* Dec. 21, 1890, 11th Annual Dinner, Attendees
Benedict, Edward G.: (F) Member Sons of New England, New England Society of the City of Brooklyn, 1890, (CMTS)*"Brooklyn Eagle,"* Dec. 21, 1890, 11th Annual Dinner, Attendees
Benedict, Ezra G.: (F) Member Masters Lodge, No. 5, 1900, Albany, NY
Benedict, H. H.: (F) Member Brooklyn Revenue Reform Club, 1886, (I)*"Brooklyn Eagle,"* Jan. ,27 1886, Attendees at a dinner
Benedict, Seelye: (F) Member Sons of New England, New England Society of the City of Brooklyn, 1887, (CMTS)*"Brooklyn Eagle,"* Dec. 22, 1887, Annual Dinner, Attendees
Benjamin, George H.: (F) Member Grand Council of the Princes of Jerusalem, 1882, Albany, NY
Benjamin, George H.: (F) Member Ineffable and Sublime Grand Lodge of Perfection, 1882, Albany, NY
Benjamin, George H.: (F) Member Masters Lodge, No. 5, 1900, Albany, NY, (CMTS) Past Master
Benjamin , Abraham T.: (F) Member Temple Lodge, No. 14, 1900, Albany, NY
Bennett, Daniel C.: (F) Member Masters Lodge, No. 5, 1900, Albany, NY
Bennett, Miss Sarah: (F) Member Independent Order of Good Templars, Westhampton Lodge No. 885, instituted Apr. 16, 1889, New Officers installed Feb. 16, 1900, (CMTS) Meeting Notes, *"Brooklyn Eagle,"* Feb. 18, 1900, Guard
Bensen, Albert V.: (F) Member Mount Vernon Lodge, No. 3, 1900, Albany, NY
Benson, John: (F) Member Temple Lodge, No. 14, 1900, Albany, NY
Bentham, H. D.: (F) Member Murray Lodge, No. 380, F. & A. M., 1906, Holley, Orleans, Co., NY
Benton, Lloyd B.: (F) Member Lowville Lodge No. 134, F. & A. M., 1929, Lowville, NY, (CO) Lewis, (JD) May 6, 1922
Benz, Pearl: (F) Member Hope Rebekah Lodge No. 10, 1949-1950, Brockport, NY, (CO) Monroe, (CMTS Property Committee
Bergen, Tunis G.: (F) Member St. Nicholas Society of Nassau Island, 1861, (CMTS)"Brooklyn Eag;e," Dec. 11, 1861, Article regarding the Anniversary Dinner, President
Berko, Max: (F) Member Arcana Lodge, No. 246, F. & A. M., 1934, New York, NY, (JD) Mar. 16, 1925
Berkorwitz, David: (F) Member Arcana Lodge, No. 246, F. & A. M., 1934, New York, NY, (JD) Oct. 12, 1926
Berler, Oscar: (F) Member Arcana Lodge, No. 246, F. & A. M., 1934,

New York, NY, (JD) Dec. 1, 1913
Berlin, Jr., Fred C.: (F) Member Temple Lodge, No. 14, 1900, Albany, NY
Berman, Joseph L.: (F) Member Arcana Lodge, No. 246, F. & A. M., 1934, New York, NY, (JD) Apr. 26, 1932
Bernheimer, Henry: (F) Member Washington Lodge, No. 85, 1900, Albany, NY, (CEN) 1880 6$^{th}$ Ward, Albany, Albany Co., NY Listed Abm. Bernheimer, 55, Dry Goods Peddler, Wuertemburg, Celia, 49, Germany, Henry, 20, Cigar Maker, Elizabeth, 14
Bernikow, Abram: (F) Member Arcana Lodge, No. 246, F. & A. M., 1934, New York, NY, (JD) Feb. 21, 1910
Bernstein, E. M.: (F) Member Arcana Lodge, No. 246, F. & A. M., 1934, New York, NY, (JD) Jan. 20, 1913
Bernstein, Moe: (F) Member Arcana Lodge, No. 246, F. & A. M., 1934, New York, NY, (JD) Jun. 26, 1928
Berri, William: (F) Member Brooklyn Choral Society, 1889, (CMTS) *"Brooklyn Eagle,"* Oct. 2, 1889, (CMTS) President of the Board of Directors
Berri, William: (F) Member Sons of New England, New England Society of the City of Brooklyn, 1890, (CMTS)*"Brooklyn Eagle,"* Dec. 21, 1890, 11th Annual Dinner, Attendees, (CEN) 1880, Brooklyn, Kings Co., NY, William H. Berri, 53, Printer, NY, Eliza, 50, Ireland, Eliza, 24, William 22, Photographer, Lewis, 20, Clerk, Chillane, 17, Charles, 13
Berry, Mrs. Charles: (F) Member Lenox Ladies Aid Society of Lenox Road M. E. Church, Brooklyn, 1900, (CMTS) *"Brooklyn Eagle,"* Mar. 13, 1900, Meeting Notice, Assistant Treasurer
Berryman, W. R.: (F) Member Society of American Magicians, Apr., 1931, New York, (RES) Brooklyn, NY, (CMTS) Life Member
Besher, John H.: (F) Member Long Island Lodge, No. 382, F. &. A. M. 1874, NY, (CMTS) Past Master
Bessor, George: (F) Member Long Island Lodge, No. 382, F. &. A. M. 1874, NY
Best, John: (F) Member Washington Lodge, No. 85, 1900, Albany, NY, (CMTS) Past Master, (CEN) 1880 11$^{th}$ Ward, Albany, Albany CO., NY, 39, Piano Maker, NY, Mary J., 39, Lizzie J., 17, Henry M., 12, Nellie B., 12, John J., 7
Beverly, G. W.: (F) Member Long Island Lodge, No. 382, F. &. A. M. 1874, NY
Beyer, Chester H.: (F) Member Lowville Lodge No. 134, F. & A. M., 1929, Lowville, NY, (CO) Lewis, (JD) Mar. 30, 1928
Bickers, Joseph E.: (F) Member Lowville Lodge No. 134, F. & A. M., 1929, Lowville, NY, (CO) Lewis, (JD) Apr. 21, 1922
Biddle, C. H.: (F) Member Brooklyn Dental Society, 1877, Brooklyn, NY,

(CMTS) *"Brooklyn Eagle,"* Dec. 15, 1877. Celebration of 10th Anniversary. Society established Dec. 14, 1867, (CMTS) Clinics Committee

Bietz, H.: (F) Member Herber Lodge, No. 698,1898, F. & A. M., New York, NY, Greenpoint area, (RES) New York City

Bigelow, John M.: (F) Member Masters Lodge, No. 5, 1900, Albany, NY, (CEN) 1880, $5^{th}$ Ward, Albany, Albany Co., NY, 33, NY, Physician

Billson, C. A.: (F) Member Washington Lodge, No. 85, 1900, Albany, NY

Bilofsky, Maxwell M.: (F) Member Arcana Lodge, No. 246, F. & A. M., 1934, New York, NY, (JD) Apr. 26, 1927

Bingham, Earl A.: (F) Member Lowville Lodge No. 134, F. & A. M., 1929, Lowville, NY, (CO) Lewis, (JD) Jul. 7, 1905, (B) Dec. 6, 1880, (BP) Martinsburg, Lewis Co., NY, (PRTS) Howard C. Bingham and Frances Louise Moore, (CMTS) Middle name is "Alexander"

Bingham, George H.: (F) Member Temple Lodge, No. 14, 1900, Albany, NY, (CEN) $11^{th}$ Ward, Albany, Albany Co., NY, 55, Ire, Boot, Shoe & Fancy Store, 55, Elizabeth M., 48, Anne M., 26, Robert G., 19, Apprentice at Printing House

Binley, George W.: (F) Member Temple Lodge, No. 14, 1900, Albany, NY, (CEN) 1880, $11^{th}$ Ward, Albany, Albany Co., NY, Listed with Elizabeth, 63, widow, Eng, George, 32, Music Teacher, Eng, Alfred, (D) May 4, 1937, (MD) May 29, 1894, (Spouse) Martha J. Scott, (PMD) Albany Co., NY

Bird, Ruth: (F) Member Hope Rebekah Lodge No. 10, 1949-1950, Brockport, NY, (CO) Monroe, (CMTS) Warden

Biscoe, H.: (F) Member Long Island Lodge, No. 382, F. &. A. M. 1874, NY

Bishara, Edward H.: (F) Member Arcana Lodge, No. 246, F. & A. M., 1934, New York, NY, (JD) Mar. 16, 1925

Bishara, H. Alfred: (F) Member Arcana Lodge, No. 246, F. & A. M., 1934, New York, NY, (JD) Feb. 9, 1932

Bishara, Habib A.: (F) Member Arcana Lodge, No. 246, F. & A. M., 1934, New York, NY, (JD) May 10, 1917

Bishop, Darwin: (F) Member Lowville Lodge No. 134, F. & A. M., 1929, Lowville, NY, (CO) Lewis, (JD) Mar. 20, 1908, (CEN) 1880 Watson, Lewis Co., NY, Listed with Edwin Bishopp, (sic), 45, NY, Farmer, Caroline, 39, Charles, 18, William, 16, Mary J., 14, Edwin, 12, Darwin, 4

Bishop, Darwin: (F) Member Lowville Chapter No. 223, R. A. M., 1929, Lowville, NY, (CO) Lewis, (JD) Jan. 19, 1909, (CEN) 1880 Watson, Lewis Co., NY, Listed with Edwin Bishopp, (sic), 45, NY, Farmer, Caroline, 39, Charles, 18, William, 16, Mary J., 14, Edwin, 12, Darwin, 4

Bishop, George C.: (F) Member Temple Lodge, No. 14, 1900, Albany,

NY, (CEN) 1880, 16th Ward, Albany, Albany Co., NY Listed with Thomas S. Bishop, 45, Newspaper Reporter, Jane E., 40, George C., 20, clerk, Mary M., 18, Carrie V., 15, Nellie J., 13, Cora A., 11, Gilbert C., 9, Addison K., 1

Bishop, Thomas J.: (F) Member Temple Lodge, No. 14, 1900, Albany, NY, (CMTS) Life Member

Blach, Lewis L.: (F) Member Masters Lodge, No. 5, 1900, Albany, NY

Blackburn, John: (F) Member Masters Lodge, No. 5, 1900, Albany, NY, (CEN) 1880 17th Ward, Albany, Albany Co., NY, 43, Ire, Coal Dealer, Nancy, 43, Ire, John T. D., 16, Sarah, 13, Robert, 12, Isaac Downing, Brother-in-law, 25, Clerk in coal office,

Blackburn, Thomas R.: (F) Member Grand Council of the Princes of Jerusalem, 1882, Albany, NY, (CEN) 1880, 17th Ward, Albany, Albany Co., NY, 49, Ire, Foreman N.Y.C. R.R., Rebecca, 47, Ire, Anna, 20, Sarah, 18, Lizzie, 16, Thomas, 13, Willie, 9, Robert, 6.

Blackburn, Thos. R.: (F) Member Ineffable and Sublime Grand Lodge of Perfection, 1882, Albany, NY

Blackford, Mrs. A.: (F) Member Mispah Circle, 1888, Brooklyn, (I) *"Brooklyn Eagle,"* Dec. 12, 1888. Mentioned in an article about a fair raising funds for a Home for the Blind

Blackmon, Gilbert A.: (F) Member Lowville Lodge No. 134, F. & A. M., 1929, Lowville, NY, (CO) Lewis, (JD) Jan. 24, 1886

Blair, Arthur: (F) Member Mount Vernon Lodge, No. 3, 1900, Albany, NY, (CEN) 5th Ward, Albany, Albany Co., NY, Listed with Nathan Blair, 50, Tailor, Bohemia, Elizabeth, 44, Bohemia, Minnie, 25, NY, Louis, 23, Physician, MA, Arutherm 20, Cutter, MA, Jacon, 16, NY, Apprentice to Tailor

Blair, Louis E.: (F) Member Mount Vernon Lodge, No. 3, 1900, Albany, NY,(CEN) 5th Ward, Albany, Albany Co., NY, Listed with Nathan Blair, 50, Tailor, Bohemia, Elizabeth, 44, Bohemia, Minnie, 25, NY, Louis, 23, Physician, MA, Arutherm 20, Cutter, MA, Jacon, 16, NY, Apprentice to Tailor

Blakeslee, George H.: (F) Member Masters Lodge, No. 5, 1900, Albany, NY

Blasie, William: (F) Member Washington Lodge, No. 85, 1900, Albany, NY, (CMTS) Past Master, (CEN) 1880, 4th Ward, Albany, Albany Co., NY, 48, NY, Barber, Catherine, 38, Isabella, 19, William, 17, Catherine, 12, George, 10, Mary, 8, Elvira, 6, Joseph, 6, Mary Blaise, 78, Mother, Prussia

Blatner, Jacob M.: (F) Member Mount Vernon Lodge, No. 3, 1900, Albany, NY

Blatner, Joseph H.: (F) Member Masters Lodge, No. 5, 1900, Albany, NY, (CEN) 14th Ward, Albany, Albany Co., NY. 31, Physician, Mary D., 28, Sandford K., 2, Leroy S., 2mo.

Blatner, Sol. H.: (F) Member Washington Lodge, No. 85, 1900, Albany, NY

Blaum, Phillip R.: (OBIT) *"The River Report,"* Apr. 25, 2004. Philip R. Blaum of Eldred, NY, a retired New York City police officer and a resident of the area since 1981, died Sunday, April 11 at New York VA Hospital in Manhattan. He was 57. The son of the late Philip F. and Catherine Mood Blaum, he was born February 11 in Queen, NY. Blaum was a United States Marine and a veteran of the Vietnam War. He was a member of the Beaver Brook Rod and Gun Club, the Eldred Mountain Stream Rod and Gun Club and the VFW Tusten-Highland Post 6427. Survivors include one brother, Richard Blaum and Richard's wife Roberta of Carmel, NY, a nephew Matthew and a niece Elizabeth. Friends were invited to call on Wednesday, April 14 at Gray-Rasmussen Funeral Home in Barryville, NY. Funeral services will be held Thursday, April 15 at 11:00 a.m. at Gray-Rasmussen. The Reverend Anthony Moore will officiate. Burial will be in the Sullivan County Veterans Cemetery in Liberty.

Blauvekt, Isaac: (F) Member Masters Lodge, No. 5, 1900, Albany, NY

Bleakney, O.: (F) Member Long Island Lodge, No. 382, F. &. A. M. 1874, NY

Blessing, Elmer A.: (F) Member Temple Lodge, No. 14, 1900, Albany, NY, (CEN) 1880, 17$^{th}$ Ward, Albany, Albany Co., NY Listed with Peter McCullach, Elmer A., 18, At School

Blessing, Ira H.: (F) Member Temple Lodge, No. 14, 1900, Albany, NY (CEN) 1880, 17$^{th}$ Ward, Albany, Albany Co., NY Listed with Peter McCullach, Ira, 15, At School

Blewer, J. Willard: (F) Member Mount Vernon Lodge, No. 3, 1900, Albany, NY

Bliss, Albert: (F) Member Lowville Lodge No. 134, F. & A. M., 1929, Lowville, NY, (CO) Lewis, (JD) Jan. 13m 1893

Bliss, Amos: (F) Member Lowville Chapter No. 223, R. A. M., 1929, Lowville, NY, (CO) Lewis, (JD) Feb. 23, 1892

Bliss, Amos K.: (F) Member Lowville Lodge No. 134, F. & A. M., 1929, Lowville, NY, (CO) Lewis, (JD) Feb. 7, 1890

Bliss, Edwin: (F) Member Murray Lodge, No. 380, F. & A. M., 1906, Holley, Orleans, Co., NY, (CMTS) Past Master, Deceased as of 1906, (CEN) 1880, Holley, Oleans Co., NY, 60, Builder, MA, Mary A. 53, Dwight, 25, (B) Jul. 13, 1819, (BP) Chicopee, Hampden Co., MA, (MD) May 30, 1849, (Spouse) Mary Seymour, (PRTS) William Bliss and Phebe Chapin, (GPRTS) William C. Bliss, b. Sep. 11, 1779, d. May 19, 1864, md. Oct. 1, 1803 and Phobe Chapin, b. May 22, 1781, d. Nov. Nov. 12, 1861. Phobe Chapin's parents are Levi Chapin and Sarah Richardson. Levi Chapin was born Aug. 23, 1751, died August 19, 1835. Levi Chapin's are Joseph Chapin and Elizabeth Felt

Bliss, George W.: (F) Member Temple Lodge, No. 14, 1900, Albany,

NY

Bliss, William H.: (F) Member Murray Lodge, No. 380, F. & A. M., 1906, Holley, Orleans, Co., NY

Blodgett, Norton P.: (F) Member Lowville Lodge No. 134, F. & A. M., 1929, Lowville, NY, (CO) Lewis, (JD) Jun. 1, 1923

Blum, Jacob: (F) Member Arcana Lodge, No. 246, F. & A. M., 1934, New York, NY, (JD) Oct. 6, 1919

Blum, Robert H.: (F) Member Arcana Lodge, No. 246, F. & A. M., 1934, New York, NY, (JD) Apr. 17, 1922

Blum, Thomas: (F) Member Herber Lodge, No. 698,1898, F. & A. M., New York, NY, Greenpoint area, (RES) New York City

Blumen, Nathan: (F) Member Arcana Lodge, No. 246, F. & A. M., 1934, New York, NY, (JD) May 7, 1917

Bock, E.: (F) Member Herber Lodge, No. 698,1898, F. & A. M., New York, NY, Greenpoint area, (RES) New York City

Bodner, Irving G,: (F) Member Arcana Lodge, No. 246, F. & A. M., 1934, New York, NY, (JD) Dec. 5, 1921

Bogen, F.: (F) Member Herber Lodge, No. 698,1898, F. & A. M., New York, NY, Greenpoint area, (RES) New York City

Bogue, Dr. S. A.: (F) Member Brooklyn Dental Society, 1877, Brooklyn, NY, (CMTS) *"Brooklyn Eagle,"* Dec. 15, 1877. Celebration of 10th Anniversary. Society established Dec. 14, 1867, (CMTS) Present from New York

Bohen, James: (F) Member Long Island Lodge, No. 382, F. &. A. M. 1874, NY

Bolte, H.: (F) Member Long Island Lodge, No. 382, F. &. A. M. 1874, NY

Bonaventuer, C.: (F) Member Long Island Lodge, No. 382, F. &. A. M. 1874, NY

Bond, L. V.: (F) Member Temple Lodge, No. 14, 1900, Albany, NY

Bond, Newton R.: (F) Member Temple Lodge, No. 14, 1900, Albany, NY

Boody, David A.: (F) Member Sons of New England, New England Society of the City of Brooklyn, 1890, (CMTS)*"Brooklyn Eagle,"* Dec. 21, 1890, 11th Annual Dinner, Attendees, (Spouse) Abbie H. Treat, (CH) Alvin (b.Jan. 26, 1862), (CEN) 1880, Brooklyn, Kings Co., NY,42, ME, Stock Broker, Abby T., 38, ME, Henry T., 14, Maud L., 12, Charles A., 9, Alvin, 7, Edgar, 5

Boody, David A.: (F) Member Sons of New England, New England Society of the City of Brooklyn, 1887, (CMTS)*"Brooklyn Eagle,"* Dec. 22, 1887, Annual Dinner, Attendees

Boody, Mayor: (F) Member Friendly Sons of St. Patrick, 1893, Brooklyn, (CMTS)*"Brooklyn Eagle,"* May 18, 1893, Article regarding the election of Andrew T. Sullivan as postmaster. In the article it mentioned that there were only 50 members in this Society. Guest. It is unknown if a member of the Society.

Bookheim, Levi: (F) Member Washington Lodge, No. 85, 1900, Albany, NY

Bookheim, Louis W.: (F) Member Washington Lodge, No. 85, 1900, Albany, NY

Boom, Leonard F.: (F) Member Temple Lodge, No. 14, 1900, Albany, NY

Boos, John: (F) Member Temple Lodge, No. 14, 1900, Albany, NY

Booth, William H.: (F) Member Temple Lodge, No. 14, 1900, Albany, NY

Boots, John: (F) Member Murray Lodge, No. 380, F. & A. M., 1906, Holley, Orleans, Co., NY

Bopp, J. H.: (F) Member Long Island Lodge, No. 382, F. &. A. M. 1874, NY

Borchard, Nathan: (F) Member Society for the Relief of Respectable Indigent Females, Brooklyn, (I) Brooklyn Eagle, Nov. 13, 1879, (CMTS) Secretary

Borgner, C. Walter: (F) Member Lowville Lodge No. 134, F. & A. M., 1929, Lowville, NY, (CO) Lewis, (JD) Feb. 21, 1913

Borow, Harry: (F) Member Arcana Lodge, No. 246, F. & A. M., 1934, New York, NY, (JD) Oct. 26, 1926

Borst, Warren R.: (F) Member Temple Lodge, No. 14, 1900, Albany, NY, (CEN) 1880, Albany, Albany Co., NY Listed with William B., 57, Amanda, 45, Alice H., 19, Warren R., 8, (BP) Middleburgh, NY, (MD) Sep. 10, 1905, (Spouse) Lillian Ireland

Borthwick, Edwin: (F) Member Washington Lodge, No. 85, 1900, Albany, NY

Boshart, Albert C.: (F) Member Lowville Lodge No. 134, F. & A. M., 1929, Lowville, NY, (CO) Lewis, (JD) Aug. 17, 1883

Boshart, C. Ralph: (F) Member Lowville Lodge No. 134, F. & A. M., 1929, Lowville, NY, (CO) Lewis, (JD) Mar. 3, 1916

Boshart, Edward J.: (F) Member Lowville Lodge No. 134, F. & A. M., 1929, Lowville, NY, (CO) Lewis, (CMTS) Past Master 1900, (CEN) 1880, Lowville, Lewis Co., NY Listed with Charles D., 50, NY, Farmer. Margaret, 50, Charles F., 19, Nellie M. E., 18, Edward J., 15, Grace E., 8, Nancy M. Boshart, 67, Sister, William Boshart, 60, Brother, Jane Quakenbush, 61, Sister-in-Law, Frank Spitzer, 26, lawyer, nephew

Boshart, Edward J.: (F) Member Lowville Lodge No. 134, F. & A. M., 1929, Lowville, NY, (CO) Lewis, (JD) Jan. 25, 1889, (OC) Attorney, Graft's Legal Directory, 1908-1909

Boshart, F. Eugene: (F) Member Lowville Lodge No. 134, F. & A. M., 1929, Lowville, NY, (CO) Lewis, (JD) Apr. 2, 1926

Boshart, John M.: (F) Member Lowville Lodge No. 134, F. & A. M., 1929, Lowville, NY, (CO) Lewis, (JD) May 1, 1906

Boshart, William E.: (F) Member Lowville Lodge No. 134, F. & A. M., 1929, Lowville, NY, (CO) Lewis, (JD) Jan. 21, 1921

Bostwick, Charles A.: (F) Member Lowville Chapter No. 223, R. A. M., 1929, Lowville, NY, (CO) Lewis, (JD) Apr. 3, 1906

Bosworth, Mather: (F) Member Lewis County Bible Society, 1812, Charter Officers, (CMTS) Deacon, (Spouse) Bathsheba Deming, (MD) Oct. 17, 1893, (PMD) Westmoreland, Oneida Co., NY

Bothamly, William B.: (F) Member Temple Lodge, No. 14, 1900, Albany, NY

Bouck, Peter C.: (F) Member Mount Vernon Lodge, No. 3, 1900, Albany, NY

Bouffer, Miss: (F) Member Nativity Sewing Society, 1900, Brooklyn, (I) *"Brooklyn Eagle,"* Feb. 3, 1900. Article regarding raising money to buy clothing for the poor.

Boughton, John W.: (F) Member Mount Vernon Lodge, No. 3, 1900, Albany, NY

Bourke, W.: (F) Member Long Island Lodge, No. 382, F. &. A. M. 1874, NY

Bowdan, Jack: (F) Member Arcana Lodge, No. 246, F. & A. M., 1934, New York, NY, (JD) Mar. 21, 1924

Bowden, Charles H.: (F) Member Foresters of America, Fort Greene No. 23, 1900, Brooklyn, (I) *"Brooklyn Eagle,"* Feb. 3, 1900. Meeting Notice, (CMTS) Secretary

Bowdish, John: (F) Member Lowville Lodge No. 134, F. & A. M., 1929, Lowville, NY, (CO) Lewis, (JD) Dec. 9, 1870, Author of a Centennial poem, 1876, Published at Canajorhari, NY, Fourth of July Orations Collection

Bowen, G. Bryon: (F) Member Lowville Lodge No. 134, F. & A. M., 1929, Lowville, NY, (CO) Lewis, (JD) Apr. 30, 1920

Bowers, Augustus: (F) Member Mount Vernon Lodge, No. 3, 1900, Albany, NY, (CMTS) Past Master 1863

Bowers, Robert J.: (F) Member Temple Lodge, No. 14, 1900, Albany, NY

Bowker, R. R.: (F) Member Brooklyn Revenue Reform Club, 1886, (I)*"Brooklyn Eagle,"* Jan. 27 1886, Attendees at a dinner

Bowman, Charles I.: (F) Member Lowville Lodge No. 134, F. & A. M., 1929, Lowville, NY, (CO) Lewis, (JD) Jun. 11, 1927

Bowman, Charles J.: (F) Member Lowville Lodge No. 134, F. & A. M., 1929, Lowville, NY, (CO) Lewis, (JD) Jul. 2, 1909

Bowman, Charles J.: (F) Member Lowville Chapter No. 223, R. A. M., 1929, Lowville, NY, (CO) Lewis, (JD) Sep. 14, 1920, (CEN) 1880 Waston, Lewis Co., NY, Listed with Isaac Bowman, 40, Framer, Francis, 32, Mary E., 13, Chas. J., 11, Nellie R., 10, Lora A., 8, Ida M., 5, Earl K., 1

Bowman, Earl K.: (F) Member Lowville Lodge No. 134, F. & A. M., 1929, Lowville, NY, (CO) Lewis, (JD) May 2, 1919 (CEN) 1880 Waston, Lewis Co., NY, Listed with Isaac Bowman, 40, Framer, Francis, 32, Mary E., 13, Chas. J., 11, Nellie R., 10, Lora A., 8, Ida M., 5, Earl K., 1

Bowman, Frank C.: (F) Member Lowville Lodge No. 134, F. & A. M., 1929, Lowville, NY, (CO) Lewis, (JD) May 22, 1896

Bowman, G. N.: (F) Member Murray Lodge, No. 380, F. & A. M., 1906, Holley, Orleans, Co., NY, (CMTS) Past Master, Deceased as of 1906

Bowman, H. B.: (F) Member Murray Lodge, No. 380, F. & A. M., 1906, Holley, Orleans, Co., NY

Bowman, Nelson C.: (F) Member Temple Lodge, No. 14, 1900, Albany, NY, (CEN) 1880 11th Ward, Albany, Albany Co., NY Listed with Chas. W. Bowman, 30, NY, Painter, Elizabeth, 25, Nelson, 10, Ida, 8, Florence, 2

Bowman, Wallace B.: (F) Member Society of American Magicians, Apr., 1931, New York, (RES) New Rochelle, NY

Bowne, W. H. D. W.: (F) Member Temple Lodge, No. 14, 1900, Albany, NY

Boyce, Miss: (F) Member Mispah Circle, 1888, Brooklyn, (I) *"Brooklyn Eagle,"* Dec. 12, 1888. Mentioned in an article about a fair raising funds for a Home for the Blind

Boyd, Joseph: (F) Member Long Island Lodge, No. 382, F. &. A. M. 1874, NY

Boyd, Mrs. E. S.: (F) Member Lenox Ladies Aid Society of Lenox Road M. E. Church, Brooklyn, 1900, (CMTS) *"Brooklyn Eagle,"* Mar. 13, 1900. Meeting Notice, Board of Managers

Boyd, Samuel Millspaugh: (OBIT) *"Liberty Register,"* Jul. 18, 1902, Liberty, Sullivan Co., NY, Died at his home in Middletown, Saturday, July 12th, 1902, of rheumatism of the heart, Samuel M. BOYD, aged 51 years. Mr. Boyd was born at Hemstead, Rockland Co., and was the son of Rev. John N. Boyd and Mary Jane Millsbaugh Boyd. His father was the minister at Liberty Presbyterian Church. He attended the Liberty Normal Institute until he was fifteen years old, when he entered the store of Clements & Messiter, general merchants, where he remained for more than a year. After attending the Jersey Shore Academy, Pa., and the Rastus Hall, at Flatbush, L.I., he entered Princeton College, from which he graduated in 1864 with honors. In 1868 he bought the Middletown Mercury and was its editor and publisher until 1873.siness. He later became partners with Major Wilbur M. Combs. Deceased was prominent in Masonic circles. Having served Hoffman Lodge in the Wardens' chairs he was chosen Worshipful Master in 1887 and served four years. He is survived by his wife, Louise, who was a daughter of the late Frederick S.

Boyd, of New York city, and by two sons, Dr. Irvin Boyd, of the Pennsylvania Railroad Medical Hospital Corps. with headquarters in Olean and Fred N., of the firm of Adams & Boyd, of Middletown. Mrs. Mary S. Berry, widow of Mayor D.W. Berry, is an only sister. George H. Boyd, of Crystal Run, is an uncle, and Charles J. Boyd, of the Press, and Samuel W. Millsbaugh, the stationer, of Middletown, were first cousins.

Boyd, William: (F) Member Mount Vernon Lodge, No. 3, 1900, Albany, NY

Boyle, Henry J.: (F) Member Grand Council of the Princes of Jerusalem, 1882, Albany, NY

Boynton, George A.: (F) Member Sons of New England, New England Society of the City of Brooklyn, 1887, (CMTS) *"Brooklyn Eagle,"* Dec. 22, 1887, Annual Dinner, Attendees

Brace, A. J.: (F) Member Murray Lodge, No. 380, F. & A. M., 1906, Holley, Orleans, Co., NY

Brach, Robert B.: (I) *"Brooklyn Eagle,"* Feb. 19, 1902. Funeral Services at the Club House of the Brooklyn Lodge, No. 22, B. P. O. Elks for Wm. H. West. Elk services were first then masonic services by New York Lodge No. 330, F. A. & M., (CMTS) Exalted Ruler, Elks

Bradish, James S.: (F) Member Society for the Acquisition of Useful Knowledge, Apr. 26, 1843, (CO) Lewis

Bradish, William F.: (F) Member Lowville Lodge No. 134, F. & A. M., 1929, Lowville, NY, (CO) Lewis, (JD) Dec. 15, 1911 William F., (B) 1883, (D) 1963, Mary Fish Bradish, (B) 1888, (D) 19??, (C) Beeches Bridge Cemetery, Watson, Lewis Co., NY

Bradish, William F.: (F) Member Lowville Chapter No. 223, R. A. M., 1929, Lowville, NY, (CO) Lewis, (JD) Jun. 12, 1923, (B) Apr. 9, 1883, (D) Jun., 1963, (BP) Greig, Lewis Co., NY, (MD) Oct. 15, 1913, (Spouse) Mary Emma Fish, (PRTS) Charles Bradish and Vienna Bento, (BPRTS) Edward Fish and Fannie Austin

Bradley, Daniel G.: (F) Member Temple Lodge, No. 14, 1900, Albany, NY

Bradley, George C.: (F) Member Sons of New England, New England Society of the City of Brooklyn, 1887, (CMTS) *"Brooklyn Eagle,"* Dec. 22, 1887, Annual Dinner, Attendees

Bradt, Fred C.: (F) Member Lowville Lodge No. 134, F. & A. M., 1929, Lowville, NY, (CO) Lewis, (CMTS) Past Master 1910, 1911

Brady, Earl J.: (F) Member Lowville Lodge No. 134, F. & A. M., 1929, Lowville, NY, (CO) Lewis, (JD) Jan. 29, 1897

Braime, Rear Admiral: (F) Member Sons of New England, New England Society of the City of Brooklyn, 1890, (CMTS) *"Brooklyn Eagle,"* Dec. 21, 1890, 11th Annual Dinner, Attendees

Brainard, Albert E.: (F) Member Masters Lodge, No. 5, 1900, Albany, NY, (CEN) 1880, 11th Ward, Albany, Albany Co., 50, Engineer,

Belle, 43, Blanche, 18, Eugene, 16, Albert, 13

Brainard, Morris F.: (F) Member Temple Lodge, No. 14, 1900, Albany, NY

Brainard, William H.: (F) Member Masters Lodge, No. 5, 1900, Albany, NY, (CEN) 1880, 7$^{th}$ Ward, Albany, Albany Co., NY, 44, Lumber Inspector, Georgeanna, 41, Emma, 21, Wm. H., 17, Works in Lumber Yard, Harrison, 12, Hattie F., 6, Bertha D., 2.

Brainerd, George C.: (F) Member Sons of New England, New England Society of the City of Brooklyn, 1887, (CMTS) *"Brooklyn Eagle,"* Dec. 22, 1887, Annual Dinner, Attendees

Brakman, Henry P.: (F) Member Murray Lodge, No. 380, F. & A. M., 1906, Holley, Orleans, Co., NY

Brand, Jr., Adam: (F) Member Temple Lodge, No. 14, 1900, Albany, NY

Brandes, Sol. D.: (F) Member Arcana Lodge, No. 246, F. & A. M., 1934, New York, NY, (JD) Dec. 1, 1919

Brandt, Charles: (F) Member Long Island Lodge, No. 382, F. &. A. M. 1874, NY

Bradt, Robert R.: (F) Akron Lodge No. 527, F. A. &, Akon, NY, (CMTS) Member Card No. 29, dated Dec. 31, 1966.

Brattig, Adolph: (F) Member Temple Lodge, No. 14, 1900, Albany, NY

Braudie, Joseph A.: (F) Member Arcana Lodge, No. 246, F. & A. M., 1934, New York, NY, (JD) Dec. 3, 1917

Brauer, D.: (F) Member Herber Lodge, No. 698,1898, F. & A. M., New York, NY, Greenpoint area, (RES) New York City

Breakenridge, Geo. T.: (F) Member Masters Lodge, No. 5, 1900, Albany, NY

Breckinridge, William P. C.: (F) Member Sons of New England, New England Society of the City of Brooklyn, 1890, (CMTS)*"Brooklyn Eagle,"* Dec. 21, 1890, 11th Annual Dinner, Attendees

Bredahl, Chris.: (F) Member Herber Lodge, No. 698,1898, F. & A. M., New York, NY, Greenpoint area, (RES) Brooklyn

Breen, Lael W.: (F) Member Lowville Lodge No. 134, F. & A. M., 1929, Lowville, NY, (CO) Lewis, (JD) Dec. 5, 1913

Breen, William N.: (F) Member Lowville Lodge No. 134, F. & A. M., 1929, Lowville, NY, (CO) Lewis, (JD) May 30, 1910

Breen, William N.: (F) Member Lowville Chapter No. 223, R. A. M., 1929, Lowville, NY, (CO) Lewis, (JD) Jun. 4, 1912

Bremer, H.: (F) Member Herber Lodge, No. 698,1898, F. & A. M., New York, NY, Greenpoint area, (RES) New York City

Brennan, M.: (F) Member Friendly Sons of St. Patrick, 1893, Brooklyn, (CMTS)*"Brooklyn Eagle,"* May 18, 1893, Article regarding the election of Andrew T. Sullivan as postmaster. In the article it mentioned that there were only 50 members in this Society., Guest. It is unknown if a member of the Society.

Brennan, W. F.: (F) Member Friendly Sons of St. Patrick, 1893, Brooklyn, (CMTS) *"Brooklyn Eagle,"* May 18, 1893, Article regarding the election of Andrew T. Sullivan as postmaster. In the article it mentioned that there were only 50 members in this Society., Guest. It is unknown if a member of the Society.

Brentman, C. J.: (F) Member Long Island Lodge, No. 382, F. &. A. M. 1874, NY

Bresler, Frederick U.: (F) Member Temple Lodge, No. 14, 1900, Albany, NY, (CEN) 1880 $5^{th}$ Ward, Albany, Albany Co., NY, 25, Bookkeeper, Mary E., 21, Frederick A., 3, Francis 10mo.

Brewster, Miss: (F) Member Mispah Circle, 1888, Brooklyn, (I) *"Brooklyn Eagle,"* Dec. 12, 1888. Mentioned in an article about a fair raising funds for a Home for the Blind

Brickwidde, Ida: (F) Member Mispah Circle, 1888, Brooklyn, (I) *"Brooklyn Eagle,"* Dec. 12, 1888. Mentioned in an article about a fair raising funds for a Home for the Blind

Bridges, Milton A.: (F) Member Society of American Magicians, Apr., 1931, New York, (RES) New York City

Briegel, Jess: (F) Member Society of American Magicians, Apr., 1931, New York, (RES) New York City

Brier, J.: (F) Member Long Island Lodge, No. 382, F. &. A. M. 1874, NY

Brilleman, Isaac: (F) Member Washington Lodge, No. 85, 1900, Albany, NY

Brimhall, Horace F.: (F) Member Temple Lodge, No. 14, 1900, Albany, NY

Brink, Alfred D.: (F) Member Washington Lodge, No. 85, 1900, Albany, NY, (CMTS) Past Members

Brisbin, William: (F) Member Mount Vernon Lodge, No. 3, 1900, Albany, NY

Brockway, A. H.: (F) Member Brooklyn Dental Society, 1877, Brooklyn, NY, (CMTS) *"Brooklyn Eagle,"* Dec. 15, 1877. Celebration of 10th Anniversary. Society established Dec. 14, 1867, (CMTS) Vice President

Brockway, A. H.: (F) Member Brooklyn Dental Society, 1877, Brooklyn, NY, (CMTS) *"Brooklyn Eagle,"* Dec. 15, 1877. Celebration of 10th Anniversary. Society established Dec. 14, 1867, (CMTS) Subjects Committee

Brodhead, William F.: (F) Member Arcana Lodge, No. 246, F. & A. M., 1934, New York, NY, (JD) Nov. 19, 1923

Brody, Julius K.: (F) Member Arcana Lodge, No. 246, F. & A. M., 1934, New York, NY, (JD) Apr. 15, 1912

Brome, Robert J.: (F) Member Monticello Lodge, No. 532, F. & A. M., (CO) Sullivan Co., NY, (CMTS) Past Master 1886, 1887, 1888,

1894, 1895, 1896, Trustee 1897

Bromley, J. H.: (F) Member Long Island Lodge, No. 382, F. &. A. M. 1874, NY

Bronson, Dr. William A.: (F) Member Brooklyn Dental Society, 1877, Brooklyn, NY, (CMTS) *"Brooklyn Eagle,"* Dec. 15, 1877. Celebration of 10th Anniversary. Society established Dec. 14, 1867, (CMTS) Present from New York

Bronson, J. A.: (F) Member Long Island Lodge, No. 382, F. &. A. M. 1874, NY

Bronson, R. O.: (F) Member Murray Lodge, No. 380, F. & A. M., 1906, Holley, Orleans, Co., NY

Brook, Ernest C.: (F) Member Mount Vernon Lodge, No. 3, 1900, Albany, NY

Brooks, E. H.: (F) Member Long Island Lodge, No. 382, F. &. A. M. 1874, NY

Brooks, Jonas H,: (F) Member Masters Lodge, No. 5, 1900, Albany, NY, (CEN) 14$^{th}$ Ward, Albany, Albany Co., NY, 32, MA, Single, Bank Teller, (B) Jan. 4, 1848, (BP) Worcester Co., MA, (PRTS) Moses Brooks and Sophronia Greenwood, (CMTS) Moses Brooks was living in Unadilla, Otesgo Co., NY in 1880, 1880 Census, 71, Saphrona G., 70, Charles G. Brooks, 29, Mary Barker, 22.

Brooks, Russell J.: (F) Member Lowville Lodge No. 134, F. & A. M., 1929, Lowville, NY, (CO) Lewis, (JD) Jun. 24, 1881, (CEN) 1880, Martinsbugh, Lewis Co., NY, 22, Farmer, Georgie, 18

Brosch, Jr., John: (F) Member Anglo Saxon Lodge No. 137, F. A. M., (CMTS) Meeting Notes, *"Brooklyn Eagle,"* Mar. 23, 1887, Senior Deacon, (CEN) 1880, 22$^{nd}$ Ward, District 7, Brooklyn, Kings Co., NY, John Brosh, 50, Germany, Park Police, Elizabeth, 41.

Brough, William: (F) Member St. Nicholas Society of Nassau Island, 1861, (CMTS)*"Brooklyn Eagle,"* Dec. 11, 1861, Article regarding the Anniversary Dinner, Sang *"All's Well,"* in duet

Brougham, Joseph H.: (F) Member Mount Vernon Lodge, No. 3, 1900, Albany, NY

Broughton, W. H.: (F) Member Brooklyn Revenue Reform Club, 1886, (I)*"Brooklyn Eagle,"* Jan. 27 1886, Attendees at a dinner

Brower, George V.: (F) Member Sons of New England, New England Society of the City of Brooklyn, 1890, (CMTS)*"Brooklyn Eagle,"* Dec. 21, 1890, 11th Annual Dinner, Attendees, President of the St. Nicholas Society, (CEN) 1880, Brooklyn, Kings Co., 39, NJ, Lawyer, Mary E., 35, Genevive, 8, Edith, 7, George, 5, Ernest, 3

Brown, Albert J.: (F) Member Arcana Lodge, No. 246, F. & A. M., 1934, New York, NY, (JD) Jun. 9, 1925

Brown, Asaph B.: (F) Member Temple Lodge, No. 14, 1900, Albany, NY, (CEN) 1880, 4$^{th}$ Ward, Albany, Albany Co., NY, 35, MA, Junk Dealer, Eva M., 28, CT

Brown, Daniel C.: (F) Member Masters Lodge, No. 5, 1900, Albany, NY

Brown, Dorrance D.: (F) Member Lowville Lodge No. 134, F. & A. M., 1929, Lowville, NY, (CO) Lewis, (JD) May 14, 1928

Brown, Emory: (I) *"Brooklyn Eagle,"* Dec. 7, 1896. 12th Annual Memorial Services, Plymouth Church, Brooklyn Lodge No. 22, B. F. O. Elks, Roll Call of the dead. Address made by Maryland Senator George L. Wellington, (CMTS) Name called., (CEN) 1$^{st}$ Ward, Brooklyn, Kings Co., 38, Clerk at P.O., Elizabeth 26, Emery A., 4, Hontesue, 11M, Sarah Arthur, 38, Sister-in-law, Kate Arthur, 28, sister-in-law

Brown, Frank J.: (F) Member Arcana Lodge, No. 246, F. & A. M., 1934, New York, NY, (JD) Feb. 10, 1919

Brown, George A.: (OBIT) Retired auto mechanic George A. Brown, 79, who died April 13 at the home of his daughter Mrs. Alfreda Lappen, was buried in Verona Cemetery.He was born at Godfrey, a son of the late Alpheus Brown and his wife, the former Martha Babcock.Mr. Brown manufactured cheese boxes at Godfrey until 1929 and then became an auto mechanics, a position he held until his retirement 10 years ago. He was a member of the United Church.Mr. Brown was a member of the Canadian Order of Foresters since 1912 and Albion Lodge 109, A.F. and A.M. at Harrowsmith from which he received a 50-year pin and life membership last summer.Surviving are a son, Bruce, Verona; a daughter, Mrs. T. B. Lappen, Verona; two sisters, Mrs. Mattie Jones, of Souris, Man., Mrs. Edna Sturgis, Wallaceburg, Ont.; size grandchildren and four great grandchildren.Pallbearers were Carmen Babcock, Jay Stewart, Rupert Storms, Cecil Babcock, Henry Jackson and Harold Kerr.

Brown, George F.: (F) Member Lowville Lodge No. 134, F. & A. M., 1929, Lowville, NY, (CO) Lewis, (JD) Sep. 21, 1928

Brown, Goodwin: (F) Member Masters Lodge, No. 5, 1900, Albany, NY, (CEN) 1880, Buffalo, Erie Co., NY, 28, NY, Attorney, Lillian, 29, CT, Fraser, 1, CT, (B) Apr. 5, 1852, (BP) Henderson, Jefferson Co., NY, (MD) Oct. 4, 1877, (Spouse) Lillian S. Woodhouse, (PMD) Hartford, CT, (CH) Frazer, b. Jun. 10, 1879.

Brown, H. L.: (F) Member Murray Lodge, No. 380, F. & A. M., 1906, Holley, Orleans, Co., NY, (CMTS) Lilliam Woodhouse's parents were Levi Woodhouse and Theodosia Sperry

Brown, J. M.: (F) Member Murray Lodge, No. 380, F. & A. M., 1906, Holley, Orleans, Co., NY

Brown, James: (F) Member Washington Lodge, No. 85, 1900, Albany, NY

Brown, John H.: (F) Member Monticello Lodge, No. 532, F. & A. M., (CO) Sullivan Co., NY, (CMTS) Past Master 1902

Brown, Lyman P.: (F) Member Mount Vernon Lodge, No. 3, 1900,

Albany, NY

Brown, Miller E.: (F) Member Long Island Lodge, No. 382, F. &. A. M. 1874, NY

Brown, Miss Ruth A.: (F) Member Independent Order of Good Templars, Westhampton Lodge No. 885, instituted Apr. 16, 1889, New Officers installed Feb. 16, 1900, (CMTS) Meeting Notes, *"Brooklyn Eagle,"* Feb. 18, 1900 ,Assistant Secretary

Brown, R. J.: (F) Member Murray Lodge, No. 380, F. & A. M., 1906, Holley, Orleans, Co., NY

Brown, Roy H.: (F) Member Lowville Lodge No. 134, F. & A. M., 1929, Lowville, NY, (CO) Lewis, (JD) Dec. 30, 1922

Brown, Roy H.: (F) Member Lowville Lodge No. 134, F. & A. M., 1929, Lowville, NY, (CO) Lewis, (JD) Dec. 30, 1922

Brown, Samuel W.: (F) Member Masters Lodge, No. 5, 1900, Albany, NY

Brown, T. H.: (F) Member Long Island Lodge, No. 382, F. &. A. M. 1874, NY

Brown, W. Howard: (F) Member Masters Lodge, No. 5, 1900, Albany, NY

Brown, William C.: (F) Member Lowville Lodge No. 134, F. & A. M., 1929, Lowville, NY, (CO) Lewis, (JD) Dec. 31, 1919

Browne, Walter A.: (F) Member Mount Vernon Lodge, No. 3, 1900, Albany, NY

Brownlow, William: (F) Member Temple Lodge, No. 14, 1900, Albany, NY, (CEN) 17th Ward, Albany, Albay Co., NY, 26, Carpenter, Mary J., 25, Mary, 1

Bruce, William: (F) Member Masters Lodge, No. 5, 1900, Albany, NY, (CEN) 11th Ward, Albany, Albany Co., Ny, Listed with Mrs. William Bruce, 55, widow, Wm. Bruce, 32, MD, Agnes, 30, MD, Jennie, 28, NY

Brumaghim, Edward C.: (F) Member Temple Lodge, No. 14, 1900, Albany, NY, (CMTS) Life Member

Brundage, John R.: (F) Member Society of American Magicians, Apr., 1931, New York, (RES) New York City

Brush, E.: (F) Member Long Island Lodge, No. 382, F. &. A. M. 1874, NY

Bryan, William J.: (F) Member Temple Lodge, No. 14, 1900, Albany, NY, (CMTS) Past Master 1896

Bryant, William C.: (F) Member Sons of New England, New England Society of the City of Brooklyn, 1887, (CMTS) *"Brooklyn Eagle,"* Dec. 22, 1887, Annual Dinner, Attendees

Bubaseck, Oscar J.: (F) Member Arcana Lodge, No. 246, F. & A. M., 1934, New York, NY, (JD) May 2, 1910

Buchanan, Charles J.: (F) Member Temple Lodge, No. 14, 1900, Albany, NY, (CMTS) Life Member

Buchmiller, H.: (F) Member Herber Lodge, No. 698,1898, F. & A. M.,

New York, NY, Greenpoint area, (RES) New York City

Buckingham, Oliver W.: (F) Member Sons of New England, New England Society of the City of Brooklyn, 1890, (CMTS)*"Brooklyn Eagle,"* Dec. 21, 1890, 11th Annual Dinner, Attendees

Buckley, Charles S.: (F) Member Temple Lodge, No. 14, 1900, Albany, NY

Buckley, James P.: (F) Member Temple Lodge, No. 14, 1900, Albany, NY

Buckman, Mrs. D. L.: (F) Member Young Ladies' Mission Circle, 1888, Brooklyn, (I) *"Brooklyn Eagle,"* Dec. 12, 1888. Article regarding Societies aiding churches, (CMTS) Helping St. John's Methodist Episcopal Church, Secretary

Budington, J. M.: (F) Member Murray Lodge, No. 380, F. & A. M., 1906, Holley, Orleans, Co., NY

Buell, Henry J.: (F) Member Murray Lodge, No. 380, F. & A. M., 1906, Holley, Orleans, Co., NY, (CMTS) Past Master

Buell, Lansing M.: (F) Member Masters Lodge, No. 5, 1900, Albany, NY, (CEN) 1880, $17^{th}$ Ward, Albany, Albany CO., NY, 53, Clerk In Hardware and Iron Store, Mary A., 53, CT, (B) Apr. 10, 1827, (PRTS) Rodbet Buell and Harriet Merchant

Buffman, Thomas A.: (F) Member Sons of New England, New England Society of the City of Brooklyn, 1890, (CMTS)*"Brooklyn Eagle,"* Dec. 21, 1890, 11th Annual Dinner, Attendees

Bugden, Herbert E.: (F) Member Temple Lodge, No. 14, 1900, Albany, NY, (CEN) $11^{th}$ Ward, Albany, Albany Co., NY, Listed with Josiah Bugden, 62, Eng, Carpenter, Mary, 55, NY, Herbert, 23, Pressman, Arthur, 10

Buhl, Gertel J.: (F) Member Temple Lodge, No. 14, 1900, Albany, NY

Bulger, Charles E.: (F) Member Mount Vernon Lodge, No. 3, 1900, Albany, NY, (CEN) $4^{th}$ Ward, Albany, Albany Co., NY. Listed With Isaac Bulger, 55, Ire, teamster, Anna, 60, Ire, Benjamin, 27, Stationery Engineer, William, 24, Stationery Engineer, Charles, 21, Carpenter

Bullwinkle, G.: (F) Member Herber Lodge, No. 698,1898, F. & A. M., New York, NY, Greenpoint area, (RES) Brooklyn

Burch, George S.: (F) Member Temple Lodge, No. 14, 1900, Albany, NY,(CEN) $17^{th}$ Ward, Albany, Albany Co., NY, Listed with John G. Birch, 52, Coal Dealer, Mary A., 47, Fred G., 21, Works In Coal Office, John G., 19, Works in Telephone Office, George S., 14, Alice M., 6.

Burckel, Christian E.: (F) Member Society of American Magicians, Apr., 1931, New York, (RES) Mt. Vernon, NY

Burdick, A. C.: (F) Member Lowville Lodge No. 134, F. & A. M., 1929, Lowville, NY, (CO) Lewis, (CMTS) Past Master 1906. 1907

Burdick, Albert C.: (F) Member Lowville Lodge No. 134, F. & A. M.,

1929, Lowville, NY, (CO) Lewis, (JD) Feb. 10, 1893

Burdick, Albert C.: (F) Member Lowville Chapter No. 223, R. A. M., 1929, Lowville, NY, (CO) Lewis, (JD) Feb. 20, 1894, (B) Aug. 11, 1871, (BP) Graig, Lewis Co., NY, (D) Jun. 14, 1931, (MD) Sep. 15, 1919, (BP) Lewis Co., NY, (Spouse) Elizabeth H. Cobb, (PRTS) Luther Calvin Burdick, (b. Apr. 7, 1846, d. Feb. 5, 1898, md. Jun. 6, 1867) and Sarah M. Stephens, (GPRTS) Albert Burdick and Emily Berrus, (CEN) 1880 Greig, Lewis Co., NY Listed with Luther Burdick, 34, NY, Dry Goods Merchant. Sarah, 27, Albert L. C., 8, Charles M., 6, Charles Stephens, 50, father-in-law

Burdick, Charles M.: (F) Member Lowville Chapter No. 223, R. A. M., 1929, Lowville, NY, (CO) Lewis, (JD) Nov. 20, 1900, (B) Aug. 26, 1873, (BP) Graig, Lewis Co., NY, (PRTS) Luther Calvin Burdick, (b. Apr. 7, 1846, d. Feb. 5, 1898, md. Jun. 6, 1867) and Sarah M. Stephens, (GPRTS) Albert Burdick and Emily Berrus, (CEN) 1880 Greig, Lewis Co., NY Listed with Luther Burdick, 34, NY, Dry Goods Merchant. Sarah, 27, Albert L. C., 8, Charles M., 6, Charles Stephens, 50, father-in-law

Burdick, E. DeForest: (F) Member Lowville Chapter No. 223, R. A. M., 1929, Lowville, NY, (CO) Lewis, (JD) Mar. 27, 1928

Burdick, Franklin G.: (F) Member Lowville Chapter No. 223, R. A. M., 1929, Lowville, NY, (CO) Lewis, (JD) Jan. 17, 1911, (B) Apr. 19, 1858, (BP) Turn, Lewis Co., NY, (PRTS) Albert Burdick and Emily Berrus

Burdick, Linneus H.: (F) Member Temple Lodge, No. 14, 1900, Albany, NY, (CEN) 1880, 11$^{th}$ Ward, Albany, Albany C., NY, Listed with Lineas H., 28, Printer, Gerturde, 27, Arthur P., 8, Florence, 6, Gertrude E., 4, Stella, 17, sister, (B) Mar. 21, 1851, (BP) DeRuyter, Madison Co., NY, (PRTS) Addison S. Burdick and Mary L. Stillman, (MD) Nov. 3, 1870, (PMD) Albany, NY, (Spouse) Gertrude Anna Putnam

Burdick, Raymond C.: (F) Member Lowville Chapter No. 223, R. A. M., 1929, Lowville, NY, (CO) Lewis, (JD) Oct. 27, 1920

Burdick, Spencer E.: (F) Member Lowville Chapter No. 223, R. A. M., 1929, Lowville, NY, (CO) Lewis, (JD) May 5, 1908, (B) Nov. 26, 1874, (D) 1931, (BP) Turn, Lewis CO., NY, (PRTS) Elhanen D. Burdick and Delaphina A. Brown, (CEN) Glendale, Lewis Co., NY Listed with E. D. Burdick, 29, Merchant, Delaphine, 29, Carrie E., 9, Ella J., 7, Spencer E., 5, Harvery D., 2

Burger, Philip G.: (F) Member Temple Lodge, No. 14, 1900, Albany, NY

Burgess, William L.: (F) Member Mount Vernon Lodge, No. 3, 1900, Albany, NY

Burham, William F.: (F) Member Temple Lodge, No. 14, 1900, Albany, NY

Burham , Edward P.: (F) Member Temple Lodge, No. 14, 1900, Albany, NY

Burhams, George M.: (F) Member Temple Lodge, No. 14, 1900, Albany, NY

Burke, Adams J.: (F) Member Mount Vernon Lodge, No. 3, 1900, Albany, NY

Burke, John: (F) Member Long Island Lodge, No. 382, F. &. A. M. 1874, NY

Burkhart, Herman L.: (F) Member Lowville Lodge No. 134, F. & A. M., 1929, Lowville, NY, (CO) Lewis, (JD) Sep. 21, 1928

Burkhart, Ora: (F) Member Hope Rebekah Lodge No. 10, 1949-1950, Brockport, NY, (CO) Monroe

Burkitt, Thomas: (F) Member Friendly Sons of St. Patrick, 1893, Brooklyn, (CMTS)*"Brooklyn Eagle,"* May 18, 1893, Article Regarding the election of Andrew T. Sullivan as postmaster. In the article it mentioned that there were only 50 members in this Society., Treasurer, Member of the Dinner Committee

Burn, Henry W.: (F) Member Temple Lodge, No. 14, 1900, Albany, NY

Burnard, R. W.: (F) Member Star of Bethlem No. 322, F. A. M., 1900, Brooklyn, (I) *"Brooklyn Eagle,"* Feb. 3, 1900. Meeting Notice., (CMTS) Junior Warden

Burnet, Max: (F) Member Arcana Lodge, No. 246, F. & A. M., 1934, New York, NY, (JD) Oct. 26, 1926

Burnett, Miss C.: (F) Member Nativity Sewing Society, 1900, Brooklyn, (I) *"Brooklyn Eagle,"* Feb. 3, 1900. Article regarding raising money to buy clothing for the poor.

Burnham, Avon C.: (F) Member National Union, Brooklyn No. 375, 1900, (I)*"Brooklyn Eagle,"* Feb. 3, 1900. Meeting Notice, (CMTS) Financial Secretary

Burns, L. G.: (F) Member Murray Lodge, No. 380, F. & A. M., 1906, Holley, Orleans, Co., NY

Burr, Morris S.: (F) Member Lowville Chapter No. 223, R. A. M., 1929, Lowville, NY, (CO) Lewis, (JD) Nov. 9, 1920

Burrows, James T.: (F) Member Society of American Magicians, Apr., 1931, New York, (RES) Valley Stream, NY

Burtis, John H.: (F) Member Brooklyn Revenue Reform Club, 1886, (I)*"Brooklyn Eagle,"* Jan. ,27 1886, Attendees at a dinner

Burwell, Charles D.: (F) Member Sons of New England, New England Society of the City of Brooklyn, 1890, (CMTS)*"Brooklyn Eagle,"* Dec. 21, 1890, 11th Annual Dinner, Attendees

Bush, Louis: (F) Member Lowville Chapter No. 223, R. A. M., 1929, Lowville, NY, (CO) Lewis, (JD) Apr. 21, 1903

Bush, William T.: (F) Member Lowville Lodge No. 134, F. & A. M., 1929, Lowville, NY, (CO) Lewis, (CMTS) Past Master 1891, 1892

Bush, William T.: (F) Member Lowville Lodge No. 134, F. & A. M.,

1929, Lowville, NY, (CO) Lewis, (JD) May 16, 1884
Bush, William T.: (F) Member Lowville Chapter No. 223, R. A. M., 1929, Lowville, NY, (CO) Lewis, (JD) Jan. 27, 1885
Butcher, Silas R.: (F) Member Sons of New England, New England Society of the City of Brooklyn, 1887, (CMTS) *"Brooklyn Eagle,"* Dec. 22, 1887, Annual Dinner, Attendees
Butler, Ladson: (F) Member Society of American Magicians, Apr., 1931, New York, (RES) New York City
Butler, Miss: (F) Member Nativity Sewing Society, 1900, Brooklyn, (I) *"Brooklyn Eagle,"* Feb. 3, 1900. Article regarding raising money to buy clothing for the poor.
Butler, Mrs.: (F) Member Nativity Sewing Society, 1900, Brooklyn, (I) *"Brooklyn Eagle,"* Feb. 3, 1900. Article regarding raising money to buy clothing for the poor.
Butler, W. Burdett: (F) Member Temple Lodge, No. 14, 1900, Albany, NY
Butler, William Henry: (F) Member Mount Vernon Lodge, No. 3, 1900, Albany, NY
Buttling, William J.: (I) *"Brooklyn Eagle,"* Feb. 19, 1902. Funeral Services at the Club House of the Brooklyn Lodge, No. 22, B. P. O. Elks for Wm. H. West. Elk services were first then masonic services by New York Lodge No. 330, F. A. & M., (CMTS) Made a floral gift.
Butts, Edward C.: (F) Member Lowville Lodge No. 134, F. & A. M., 1929, Lowville, NY, (CO) Lewis, (JD) Nov. 15, 1889
Butts, Hayden H.: (F) Member Sons of New England, New England Society of the City of Brooklyn, 1890, (CMTS) *"Brooklyn Eagle,"* Dec. 21, 1890, 11th Annual Dinner, Attendees
Buxton, James H.: (F) Member Lowville Lodge No. 134, F. & A. M., 1929, Lowville, NY, (CO) Lewis, (JD) Jun. 7, 1912, (CEN) 1880 Harrisburg, Lewis Co., NY, 18, Farm Laborer
Buys, Frederick C.: (F) Member Brooklyn Choral Society, 1889, (CMTS) *"Brooklyn Eagle,"* Oct. 2, 1889, (CMTS) Secretary
Byrne, Miss Rose: (F) Member Nativity Sewing Society, 1900, Brooklyn, (I) *"Brooklyn Eagle,"* Feb. 3, 1900. Article regarding raising money to buy clothing for the poor.
Cady, F. W.: (F) Member Murray Lodge, No. 380, F. & A. M., 1906, Holley, Orleans, Co., NY
Cahalmers, Robert: (F) Member Temple Lodge, No. 14, 1900, Albany, NY
Caldwell, Walter Lee: (F) Member Temple Lodge, No. 14, 1900, Albany, NY
Callen, Peter J.: (F) Member Temple Lodge, No. 14, 1900, Albany, NY
Calligan, Mrs. George: (F) Member Mispah Circle, 1888, Brooklyn, (I)

*"Brooklyn Eagle,"* Dec. 12, 1888. Mentioned in an article about a fair raising funds for a Home for the Blind

Cameron, Edward M.: (F) Member Masters Lodge, No. 5, 1900, Albany, NY

Cameron, Frederick W.: (F) Member Temple Lodge, No. 14, 1900, Albany, NY

Cameron, Henry Griggs: (OBIT) *"News Journal"* Friday, Oct. 20, 2000. Henry Griggs Cameron, 82, of Sarasota, FL, formerly of Irvington-on-Hudson, NY, born July 21, 1918, died October 16, 2000. A retired owner of an Advertising and Printing Business, "SE Same Press." Graduated from NY School of Banking, NYU. Served in the US Coast Guard. Attended St. Andrews United Church of Christ, was a Master Mason at Hiawatha Lodge, Pleasantville, NY; Docent of Mote Marine Aquarium, Sun Coast Mummers String Band of Bradenton, FL. Survived by wife, Louise Marie Cameron, Sarasota, FL; daughter, Laurie Griggs Cameron, Buffalo, MN; sons, Bruce L. Cameron, La Mesa, CA, Bradner Scott Cameron, Bridgeport, CT; sister, Margaret Cameron Sears, Washingtonville, NY; daughters- in-law Mrs. Betty Cameron, Mrs. Isabel Cameron; grandchildren, Andrew and Sean Siffert. Predeceased by Miriam Fulton Vande Mark and Henry G. Cameron, Sr. Memorial service Friday, October 20, 2000 at 10 am, St. Andrew's United Church of Christ, Sarasota, FL, Masonic services to follow.

Campbell, Charles C.: (F) Member Mount Vernon Lodge, No. 3, 1900, Albany, NY

Campbell, Felix: (F) Member Friendly Sons of St. Patrick, 1893, Brooklyn, (CMTS)*"Brooklyn Eagle,"* May 18, 1893, Article regarding the election of Andrew T. Sullivan as postmaster. In the article it mentioned that there were only 50 members in this Society. It is unknown if a member of the Society.

Campbell, J. W.: (F) Member Long Island Lodge, No. 382, F. &. A. M. 1874, NY

Campbell, Lawrence M.: (F) Member Lowville Chapter No. 223, R. A. M., 1929, Lowville, NY, (CO) Lewis, (JD) May 10. 1927

Campbell, W. A.: (F) Member Brooklyn Dental Society, 1877, Brooklyn, NY, (CMTS) *"Brooklyn Eagle,"* Dec. 15, 1877. Celebration of 10th Anniversary. Society established Dec. 14, 1867, (CMTS) Executive Committee

Campbell, William H.: (F) Member Mount Vernon Lodge, No. 3, 1900, Albany, NY

Candler, F. B.: (F) Member Sons of New England, New England Society of the City of Brooklyn, 1890, (CMTS)*"Brooklyn Eagle,"* Dec. 21, 1890, 11th Annual Dinner, Attendees

Canfield, John: (F) Member Denmark Ecclesiastical Society, Sep. 21, 1810, (CO) Lewis, (CMTS) Trustee

Canfield, Rev. A. J.: (F) Member Brooklyn Revenue Reform Club, 1886,

(I)*"Brooklyn Eagle,"* Jan. ,27 1886, Attendees at a dinner

Cantine, Edward B.: (F) Member Temple Lodge, No. 14, 1900, Albany, NY, (CEN) 1880, Rome, Oneida CO., NY, Listed with George H. Cantine, 40, Manager Life Insurance Agency, Marrion, J., 39, Edward B. VT, 19, Law Student, France M., 4, sister, Alace, 21, Sister, (AKA) Edward Byron Cantini, (B) Aug. 4, 1860, (BP) Rutalnd, VT, (PRTS) George Cantine and Marion Josina Cook.

Canton, T.: (F) Member Long Island Lodge, No. 382, F. &. A. M. 1874, NY

Cardini, Richard: (F) Member Society of American Magicians, Apr., 1931, New York, (RES) Jamaica, L. I., NY

Carine, Miss Lillie: (F) Member Mispah Circle, 1888, Brooklyn, (I) *"Brooklyn Eagle,"* Dec. 12, 1888. Mentioned in an article about a fair raising funds for a Home for the Blind

Carine, Miss Mattie: (F) Member Mispah Circle, 1888, Brooklyn, (I) *"Brooklyn Eagle,"* Dec. 12, 1888. Mentioned in an article about a fair raising funds for a Home for the Blind

Carine, Miss Susie: (F) Member Mispah Circle, 1888, Brooklyn, (I) *"Brooklyn Eagle,"* Dec. 12, 1888. Mentioned in an article about a fair raising funds for a Home for the Blind

Carine, Mrs.: (F) Member Mispah Circle, 1888, Brooklyn, (I) *"Brooklyn Eagle,"* Dec. 12, 1888. Mentioned in an article about a fair raising funds for a Home for the Blind

Carlsen, A. W.: (F) Member Long Island Lodge, No. 382, F. &. A. M. 1874, NY

Carlson, Charles A.: (F) Member Murray Lodge, No. 380, F. & A. M., 1906, Holley, Orleans, Co., NY

Carlton, Clifford B.: (F) Member Lowville Lodge No. 134, F. & A. M., 1929, Lowville, NY, (CO) Lewis, (JD) Nov. 2, 1924

Carman, Jr., N. G.: (F) Member Sons of New England, New England Society of the City of Brooklyn, 1890, (CMTS)*"Brooklyn Eagle,"* Dec. 21, 1890, 11th Annual Dinner, Attendees

Carpenter, Lois: (F) Member Hope Rebekah Lodge No. 10, 1949-1950, Brockport, NY, (CO) Monroe

Carpenter, Stanton P.: (F) Member Lowville Lodge No. 134, F. & A. M., 1929, Lowville, NY, (CO) Lewis, (JD) Mar. 30, 1928

Carpenter, W. D.: (I) *"Brooklyn Eagle,"* Dec. 7, 1896. 12th Annual Memorial Services, Plymouth Church, Brooklyn Lodge No. 22, B. F. O. Elks, Roll Call of the dead. Address made by Maryland Senator George L. Wellington. , (CMTS) Name called.

Carpenter, Jr., Geo. W.: (F) Member Masters Lodge, No. 5, 1900, Albany, NY

Carr, Dr. William: (F) Member Brooklyn Dental Society, 1877, Brooklyn, NY, (CMTS) *"Brooklyn Eagle,"* Dec. 15, 1877. Celebration of 10th Anniversary. Society established Dec. 14, 1867, (CMTS) Present from New York

Carriere, Jr., John B.: (F) Member Temple Lodge, No. 14, 1900, Albany, NY

Carroll, Joseph W.: (F) Member Sons of New England, New England Society of the City of Brooklyn, 1890, (CMTS)*"Brooklyn Eagle,"* Dec. 21, 1890, 11th Annual Dinner, Attendees

Carroll, Mrs. S.: (F) Member Nativity Sewing Society, 1900, Brooklyn, (I) *"Brooklyn Eagle,"* Feb. 3, 1900. Article regarding raising money to buy clothing for the poor.

Carson, Miss Grace: (F) Member Mispah Circle, 1888, Brooklyn, (I) *"Brooklyn Eagle,"* Dec. 12, 1888. Mentioned in an article about a fair raising funds for a Home for the Blind

Carson, T.: (F) Member Long Island Lodge, No. 382, F. &. A. M. 1874, NY

Carter, Clarence L.: (F) Member Lowville Lodge No. 134, F. & A. M., 1929, Lowville, NY, (CO) Lewis, (JD) May 2, 1919

Carter, Edith: (F) Member Hope Rebekah Lodge No. 10, 1949-1950, Brockport, NY, (CO) Monroe, (CMTS) treasurer

Carter, Milton: (F) Member Lowville Lodge No. 134, F. & A. M., 1929, Lowville, NY, (CO) Lewis, (JD) Aug. 28, 1915

Carter, William H.: (F) Member Mount Vernon Lodge, No. 3, 1900, Albany, NY

Carter , Charles A.: (F) Member Lowville Lodge No. 134, F. & A. M., 1929, Lowville, NY, (CO) Lewis, (JD) Oct. 15, 1920

Carty, Frank: (F) Member Temple Lodge, No. 14, 1900, Albany, NY

Carvan, Christopher C.: (F) Member Society of American Magicians, Apr., 1931, New York, (RES) New York City

Cary, I. B.: (F) Member Murray Lodge, No. 380, F. & A. M., 1906, Holley, Orleans, Co., NY

Cary, Isaac B.: (F) Member Sons of New England, New England Society of the City of Brooklyn, 1887, (CMTS)*"Brooklyn Eagle,"* Dec. 22, 1887, Annual Dinner, Attendees

Cary, Isaac H.: (F) Member Sons of New England, New England Society of the City of Brooklyn, 1890, (CMTS)*"Brooklyn Eagle,"* Dec. 21, 1890, 11th Annual Dinner, Attendees

Case, Mrs. John A.: (F) Member Lenox Ladies Aid Society of Lenox Road M. E. Church, Brooklyn, 1900, (CMTS) *"Brooklyn Eagle,"* Mar. 13, 1900. Meeting Notice, Board of Managers

Case, Spencer T.: (F) Member Mount Vernon Lodge, No. 3, 1900, Albany, NY

Casey, John M.: (F) Member Long Island Lodge, No. 382, F. &. A. M. 1874, NY

Cassidy, Miss: (F) Member Nativity Sewing Society, 1900, Brooklyn, (I) *"Brooklyn Eagle,"* Feb. 3, 1900. Article regarding raising money to buy clothing for the poor.

Cassidy, Mrs. J. J.: (F) Member Nativity Sewing Society, 1900,

Brooklyn, (I) *"Brooklyn Eagle,"* Feb. 3, 1900. Article regarding raising money to buy clothing for the poor.

Castle, Thomas S.: (F) Member Mount Vernon Lodge, No. 3, 1900, Albany, NY

Caswell, Miss K.: (F) Member Ladies Aid Society of Flatbush, Brooklyn, 1888, (CMTS) *"Brooklyn Eagle,"* Oct. 7, 1888, Meeting Notice, Secretary

Catlin, General Isaac S.: (F) Member Sons of New England, New England Society of the City of Brooklyn, 1890, (CMTS)*"Brooklyn Eagle,"* Dec. 21, 1890, 11th Annual Dinner, Attendees

Caton, Frank C.: (F) Member Society of American Magicians, Apr., 1931, New York, (RES) Caldwell, NJ

Chamberlain, Frank F.: (F) Member Masters Lodge, No. 5, 1900, Albany, NY, (CMTS) Past Master

Chamberlain, Rev. Dr. L. T.: (F) Member Sons of New England, New England Society of the City of Brooklyn, 1887, (CMTS)*"Brooklyn Eagle,"* Dec. 22, 1887, Annual Dinner, Attendees

Champlin, Charles S.: (F) Member Grand Council of the Princes of Jerusalem, 1882, Albany, NY

Champlin, Charles S.: (F) Member Ineffable and Sublime Grand Lodge of Perfection, 1882, Albany, NY

Chanberlain, E. T.: (F) Member Masters Lodge, No. 5, 1900, Albany, NY

Chapelle, M. S.: (I) *"Brooklyn Eagle,"* Feb. 19, 1902. Funeral Services at the Club House of the Brooklyn Lodge, No. 22, B. P. O. Elks for Wm. H. West. Elk services were first then masonic services by New York Lodge No. 330, F. A. & M., (CMTS) Made a floral gift.

Chapin, Mayor Alfred: (F) Member Sons of New England, New England Society of the City of Brooklyn, 1890, (CMTS)*"Brooklyn Eagle,"* Dec. 21, 1890, 11th Annual Dinner, Attendees

Chapin, Mayor-Elect: (F) Member Sons of New England, New England Society of the City of Brooklyn, 1887, (CMTS)*"Brooklyn Eagle,"* Dec. 22, 1887, Annual Dinner, Attendees

Chapman, A. N.: (F) Member Brooklyn Dental Society, 1877, Brooklyn, NY, (CMTS) *"Brooklyn Eagle,"* Dec. 15, 1877. Celebration of 10th Anniversary. Society established Dec. 14, 1867, (CMTS) Executive Committee

Chapman, Clarence C.: (F) Member Masters Lodge, No. 5, 1900, Albany, NY, (B) Jul. 25, 1853, (BP) Albany, Albany Co., NY, (PRTS) Isaac Chapman

Chapman, Napoleon B.: (F) Member Temple Lodge, No. 14, 1900, Albany, NY , (CEN) 1880, $15^{th}$ Ward, Albany, Albany Co., NY, 42, Bookkeeper, Mary, 32, William, 8, Edwin, 5, (B) Aug. 6, 1839, (BP) Rensselaerville, Albany Co., NY, (PRTS) William S. Chapman and Emily Winans

Chappel, J. H.: (F) Member Long Island Lodge, No. 382, F. &. A. M.

1874, NY

Chase, Helen: (F) Member Hope Rebekah Lodge No. 10, 1949-1950, Brockport, NY, (CO) Monroe, (CMTS) Financial Secretary

Chayes, Arthur: (F) Member Arcana Lodge, No. 246, F. & A. M., 1934, New York, NY, (JD) May 7, 1923

Chiguoine, V. P.: (F) Member Long Island Lodge, No. 382, F. &. A. M. 1874, NY

Chism, George M.: (F) Member Temple Lodge, No. 14, 1900, Albany, NY, (CEN) 1880, 5th Ward, Albany, Albany Co., NY, Living at a Hotel, 35, NY, cigarmaker

Chism, Jr., John Davis: (F) Member Temple Lodge, No. 14, 1900, Albany, NY

Christie, D. E.: (F) Member Home Circle, 1900, Brooklyn, (I) *"Brooklyn Eagle,"* Feb. 3, 1900. Meeting Notice., (CMTS) Secretary

Church, A. B.: (F) Member Murray Lodge, No. 380, F. & A. M., 1906, Holley, Orleans, Co., NY

Citron, Solomon L.: (F) Member Arcana Lodge, No. 246, F. & A. M., 1934, New York, NY, (JD) May 11, 1926

Claghorn, Charles: (F) Member Brooklyn Revenue Reform Club, 1886, (I) *"Brooklyn Eagle,"* Jan. 27, 1886, Attendees at a dinner

Clairmont, Henry B.: (F) Member Temple Lodge, No. 14, 1900, Albany, NY

Clark, C. L.: (F) Member Long Island Lodge, No. 382, F. &. A. M. 1874, NY

Clark, Eli Clinton: (F) Member Masters Lodge, No. 5, 1900, Albany, NY, (CMTS) Past Master

Clark, G. T.: (F) Member Society for the Relief of Respectable Indigent Females, Brooklyn, (I) Brooklyn Eagle, Nov. 13, 1879, (CMTS) Superintendent Female Old Folks Home

Clark, Henry: (F) Member Temple Lodge, No. 14, 1900, Albany, NY

Clark, John: (F) Member Friendly Sons of St. Patrick, 1893, Brooklyn, (CMTS) *"Brooklyn Eagle,"* May 18, 1893, Article regarding the election of Andrew T. Sullivan as postmaster. In the article it mentioned that there were only 50 members in this Society. It is unknown if a member of the Society.

Clark, John P.: (F) Member Educational Society of Lewis Co., NY, Nov. 14, 1845, (CMTS) Treasurer

Clark, John S.: (F) Member Harrisburgh Ecclesiastical Society, Jul. 9, 1805, (CO) Lewis, (B) Aug. 18, 1778, (BP) Barre, MA, (Spouse) Abigail White, (PRTS) William Clark

Clark, Miss J.: (F) Member Nativity Sewing Society, 1900, Brooklyn, (I) *"Brooklyn Eagle,"* Feb. 3, 1900. Article regarding raising money to buy clothing for the poor.

Clark, Mrs. J. T.: (F) Member Nativity Sewing Society, 1900, Brooklyn, (I) *"Brooklyn Eagle,"* Feb. 3, 1900. Article regarding

raising money to buy clothing for the poor.

Clark, S. Beers: (F) Member Long Island Lodge, No. 382, F. &. A. M. 1874, NY

Clark, W. W.: (F) Member Long Island Lodge, No. 382, F. &. A. M. 1874, NY

Clark, Jr., Eli C.: (F) Member Grand Council of the Princes of Jerusalem, 1882, Albany, NY

Clarke, Charles M.: (F) Member Sons of New England, New England Society of the City of Brooklyn, 1887, (CMTS) *"Brooklyn Eagle,"* Dec. 22, 1887, Annual Dinner, Attendees

Clarke, Walter V.: (F) Member Society of American Magicians, Apr., 1931, New York, (RES) New York City

Clausen, Frederick W.: (F) Member Arcana Lodge, No. 246, F. & A. M., 1934, New York, NY, (JD) May 2, 1921

Cleary, Mrs. Anna: (F) Member Ladies Catholic Benevolent Association, St. Augustines No. 214, 1900, Brooklyn, (I) *"Brooklyn Eagle,"* Feb. 3, 1900. Meeting Notice, (CMTS) Financial Secretary

Clement, Judge Nathaniel: (F) Member Sons of New England, New England Society of the City of Brooklyn, 1890, (CMTS) *"Brooklyn Eagle,"* Dec. 21, 1890, 11th Annual Dinner, Attendees

Clerc, L.: (F) Member Long Island Lodge, No. 382, F. &. A. M. 1874, NY

Clidden, Charles W.: (F) Member Murray Lodge, No. 380, F. & A. M., 1906, Holley, Orleans, Co., NY

Clinton, Francis W.: (F) Member Society of American Magicians, Apr., 1931, New York, (RES) Brooklyn, NY

Clinton, Rev. Isaac: (F) Member Lewis County Bible Society, 1812, Charter Officers, (CMTS) Vice President, (B) Jan. 21, 1759, (D) Mar. 18, 1840, (DP) Lowville, NY, (PRTS) Lawrence Clinton and Sarah Tryal, (Spouse) Charit Welles

Clough, C. W.: (F) Member Murray Lodge, No. 380, F. & A. M., 1906, Holley, Orleans, Co., NY

Clough, F. A.: (F) Member Murray Lodge, No. 380, F. & A. M., 1906, Holley, Orleans, Co., NY

Clough, G. P.: (F) Member Long Island Lodge, No. 382, F. &. A. M. 1874, NY

Clough, Jeremiah: (F) Member Murray Lodge, No. 380, F. & A. M., 1906, Holley, Orleans, Co., NY, (CMTS) Past Master, Deceased as of 1906

Clowes, Dr. J. W.: (F) Member Brooklyn Dental Society, 1877, Brooklyn, NY, (CMTS) *"Brooklyn Eagle,"* Dec. 15, 1877. Celebration of 10th Anniversary. Society established Dec. 14, 1867, (CMTS) Present from New York

Clugstone, G. B.: (F) Member Arcana Lodge, No. 246, F. & A. M., 1934, New York, NY, (JD) Feb. 17, 1902, Life Member

Cnouse, Richard C.: (OBIT) *"The River Reporter,"* Apr. 19, 2001,

Narrowsburg, NY. Richard "Dick" C. Canouse of Milford, an 18-year Milford supervisor and 13-year chairman of the Milford Township Planning Commission, died Monday, April 9, 2001 in Bon Secours Community Hospital in Port Jervis. He was 69. Son of Leona Wright Canouse and the late Clyde Canouse, he was born September 23, 1931 in Milford. He was a U.S. Army veteran serving as Corporal. He studied under the G.I. Bill at the International Correspondence School in the field of plumbing and heating. He went into business as a contractor. He purchased the summer resort Moon Valley Park that he operated with his and was a member of the Pike County Chamber of Commerce; Lake Wallenpaupack Association; Pennsylvania Tourist Association and the Pocono Mountain Vacation Bureau. He was a life member of the Milford Fire Department, serving twice as chief and also as president. He was appointed as Pike County Coordinator of the Fireman's Federation. He was a volunteer dispatcher for the Milford Fire Department for 15 years in Pike Countyand a member of the Milford Fire Department Ambulance Corps for more than 25 years. He was an original member of the Advisory Board for the Pike County Communication Center. He was a member of the Pike County Fire Police Association, the NRA and the Marsch-Kellogg American Legion Post #139 in Milford. Survivors include his mother, of Milford; his wife, Viola Kern Canouse at home; two daughters, Lorelei Davis and husband Steven of Milford and Jacqueline Carey and husband William of Westfield; and four grandchildren. Memorial services were held April 18, 7:30 p.m. in the First Presbyterian Church of Milford on Broad Street. Burial will be in Milford Cemetery, Dingman Township at the convenience of the family.

Cocks, Charles P.: (F) Member Brooklyn Revenue Reform Club, 1886, (I)*"Brooklyn Eagle,"* Jan. ,27 1886, Attendees at a dinner

Coddington, J.: (F) Member Long Island Lodge, No. 382, F. &. A. M. 1874, NY

Coe, Charles G.: (F) Member Anglo Saxon Lodge No. 137, F. A. M., (CMTS) Meeting Notes, *"Brooklyn Eagle,"* Mar. 13, 1887, Entered the Apprentice Degree by W. M. Jerome E. Morse

Coe, Henry L.: (F) Member Sons of New England, New England Society of the City of Brooklyn, 1890, (CMTS)*"Brooklyn Eagle,"* Dec. 21, 1890, 11th Annual Dinner, Attendees, (CEN) 1880, Brooklyn, Kings Co., NY, 41, Brass Manufacturer, Martha H., 37, Mary J., 15, Florence, 11, Blanch, 8

Coe, Ray D.: (F) Member Lowville Lodge No. 134, F. & A. M., 1929, Lowville, NY, (CO) Lewis, (JD) Jun. 20, 1924

Coffin, Harry R.: (F) Member Lowville Lodge No. 134, F. & A. M., 1929, Lowville, NY, (CO) Lewis, (JD) Nov. 18, 1927

Cohen, Abram: (F) Member Arcana Lodge, No. 246, F. & A. M., 1934,

New York, NY, (JD) Jun. 4, 1923
Cohen, Harry: (F) Member Arcana Lodge, No. 246, F. & A. M., 1934, New York, NY, (JD) Oct. 20, 1919
Cohen, Joseph: (F) Member Arcana Lodge, No. 246, F. & A. M., 1934, New York, NY, (JD) Mar. 26, 1929
Cohen, Max: (F) Member Arcana Lodge, No. 246, F. & A. M., 1934, New York, NY, (JD) Feb. 9, 1932
Cohen, Ralph: (F) Member Arcana Lodge, No. 246, F. & A. M., 1934, New York, NY, (JD) Mar. 26, 1929
Cohen, Samuel: (F) Member Arcana Lodge, No. 246, F. & A. M., 1934, New York, NY, (JD) Jun. 23, 1931
Cohn, Arthur: (F) Member Arcana Lodge, No. 246, F. & A. M., 1934, New York, NY, (JD) May 3, 1920
Coit, William: (F) Member Sons of New England, New England Society of the City of Brooklyn, 1890, (CMTS)*"Brooklyn Eagle,"* Dec. 21, 1890, 11th Annual Dinner, Attendees
Cole, C. H.: (F) Member Long Island Lodge, No. 382, F. &. A. M. 1874, NY
Cole, Charles W.: (F) Member Temple Lodge, No. 14, 1900, Albany, NY
Cole, Dorothy: (F) Member Hope Rebekah Lodge No. 10, 1949-1950, Brockport, NY, (CO) Monroe
Cole, Edward H.: (F) Member Temple Lodge, No. 14, 1900, Albany, NY
Cole, Frederick W.: (F) Member Temple Lodge, No. 14, 1900, Albany, NY
Cole, G. P.: (F) Member Murray Lodge, No. 380, F. & A. M., 1906, Holley, Orleans, Co., NY
Cole, I. U.: (F) Member Murray Lodge, No. 380, F. & A. M., 1906, Holley, Orleans, Co., NY
Cole, N. L.: (F) Member Murray Lodge, No. 380, F. & A. M., 1906, Holley, Orleans, Co., NY
Cole, Harry E.: (F) Member Temple Lodge, No. 14, 1900, Albany, NY
Colletti, J.: (F) Member Long Island Lodge, No. 382, F. &. A. M. 1874, NY
Collier, DuBois: (F) Member Ineffable and Sublime Grand Lodge of Perfection, 1882, Albany, NY
Collier, DuBoise: (F) Member Grand Council of the Princes of Jerusalem, 1882, Albany, NY
Collier, Rev. R. Price: (F) Member Sons of New England, New England Society of the City of Brooklyn, 1890, (CMTS)*"Brooklyn Eagle,"* Dec. 21, 1890, 11th Annual Dinner, Attendees
Collins, Albert E.: (F) Member Temple Lodge, No. 14, 1900, Albany, NY
Collins, Charles C.: (F) Member Friendly Sons of St. Patrick, 1893,

Brooklyn, (CMTS)*"Brooklyn Eagle,"* May 18, 1893, Article regarding the election of Andrew T. Sullivan as postmaster. In the article it mentioned that there were only 50 members in this Society. It is unknown if a member of the Society.

Collins, Edward H.: (F) Member Arcana Lodge, No. 246, F. & A. M., 1934, New York, NY, (JD) Jun. 10, 1930

Collins, John J.: (F) Member Society of American Magicians, Apr., 1931, New York

Collins, Seymour: (F) Member Arcana Lodge, No. 246, F. & A. M., 1934, New York, NY, (JD) Nov. 14, 1933

Collins, William D.: (F) Member Arcana Lodge, No. 246, F. & A. M., 1934, New York, NY, (JD) Oct. 16, 1922

Collison, Thomas J.: (F) Member Lowville Chapter No. 223, R. A. M., 1929, Lowville, NY, (CO) Lewis, (JD) Jan. 30, 1912

Collyear, Rev. Dr. Robert: (F) Member Society for the Relief of Respectable Indigent Females, Brooklyn, (I) *Brooklyn Eagle,* Nov. 13, 1879, (CMTS) Paster of Church of the Messiah

Colton, Aaron: (F) Member Grand Council of the Princes of Jerusalem, 1882, Albany, NY

Colton, Aaron: (F) Member Ineffable and Sublime Grand Lodge of Perfection, 1882, Albany, NY

Coltson, J.: (F) Member Long Island Lodge, No. 382, F. &. A. M. 1874, NY

Colyer, C. R.: (F) Member Long Island Lodge, No. 382, F. &. A. M. 1874, NY

Colyer, G. B.: (F) Member Long Island Lodge, No. 382, F. &. A. M. 1874, NY

Colyer, Mrs. J.: (F) Member Lenox Ladies Aid Society of Lenox Road M. E. Church, Brooklyn, 1900, (CMTS) *"Brooklyn Eagle,"* Mar. 13, 1900. Meeting Notice, Assistant Secretary

Combs, A. B.: (F) Member Home Circle, 1900, Brooklyn, (I) *"Brooklyn Eagle,"* Feb. 3, 1900. Meeting Notice, (CMTS) Financier

Combs, Frank B.: (F) Member Temple Lodge, No. 14, 1900, Albany, NY

Combs, Lewis B.: (F) Member Temple Lodge, No. 14, 1900, Albany, NY

Comerford, Peter: (F) Member Friendly Sons of St. Patrick, 1899, Brooklyn, (CMTS)*"Brooklyn Eagle,"* Dec. 9, 1899, Article regarding the election of officers for 1900, (CMTS) Trustee

Comerford, Peter: (F) Member Friendly Sons of St. Patrick, 1893, Brooklyn, (CMTS)*"Brooklyn Eagle,"* May 18, 1893, Article regarding the election of Andrew T. Sullivan as postmaster. In the article it mentioned that there were only 50 members in this Society, Member of the Dinner Committee

Conaty, J. A.: (F) Member Long Island Lodge, No. 382, F. &. A. M. 1874, NY

Condit, John: (F) Member Clyde Lodge No. 341, F. A. M., 1905, Clyde, NY, (CO) Wayne, (CMTS) Past Master 1854, 1855

Conkey, David L.: (F) Member Lowville Lodge No. 134, F. & A. M., 1929, Lowville, NY, (CO) Lewis, (JD) Jan. 24, 1902

Conkey, David L.: (F) Member Lowville Chapter No. 223, R. A. M., 1929, Lowville, NY, (CO) Lewis, (JD) Nov. 23, 1903

Conkey, William J.: (F) Member Temple Lodge, No. 14, 1900, Albany, NY

Conklin, C. W.: (F) Member Catholic Knights of Amercia, 1900, Brooklyn, (I) *"Brooklyn Eagle,"* Feb. 3, 1900. Meeting Notice. (CMTS) State Secretary

Conley, Walter H.: (F) Member Masters Lodge, No. 5, 1900, Albany, NY

Connors, Miss Maudie: (F) Member Mispah Circle, 1888, Brooklyn, (I) *"Brooklyn Eagle,"* Dec. 12, 1888. Mentioned in an article about a fair raising funds for a Home for the Blind

Conover, John: (F) Member Lowville Lodge No. 134, F. & A. M., 1929, Lowville, NY, (CO) Lewis, (CMTS) Past Master 1857. 1862, 1863

Constantine, John: (F) Member Long Island Lodge, No. 382, F. &. A. M. 1874, NY, (CEN) 1880, 14th Ward, Albany, Albany Co., NY. Appears to be living in a boarding house run by two sisters, Agness Hotaling and Sophia Williams. John Constantine, 31, Ire, Stone Cutter. Also living in the house was a Dennis Constantine, 41, Stone Cutter, Ire.

Constick, Franklin: (F) Member Temple Lodge, No. 14, 1900, Albany, NY

Converse, Henry T.: (F) Member Masters Lodge, No. 5, 1900, Albany, NY, (CEN) 1880, 7th Ward, Albany, Albany Co., NY, 24, Wholesale Shoes, Alice, 25, Franklin, 53, father, wholesale shoes, Frabk B. 21, brother, shoe store clerk.

Conway, Mrs. J. T.: (F) Member Nativity Sewing Society, 1900, Brooklyn, (I) *"Brooklyn Eagle,"* Feb. 3, 1900. Article regarding raising money to buy clothing for the poor.

Coogan, William C.: (F) Member Temple Lodge, No. 14, 1900, Albany, NY

Cook, Adam: (F) Member Ineffable and Sublime Grand Lodge of Perfection, 1882, Albany, NY

Cook, Charles G.: (F) Member Grand Council of the Princes of Jerusalem, 1882, Albany, NY

Cook, Francis D.: (F) Member Lowville Lodge No. 134, F. & A. M., 1929, Lowville, NY, (CO) Lewis, (JD) Jan. 15, 1926

Cook, George H.: (F) Member Sons of New England, New England Society of the City of Brooklyn, 1890, (CMTS)*"Brooklyn Eagle,"* Dec. 21, 1890, 11th Annual Dinner, Attendees

Cook, George R.: (F) Member Lowville Lodge No. 134, F. & A. M.,

1929, Lowville, NY, (CO) Lewis, (JD) Apr. 2, 1915
- Cook, Henry: (F) Member Grand Council of the Princes of Jerusalem, 1882, Albany, NY
- Cook, John T.: (F) Member Mount Vernon Lodge, No. 3, 1900, Albany, NY, (CMTS) Past Master 1898
- Cook, Miss: (F) Member Nativity Sewing Society, 1900, Brooklyn, (I) *"Brooklyn Eagle,"* Feb. 3, 1900. Article regarding raising money to buy clothing for the poor.
- Cook, Robert P.: (F) Member Temple Lodge, No. 14, 1900, Albany, NY
- Cook, Seth P.: (F) Member Temple Lodge, No. 14, 1900, Albany, NY
- Cooke, C. D.: (F) Member Brooklyn Dental Society, 1877, Brooklyn, NY, (CMTS) *"Brooklyn Eagle,"* Dec. 15, 1877. Celebration of 10th Anniversary. Society established Dec. 14, 1867, (CMTS) Ethics Committee
- Cooke, Francis D.: (F) Member Lowville Chapter No. 223, R. A. M., 1929, Lowville, NY, (CO) Lewis, (JD) Mar. 27, 1928
- Cookingham, M. F.: (F) Member Temple Lodge, No. 14, 1900, Albany, NY
- Cooley, John L.: (F) Member Lowville Lodge No. 134, F. & A. M., 1929, Lowville, NY, (CO) Lewis, (JD) Mar. 2, 1928
- Cooley, Nellie: (F) Member Hope Rebekah Lodge No. 10, 1949-1950, Brockport, NY, (CO) Monroe
- Coombs, William J.: (F) Member Brooklyn Revenue Reform Club, 1886, (I)*"Brooklyn Eagle,"* Jan. ,27 1886, Attendees at a dinner
- Cooper, A. G.: (F) Member Lexington Lodge, 310, F. A. & M., 1900, Brooklyn, (I) *"Brooklyn Eagle,"* Feb. 3, 1900. Meeting Notice, (CMTS) Senior Warden
- Cooper, George L.: (F) Member Grand Council of the Princes of Jerusalem, 1882, Albany, NY
- Cooper, John G.: (F) Member Ineffable and Sublime Grand Lodge of Perfection, 1882, Albany, NY
- Cooper, John L.: (F) Member Masters Lodge, No. 5, 1900, Albany, NY
- Cooper, Mrs.: (F) Member Nativity Sewing Society, 1900, Brooklyn, (I) *"Brooklyn Eagle,"* Feb. 3, 1900. Article regarding raising money to buy clothing for the poor.
- Cooper, W. L.: (F) Member National Provident Union, Lafayette No. 28, 1900, Brooklyn, (I) *"Brooklyn Eagle,"* Feb. 3, 1900. Meeting Notice, (CMTS) Secretary
- Cooper, Walter A.: (I) *"Brooklyn Eagle,"* Feb. 19, 1902. Funeral Services at the Club House of the Brooklyn Lodge, No. 22, B. P. O. Elks for Wm. H. West. Elk services were first then masonic services by New York Lodge No. 330, F. A. & M., (CMTS) Reader at the services and pallbearer

Cooper, Wm.: (F) Member Arcana Lodge, No. 246, F. & A. M., 1934, New York, NY, (JD) Nov. 18, 1918

Copely, Albert A.: (F) Member Lowville Lodge No. 134, F. & A. M., 1929, Lowville, NY, (CO) Lewis, (JD) Apr. 7, 1911

Cordier, August J.: (F) Member Sons of New England, New England Society of the City of Brooklyn, 1890, (CMTS)*"Brooklyn Eagle,"* Dec. 21, 1890, 11th Annual Dinner, Attendees

Cordts, Brother: (F) Member Lessing Lodge No. 608, (CMTS) Meeting Notes, *"Brooklyn Eagle,"* Mar. 23, 1887, Past Master in attendance

Corey, Charles H.: (F) Member Temple Lodge, No. 14, 1900, Albany, NY

Corliss, Stephen P.: (F) Member Temple Lodge, No. 14, 1900, Albany, NY

Cornell, Fenimore L.: (F) Member Temple Lodge, No. 14, 1900, Albany, NY

Cornell, John F.: (F) Member Friendly Sons of St. Patrick, 1893, Brooklyn, (CMTS)*"Brooklyn Eagle,"* May 18, 1893, Article regarding the election of Andrew T. Sullivan as postmaster. In the article it mentioned that there were only 50 members in this Society., Guest. It is unknown if a member of the Society.

Cornish, George B.: (F) Member Lowville Lodge No. 134, F. & A. M., 1929, Lowville, NY, (CO) Lewis, (JD) May 2, 1919

Cornish, H. Rea: (F) Member Lowville Chapter No. 223, R. A. M., 1929, Lowville, NY, (CO) Lewis, (JD) Feb. 17, 1908

Cornu, G. G.: (F) Member Long Island Lodge, No. 382, F. &. A. M. 1874, NY

Cornwall, H. Davenport: (F) Member Lowville Chapter No. 223, R. A. M., 1929, Lowville, NY, (CO) Lewis, (JD) Jun. 19, 1906

Corrin, E.Q.: (F) Member Clyde Lodge No. 341, F. A. M., 1905, Clyde, NY, (CO) Wayne, (CMTS) Past Master 1900, 1901

Cortright, Eleanor: (F) Member Hope Rebekah Lodge No. 10, 1949-1950, Brockport, NY, (CO) Monroe, (CMTS) Recording Secretary

Corwin, Ray D.: (F) Member Lowville Lodge No. 134, F. & A. M., 1929, Lowville, NY, (CO) Lewis, (JD) Apr. 13, 1923

Cottrell, Fred H.: (F) Member First District Suffolk, Adah Chapter. No. 52, 1923, Northport, NY, (CMTS) Patron, (RES) Northport

Couch, Joseph J.: (F) Member Joppa Lodge No. 201, (CMTS) Meeting Notes, *"Brooklyn Eagle,"* Mar. 13, 1887

Couch, Melvin J.: (F) Member Monticello Lodge, No. 532, F. & A. M., (CO) Sullivan Co., NY, (CMTS) Past Master 1891

Coughler, Elijah E.: (F) Member Lowville Lodge No. 134, F. & A. M., 1929, Lowville, NY, (CO) Lewis, (JD) Mar. 2, 1923

Courtney, George L.: (F) Member Temple Lodge, No. 14, 1900, Albany, NY

Courts, Claude P.: (F) Member Lowville Lodge No. 134, F. & A. M.,

1929, Lowville, NY, (CO) Lewis, (JD) May 25, 2920
Couse, Andrew: (F) Member Masters Lodge, No. 5, 1900, Albany, NY
Covert, J.: (F) Member Long Island Lodge, No. 382, F. &. A. M. 1874, NY
Cowell, Thomas J.: (F) Member Washington Lodge, No. 85, 1900, Albany, NY, (CMTS) Past Members
Cowlbeck, Hiram W.: (F) Member Masters Lodge, No. 5, 1900, Albany, NY
Cowlbeck, Thomas A R.: (F) Member Masters Lodge, No. 5, 1900, Albany, NY
Cox, Edward G.: (F) Member Masters Lodge, No. 5, 1900, Albany, NY
Cox, James W.: (F) Member Grand Council of the Princes of Jerusalem, 1882, Albany, NY
Cox, James W.: (F) Member Ineffable and Sublime Grand Lodge of Perfection, 1882, Albany, NY
Cox, Rodman D.: (F) Member Mount Vernon Lodge, No. 3, 1900, Albany, NY
Cox, Samuel R.: (F) Member Astromical Society, Brooklyn Observatory, Mar. 16, 1850, Brooklyn, NY, (I) *"Brooklyn Eagle,"* Mar. 21, 1850
Coyle, Stephen M.: (F) Member Catholic Benevolent Legion, New York State Council District No. 1, 1900, Brooklyn, (I) *"Brooklyn Eagle,"* Feb. 3, 1900. Meeting Notice., (CMTS) Dtrict Deputy
Craig, Joseph D.: (F) Member Masters Lodge, No. 5, 1900, Albany, NY, (CMTS) Past Master
Craley, Franklin S.: (F) Member Temple Lodge, No. 14, 1900, Albany, NY
Cramp, Ralph W.: (F) Member Temple Lodge, No. 14, 1900, Albany, NY
Crandall, R. P.: (F) Member Long Island Lodge, No. 382, F. &. A. M. 1874, NY
Crandeil, C. P.: (F) Member Brooklyn Dental Society, 1877, Brooklyn, NY, (CMTS) *"Brooklyn Eagle,"* Dec. 15, 1877. Celebration of 10th Anniversary. Society established Dec. 14, 1867, (CMTS) Recording Secretary, Subjects Committee
Crane, Frederick: (F) Member Lowville Lodge No. 134, F. & A. M., 1929, Lowville, NY, (CO) Lewis
Crane, John M.: (F) Member Sons of New England, New England Society of the City of Brooklyn, 1887, (CMTS)*"Brooklyn Eagle,"* Dec. 22, 1887, Annual Dinner, Attendees
Crane, T.: (F) Member Long Island Lodge, No. 382, F. &. A. M. 1874, NY
Crannell, Charles R.: (F) Member Temple Lodge, No. 14, 1900, Albany, NY

Crannell, Jr., F. F.: (F) Member Temple Lodge, No. 14, 1900, Albany, NY

Crary, Lillian: (F) Member Hope Rebekah Lodge No. 10, 1949-1950, Brockport, NY, (CO) Monroe, (CMTS Property Committee

Craven, Christopher J.: (F) Member Temple Lodge, No. 14, 1900, Albany, NY, (CEN) 1880, 8$^{th}$ Ward, Albany, Albany Co., NY, 47, Eng, Wood Polisher, Mary, 50, Elmer, 18, Carriage Maker, Frank, 16, Printer, (MD) Jan. 1, 1855, (PMD) First Lutheran Church, Albany, NY, (Spouse) Mary Grounds

Craver, Moses: (F) Member Temple Lodge, No. 14, 1900, Albany, NY, (CEN) 1880, Albany, Albany, NY, 35, Clerk at RR.R., Elanor, 30, Grace, 6., (D) 1922, (MD) Sep. 17, 1872, (PMD) Saratoga, NY. (Spouse) Eleanor Warriner

Craver, Jr., Moses: (F) Member Grand Council of the Princes of Jerusalem, 1882, Albany, NY, (CEN) 1880, 12$^{th}$ Ward, Albany, Albany Co., NY, 69, Catherine, 69, Rachel, 40, Christina, 38, Abram, 36, Frances, 29, daughter-in-law, David, 7, grandson

Craver, Jr., Moses: (F) Member Ineffable and Sublime Grand Lodge of Perfection, 1882, Albany, NY

Crawford, Charles H.: (F) Member Temple Lodge, No. 14, 1900, Albany, NY

Crawford, Eugene: (F) Member Mount Vernon Lodge, No. 3, 1900, Albany, NY

Crawford, Ezex (sic) McI.: (F) Member Masters Lodge, No. 5, 1900, Albany, NY

Creamer, Frank D.: (F) Member Friendly Sons of St. Patrick, 1893, Brooklyn, (CMTS)*"Brooklyn Eagle,"* May 18, 1893, Article regarding the election of Andrew T. Sullivan as postmaster. In the article it mentioned that there were only 50 members in this Society. It is unknown if a member of the Society.

Creamer, William G.: (F) Member Sons of New England, New England Society of the City of Brooklyn, 1890, (CMTS)*"Brooklyn Eagle,"* Dec. 21, 1890, 11th Annual Dinner, Attendees

Crego, E. C.: (F) Member Murray Lodge, No. 380, F. & A. M., 1906, Holley, Orleans, Co., NY

Crewe, Fred H.: (F) Member Lowville Lodge No. 134, F. & A. M., 1929, Lowville, NY, (CO) Lewis, (JD) May 16, 1924

Crippen, Charles S.: (F) Member Masters Lodge, No. 5, 1900, Albany, NY, (CEN) 1880, 16$^{th}$ Ward, Albany, Albany CO., NY, 32, Clerk, NY

Croissant, Charles: (F) Member Mount Vernon Lodge, No. 3, 1900, Albany, NY, (CEN) 1880, 13$^{th}$ Ward, Albany, Albany Co., NY, Listed with Martin Croissant, 55, Bavaria, Hardware Dealer, Phillipina, 49, Charles, 21, clerk, Phillipina, 19, John, 16, clerk

Croissant, John: (F) Member Mount Vernon Lodge, No. 3, 1900, Albany, NY (CEN) 1880, 13$^{th}$ Ward, Albany, Albany Co., NY,

Listed with Martin Croissant, 55, Bavaria, Hardware Dealer, Phillipina, 49, Charles, 21, clerk, Phillipina, 19, John, 16, clerk

Cromwell, Frederick: (F) Member Sons of New England, New England Society of the City of Brooklyn, 1890, (CMTS) *"Brooklyn Eagle,"* Dec. 21, 1890, 11th Annual Dinner, Attendees

Cross, Alfred T.: (F) Member Sons of New England, New England Society of the City of Brooklyn, 1890, (CMTS) *"Brooklyn Eagle,"* Dec. 21, 1890, 11th Annual Dinner, Attendees

Cross, William T.: (F) Member Sons of New England, New England Society of the City of Brooklyn, 1890, (CMTS) *"Brooklyn Eagle,"* Dec. 21, 1890, 11th Annual Dinner, Attendees

Crotty, Miss C.: (F) Member Nativity Sewing Society, 1900, Brooklyn, (I) *"Brooklyn Eagle,"* Feb. 3, 1900. Article regarding raising money to buy clothing for the poor.

Crum, Miss A.: (F) Member Nativity Sewing Society, 1900, Brooklyn, (I) *"Brooklyn Eagle,"* Feb. 3, 1900. Article regarding raising money to buy clothing for the poor.

Cullen, Judge Edgar M.: (F) Member Sons of New England, New England Society of the City of Brooklyn, 1890, (CMTS) *"Brooklyn Eagle,"* Dec. 21, 1890, 11th Annual Dinner, Attendees

Cullington, W.: (F) Member Long Island Lodge, No. 382, F. &. A. M. 1874, NY

Culver, Cyrus W.: (F) Member Lowville Lodge No. 134, F. & A. M., 1929, Lowville, NY, (CO) Lewis, (JD) Dec. 5, 1913

Cundall, Henry E.: (F) Member Temple Lodge, No. 14, 1900, Albany, NY

Cunningham, A. C.: (F) Member Masters Lodge, No. 5, 1900, Albany, NY

Cunningham, Hugh: (F) Member Mount Vernon Lodge, No. 3, 1900, Albany, NY, (CEN) 1880, $10^{th}$ Ward, Albany Albany Co., NY, Listed with Philip Cunningham, 25, Eng, Works in Skin Factory, Catherine, 23, Hugh, 2, Ellen, 6M

Cureton, Charles O.: (F) Member Temple Lodge, No. 14, 1900, Albany, NY, (CEN) 1880, $6^{th}$ Ward, Albany, Albany Co., NY, Listed With William Cureton, 34, Clerk in Box Factory, Cecilia, 36, Charles, 6, Maria, 67, Mother

Curtis, John T.: (F) Member Monticello Lodge, No. 532, F. & A. M., (CO) Sullivan Co., NY, (CMTS) Past Master 1919

Cusack, James: (F) Member Friendly Sons of St. Patrick, 1893, Brooklyn, (CMTS) *"Brooklyn Eagle,"* May 18, 1893, Article regarding the election of Andrew T. Sullivan as postmaster. In the article it mentioned that there were only 50 members in this Society., Guest. It is unknown if a member of the Society.

Cusack, Thomas: (F) Member Friendly Sons of St. Patrick, 1899, Brooklyn, (CMTS) *"Brooklyn Eagle,"* Dec. 9, 1899, Article regarding the election of officers for 1900, (CMTS) Trustee

Cushing, Dr.: (F) Member Society for the Relief of Respectable Indigent Females, Brooklyn, (I) Brooklyn Eagle, Nov. 13, 1879

Cushman, Harry C.: (F) Member Masters Lodge, No. 5, 1900, Albany, NY

Cutler, Lorenzo: (F) Member Temple Lodge, No. 14, 1900, Albany, NY

Cutler, Walter P.: (F) Member Masters Lodge, No. 5, 1900, Albany, NY

Dailey, Ansel: (F) Member Temple Lodge, No. 14, 1900, Albany, NY

Dailey, Peter F.: (I) *"Brooklyn Eagle,"* Feb. 19, 1902. Funeral Services at the Club House of the Brooklyn Lodge, No. 22, B. P. O. Elks for Wm. H. West. Elk services were first then masonic services by New York Lodge No. 330, F. A. & M., (CMTS) Pallbearer

Daily, Mrs. Peter: (I) *"Brooklyn Eagle,"* Feb. 19, 1902. Funeral Services at the Club House of the Brooklyn Lodge, No. 22, B. P. O. Elks for Wm. H. West. Elk services were first then masonic services by New York Lodge No. 330, F. A. & M., (CMTS) Made a floral gift.

Daily, Peter: (I) *"Brooklyn Eagle,"* Feb. 19, 1902. Funeral Services at the Club House of the Brooklyn Lodge, No. 22, B. P. O. Elks for Wm. H. West. Elk services were first then masonic services by New York Lodge No. 330, F. A. & M., (CMTS) Made a floral gift.

Dale, John: (F) Member Lowville Lodge No. 134, F. & A. M., 1929, Lowville, NY, (CO) Lewis, (CMTS) Past Master 1901 1902

Dale, John W.: (F) Member Lowville Lodge No. 134, F. & A. M., 1929, Lowville, NY, (CO) Lewis, (JD) Mar. 15, 1895

Dallon, Mrs. George: (F) Member Nativity Sewing Society, 1900, Brooklyn, (I) *"Brooklyn Eagle,"* Feb. 3, 1900. Article regarding raising money to buy clothing for the poor.

Dalton, Philip W.: (F) Member Grand Council of the Princes of Jerusalem, 1882, Albany, NY

Dalton, Philip W.: (F) Member Ineffable and Sublime Grand Lodge of Perfection, 1882, Albany, NY

Daly, John E.: (F) Member Friendly Sons of St. Patrick, 1893, Brooklyn, (CMTS)*"Brooklyn Eagle,"* May 18, 1893, Article regarding the election of Andrew T. Sullivan as postmaster. In the article it mentioned that there were only 50 members in this Society., Guest. It is unknown if a member of the Society.

Damuth, Roy L.: (F) Member Lowville Lodge No. 134, F. & A. M., 1929, Lowville, NY, (CO) Lewis, (JD) Jun. 4, 1915

Danegar, G. W.: (F) Member Long Island Lodge, No. 382, F. &. A. M. 1874, NY

Daney, Joseph : (F) Member Society of American Magicians, Apr., 1931, New York, (RES) New York City

Daniels, Chas. F.: (F) Member Arcana Lodge, No. 246,

F. & A. M., 1934, New York, NY, (JD) Mar. 7, 1892, Life
Member

Dano, Alonzo S.: (F) Member Lowville Lodge No. 134, F. & A. M.,
1929, Lowville, NY, (CO) Lewis, (CMTS) Past Master 1904, 1905

Danziger, William J.: (F) Member Arcana Lodge, No. 246,
F. & A. M., 1934, New York, NY, (JD) Dec. 8, 1925

Darling, Wallace J.: (F) Member Lowville Lodge No. 134, F. & A. M.,
1929, Lowville, NY, (CO) Lewis, (JD) Mar. 29, 1912, (CEN) New
Bremen, Lewis Co., NY Listed with John Darling, 55, Farmer,
NY, Cyrena, 56, NY, Jerome, 11, Estella, 9, Gertie, 8, Wallace J.,
5

Darring, Howard F.: (F) Member Lowville Lodge No. 134, F. & A. M.,
1929, Lowville, NY, (CO) Lewis, (JD) Mar. 2, 1928, (CEN) 1880
New Bremen, Lewis Co., NY, 41, NY, Farmer, catherine, 41, wife,
France, Geo. H., 10, Minnie L., 6, Albert L., 4, Howard, 3, Adella
S., 1, William, 12, Sarah Daring, 77, Mother, France

Darrow, Jr., Jedediah: (F) Member Lewis County Bible Society, 1812,
Charter Officers, (CMTS) Deacon

Dart, Edward W.: (F) Member Society of American Magicians,
Apr., 1931, New York, (RES) New York City

Dauber, Harry: (F) Member Arcana Lodge, No. 246, F. & A. M., 1934,
New York, NY, (JD) Dec. 1, 1919

Dauber, Irving G.: (F) Member Arcana Lodge, No. 246, F. & A. M., 1934,
New York, NY, (JD) Jul. 16, 1918

Davenport, Ashley: (F) Member Lowville Lodge No. 134, F. & A. M.,
1929, Lowville, NY, (CO) Lewis, (CMTS) Past Master 1850, (B)
Feb. 11, 1794, (BP) Lowville, NY, (PRTS) Charles Davenport and
Elizabeth Taylor, (SIB) Benjamin, Alexander, Sally, Charles, Ira,
Betsy. Roxanna, John B., (CMTS) 1875 Atlas Lowville, A.
Davenport

Davenport, C. B.: (F) Member Sons of New England, New England
Society of the City of Brooklyn, 1890, (CMTS)*"Brooklyn Eagle,"*
Dec. 21, 1890, 11th Annual Dinner, Attendees

Davenport, Franklin R.: (F) Member Temple Lodge, No. 14, 1900,
Albany, NY

Davenport, Leonard C.: (F) Member Lowville Lodge No. 134, F. & A. M.,
1929, Lowville, NY, (CO) Lewis, (CMTS) Past Master 1858,
Lowville Business Directory, 1867-1868, L. C. Davenport, (OC)
Attorney, (CEN) 1880 Lowville, Lewis Co., NY Census, 55. Ny,
Lawyer, Jerusha, wife, 50, NY, Louisa, 15, May, 12, Charles, 11,
(B) Oct. 25, 1823, (D) Jul. 31, 1885, (MD) Dec. 29, 1857,
(Spouse) Jerusha Lydia Avery, (PRTS) Charles Davenport and
Anna Cole, (CH) Leonard Charles Davenport (b. Mar. 6, 1869)

Davenport, Leroy J.: (F) Member Lowville Lodge No. 134, F. & A. M.,
1929, Lowville, NY, (CO) Lewis, (JD) Apr. 19, 1918

Davenport, Samuel J.: (F) Member Temple Lodge, No. 14, 1900, Albany,

NY

Davenport, William B.: (F) Member Sons of New England, New England Society of the City of Brooklyn, 1890, (CMTS)*"Brooklyn Eagle,"* Dec. 21, 1890, 11th Annual Dinner, Attendees

Davenport, A. Clark: (F) Member Lowville Lodge No. 134, F. & A. M., 1929, Lowville, NY, (CO) Lewis, (CMTS) Past Master 1903

Davey, George W.: (F) Member Mount Vernon Lodge, No. 3, 1900, Albany, NY

Davids, Ernest: (F) Member Society of American Magicians, Apr., 1931, New York, (RES) West New York, NJ

Davids, Fannie: (F) Member Mispah Circle, 1888, Brooklyn, (I) *"Brooklyn Eagle,"* Dec. 12, 1888. Mentioned in an article about a fair raising funds for a Home for the Blind

Davids, Mrs.: (F) Member Mispah Circle, 1888, Brooklyn, (I) *"Brooklyn Eagle,"* Dec. 12, 1888. Mentioned in an article about a fair raising funds for a Home for the Blind

Davidson, George G.: (F) Member Masters Lodge, No. 5, 1900, Albany, NY

Davidson, Irwin D.: (F) Member Society of American Magicians, Apr., 1931, New York, (RES) New York City

Davidson, Robert: (F) Member Temple Lodge, No. 14, 1900, Albany, NY, (CEN) 1880, 11th Ward, Albany, Albany Co., NY, 46, Capt. of Police, Margaret, 46, Anna, 19, daughter, Wn., 16, son, David, 30, brother, single, engineer, Margaret, 38, sister, Rachael, 28, sister

Davies, A. David: (F) Member Lowville Lodge No. 134, F. & A. M., 1929, Lowville, NY, (CO) Lewis, (JD) Jun. 20, 1919

Davis, Charles E.: (F) Member Masters Lodge, No. 5, 1900, Albany, NY, (CEN) 1880, 7th Ward, Albay, Albany Co., NY, 52, Lumber Inspector, Eliza D., 50

Davis, Charles G.: (F) Member Temple Lodge, No. 14, 1900, Albany, NY

Davis, Charles J.: (F) Member Temple Lodge, No. 14, 1900, Albany, NY

Davis, G. H.: (F) Member Murray Lodge, No. 380, F. & A. M., 1906, Holley, Orleans, Co., NY

Davis, G. W.: (F) Member Long Island Lodge, No. 382, F. &. A. M. 1874, NY

Davis, John A.: (F) Member Ineffable and Sublime Grand Lodge of Perfection, 1882, Albany, NY, (CEN) 1880 7th Ward, Albany, Albany CO., NY, 47, Ship Builder, Susan M., 42, James H., 21, Catalena, 15, Elmina, 11, August, 8, Edgar S., 6, Anna G., 2

Davis, John M.: (F) Member Society of American Magicians, Apr., 1931, New York, (RES) Hudson Terminal, NY

Davis, Leon A.: (F) Member Lowville Lodge No. 134, F. & A. M., 1929, Lowville, NY, (CO) Lewis, (JD) Dec. 9, 1922

Davis, Will J.: (I) *"Brooklyn Eagle,"* Feb. 19, 1902. Funeral Services at the Club House of the Brooklyn Lodge, No. 22, B. P. O. Elks for Wm. H. West. Elk services were first then masonic services by New York Lodge No. 330, F. A. & M., (CMTS) Made a floral gift.

Davis, William T.: (F) Member Sons of New England, New England Society of the City of Brooklyn, 1890, (CMTS) *"Brooklyn Eagle,"* Dec. 21, 1890, 11th Annual Dinner, Attendees

Davison, A. H.: (F) Member Long Island Lodge, No. 382, F. &. A. M. 1874, NY, (CMTS) Past Master

Dawson, E. P.: (F) Member Long Island Lodge, No. 382, F. &. A. M. 1874, NY

Dawson, J. W.: (F) Member Long Island Lodge, No. 382, F. &. A. M. 1874, NY

Dayan, Chas.: (F) Member Lowville Lodge No. 134, F. & A. M., 1929, Lowville, NY, (CO) Lewis, (CMTS) Past Master 1848, 1849, 1854, 1855, (CEN) 1825 Lowville, Lewis Co., NY, 1835 Lowville, Lewis Co., NY Census, (C) West Martinsburg Cemetery, No Dates on Stone

De Riestinal, A.: (F) Member Sons of New England, New England Society of the City of Brooklyn, 1890, (CMTS) *"Brooklyn Eagle,"* Dec. 21, 1890, 11th Annual Dinner, Attendees

De Riiesthal, A.: (F) Member Sons of New England, New England Society of the City of Brooklyn, 1887, (CMTS) *"Brooklyn Eagle,"* Dec. 22, 1887, Annual Dinner, Attendees

De Silver, Carl: (F) Member Sons of New England, New England Society of the City of Brooklyn, 1890, (CMTS) *"Brooklyn Eagle,"* Dec. 21, 1890, 11th Annual Dinner, Attendees

De Vries, Frederick W.: (F) Member Arcana Lodge, No. 246, F. & A. M., 1934, New York, NY, (JD) Mar. 6, 1911

Deakin, W. Albert: (F) Member Lowville Lodge No. 134, F. & A. M., 1929, Lowville, NY, (CO) Lewis, (JD) Dec. 29, 1915

Dean, Frederick A.: (F) Member Temple Lodge, No. 14, 1900, Albany, NY , (CEN) 1880, 11th Ward, Albany, Albany Co., NY, Listed With Eliza A. Dean, 60, widow, Frederick A., 31, son, Josephine D., 23, daughter, Joanna A., 19, daughter

Dean, Samuel : (F) Member Lewis County Bible Society, 1812, Charter Officers, (CMTS) Committee

Dean, Sydney D.: (OBIT) *"News Journal,"* Sunday, May 7, 2000, Sydney D. Dean of Carmel, NY died on May 5, 2000 at Westchester Medical Center.. He was 78. He was born on June 18, 1921 in Manchester, England to Hannah Booth and George H. Dean. On June 15, 1947. He married Florence Clarke Dean in Goshen, NY. He was a member of Goshen Masonic Lodge, a 32 Degree Mason in the Scottish Rite, Valley of Albany and a Shriner in Cypress Temple, Albany. He was a life member of the Carmel Fire Department and Past President and a Charter Member of the

Carmel Ambulance Corp. He was a member of the Drew United Methodist Church. Mr. Dean was Captain of Corrections with the New York State Department of Corrections, retiring in 1982. He also worked as a Court Officer for the Putnam County Sheriff Department. He was a Veteran of World War II, Army Air Corp. He is survived by his children, Mr. and Mrs. James and Marianne Dean, Kathryn Collins and Mr. and Mrs. Ted and Meg Kuhn; 1 brother, Walter H. Dean; and 7 grandchildren, Jennifer, Shawn and Amanda Collins, Allyson, Stephanie and Teddy Kuhn and Erica Dean. The funeral is on Monday at 11 am at Drew United Methodist Church, Carmel, NY. Interment at Raymond Hill Cemetery.

Dearstyne, Chester F.: (F) Member Masters Lodge, No. 5, 1900, Albany, NY, (CEN) 1880, 13th Ward, Albany, Albany Co., NY, 29, Cigar maker, Jane, 27, wife

Dearstyne, Edmund C.: (F) Member Temple Lodge, No. 14, 1900, Albany, NY

Dearstyne, Frank S.: (F) Member Temple Lodge, No. 14, 1900, Albany, NY

DeBarthe, William E.: (F) Member Temple Lodge, No. 14, 1900, Albany, NY, (CEN) 4th Ward, Albany, Albany Co., NY, single, 23, CT, Cigar maker

Degenhardt, G.: (F) Member Herber Lodge, No. 698,1898, F. & A. M., New York, NY, Greenpoint area, (RES) Brooklyn

DeGroot, Peter J.: (F) Member Temple Lodge, No. 14, 1900, Albany, NY

Dekin, Albert A.: (F) Member Lowville Lodge No. 134, F. & A. M., 1929, Lowville, NY, (CO) Lewis, (JD) Mar. 4, 1904, (B) Apr. 22, 1860, (MD) Aug. 29, 1882, (Spouse) Rosina Bliss

Dekin, Claude A.: (F) Member Lowville Lodge No. 134, F. & A. M., 1929, Lowville, NY, (CO) Lewis, (JD) Apr. 16, 1909, (B) Feb., 1888, (PRTS) Albert A. Dekin

Dekin, Dewey A.: (F) Member Lowville Lodge No. 134, F. & A. M., 1929, Lowville, NY, (CO) Lewis, (CMTS) Past Master 1925

Dekin, Dewey A.: (F) Member Lowville Lodge No. 134, F. & A. M., 1929, Lowville, NY, (CO) Lewis, (JD) Nov. 7, 1917, (B) Aug. 6, 1898, (D) Sep., 1980, (RES) Chase Lake, Glendale, Glenfield, Otter Creek, Pine Grove, Lewis Co., NY

Dekin, Dewey A.: (F) Member Lowville Chapter No. 223, R. A. M., 1929, Lowville, NY, (CO) Lewis, (JD) Jun. 7, 1921

Dekin, Murray A.: (F) Member Lowville Lodge No. 134, F. & A. M., 1929, Lowville, NY, (CO) Lewis, (JD) Dec. 5, 1919

Dekin , Claude A.: (F) Member Lowville Chapter No. 223, R. A. M., 1929, Lowville, NY, (CO) Lewis, (JD) Apr. 1, 1913

Delavan, John Savage: (F) Member Grand Council of the Princes of Jerusalem, 1882, Albany, NY

Delavan, John Savage: (F) Member Ineffable and Sublime Grand Lodge of Perfection, 1882, Albany, NY

Deluhery, Miss M. M.: (F) Member Nativity Sewing Society, 1900, Brooklyn, (I) *"Brooklyn Eagle,"* Feb. 3, 1900. Article regarding raising money to buy clothing for the poor.

Demarest, Miss Grace: (F) Member Childrens's Mission Band, 1888, Brooklyn, (I) *"Brooklyn Eagle,"* Dec. 12, 1888. Article regarding Societies aiding churches., (CMTS) Helping St. John's Methodist Episcopal Church, Secretary

Deming, Horace E.: (F) Member Brooklyn Revenue Reform Club, 1886, (I) *"Brooklyn Eagle,"* Jan. ,27 1886, Attendees at a dinner

Dence, John D.: (F) Member Lowville Lodge No. 134, F. & A. M., 1929, Lowville, NY, (CO) Lewis, (JD) Apr. 23, 1897, (AKA) John Doig Dence, (B) Jul. 25, 1873, (BP) Lowville, NY, (MD) Jun. 29, 1898, (Spouse) Mollie Phalon, (PRTS) John Dence and Harriet Poole, (b. Feb. 16, 1829, d. Jun. 29, 1898, (GRDPRTS) Dance Dence and Margaret DeWanderlear, (CEN) 1880 Lowville, Lewis Co., NY, Listed with John Dense, 50, Farmer, Harriet, 47, NY, Lillian, 15, John D., 6

Dence, John D.: (F) Member Lowville Chapter No. 223, R. A. M., 1929, Lowville, NY, (CO) Lewis, (JD) Jun. 3, 1902

Dening, Lyston E.: (F) Member Lowville Lodge No. 134, F. & A. M., 1929, Lowville, NY, (CO) Lewis, (JD) Apr. 7, 1922

Denison, Frank: (F) Member Mount Vernon Lodge, No. 3, 1900, Albany, NY

Denison, Fred P.: (F) Member Masters Lodge, No. 5, 1900, Albany, NY

Dennen, Marie L.: (F) Member Ladies Catholic Benevolent Association, St. Augustines No. 214, 1900, Brooklyn, (I) *"Brooklyn Eagle,"* Feb. 3, 1900. Meeting Notice., (CMTS) Recorder

Denning, William B.: (F) Member Lowville Lodge No. 134, F. & A. M., 1929, Lowville, NY, (CO) Lewis, (JD) May 2, 1919

Derbyshire, Wm.: (F) Member Daughters of Temperances, Hope of the Fallen Union, Martinsburgh, NY, Jan. 9, 1851, (CO) Lewis, (Spouse) Laura Trowbridge, (MD) Nov. 17, 1806, (PMD) Denmark, NY, (CH) William Trowbridge, b. Dec. 8, 1809.

Derrick, E. C.: (F) Member Murray Lodge, No. 380, F. & A. M., 1906, Holley, Orleans, Co., NY

Desgrey, Arthur H.: (F) Member Society of American Magicians, Apr., 1931, New York, (RES) Yonkers, NY

Desobe, Joseph O.: (F) Member Masters Lodge, No. 5, 1900, Albany, NY

Devine, William : (I) *"Brooklyn Eagle,"* Jun. 2, 1879, Dedication of the burial plot of the Order of Elks in Evergreen Cemetery, (CMTS) Esteemed Loyal Knight

DeVoe, Alex. .: (F) Member Lowville Lodge No. 134, F. & A. M.,

1929, Lowville, NY, (CO) Lewis, (CMTS) Past Master 1895

Dewart, James: (F) Member Long Island Lodge, No. 382, F. &. A. M. 1874, NY

Dewey, William H.: (F) Member Lowville Chapter No. 223, R. A. M., 1929, Lowville, NY, (CO) Lewis, (JD) Oct. 27, 1920

Diamond, Jacob L.: (F) Member Arcana Lodge, No. 246, F. & A. M., 1934, New York, NY, (JD) Dec. 8, 1925

Dickerman, John S.: (F) Member Grand Council of the Princes of Jerusalem, 1882, Albany, NY

Dickerman, John S.: (F) Member Ineffable and Sublime Grand Lodge of Perfection, 1882, Albany, NY

Dickinson, Everett M.: (F) Member Temple Lodge, No. 14, 1900, Albany, NY

Dickman, Irving: (F) Member Arcana Lodge, No. 246, F. & A. M., 1934, New York, NY, (JD) Aug. 6, 1918

Dickson, Walter : (F) Member Ineffable and Sublime Grand Lodge of Perfection, 1882, Albany, NY

Dickson, Walter F.: (F) Member Grand Council of the Princes of Jerusalem, 1882, Albany, NY

Diedrick, R.: (F) Member Long Island Lodge, No. 382, F. &. A. M., 1874, NY

Diehlmann, Brother: (F) Member Lessing Lodge No. 608, (CMTS) Meeting Notes, *"Brooklyn Eagle,"* Mar. 23, 1887, Past Master in attendance

Diersing, John A.: (F) Member Arcana Lodge, No. 246, F. & A. M., 1934, New York, NY, (JD) Jul. 17, 1911

Diez, L.: (F) Member Herber Lodge, No. 698,1898, F. & A. M., New York, NY, Greenpoint area, (RES) New York City

Dillow, Jr., Richard : (F) Member Temple Lodge, No. 14, 1900, Albany, NY

Dixon, Frederick: (F) Member Mount Vernon Lodge, No. 3, 1900, Albany, NY

Dockstader, Lew: (I) *"Brooklyn Eagle,"* Feb. 19, 1902. Funeral Services at the Club House of the Brooklyn Lodge, No. 22, B. P. O. Elks for Wm. H. West. Elk services were first then masonic services by New York Lodge No. 330, F. A. & M., (CMTS) Made a floral gift.

Dockstader, Mrs. Lew: (I) *"Brooklyn Eagle,"* Feb. 19, 1902. Funeral Services at the Club House of the Brooklyn Lodge, No. 22, B. P. O. Elks for Wm. H. West. Elk services were first then masonic services by New York Lodge No. 330, F. A. & M., (CMTS) Made a floral gift.

Doherty, Miss: (F) Member Nativity Sewing Society, 1900, Brooklyn, (I) *"Brooklyn Eagle,"* Feb. 3, 1900. Article regarding raising money to buy clothing for the poor.

Doherty, Miss S.: (F) Member Nativity Sewing Society, 1900, Brooklyn, (I) *"Brooklyn Eagle,"* Feb. 3, 1900. Article regarding

raising money to buy clothing for the poor.
Doherty, Mrs. William : (F) Member Nativity Sewing Society, 1900, Brooklyn, (I) *"Brooklyn Eagle,"* Feb. 3, 1900. Article regarding raising money to buy clothing for the poor.
Doig, Charles K.: (F) Member Lowville Lodge No. 134, F. & A. M., 1929, Lowville, NY, (CO) Lewis, (JD) May 5, 1876
Doig, Charles K.: (F) Member Lowville Lodge No. 134, F. & A. M., 1929, Lowville, NY, (CO) Lewis, (JD) May 5, 1876, (AKA) Charles Knox Doig, (B) Nov. 28, 1853, (D)Mar. 9, 1936 1909, (C) Lowville Rural Cemetery, (PRTS) John C. Doig and Maria Augusta Knox, (MD) Feb. 12, 1877, (OC) Druggist, Doig & Pelton, Later changed to Doig Brothers Drug Store
Doig, Frank C.: (F) Member Lowville Lodge No. 134, F. & A. M., 1929, Lowville, NY, (CO) Lewis, (CMTS) Past Master 1878, (AKA) Frank Collins Doig, (B) Aug. 19, 1851, (D) Apr. 2, 1909, (C) Lowville Rural Cemetery, (PRTS) John C. Doig and Maria Augusta Knox, (MD) Feb. 12, 1877, (Spouse) Kate Jones, (OC) Druggist, Doig & Pelton, (F) Other Memberships were: Lowville Club, President 1894-1899, Member of Trinity Church, (CH) Julia Mitchell, (b. Oct. 22, 1881), Maria, (b. Jan. 6, 1885)
Doig, John: (F) Member Lowville Lodge No. 134, F. & A. M., 1929, Lowville, NY, (CO) Lewis, (CMTS) Past Master 1856, (B) May 15, 1820, (D) Nov. 15, 1867, (C) Lowville Rural Cemetery, (MD) May 1, 1848, (Spouse) Maria Augusta Knox, (OC) Druggist, Director of Bank of Lowville, Trustee & treasurer for Lowville Academy
Dolbeare, F. W.: (F) Member Brooklyn Dental Society, 1877, Brooklyn, NY, (CMTS) *"Brooklyn Eagle,"* Dec. 15, 1877. Celebration of 10th Anniversary. Society established Dec. 14, 1867, (CMTS) Treasurer
Donaldson, John: (F) Member Friendly Sons of St. Patrick, 1893, Brooklyn, (CMTS)*"Brooklyn Eagle,"* May 18, 1893, Article Regarding the election of Andrew T. Sullivan as postmaster. In the article it mentioned that there were only 50 members in this Society., Guest. It is unknown if a member of the Society.
Donaldson, P.: (F) Member Long Island Lodge, No. 382, F. &. A. M., 1874, NY
Donnelly, Mrs. Joseph: (I) *"Brooklyn Eagle,"* Feb. 19, 1902. Funeral Services at the Club House of the Brooklyn Lodge, No. 22, B. P. O. Elks for Wm. H. West. Elk services were first then masonic services by New York Lodge No. 330, F. A. & M., (CMTS) Made a floral gift.
Donnlley, Rev. J. J.: (F) Member Nativity Sewing Society, 1900, Brooklyn, (I) *"Brooklyn Eagle,"* Feb. 3, 1900. Article regarding raising money to buy clothing for the poor.
Donoghue, Peter J.: (F) Member Friendly Sons of St. Patrick, 1893,

Brooklyn, (CMTS)*"Brooklyn Eagle,"* May 18, 1893, Article Regarding the election of Andrew T. Sullivan as postmaster. In the article it mentioned that there were only 50 members in this Society., Guest. It is unknown if a member of the Society.

Donovan, John F.: (F) Member Friendly Sons of St. Patrick, 1893, Brooklyn, (CMTS)*"Brooklyn Eagle,"* May 18, 1893, Article Regarding the election of Andrew T. Sullivan as postmaster. In the article it mentioned that there were only 50 members in this Society., Guest. It is unknown if a member of the Society.

Dorrance, Charles: (I) *"Brooklyn Eagle,"* Feb. 19, 1902. Funeral Services at the Club House of the Brooklyn Lodge, No. 22, B. P. O. Elks for Wm. H. West. Elk services were first then masonic services by New York Lodge No. 330, F. A. & M., (CMTS) Made a floral gift.

Dorrance, Mrs. Charles : (I) *"Brooklyn Eagle,"* Feb. 19, 1902. Funeral Services at the Club House of the Brooklyn Lodge, No. 22, B. P. O. Elks for Wm. H. West. Elk services were first then masonic services by New York Lodge No. 330, F. A. & M., (CMTS) Made a floral gift.

Dorsey, T. F.: (F) Member Long Island Lodge, No. 382, F. &. A. M., 1874, NY

Doty, Chillus: (F) Member Daughters of Temperances, Hope of the Fallen Union, Martinsburgh, NY, Jan. 9, 1851, (CO) Lewis

Doty, Ethan Allan: (F) Member Sons of New England, New England Society of the City of Brooklyn, 1887, (CMTS)*"Brooklyn Eagle,"* Dec. 22, 1887, Annual Dinner, Attendees

Doty, Ethan Allen: (F) Member Sons of New England, New England Society of the City of Brooklyn, 1890, (CMTS)*"Brooklyn Eagle,"* Dec. 21, 1890, 11th Annual Dinner, Attendees

Dougherty, J. H.: (F) Member Brooklyn Revenue Reform Club, 1886, (I)*"Brooklyn Eagle,"* Jan. ,27 1886, Attendees at a dinner

Douglas, Duncan: (F) Member Masters Lodge, No. 5, 1900, Albany, NY

Douglas, Edward: (F) Member Grand Council of the Princes of Jerusalem, 1882, Albany, NY

Douglas, Kenneth R.: (F) Member Masters Lodge, No. 5, 1900, Albany, NY

Douglass, H. H.: (F) Member Brooklyn Revenue Reform Club, 1886, (I)*"Brooklyn Eagle,"* Jan. ,27 1886, Attendees at a dinner

Douglass, John J.: (F) Member Joppa Lodge No. 201, (CMTS) Meeting Notes, *"Brooklyn Eagle,"* Mar. 13, 1887, W. M.

Douton, Wm. J.: (F) Member Murray Lodge, No. 380, F. & A. M., 1906, Holley, Orleans, Co., NY

Downs, Daniel: (F) Member Monticello Lodge, No. 532, F. & A. M., (CO) Sullivan Co., NY, (CMTS) Trustee 1897

Downs, W. A.: (F) Member Murray Lodge, No. 380, F. & A. M., 1906, Holley, Orleans, Co., NY

Doyle, Mrs. L.: (F) Member Nativity Sewing Society, 1900,

Brooklyn, (I) *"Brooklyn Eagle,"* Feb. 3, 1900. Article regarding raising money to buy clothing for the poor.
- Doyle, Nicholas: (I) *"Brooklyn Eagle,"* Feb. 19, 1902. Funeral Services at the Club House of the Brooklyn Lodge, No. 22, B. P. O. Elks for Wm. H. West. Elk services were first then masonic services by New York Lodge No. 330, F. A. & M., (CMTS) Member of Metropolitian Male Quartet. Member of the Elks
- Draizin, David: (F) Member Arcana Lodge, No. 246, F. & A. M., 1934, New York, NY, (JD) May 5, 1919
- Draper, Harry G.: (F) Member Temple Lodge, No. 14, 1900, Albany, NY, (CEN) 1880, $16^{th}$ Ward, Albany, Albany Co., NY, Listed with Henry W. Draper, 25, Wood Box Maker, Louise M., 24, Harry G., 3
- Drew, Mrs. C.: (F) Member Mispah Circle, 1888, Brooklyn, (I) *"Brooklyn Eagle,"* Dec. 12, 1888. Mentioned in an article about a fair raising funds for a Home for the Blind
- Drislane, William E.: (F) Member Temple Lodge, No. 14, 1900, Albany, NY
- Drucker, J.: (F) Member Herber Lodge, No. 698,1898, F. & A. M., New York, NY, Greenpoint area, (RES) Brooklyn
- Dryfood, Sideny O. E.: (F) Member Society of American Magicians, Apr., 1931, New York, (RES) New York City
- DuBois, James: (F) Member Long Island Lodge, No. 382, F. &. A. M., 1874, NY
- DuBois, John C.: (F) Member Ineffable and Sublime Grand Lodge of Perfection, 1882, Albany, NY
- DuBoius, John C.: (F) Member Grand Council of the Princes of Jerusalem, 1882, Albany, NY
- Duck, J. L.: (F) Member Long Island Lodge, No. 382, F. &. A. M. 1874, NY
- Ducrot, Frank: (F) Member Society of American Magicians, Apr., 1931, New York, (RES) New York City
- Duffy, J. Chas.: (F) Member Knights of Columbus, Columbus Council No. 126, 1900, Brooklyn, (I) *"Brooklyn Eagle,"* Feb. 3, 1900. Meeting Notice., (CMTS) Financial Secretary
- Duffy, Miss: (F) Member Nativity Sewing Society, 1900, Brooklyn, (I) *"Brooklyn Eagle,"* Feb. 3, 1900. Article regarding raising money to buy clothing for the poor.
- Duffy, Miss G.: (F) Member Nativity Sewing Society, 1900, Brooklyn, (I) *"Brooklyn Eagle,"* Feb. 3, 1900. Article regarding raising money to buy clothing for the poor.
- Dumary, T. Henry: (F) Member Temple Lodge, No. 14, 1900, Albany, NY
- Dunaway, Fred G.: (F) Member Lowville Lodge No. 134, F. & A. M., 1929, Lowville, NY, (CO) Lewis, (JD) Nov. 29, 1919
- Dunbar, Albert C.: (F) Member Lowville Lodge No. 134, F. & A. M.,

1929, Lowville, NY, (CO) Lewis, (JD) May 26, 1899
Dunker, Charles F.: (F) Member Arcana Lodge, No. 246, F. & A. M., 1934, New York, NY, (JD) May 29, 1911
Dunn, Desmond: (F) Member Brooklyn Revenue Reform Club, 1886, (I) *"Brooklyn Eagle,"* Jan. ,27 1886, Attendees at a dinner
Dunn, John J.: (F) Member Arcana Lodge, No. 246, F. & A. M., 1934, New York, NY, (JD) Nov. 7, 1910
Durack, Walter L.: (F) Member Friendly Sons of St. Patrick, 1893, Brooklyn, (CMTS) *"Brooklyn Eagle,"* May 18, 1893, Article regarding the election of Andrew T. Sullivan as postmaster. In the article it mentioned that there were only 50 members in this Society., Guest. It is unknown if a member of the Society.
Duren, Henry: (F) Member Long Island Lodge, No. 382, F. &. A. M. 1874, NY
Durham, T. P.: (F) Member Long Island Lodge, No. 382, F. &. A. M. 1874, NY
Durwald, G.: (F) Member Herber Lodge, No. 698,1898, F. & A. M., New York, NY, Greenpoint area, (RES) New York City
Dutcher, Coles O.: (F) Member Lowville Lodge No. 134, F. & A. M., 1929, Lowville, NY, (CO) Lewis, (JD) Jan. 16, 1920 , (B) Feb. 28,1893, (D) Jan. 1971
Dwight, M. W.: (F) Member Astromical Society, Brooklyn Observatory, Mar. 16, 1850, Brooklyn, NY, (I) *"Brooklyn Eagle,"* Mar. 21, 1852
Dwight, Timothy: (F) Member Sons of New England, New England Society of the City of Brooklyn, 1887, (CMTS) *"Brooklyn Eagle,"* Dec. 22, 1887, Annual Dinner, Attendees, President of Yale Universaity
Dyer, William S.: (F) Member Masters Lodge, No. 5, 1900, Albany, NY
Dykman, William N.: (F) Member Sons of New England, New England Society of the City of Brooklyn, 1890, (CMTS) *"Brooklyn Eagle,"* Dec. 21, 1890, 11th Annual Dinner, Attendees
Earl, Charles T.: (I) *"Brooklyn Eagle,"* Feb. 19, 1902. Funeral Services at the Club House of the Brooklyn Lodge, No. 22, B. P. O. Elks for Wm. H. West. Elk services were first then masonic services by New York Lodge No. 330, F. A. & M., (CMTS) Made a floral gift.
Earle, Edward : (F) Member Brooklyn Revenue Reform Club, 1886, (I) *"Brooklyn Eagle,"* Jan. ,27 1886, Attendees at a dinner
Earle, T. F.: (F) Member Long Island Lodge, No. 382, F. &. A. M. 1874, NY
Easton, A. S.: (F) Member Educational Society of Lewis Co., NY, Nov. 14, 1845, (CMTS) Recording Secretary
Easton, Frederick: (F) Member Masters Lodge, No. 5, 1900, Albany, NY
Easton, Gilbert R.: (F) Member Lowville Lodge No. 134, F. & A. M., 1929, Lowville, NY, (CO) Lewis, (CMTS) Past Master 1898, 1899
Easton, Giles N.: (F) Member Lowville Lodge No. 134, F. & A. M.,

1929, Lowville, NY, (CO) Lewis, (JD) Aug. 1, 1913
Easton, Giles N.: (F) Member Lowville Chapter No. 223, R. A. M., 1929, Lowville, NY, (CO) Lewis, (JD) Nov. 13, 1913
Easton, William: (F) Member Grand Council of the Princes of Jerusalem, 1882, Albany, NY
Easton, William: (F) Member Ineffable and Sublime Grand Lodge of Perfection, 1882, Albany, NY
Easton, William: (F) Member Masters Lodge, No. 5, 1900, Albany, NY
Easton, William L.: (F) Member Lowville Lodge No. 134, F. & A. M., 1929, Lowville, NY, (CO) Lewis, (JD) Jun. 8, 1928
Eaton, Calvin W.: (F) Member Masters Lodge, No. 5, 1900, Albany, NY, (CMTS) Past Master
Eaton, James W.: (F) Member Masters Lodge, No. 5, 1900, Albany, NY
Eaton, Miss Alice M.: (F) Member The Young Women's Guild, 1888, Brooklyn, (I) *"Brooklyn Eagle,"* Dec. 12, 1888. Article regarding Societies aiding churches., (CMTS) Helping Plymouth Church, Vice President
Eaton, William T.: (F) Member Lowville Chapter No. 223, R. A. M., 1929, Lowville, NY, (CO) Lewis, (JD) Dec. 3, 1923
Ebel, William G.: (F) Member Temple Lodge, No. 14, 1900, Albany, NY
Eckhaus, Chas.: (F) Member Arcana Lodge, No. 246, F. & A. M., 1934, New York, NY, (JD) Nov. 16, 1914
Eckhaus, Samuel: (F) Member Arcana Lodge, No. 246, F. & A. M., 1934, New York, NY, (JD) Jun. 5, 1922
Eckstein, C.: (F) Member Long Island Lodge, No. 382, F. &. A. M., 1874, NY
Edelman, I. Alfred: (F) Member Arcana Lodge, No. 246, F. & A. M., 1934, New York, NY, (JD) May 12, 1931
Edelman, N. D.: (F) Member Arcana Lodge, No. 246, F. & A. M., 1934, New York, NY, (JD) Feb. 10, 1931
Edelson, Morris: (F) Member Arcana Lodge, No. 246, F. & A. M., 1934, New York, NY, (JD) Jun. 13, 1933
Edgerton, Frederick W.: (F) Member Temple Lodge, No. 14, 1900, Albany, NY
Edgin, Geo. H.: (F) Member Arcana Lodge, No. 246, F. & A. M., 1934, New York, NY, (JD) Nov. 15, 1909
Edick, Fred T.: (F) Member Lowville Lodge No. 134, F. & A. M., 1929, Lowville, NY, (CO) Lewis, (JD) Mar. 2, 1923
Edick, Fred T.: (F) Member Lowville Chapter No. 223, R. A. M., 1929, Lowville, NY, (CO) Lewis, (JD) Mar. 8, 1927
Edwards, D. L.: (F) Member Clyde Lodge No. 341, F. A. M., 1905, Clyde, NY, (CO) Wayne, (CMTS) Past Master 1902, 1903
Edwards, F. A.: (F) Member Murray Lodge, No. 380, F. & A. M., 1906, Holley, Orleans, Co., NY
Edwards, G. P.: (F) Member Friendly Sons of St. Patrick, 1893, Brooklyn, (CMTS)*"Brooklyn Eagle,"* May 18, 1893, Article regarding

the election of Andrew T. Sullivan as postmaster. In the article it mentioned that there were only 50 members in this Society., Guest. It is unknown if a member of the Society.

Edwards, Leand: (F) Member Temple Lodge, No. 14, 1900, Albany, NY

Edwards, Mrs.: (F) Member Ladies' Home and Foreign Mission Society, 1888, Brooklyn, (I) *"Brooklyn Eagle,"* Dec. 12, 1888. Article regarding Societies aiding churches., (CMTS) Helping Green Avenue Presbyterian Church, Vice President

Edwards, Thomas: (F) Member Long Island Lodge, No. 382, F. &. A. M., 1874, NY

Ege, Wald O.: (F) Member Society of American Magicians, Apr., 1931, New York, (RES) Brooklyn, NY

Egerton, William S.: (F) Member Masters Lodge, No. 5, 1900, Albany, NY

Eggers, John W.: (F) Member Society of American Magicians, Apr., 1931, New York, (RES) Summitt, NJ

Eggers, R.: (F) Member Herber Lodge, No. 698,1898, F. & A. M., New York, NY, Greenpoint area, (RES) New York City

Eggleston, N.: (F) Member Long Island Lodge, No. 382, F. &. A. M., 1874, NY

Ehlers, August: (F) Member Temple Lodge, No. 14, 1900, Albany, NY

Ehrlich, Leon: (F) Member Arcana Lodge, No. 246, F. & A. M., 1934, New York, NY, (JD) Jun. 20, 1921

Einstein, Edward H.: (F) Member Arcana Lodge, No. 246, F. & A. M., 1934, New York, NY, (JD) Jun. 22, 1922

Elbert, Wm.: (F) Member Herber Lodge, No. 698,1898, F. & A. M., New York, NY, Greenpoint area, (RES) New York City

Eldred, A.: (F) Member Long Island Lodge, No. 382, F. &. A. M. 1874, NY

Eldridge, Herbert C.: (F) Member Masters Lodge, No. 5, 1900, Albany, NY

Elgie, Augustus: (F) Member Mount Vernon Lodge, No. 3, 1900, Albany, NY

Elias, Charles F.: (F) Member Arcana Lodge, No. 246, F. & A. M., 1934, New York, NY, (JD) Mar. 9, 1926

Ellers, Charles E.: (F) Member Mount Vernon Lodge, No. 3, 1900, Albany, NY

Elliott, Brother: (F) Member Acanthus Lodge No. 719, F. A. M., (CMTS) Meeting Notes, *"Brooklyn Eagle,"* Mar. 13, 1887

Elliott, Dr. George: (F) Member Brooklyn Dental Society, 1877, Brooklyn, NY, (CMTS) *"Brooklyn Eagle,"* Dec. 15, 1877. Celebration of 10th Anniversary. Society established Dec. 14, 1867, (CMTS) Present from New York

Elliott, Leon: (F) Member Arcana Lodge, No. 246, F. & A. M., 1934, New York, NY, (JD) Feb. 15, 1915

Elliott, W.G.: (F) Member Clyde Lodge No. 341, F. A. M., 1905, Clyde,

NY, (CO) Wayne, (CMTS) Past Master 1857
Elliott, M.D., Joseph B.: (F) Member Sons of New England, New England Society of the City of Brooklyn, 1890, (CMTS)*"Brooklyn Eagle,"* Dec. 21, 1890, 11th Annual Dinner, Attendees
Ellison, S.: (F) Member Long Island Lodge, No. 382, F. &. A. M. 1874, NY
Elmer, Spencer A.: (F) Member Lowville Lodge No. 134, F. & A. M., 1929, Lowville, NY, (CO) Lewis, (JD) Feb 19, 1926, (B) Jan. 15, 1880, (BP) Harrisburg, NY, (D) Jun. 12, 1948, (DP) Long Beach, CA, (Spouse) Ada Loomis
Elste, L.: (F) Member Herber Lodge, No. 698,1898, F. & A. M., New York, NY, Greenpoint area, (RES) New York City
Emmons, Willis J.: (F) Member Lowville Lodge No. 134, F. & A. M., 1929, Lowville, NY, (CO) Lewis, (JD) Jun. 11, 1926
Endris, Jacob: (F) Member Long Island Lodge, No. 382, F. &. A. M., 1874, NY
Endris, John: (F) Member Long Island Lodge, No. 382, F. &. A. M., 1874, NY
Engel, Jacob: (F) Member Arcana Lodge, No. 246, F. & A. M., 1934, New York, NY, (JD) Oct. 11, 1927
Engle, Stewart: (F) Member Society of American Magicians, Apr., 1931, New York, (RES) Brooklyn, NY
Epke, Wilma D.: (F) Member Hope Rebekah Lodge No. 10, 1949-1950, Brockport, NY, (CO) Monroe
Erdmann, Wm. G. B.: (F) Member Temple Lodge, No. 14, 1900, Albany, NY
Erhler, A.: (F) Member Long Island Lodge, No. 382, F. &. A. M., 1874, NY
Ernest, Bernard M. L.: (F) Member Society of American Magicians, Apr., 1931, New York, (RES) New York City
Ernst, Joseph A.: (F) Member Temple Lodge, No. 14, 1900, Albany, NY
Ertzberger, Archibald S.: (F) Member Temple Lodge, No. 14, 1900, Albany, NY
Esquirol, Mrs. J. J. H.: (F) Member Lenox Ladies Aid Society of Lenox Road M. E. Church, Brooklyn, 1900, (CMTS) *"Brooklyn Eagle,"* Mar. 13, 1900. Meeting Notice, Board of Managers
Estes, B. W.: (F) Member Long Island Lodge, No. 382, F. &. A. M. 1874, NY
Estes, Benjamin: (F) Member Sons of New England, New England Society of the City of Brooklyn, 1887, (CMTS)*"Brooklyn Eagle,"* Dec. 22, 1887, Annual Dinner, Attendees
Estes, William : (F) Member Arcana Lodge, No. 246, F. & A. M., 1934, New York, NY, (JD) Nov. 10, 1931
Evans, Charles: (F) Member Lowville Lodge No. 134, F. & A. M., 1929, Lowville, NY, (CO) Lewis, (JD) Mar. 29, 1912

Evans, Edward R.: (F) Member Masters Lodge, No. 5, 1900, Albany, NY

Evans, Edwin L.: (F) Member Lowville Lodge No. 134, F. & A. M., 1929, Lowville, NY, (CO) Lewis, (JD) Mar. 29, 1912, (B) Jan. 5, 1875, (BP) Martinsburg, Lewis Co., NY, (MD) Aug. 16, 1899, (Spouse) Edith C. Loucks

Evans, J. Duane: (F) Member Lowville Lodge No. 134, F. & A. M., 1929, Lowville, NY, (CO) Lewis, (JD) Mar. 15, 1889

Evans, John L.: (F) Member Monticello Lodge, No. 532, F. & A. M., (CO) Sullivan Co., NY, (CMTS) Past Master 1876, 1881

Evans, John W.: (F) Member Commonwealth Lodge No. 409, (CMTS) Meeting Notes, *"Brooklyn Eagle,"* Mar. 13, 1887

Evans, Mrs. J.: (F) Member Ladies Loyal Orange Legion, Princess of Orange No. 6, 1900, Brooklyn, (I) *"Brooklyn Eagle,"* Feb. 3, 1900. Meeting Notice., (CMTS) Whorshipful Matron

Evans, W.: (F) Member Long Island Lodge, No. 382, F. &. A. M., 1874, NY

Evans, William G.: (F) Member Lowville Lodge No. 134, F. & A. M., 1929, Lowville, NY, (CO) Lewis, (JD) Feb. 3, 1903

Faeber, Murray: (F) Member Arcana Lodge, No. 246, F. & A. M., 1934, New York, NY, (JD) Apr. 26, 1927

Fagan, Miss: (F) Member Nativity Sewing Society, 1900, Brooklyn, (I) *"Brooklyn Eagle,"* Feb. 3, 1900. Article regarding raising money to buy clothing for the poor., (CMTS) Two separate people present.

Faggiana, S.: (F) Member Long Island Lodge, No. 382, F. &. A. M. 1874, NY

Fahnestock, Gates D.: (F) Member Sons of New England, New England Society of the City of Brooklyn, 1890, (CMTS) *"Brooklyn Eagle,"* Dec. 21, 1890, 11th Annual Dinner, Attendees

Failing, Harold A.: (F) Member Lowville Lodge No. 134, F. & A. M., 1929, Lowville, NY, (CO) Lewis, (JD) Mar. 18, 1927

Failing, Philander D.: (F) Member Lowville Lodge No. 134, F. & A. M., 1929, Lowville, NY, (CO) Lewis, (JD) Apr. 22, 1921, (AKA)

Faling, (CEN) 1880 Montague, Lews CO., NY Listed with Philander Faling 39, NY, E. Mary, 35, Everette, 17, Edward, 15, Dette, 14, Berdett, 9, Philander, 7, Alexander, 5, Ira, 4, Ernest, 2

Fairchild, Charles H.: (F) Member Lowville Lodge No. 134, F. & A. M., 1929, Lowville, NY, (CO) Lewis, (JD) Apr. 15, 1921, (AKA) Charles Henry Fairchild, (B) Mar. 15, 1882, (BP) Port Leyden, (D) Sep. 10, 1959, (DP) Port Leyden, (MD) Sep. 20, 1906, (Spouse) Alma Edith Wilcox, (PRTS) Fellus Fairchild, (b. Aug. 28, 1845, d. May 26, 1884) and Emma Maria Plumb, (GPRTS) David Fairchild and Eliza M. Taylor

Fairchild, Harold A.: (F) Member Lowville Lodge No. 134, F. & A. M., 1929, Lowville, NY, (CO) Lewis, (CMTS) Past Master 1926

Fairchild, Harold A.: (F) Member Lowville Lodge No. 134, F. & A. M., 1929, Lowville, NY, (CO) Lewis, (JD) Nov. 17, 1916

Fairchild, Harold A.: (F) Member Lowville Chapter No. 223, R. A. M., 1929, Lowville, NY, (CO) Lewis, (JD) Nov. 11, 1919

Fairchild, Herbert D.: (F) Member Lowville Lodge No. 134, F. & A. M., 1929, Lowville, NY, (CO) Lewis, (JD) Oct. 4, 1907, (AKA) (CEN) 1880 Leyden, Lewis Co., NY, Fellus E., 34, Jobber, Emma M., 34, Herbert D., 11, Emma, 3, Ella, 3, (GPRTS) David Fairchild and Eliza M. Taylor

Fairchild, Herbert D.: (F) Member Lowville Chapter No. 223, R. A. M., 1929, Lowville, NY, (CO) Lewis, (JD) May 27, 1906, (B) Jan. 14, 1869, (BP) West Turn, (D) Nov. 15, 1941, (Spouse) Minnie McMoran, (MD) Jun. 15, 1892, (PRTS) Fellus Fairchild (b. Aug. 28,1845, d. May 26, 1884) and Emma Maria Plumb, (b. Aug. 23, 1845, d. Nov. 15, 1935, (AKA) Herbert David Fairchild, (PGPRTS) David Fairchild and Elizabeth Mae Taylor, (MGPRTS) Eleazer Plumb and Matilda Miller

Falk, Ph.D., K. George: (F) Member Society of American Magicians, Apr., 1931, New York, (RES) New York City

Falk, Ph.D., Myron S.: (F) Member Society of American Magicians, Apr., 1931, New York, (RES) New York City

Farley, Rev. Dr.: (F) Member Society for the Relief of Respectable Indigent Females, Brooklyn, (I) Brooklyn Eagle, Nov. 13, 1879

Farley, Rev. Dr. F. A.: (F) Member Sons of New England, New England Society of the City of Brooklyn, 1887, (CMTS) *"Brooklyn Eagle,"* Dec. 22, 1887, Annual Dinner, Attendees

Farney, Ezra J.: (F) Member Lowville Lodge No. 134, F. & A. M., 1929, Lowville, NY, (CO) Lewis, (JD) Mar. 30, 1928, (B) Jan. 10, 1895, (BP) New Bremen, Lewis CO., NY, (D) Feb. 28, 1963, (PRTS) Joseph P. Farney and Emma Zehr

Farney, George M.: (F) Member Lowville Lodge No. 134, F. & A. M., 1929, Lowville, NY, (CO) Lewis, (JD) Feb. 20, 1922, (B) Mar. 12, 1890, (BP) New Bremen, Lewis Co., NY, (D) Feb. 4, 1946, (PRTS) Michael Farney, (b. Jan. 14, 1850, d. Jul. 9, 1915, md. Feb. 15, 1877) and Amelia Mills, (b. Jun. 15, 1851, d. Sep. 28, 1897), (SIB) Clinton David, Henry Joseph, Jessie Magdelena

Farnsworth, R. C.: (F) Member Murray Lodge, No. 380, F. & A. M., 1906, Holley, Orleans, Co., NY

Farrar, J. L.: (F) Member Brooklyn Dental Society, 1877, Brooklyn, NY, (CMTS) *"Brooklyn Eagle,"* Dec. 15, 1877. Celebration of 10th Anniversary. Society established Dec. 14, 1867, (CMTS) Clinics Committee

Farrell, Thomas F.: (F) Member Friendly Sons of St. Patrick, 1893, Brooklyn, (CMTS) *"Brooklyn Eagle,"* May 18, 1893, Article regarding the election of Andrew T. Sullivan as postmaster. In the article it mentioned that there were only 50 members in this Society., Guest. It is unknown if a member of the Society.

Farrington, Harvey F.: (F) Member Lowville Lodge No. 134, F. & A. M., 1929, Lowville, NY, (CO) Lewis, (JD) Dec. 6, 1907

Farrington, Harvey F.: (F) Member Lowville Chapter No. 223, R. A. M., 1929, Lowville, NY, (CO) Lewis, (JD) Jan. 19, 1909

Fasoldt, Otto H.: (F) Member Masters Lodge, No. 5, 1900, Albany, NY

Faulkner, John: (F) Member Long Island Lodge, No. 382, F. &. A. M. 1874, NY

Feingold, Robert H.: (F) Member Arcana Lodge, No. 246, F. & A. M., 1934, New York, NY, (JD) Jun. 9, 1925

Feingold, Samuel: (F) Member Arcana Lodge, No. 246, F. & A. M., 1934, New York, NY, (JD)Apr. 15, 1918

Feldman, Jacob: (F) Member Arcana Lodge, No. 246, F. & A. M., 1934, New York, NY, (JD) Jun. 3,1 192 1

Feldman, N. S.: (F) Member Arcana Lodge, No. 246, F. & A. M., 1934, New York, NY, (JD) Feb. 15, 1904, Life Member

Fero, DeMyre S.: (F) Member Grand Council of the Princes of Jerusalem, 1882, Albany, NY

Ferron, Charles H.: (I) *"Brooklyn Eagle,"* Dec. 7, 1896. 12th Annual Memorial Services, Plymouth Church, Brooklyn Lodge No. 22, B. F. O. Elks, Roll Call of the dead. Address made by Maryland Senator George L. Wellington. , (CMTS) Name called.

Fessendsen, Oliver G.: (F) Member Sons of New England, New England Society of the City of Brooklyn, 1890, (CMTS)*"Brooklyn Eagle,"* Dec. 21, 1890, 11th Annual Dinner, Attendees

Feust, Sidney: (F) Member Society of American Magicians, Apr., 1931, New York, (RES) New York City

Fichtel, Miss D.: (F) Member Mispah Circle, 1888, Brooklyn, (I) *"Brooklyn Eagle,"* Dec. 12, 1888. Mentioned in an article about a fair raising funds for a Home for the Blind

Fiedler, Wm R.: (F) Member Herber Lodge, No. 698,1898, F. & A. M., New York, NY, Greenpoint area, (RES) New York City

Field, Fred A.: (F) Member Monticello Lodge, No. 532, F. & A. M., (CO) Sullivan Co., NY, (CMTS) Past Master 1865, 1866, 1867

Field, W. E.: (F) Member Long Island Lodge, No. 382, F. &. A. M. 1874, NY

Field, W.N.: (F) Member Clyde Lodge No. 341, F. A. M., 1905, Clyde, NY, (CO) Wayne, (CMTS) Past Master 1883

Field, William D.: (F) Member Grand Council of the Princes of Jerusalem, 1882, Albany, NY

Field, William D.: (F) Member Ineffable and Sublime Grand Lodge of Perfection, 1882, Albany, NY

Field, William G.: (F) Member Temple Lodge, No. 14, 1900, Albany, NY

Fields, Al S.: (I) *"Brooklyn Eagle,"* Feb. 19, 1902. Funeral Services at the

Club House of the Brooklyn Lodge, No. 22, B. P. O. Elks for Wm. H. West. Elk services were first then masonic services by New York Lodge No. 330, F. A. & M., (CMTS) Made a floral gift.

Fields, Lew M.: (I) *"Brooklyn Eagle,"* Feb. 19, 1902. Funeral Services at the Club House of the Brooklyn Lodge, No. 22, B. P. O. Elks for Wm. H. West. Elk services were first then masonic services by New York Lodge No. 330, F. A. & M., (CMTS) Pallbearer

Fiening, H.: (F) Member Herber Lodge, No. 698,1898, F. & A. M., New York, NY, Greenpoint area, (RES) New York City

Finch, Charles C.: (F) Member Masters Lodge, No. 5, 1900, Albany, NY

Finch, Wellington: (F) Member Mount Vernon Lodge, No. 3, 1900, Albany, NY

Fine, Abram J.: (F) Member Arcana Lodge, No. 246, F. & A. M., 1934, New York, NY, (JD) Jun. 9, 1925

Fine, Lewis: (F) Member Arcana Lodge, No. 246, F. & A. M., 1934, New York, NY, (JD) Feb. 20, 1922

Fine, Sampson: (F) Member Arcana Lodge, No. 246, F. & A. M., 1934, New York, NY, (JD) Jan. 20, 1913

Finger, J.: (F) Member Herber Lodge, No. 698,1898, F. & A. M., New York, NY, Greenpoint area, (RES) New York City

Finherty, J. W.: (F) Member Friendly Sons of St. Patrick, 1893, Brooklyn, (CMTS)*"Brooklyn Eagle,"* May 18, 1893, Article regarding the election of Andrew T. Sullivan as postmaster. In the article it mentioned that there were only 50 members in this Society., Guest. It is unknown if a member of the Society.

Finkel, Albert D.: (F) Member Temple Lodge, No. 14, 1900, Albany, NY

Finkel, Jacob: (F) Member Arcana Lodge, No. 246, F. & A. M., 1934, New York, NY, (JD) Jun. 3, 1912

Finkelman, Maurice: (F) Member Arcana Lodge, No. 246, F. & A. M., 1934, New York, NY, (JD) Sep. 16, 1918

Finkelman, Samuel J.: (F) Member Arcana Lodge, No. 246, F. & A. M., 1934, New York, NY, (JD) Dec. 5, 1921, (Spouse) Jennie Jackson, (MD) Aug. 23, 1904. (PMD) Manhattan, NY

Finkleman, John: (F) Member Murray Lodge, No. 380, F. & A. M., 1906, Holley, Orleans, Co., NY

First, Chas. S. M.: (F) Member Arcana Lodge, No. 246, F. & A. M., 1934, New York, NY, (JD) Nov. 17, 1924

Fischer, Chas. J.: (F) Member Herber Lodge, No. 698,1898, F. & A. M., New York, NY, Greenpoint area, (RES) New York City

Fischer, H C.: (F) Member Herber Lodge, No. 698,1898, F. & A. M., New York, NY, Greenpoint area, (RES) New York City

Fischer, Louis: (F) Member Long Island Lodge, No. 382, F. &. A. M. 1874, NY

Fishbone, Meyer B.: (F) Member Arcana Lodge, No. 246, F. & A. M., 1934, New York, NY, (JD) Oct. 12, 1926

Fishbough, Wm.: (F) Member Brooklyn Dental Society, 1877, Brooklyn,

NY, (CMTS) *"Brooklyn Eagle,"* Dec. 15, 1877. Celebration of 10th Anniversary. Society established Dec. 14, 1867, (CMTS) Executive Committee, (CEN) 1880, Brooklyn, Kings Co., 66, NJ, Dentist, Eliza, 63, wife, Philadelphia, Mary E., 39, MA, daughter, Music and English Teacher, Morris A. Davis, son-in-law, Commercial Art Agent, Ella Davis, daughter, 30

Fisher, Clarence L.: (F) Member Lowville Chapter No. 223, R. A. M., 1929, Lowville, NY, (CO) Lewis, (JD) Jan. 30, 1912

Fisher, George H.: (F) Member Sons of New England, New England Society of the City of Brooklyn, 1890, (CMTS) *"Brooklyn Eagle,"* Dec. 21, 1890, 11th Annual Dinner, Attendees

Fisher, George H.: (F) Member Sons of New England, New England Society of the City of Brooklyn, 1890, (CMTS) *"Brooklyn Eagle,"* Dec. 21, 1890, 11th Annual Dinner, Attendees

Fisher, George H.: (F) Member Sons of New England, New England Society of the City of Brooklyn, 1887, (CMTS) *"Brooklyn Eagle,"* Dec. 22, 1887, Annual Dinner, Attendees

Fisher, Robert J.: (F) Member Society of American Magicians, Apr., 1931, New York, (RES) Brooklyn, NY

Fisher, William: (F) Member Grand Council of the Princes of Jerusalem, 1882, Albany, NY

Fisher, William: (F) Member Ineffable and Sublime Grand Lodge of Perfection, 1882, Albany, NY, (B) Jul. 17, 1845, (PRTS) Samuel W. Fisher and Jane Jackson

Fisk, A. H.: (F) Member Murray Lodge, No. 380, F. & A. M., 1906, Holley, Orleans, Co., NY

Fisk, Frank H.: (F) Member Temple Lodge, No. 14, 1900, Albany, NY

Fiske, W. J. M.: (F) Member Sons of New England, New England Society of the City of Brooklyn, 1887, (CMTS) *"Brooklyn Eagle,"* Dec. 22, 1887, Annual Dinner, Attendees

Fitch, William E.: (F) Member Grand Council of the Princes of Jerusalem, 1882, Albany, NY

Fitch, William E.: (F) Member Ineffable and Sublime Grand Lodge of Perfection, 1882, Albany, NY

Fitzgibbons, W. L.: (F) Member Friendly Sons of St. Patrick, 1893, Brooklyn, (CMTS) *"Brooklyn Eagle,"* May 18, 1893, Article regarding the election of Andrew T. Sullivan as postmaster. In the article it mentioned that there were only 50 members in this Society., Member ofDinner Committee

Fitzpatrick, James W.: (F) Member Friendly Sons of St. Patrick, 1893, Brooklyn, (CMTS) *"Brooklyn Eagle,"* May 18, 1893, Article Regarding the election of Andrew T. Sullivan as postmaster. In the article it mentioned that there were only 50 members in this Society., Guest. It is unknown if a member of the Society.

Fitzpatrick, Mrs. J.: (F) Member Nativity Sewing Society, 1900, Brooklyn, (I) *"Brooklyn Eagle,"* Feb. 3, 1900. Article regarding

raising money to buy clothing for the poor.
Fitzpatrick, P. A.: (F) Member Friendly Sons of St. Patrick, 1893, Brooklyn, (CMTS) *"Brooklyn Eagle,"* May 18, 1893, Article regarding the election of Andrew T. Sullivan as postmaster. In the article it mentioned that there were only 50 members in this Society., Guest. It is unknown if a member of the Society.
Flachner, Louis: (F) Member Arcana Lodge, No. 246, F. & A. M., 1934, New York, NY, (JD) Jun. 28, 1927
Fletcher, Abram M.: (F) Member Arcana Lodge, No. 246, F. & A. M., 1934, New York, NY, (JD) Jun. 7, 1920
Floyd, Albion Ward: (F) Member Temple Lodge, No. 14, 1900, Albany, NY
Flug, William J.: (F) Member Arcana Lodge, No. 246, F. & A. M., 1934, New York, NY, (JD) Jun. 9, 1925
Flyn, Mrs. A. D.: (F) Member Nativity Sewing Society, 1900, Brooklyn, *"Brooklyn Eagle,"* Feb. 3, 1900. Article regarding raising money to buy clothing for the poor.
Flynn, Maggie: (F) Member Mispah Circle, 1888, Brooklyn, (I) *"Brooklyn Eagle,"* Dec. 12, 1888. Mentioned in an article about a fair raising funds for a Home for the Blind
Flynn, Miss Annie: (F) Member Mispah Circle, 1888, Brooklyn, (I) *"Brooklyn Eagle,"* Dec. 12, 1888. Mentioned in an article about a fair raising funds for a Home for the Blind
Flynn, Robert: (I) *"Brooklyn Eagle,"* Feb. 19, 1902. Funeral Services at the Club House of the Brooklyn Lodge, No. 22, B. P. O. Elks for Wm. H. West. Elk services were first then masonic services by New York Lodge No. 330, F. A. & M., (CMTS) Made a floral gift.
Fogel, Philip G.: (F) Member Arcana Lodge, No. 246, F. & A. M., 1934, New York, NY, (JD) Feb. 8, 1927
Foley, Mrs. James: (F) Member Mispah Circle, 1888, Brooklyn, (I) *"Brooklyn Eagle,"* Dec. 12, 1888. Mentioned in an article about a fair raising funds for a Home for the Blind
Follette, Mark: (F) Member Lowville Chapter No. 223, R. A. M., 1929, Lowville, NY, (CO) Lewis, (JD) Feb. 24, 1925
Follmer, G. A.: (F) Member Long Island Lodge, No. 382, F. &. A. M. 1874, NY
Fonda, Douw (sic) H.: (F) Member Temple Lodge, No. 14, 1900, Albany, NY
Fonda, John: (F) Member Mount Vernon Lodge, No. 3, 1900, Albany, NY, (CMTS) Life Member, Past Master 1866
Fondey, Townsend: (F) Member Grand Council of the Princes of Jerusalem, 1882, Albany, NY , (B) Dec. 22, 1817, (BAPT) Jan. 27, 1818, First Dutch Reformed Church, Albany, Albany Co., NY, (PRTS) Isaac Fonday
Fondey, Townsend: (F) Member Ineffable and Sublime Grand Lodge of Perfection, 1882, Albany, NY

Fookes, Henry H.: (F) Member Temple Lodge, No. 14, 1900, Albany, NY

Foot, G. H.: (F) Member Murray Lodge, No. 380, F. & A. M., 1906, Holley, Orleans, Co., NY

Foote, Duane C.: (F) Member Lowville Lodge No. 134, F. & A. M., 1929, Lowville, NY, (CO) Lewis, (JD) Apr. 21, 1899, (AKA) Duane Christian Foote, (B) Dec. 2, 1875, (BP) Lowville, Lewis Co., NY, (PRTS) Ellis Evans Foote, (b. Jan. 25, 1850, bp. Martinsburg, prts. Duan D. Foote and Margaret Ann Evans, md. Aug. 14, 1872, bmd. Herkimer Co.) and Emma Shoemaker, (b. Oct. 20, 1850, d. Mar. 26, 1928), (CEN) 1880 West Turin, Lewis Co., NY Listed with Ellis C. Foot, 30, Farmer, Emma, 30, Leigh S., Dunace C., 4, Margaretta, 2

Foote, Harold H.: (F) Member Lowville Lodge No. 134, F. & A. M., 1929, Lowville, NY, (CO) Lewis, (JD) May 16, 1924, (AKA) Harold Harrison Foote, (B) Dec. 28, 1888, (BP) Lowville, Lewis Co., NY, (PRTS) Ellis Evans Foote, (b. Jan. 25, 1850, bp. Martinsburg, prts. Duan D. Foote and Margaret Ann Evans, md. Aug. 14, 1872, bmd. Herkimer Co.) and Emma Shoemaker, (b. Oct. 20, 1850, d. Mar. 26, 1928)

Foote, Harold H.: (F) Member Lowville Chapter No. 223, R. A. M., 1929, Lowville, NY, (CO) Lewis, (JD) Nov. 27, 1928

Foote, J. Max: (F) Member Lowville Lodge No. 134, F. & A. M., 1929, Lowville, NY, (CO) Lewis, (JD) Oct. 7, 1910

Ford, A. H.: (F) Member Murray Lodge, No. 380, F. & A. M., 1906, Holley, Orleans, Co., NY

Ford, Albert G.: (F) Member Lowville Lodge No. 134, F. & A. M., 1929, Lowville, NY, (CO) Lewis, (JD) Feb. 21, 1913

Ford, Clarence D.: (F) Member Lowville Chapter No. 223, R. A. M., 1929, Lowville, NY, (CO) Lewis, (JD) May 10, 1927

Ford, Gordon L.: (F) Member Sons of New England, New England Society of the City of Brooklyn, 1887, (CMTS)*"Brooklyn Eagle,"* Dec. 22, 1887, Annual Dinner, Attendees

Ford, Gordon L.: (F) Member Brooklyn Revenue Reform Club, 1886, (I)*"Brooklyn Eagle,"* Jan. ,27 1886, Attendees at a dinner

Ford, Miss M.: (F) Member Nativity Sewing Society, 1900, Brooklyn, (I) *"Brooklyn Eagle,"* Feb. 3, 1900. Article regarding raising money to buy clothing for the poor.

Forrest, Mrs. P. R.: (F) Member Nativity Sewing Society, 1900, Brooklyn, (I) *"Brooklyn Eagle,"* Feb. 3, 1900. Article regarding raising money to buy clothing for the poor.

Forrister, Robert W.: (F) Member Temple Lodge, No. 14, 1900, Albany, NY

Forshew, William : (F) Member Anglo Saxon Lodge No. 137, F. A. M., (CMTS) Meeting Notes, *"Brooklyn Eagle,"* Mar. 23, 1887, Organist presented new musicals

Fort, Charles N.: (F) Member Masters Lodge, No. 5, 1900, Albany, NY

Foster, George F.: (F) Member Anglo Saxon Lodge No. 137, F. A. M., (CMTS) Meeting Notes, *"Brooklyn Eagle,"* Mar. 13, 1887, Entered the Apprentice Degree by W. M. Jerome E. Morse

Foster, Harry S.: (F) Member Temple Lodge, No. 14, 1900, Albany, NY, (CEN) 1880, 16$^{th}$ Ward, Albany, Albany CO., NY. Listed with John N. Foster, 43, Supt. Insurance Patrol, Mary A., 40, Fred H., 18, Insurance Clerk, Kitty F., 17, Harry S., 14, Angie B., 13, May G., 9, Allie N., 7.

Foster, William: (F) Member Long Island Lodge, No. 382, F. &. A. M., 1874, NY

Fowler, Philip H.: (F) Member Lowville Lodge No. 134, F. & A. M., 1929, Lowville, NY, (CO) Lewis, (JD) Feb. 1, 1924

Fowler, Philip H.: (F) Member Lowville Chapter No. 223, R. A. M., 1929, Lowville, NY, (CO) Lewis, (JD) Apr. 8, 1924

Fowler, T. H.: (F) Member Murray Lodge, No. 380, F. & A. M., 1906, Holley, Orleans, Co., NY

Fowler , George W.: (F) Member Lowville Lodge No. 134, F. & A. M., 1929, Lowville, NY, (CO) Lewis, (JD) Nov. 20, 1908

Fowler , George W.: (F) Member Lowville Chapter No. 223, R. A. M., 1929, Lowville, NY, (CO) Lewis, (JD) Jun. 21, 1917

Fowler, Jr., Edward E.: (F) Member Lowville Lodge No. 134, F. & A. M., 1929, Lowville, NY, (CO) Lewis, (JD) Jul. 7, 1905

Fowler, Jr., Edward E.: (F) Member Lowville Chapter No. 223, R. A. M., 1929, Lowville, NY, (CO) Lewis, (JD) Feb. 11, 1908

Fox, George I.: (F) Member Friendly Sons of St. Patrick, 1893, Brooklyn, (CMTS)*"Brooklyn Eagle,"* May 18, 1893, Article regarding the election of Andrew T. Sullivan as postmaster. In the article it mentioned that there were only 50 members in this Society., Guest. It is unknown if a member of the Society.

Fox, Joseph: (F) Member Hyatt Lodge No. 205, (CMTS) Meeting Notes, *"Brooklyn Eagle,"* Mar. 13, 1887, Past Master

Frad, Harry: (F) Member Arcana Lodge, No. 246, F. & A. M., 1934, New York, NY, (JD) Apr. 26, 1927

Frampton, C. G.: (F) Member Long Island Lodge, No. 382, F. &. A. M., 1874, NY

Francos, Dr. C. H.: (F) Member Brooklyn Dental Society, 1877, Brooklyn, NY, (CMTS) *"Brooklyn Eagle,"* Dec. 15, 1877. Celebration of 10th Anniversary. Society established Dec. 14, 1867, (CMTS) Present from New York

Frank, Jacob H,: (F) Member Arcana Lodge, No. 246, F. & A. M., 1934, New York, NY, (JD) Nov. 19, 1900, Life Member

Frank, Joseph: (F) Member Arcana Lodge, No. 246, F. & A. M., 1934, New York, NY, (JD) Apr. 22, 1930

Frank, Max: (F) Member Arcana Lodge, No. 246, F. & A. M., 1934, New York, NY, (JD) Nov. 2, 1903, Life

Member
Frank, Samuel L.: (F) Member Arcana Lodge, No. 246, F. & A. M., 1934, New York, NY, (JD) Nov. 17, 1924

Franklin, Daniel: (OBIT) *"Delaware Gazette,"* Ex-sheriff Daniel Franklin, whose death occurred just as we were going to press last week, was 57 years old. His death was caused by a cystic tumor of the bowels. Last March an operation was performed but the conditions were so serious that a complete removal was not considered safe. On Tuesday last Drs. Gates, Goodrich, Ormiston and Schumann performed a second operation but Mr. Franklin was not able to endure the shock and died before recovering from the anesthtic administered. Mr. Franklin was born in this town on the Little Delaware but lived many years in the town of Andes. In 1885 he was elected sheriff and came to Delhi where he has since resided except for about 5 years during which he lived in Oneonta. Mr. Franklin was a man who made many friends and they have felt great interest for him during his serious affliction. He leaves a wife, three sons, Andrew, Charles and Daniel, and two daughters, Mrs. John O. Gladstone and Mrs. John Douglas all of whom are residents of this village. His funeral was held Thursday from the M E Church, the Rev. A. E. Cord officiating. His remains were taken to Andes for burial under the aupices of the Masonic fraternity.

Franks, Ald.: (F) Member St. Nicholas Society of Nassau Island, 1861, (CMTS*)"Brooklyn Eagle,"* Dec. 11, 1861, Article regarding the Anniversary Dinner, Guest, President of the Friendly Sons of St. Patrick

Fransloli, Mrs. A.: (F) Member Nativity Sewing Society, 1900, Brooklyn, (I) *"Brooklyn Eagle,"* Feb. 3, 1900. Article regarding raising money to buy clothing for the poor.

Fredenburg, Grover C.: (F) Member Lowville Lodge No. 134, F. & A. M., 1929, Lowville, NY, (CO) Lewis, (JD) Jun. 4, 1926, (AKA) Grover Cleveland Fredenburg, (B) Jun. 19, 1887, Great Bend, Jefferson Co., NY, (D) Apr. 11, 1963, (DP) Beaver Falls, Lewis Co., NY, (PRTS) William Henry Fredenburg and Sally Ann Francis, (SIB) Egbert W., Francis H., Mary, John G.

Fredrick, Charles F.: (F) Member Mount Vernon Lodge, No. 3, 1900, Albany, NY

Fredrick, John E.: (F) Member Mount Vernon Lodge, No. 3, 1900, Albany, NY

Freeman, Theodore: (F) Member Arcana Lodge, No. 246, F. & A. M., 1934, New York, NY, (JD) Apr. 22, 1930

French, R. H.: (F) Member Anglo Saxon Lodge No. 137, F. A. M., (CMTS) Meeting Notes, *"Brooklyn Eagle,"* Mar. 23, 1887, Stood as guardian at the meeting

French, M.D., Thomas R.: (F) Member Sons of New England, New

England Society of the City of Brooklyn, 1890, (CMTS) *"Brooklyn Eagle,"* Dec. 21, 1890, 11th Annual Dinner, Attendees

Freyberger, Julius F.: (OBIT) *"The River Reporter,"* Jul. 22, 2004, Narrowsburg, NY. Julius F. Freyberger, a resident of Callicoon, died April 5, 2004 at Catskill Regional Medical Center in Harris, NY. He was 94.The son of the late Frederick and Pauline Molusky Freyberger, he was born December 4, 1909 in Hortonville. He attended Callicoon High School and enlisted in the Army in April of 1942. After training as a high-speed radio operator, he was assigned to the 10th Air Force and served in the China-Burma-India Theatre during World War II. Upon leaving the service, he became an auto mechanic and eventually opened Freyberger and Rubino's Garage in Fremont Center with Ray Rubino. This garage met the needs of the surrounding community for over 40 years. He was a Masonic member for 65 years. He received many honors and held many offices. Freyberger was a former member of the Hortonville Presbyterian Church and a familiar face at the Callicoon United Methodist Church. Survivors include a niece, Beverly Mitterwager and her husband, Kenneth of Callicoon; a grandniece Jody Gilbert of Beach Lake, PA; and grandnephews Morgan Mitterwager of Hankins and Jason Mitterwager of Callicoon. He was predeceased by a sister, Amelia, two brothers, Alfred and Walter, and a niece Elaine Callahan. Masonic services were held on April 7 at Stewart-Murphy Funeral Home, Callicoon. Funeral services were held April 8 at the funeral home, Pastor Peg VanSiclen officiating. Interment was in Hortonville Cemetery

Freybourg, William E.: (F) Member Society of American Magicians, Apr., 1931, New York, (RES) Mt. Vernon, NY

Fribourg, Walter A.: (F) Member Arcana Lodge, No. 246, F. & A. M., 1934, New York, NY, (JD) Mar. 2, 1914

Friedman, Jacob P.: (F) Member Arcana Lodge, No. 246, F. & A. M., 1934, New York, NY, (JD) Oct. 6, 1919

Friedman, Lopold: (F) Member Arcana Lodge, No. 246, F. & A. M., 1934, New York, NY, (JD) Jun. 3, 1918

Friedman, Jr., Jacob S.: (F) Member Temple Lodge, No. 14, 1900, Albany, NY, (CMTS) Life Member, (CEN) 1880, 14th Ward, Albany, Albany Co., NY, 30, Wholesale Cloth dealer, Mary, 19, Wife

Fries, M.D., Joseph H.: (F) Member Society of American Magicians, Apr., 1931, New York, (RES) Brooklyn, NY

Frisbee, Luther: (F) Member Temple Lodge, No. 14, 1900, Albany, NY, (CEN) 15th Ward, Albany, Albany Co., NY, 37, Book Binder, Euncie C., 35, MA, Charles E., 13, Mary E.Gardner, 22, sister-In-law, works in book binder , (B) Sep. 10, 1842, (BP) Albany, NY, (PRTS) Luther Frisbee, b. Dec. 29, 1794, d. Sep. 19, 1864, Bp. Dehli, Delaware Co., NY, and Ann Tomkins, md. Sep. 23, 1839. (CMTS) Luther Frisbee's parents were Philip Frisbee, and Jerusha Hammond

Frisbie, Edward : (F) Member Harrisburgh Ecclesiastical Society, Jul. 9, 1805, (CO) Lewis

Frost, Cuthbert C.: (F) Member Lowville Lodge No. 134, F. & A. M., 1929, Lowville, NY, (CO) Lewis, (JD) Nov. 3, 1905

Frost, Cuthbert C.: (F) Member Lowville Chapter No. 223, R. A. M., 1929, Lowville, NY, (CO) Lewis, (JD) Jun. 19, 1906

Frost, Frank L.: (F) Member Masters Lodge, No. 5, 1900, Albany, NY, (CEN) 1880, 5$^{th}$ Ward, Albany, Albany Co., NY, Listed with Jack Stackhouse, 43, Butcher, Mary A., 45, Mary Frost, 23, Stepdaughter, Frank L., 12, stepson.

Frost, Louis W.: (F) Member Anglo Saxon Lodge No. 137, F. A. M., (CMTS) Meeting Notes, *"Brooklyn Eagle,"* Mar. 13, 1887, Entered the Apprentice Degree by W. M. Jerome E. Morse

Frost, William K.: (F) Member Masters Lodge, No. 5, 1900, Albany, NY

Fuller, Amasa: (F) Member Ineffable and Sublime Grand Lodge of Perfection, 1882, Albany, NY

Fuller, Amza: (F) Member Grand Council of the Princes of Jerusalem, 1882, Albany, NY

Fuller, Benjamin H.: (F) Member Temple Lodge, No. 14, 1900, Albany, NY, (CEN) 5$^{th}$ Ward, Albany, Albany Co., NY. Listed with David F. Fuller, 66, grocer, Mary F., 64, Mary F., 40, Benjamin H., 38, David, 35, Alfred A., 30.

Fuller, Howard N.: (F) Member Temple Lodge, No. 14, 1900, Albany, NY

Fuller, Joseph W.: (F) Member Mount Vernon Lodge, No. 3, 1900, Albany, NY, (CEN) 1880, 14$^{th}$ Ward, Albany, Albany Co., NY. Listed with Orrin B. Fuller, 61, Phoebe B., 61, Orrin A., 37, Joseph W., 21, Augustus J., 26, Anna S., 26.

Fuller, M. T.: (F) Member Murray Lodge, No. 380, F. & A. M., 1906, Holley, Orleans, Co., NY

Fuller, Sue: (F) Member Hope Rebekah Lodge No. 10, 1949-1950, Brockport, NY, (CO) Monroe, (CMTS) Sick Committee

Fulton, William H.: (F) Member Lowville Chapter No. 223, R. A. M., 1929, Lowville, NY, (CO) Lewis, (JD) Jun. 12, 1923

Furey, James G.: (F) Member Friendly Sons of St. Patrick, 1893, Brooklyn, (CMTS) *"Brooklyn Eagle,"* May 18, 1893, Article regarding the election of Andrew T. Sullivan as postmaster. In the article it mentioned that there were only 50 members in this Society., Guest. It is unknown if a member of the Society.

Fursman, Jesse W.: (F) Member Temple Lodge, No. 14, 1900, Albany, NY, (B) 1867, (D) 1931, (Spouse) Cathe Dwyer

Gaff, Thos. C.: (F) Member Long Island Lodge, No. 382, F. &. A. M. 1874, NY

Galaffaro, Charles: (F) Member Temple Lodge, No. 14, 1900, Albany, NY

Galaway, Mrs. M.: (F) Member Nativity Sewing Society, 1900, Brooklyn, (I) *"Brooklyn Eagle,"* Feb. 3, 1900. Article regarding raising money to buy clothing for the poor.

Gallager, B.: (F) Member Friendly Sons of St. Patrick, 1893, Brooklyn, (CMTS)*"Brooklyn Eagle,"* May 18, 1893, Article regarding the election of Andrew T. Sullivan as postmaster. In the article it mentioned that there were only 50 members in this Society., Guest. It is unknown if a member of the Society.

Gallager, Bernard: (F) Member Friendly Sons of St. Patrick, 1899, Brooklyn, (CMTS)*"Brooklyn Eagle,"* Dec. 9, 1899, Article regarding the election of officers for 1900, (CMTS) President, (B) Apr. 1, 1853, (PRTS) Michael Gallager and Bridget McGrath, (Spouse) Elizabeth Thompson

Gallager, Bernard: (F) Member Friendly Sons of St. Patrick, 1893, Brooklyn, (CMTS)*"Brooklyn Eagle,"* May 18, 1893, Article regarding the election of Andrew T. Sullivan as postmaster. In the article it mentioned that there were only 50 members in this Society., Chairman of the Dinner Committee

Gallager, George E.: (F) Member Friendly Sons of St. Patrick, 1893, Brooklyn, (CMTS)*"Brooklyn Eagle,"* May 18, 1893, Article Regarding the election of Andrew T. Sullivan as postmaster. In the article it mentioned that there were only 50 members in this Society., Guest. It is unknown if a member of the Society.

Gallatbovich, Raymond S.: (F) Member Society of American Magicians, Apr., 1931, New York, (RES) Gerrittsen Beach, L. I., NY

Galler, Morris S.: (F) Member Arcana Lodge, No. 246, F. & A. M., 1934, New York, NY, (JD) Jun. 4, 1923

Gallic, F.: (F) Member Long Island Lodge, No. 382, F. &. A. M. 1874, NY

Gallien, Henry T.: (F) Member Masters Lodge, No. 5, 1900, Albany, NY, (CEN) 14$^{th}$ Ward, Albany, Albany Co., NY, 44, Germany, Dept. Comptroller, Eliza M., 46, England, Edward J., 21, Bank Clerk, Brace M., 20, Henry, 18, Clerk, Addison J., 15, Clark K., 7.

Galloway, Walter: (F) Member Lowville Lodge No. 134, F. & A. M., 1929, Lowville, NY, (CO) Lewis, (JD) Mar. 9, 1921, (B) Jul. 8, 1889, (D) Oct. 21, 1971, (BP) Lowville, NY

Galloway, Walter: (F) Member Lowville Chapter No. 223, R. A. M., 1929, Lowville, NY, (CO) Lewis, (JD) Jun. 19, 1923

Ganopol, Isaac: (F) Member Arcana Lodge, No. 246, F. & A. M., 1934, New York, NY, (JD) Apr. 27, 1912

Ganz, Wm. L.: (F) Member Arcana Lodge, No. 246, F. & A. M., 1934, New York, NY, (JD) Apr. 2, 1923, (B) Jan. 8, 1896, (BP) Yonkers, NY, (D) Jun. 19, 1960, (DP) Teaneck, NJ, (MD) Apr. 12, 1924, (Spouse) Bella Epstein, (PRTS) Charles A. Gantz and Clara

Goetz

Gardiner, Charles E.: (F) Member Temple Lodge, No. 14, 1900, Albany, NY

Gardiner, Mrs. J. T.: (F) Member Nativity Sewing Society, 1900, Brooklyn, (I) *"Brooklyn Eagle,"* Feb. 3, 1900. Article regarding raising money to buy clothing for the poor.

Gardner, George R.: (F) Member Arcana Lodge, No. 246, F. & A. M., 1934, New York, NY, (JD) Apr. 26, 1927

Gardner, J. M.: (F) Member Long Island Lodge, No. 382, F. &. A. M., 1874, NY

Garnham, Niles F.: (F) Member Lowville Lodge No. 134, F. & A. M., 1929, Lowville, NY, (CO) Lewis, (JD) Mar. 20, 1925

Garnsey, W. Miller: (F) Member Lowville Lodge No. 134, F. & A. M., 1929, Lowville, NY, (CO) Lewis, (JD) May 31, 1915

Garre, Miss Jennie: (F) Member Mispah Circle, 1888, Brooklyn, (I) *"Brooklyn Eagle,"* Dec. 12, 1888. Mentioned in an article about a fair raising funds for a Home for the Blind

Garrettson, Professor: (F) Member Brooklyn Dental Society, 1877, Brooklyn, NY, (CMTS) *"Brooklyn Eagle,"* Dec. 15, 1877. Celebration of 10th Anniversary. Society established Dec. 14, 1867, (CMTS) Present from Philadelphia

Garson, William E.: (F) Member Society of American Magicians, Apr., 1931, New York, (RES) New York City

Garvey, Thomas J.: (F) Member Temple Lodge, No. 14, 1900, Albany, NY, (CEN) 1880, 14$^{th}$ Ward, Albany, Albany Co., NY, 38, Clerk, Maria G., 39, Anna A., 7, May C., 5.

Gasser, J. Ralph: (F) Member Lowville Lodge No. 134, F. & A. M., 1929, Lowville, NY, (CO) Lewis, (JD) Mar. 20, 1925

Gates, Nelson J.: (F) Member Sons of New England, New England Society of the City of Brooklyn, 1890, (CMTS)*"Brooklyn Eagle,"* Dec. 21, 1890, 11th Annual Dinner, Attendees

Gates, Nelson J.: (F) Member Brooklyn Revenue Reform Club, 1886, (I)*"Brooklyn Eagle,"* Jan. ,27 1886, Attendees at a dinner

Gaul, Edward L.: (F) Member Grand Council of the Princes of Jerusalem, 1882, Albany, NY

Gaul, Edward L.: (F) Member Ineffable and Sublime Grand Lodge of ' Perfection, 1882, Albany, NY

Gaus, Louis H.: (F) Member Masters Lodge, No. 5, 1900, Albany, NY

Gay, Eugene A.: (F) Member Temple Lodge, No. 14, 1900, Albany, NY, (CEN) 1880, 4$^{th}$ Ward, Albany, Albany Co.,NY, Listed with Ellen Gay, widow, 64, Ireland, Susan, 41, daughter, Eugene A., 30, Telegrapher, Charles H., 26, Photographer

Gay, Gilbert H.: (F) Member Mount Vernon Lodge, No. 3, 1900, Albany, NY, (CEN) 1880, 5$^{th}$ Ward, Albany, Albany Co., NY, Listed with John Gay, 60, Retired, Betsy Jane, 59, Gilbert H., 34, Bookkeeper, Anna K., 29, daughter-in-law

Gaylor, Edward F.: (F) Member Sons of New England, New England Society of the City of Brooklyn, 1887, (CMTS) *"Brooklyn Eagle,"* Dec. 22, 1887, Annual Dinner, Attendees

Gaylor, John H.: (F) Member Mount Vernon Lodge, No. 3, 1900, Albany, NY

Gaylor, William J.: (F) Member Mount Vernon Lodge, No. 3, 1900, Albany, NY

Gaylord, Levi P. M.: (F) Member Lowville Lodge No. 134, F. & A. M., 1929, Lowville, NY, (CO) Lewis, (JD) Jan. 20, 1923

Gaynor, W. J.: (F) Member Sons of New England, New England Society of the City of Brooklyn, 1890, (CMTS) *"Brooklyn Eagle,"* Dec. 21, 1890, 11th Annual Dinner, Attendees

Gaynor, W. J.: (F) Member Sons of New England, New England Society of the City of Brooklyn, 1890, (CMTS) *"Brooklyn Eagle,"* Dec. 21, 1890, 11th Annual Dinner, Attendees

Gaynor, W. J.: (F) Member Brooklyn Revenue Reform Club, 1886, (I) *"Brooklyn Eagle,"* Jan. ,27 1886, Attendees at a dinner

Geary, A. Lincoln: (F) Member Mount Vernon Lodge, No. 3, 1900, Albany, NY

Gebhard, John G.: (F) Member Temple Lodge, No. 14, 1900, Albany, NY

Gebhardt, J S.: (F) Member Herber Lodge, No. 698,1898, F. & A. M., New York, NY, Greenpoint area, (RES) New York City

Geer, Arthur H.: (F) Member Masters Lodge, No. 5, 1900, Albany, NY

Geer, Frederick L.: (F) Member Temple Lodge, No. 14, 1900, Albany, NY

Geer, Robert: (F) Member Temple Lodge, No. 14, 1900, Albany, NY

Gelb, Julius L.: (F) Member Arcana Lodge, No. 246,F. & A. M., 1934, New York, NY, (JD) Oct. 4, 1915

Geller, Charles C.: (F) Member Mount Vernon Lodge, No. 3, 1900, Albany, NY

Gentes, A. F.: (F) Member Long Island Lodge, No. 382, F. &. A. M., 1874, NY

George, David L.: (F) Member Society of American Magicians, Apr., 1931, New York, (RES) S. Orange, NJ

George, Henry: (F) Member Mount Vernon Lodge, No. 3, 1900, Albany, NY

Georgi, L. E.: (I) *"Brooklyn Eagle,"* Jun. 2, 1879, Dedication of the burial plot of the Order of Elks in Evergreen Cemetery, (CMTS) Esteemed Lecturing Knight

Georgi, Rev. Adolph E.: (I) *"Brooklyn Eagle,"* Jun. 2, 1879, Dedication of the burial plot of the Order of Elks in Evergreen Cemetery, (CMTS) Chaplain

Geowey, Philip D. F.: (F) Member Temple Lodge, No. 14, 1900, Albany, NY

Geowey, William D.: (F) Member Temple Lodge, No. 14, 1900, Albany, NY

Gerard, Harry B.: (F) Member Lowville Lodge No. 134, F. & A. M., 1929, Lowville, NY, (CO) Lewis, (JD) Nov. 26, 1926

Gerber, E.: (F) Member Herber Lodge, No. 698,1898, F. & A. M., New York, NY, Greenpoint area, (RES) New York City

German, Paul G.: (F) Member Lowville Lodge No. 134, F. & A. M., 1929, Lowville, NY, (CO) Lewis, (JD) Jun. 8, 1928

Gerow, J. W.: (F) Member Long Island Lodge, No. 382, F. &. A. M. 1874, NY

Gerrard, Reginald D.: (F) Member Lowville Lodge No. 134, F. & A. M., 1929, Lowville, NY, (CO) Lewis, (JD) Nov. 26, 1926, (B) Mar. 21, 1898, (D) Aug., 1975, (DP) Lewis Co., NY

Gersten, A.: (F) Member Long Island Lodge, No. 382, F. &. A. M., 1874, NY

Gervis, Abbott A.: (F) Member Arcana Lodge, No. 246, F. & A. M., 1934, New York, NY, (JD) Jun. 23, 1914

Getty, Edmond C.: (F) Member Grand Council of the Princes of Jerusalem, 1882, Albany, NY

Getty, Edmund C.: (F) Member Ineffable and Sublime Grand Lodge of Perfection, 1882, Albany, NY

Giassa, W.: (F) Member Long Island Lodge, No. 382, F. &. A. M., 1874, NY

Gibbs, Lyman S.: (F) Member Masters Lodge, No. 5, 1900, Albany, NY

Giblin, Allie: (F) Member Hope Rebekah Lodge No. 10, 1949-1950, Brockport, NY, (CO) Monroe

Gibson, Robert W.: (F) Member Masters Lodge, No. 5, 1900, Albany, NY

Gieselberg, G. H.: (F) Member Arcana Lodge, No. 246, F. & A. M., 1934, New York, NY, (JD) Nov. 19, 1906, Life Member

Gieselberg, W. T.: (F) Member Arcana Lodge, No. 246, F. & A. M., 1934, New York, NY, (JD) Feb. 10, 1903

Gilbert, Frank R.: (F) Member Masters Lodge, No. 5, 1900, Albany, NY

Gilbert, George W.: (F) Member Mount Vernon Lodge, No. 3, 1900, Albany, NY

Gilbert, Harry: (I) *"Brooklyn Eagle,"* Dec. 7, 1896. 12th Annual Memorial Services, Plymouth Church, Brooklyn Lodge No. 22, B. F. O. Elks, Roll Call of the dead. Address made by Maryland Senator George L. Wellington., (CMTS) Name called.

Gilbert, Jasper W.: (F) Member Sons of New England, New England Society of the City of Brooklyn, 1887, (CMTS)*"Brooklyn Eagle,"* Dec. 22, 1887, Annual Dinner, Attendees

Gilbert, Joseph: (F) Member Washington Lodge, No. 85, 1900, Albany, NY, (CMTS) Past Members

Gilchrist, George M.: (F) Member Temple Lodge, No. 14, 1900,

Albany, NY
Giles, Henry W.: (F) Member Temple Lodge, No. 14, 1900, Albany, NY
Gill , George C.: (F) Member Brooklyn Consistory No. 24, A. A. S. R., (CMTS) Meeting Notes, *"Brooklyn Eagle,"* Mar. 13, 1887, Grand Commander giving an address
Gillespie, Frank C.: (F) Member Temple Lodge, No. 14, 1900, Albany, NY
Gillespie, W. A.: (F) Member The Plymouth League, 1888, Brooklyn, (I) *"Brooklyn Eagle,"* Dec. 12, 1888. Article regarding Societies aiding churches., (CMTS) Helping Plymouth Church, Treasurer
Gillespie, William: (F) Member Temple Lodge, No. 14, 1900, Albany, NY
Ginger, Miss Lillie: (F) Member Mispah Circle, 1888, Brooklyn, (I) *"Brooklyn Eagle,"* Dec. 12, 1888. Mentioned in an article about a fair raising funds for a Home for the Blind
Gingrich, William H.: (F) Member Temple Lodge, No. 14, 1900, Albany, NY
Ginsburg, Alex.: (F) Member Arcana Lodge, No. 246, F. & A. M., 1934, New York, NY, (JD) Jun. 30, 1919
Ginsburg, George J.: (F) Member Arcana Lodge, No. 246, F. & A. M., 1934, New York, NY, (JD) Jun. 5, 1922
Gladding, William H.: (F) Member Grand Council of the Princes of Jerusalem, 1882, Albany, NY
Gladding, William H.: (F) Member Ineffable and Sublime Grand Lodge of Perfection, 1882, Albany, NY
Glasser, Benj.: (F) Member Arcana Lodge, No. 246, F. & A. M., 1934, New York, NY, (JD) Feb. 2, 1925
Glasser, Isidore: (F) Member Arcana Lodge, No. 246, F. & A. M., 1934, New York, NY, (JD) Feb. 20, 1922
Glasser, Louis: (F) Member Arcana Lodge, No. 246, F. & A. M., 1934, New York, NY, (JD) May 2, 1923
Glasser, Rudolph: (F) Member Arcana Lodge, No. 246, F. & A. M., 1934, New York, NY, (JD) Nov. 17, 1924
Glassheim, N. : (F) Member Arcana Lodge, No. 246, F. & A. M., 1934, New York, NY, (JD) Feb. 10, 1903, Life Member
Gleasman, Newton A.: (F) Member Lowville Chapter No. 223, R. A. M., 1929, Lowville, NY, (CO) Lewis, (JD) Feb. 24, 1925
Gledhill, J. Edward: (F) Member Temple Lodge, No. 14, 1900, Albany, NY
Gledhill, William E.: (F) Member Temple Lodge, No. 14, 1900, Albany, NY
Glen, Cornelius: (F) Member Grand Council of the Princes of Jerusalem, 1882, Albany, NY
Glen, Cornelius: (F) Member Ineffable and Sublime Grand Lodge of Perfection, 1882, Albany, NY

Glenn, Arthur T.: (F) Member Lowville Chapter No. 223, R. A. M., 1929, Lowville, NY, (CO) Lewis, (JD) Apr. 17, 1923

Glenn, T. Howard: (F) Member Lowville Chapter No. 223, R. A. M., 1929, Lowville, NY, (CO) Lewis, (JD) May 9, 1922

Glenn, William H.: (F) Member Lowville Chapter No. 223, R. A. M., 1929, Lowville, NY, (CO) Lewis, (JD) Mar. 7, 1905

Glenn , Arthur T,: (F) Member Lowville Lodge No. 134, F. & A. M., 1929, Lowville, NY, (CO) Lewis, (JD) Jul. 2, 1920

Glenn , T. Howard: (F) Member Lowville Lodge No. 134, F. & A. M., 1929, Lowville, NY, (CO) Lewis, (JD) Mar. 5, 1920

Glick, Max: (F) Member Arcana Lodge, No. 246,F. & A. M., 1934, New York, NY, (JD) Nov. 26, 1929

Glickman, H. Harry: (F) Member Arcana Lodge, No. 246, F. & A. M., 1934, New York, NY, (JD) Jun. 23, 1931

Glidden, F. W.: (F) Member Murray Lodge, No. 380, F. & A. M., 1906, Holley, Orleans, Co., NY, (CMTS) Past Master

Glidden, H. R.: (F) Member Murray Lodge, No. 380, F. & A. M., 1906, Holley, Orleans, Co., NY

Glidden, Simeon: (F) Member Murray Lodge, No. 380, F. & A. M., 1906, Holley, Orleans, Co., NY

Gloeckner, Louis B.: (F) Member Temple Lodge, No. 14, 1900, Albany, NY

Goddard, Mrs.: (F) Member Mispah Circle, 1888, Brooklyn, (I) *"Brooklyn Eagle,"* Dec. 12, 1888. Mentioned in an article about a fair raising funds for a Home for the Blind

Godsmark, George: (F) Member Mount Vernon Lodge, No. 3, 1900, Albany, NY, (CMTS) Past Master 1895

Goeway, Philip D. F.: (F) Member Grand Council of the Princes of Jerusalem, 1882, Albany, NY

Goewey, Philip D. F.: (F) Member Ineffable and Sublime Grand Lodge of Perfection, 1882, Albany, NY

Goff, J. H.: (F) Member Long Island Lodge, No. 382, F. &. A. M. 1874, NY

Goffe, John H.: (F) Member Temple Lodge, No. 14, 1900, Albany, NY

Gold, Harry A.: (F) Member Arcana Lodge, No. 246, F. & A. M., 1934, New York, NY, (JD) Mar. 16, 1925

Gold, Max: (F) Member Arcana Lodge, No. 246, F. & A. M., 1934, New York, NY, (JD) Oct. 6, 1924

Goldberg, Daniel M.: (F) Member Arcana Lodge, No. 246, F. & A. M., 1934, New York, NY, (JD) Jun. 22, 1926

Goldberg, Nathan: (F) Member Arcana Lodge, No. 246, F. & A. M., 1934, New York, NY, (JD) Mar. 19, 1917

Goldin, Barney T.: (F) Member Arcana Lodge, No. 246, F. & A. M., 1934, New York, NY, (JD) May 19, 1924

Goldin, I. Frank: (F) Member Arcana Lodge, No. 246, F. & A. M., 1934, New York, NY, (JD) Mar. 31, 1924

Goldman, Abram: (F) Member Arcana Lodge, No. 246, F. & A. M., 1934, New York, NY, (JD) Jun. 4, 1923

Goldstein, Jacob J.: (F) Member Arcana Lodge, No. 246, F. & A. M., 1934, New York, NY, (JD) Jun. 8, 1926

Goldstein, Samuel: (F) Member Arcana Lodge, No. 246, F. & A. M., 1934, New York, NY, (JD) Mar. 31, 1924

Goldworm, Mathew L.: (F) Member Arcana Lodge, No. 246, F. & A. M., 1934, New York, NY, (JD) Nov. 7, 1921

Goodman, Samuel H.: (F) Member Grand Council of the Princes of Jerusalem, 1882, Albany, NY

Goodman, Samuel W.: (F) Member Masters Lodge, No. 5, 1900, Albany, NY

Goodrich, H. C.: (F) Member Long Island Lodge, No. 382, F. &. A. M. 1874, NY

Goodrich, Thomas F.: (F) Member Sons of New England, New England Society of the City of Brooklyn, 1890, (CMTS) *"Brooklyn Eagle,"* Dec. 21, 1890, 11th Annual Dinner, Attendees

Goodwin, Scott D. M.: (F) Member Ineffable and Sublime Grand Lodge of Perfection, 1882, Albany, NY

Goodwin, Scott D'M.: (F) Member Grand Council of the Princes of Jerusalem, 1882, Albany, NY

Goodwin, Scott D'M.: (F) Member Masters Lodge, No. 5, 1900, Albany, NY, (CMTS) Past Master

Goodwin, William: (F) Member Long Island Lodge, No. 382, F. &. A. M. 1874, NY

Gorden, Meyer: (F) Member Arcana Lodge, No. 246, F. & A. M., 1934, New York, NY, (JD) Apr. 17, 1922

Gordon, Asa W.: (F) Member Lowville Lodge No. 134, F. & A. M., 1929, Lowville, NY, (CO) Lewis, (JD) Mar. 18, 1927

Gordon, Charles C.: (F) Member Lowville Lodge No. 134, F. & A. M., 1929, Lowville, NY, (CO) Lewis, (JD) Jun. 1, 1908

Gordon, Chas.: (F) Member Arcana Lodge, No. 246, F. & A. M., 1934, New York, NY, (JD) Jun. 16, 1919

Gordon, Harry : (F) Member Arcana Lodge, No. 246, F. & A. M., 1934, New York, NY, (JD) Jun. 11, 1929

Gordon, Uriah: (F) Member Independent Order of Good Templars, Westhampton Lodge No. 885, instituted Apr. 16, 1889, New Officers installed Feb. 16, 1900, (CMTS) Meeting Notes, *"Brooklyn Eagle,"* Feb. 18, 1900, Sentinel

Gordon, William H.: (F) Member Grand Council of the Princes of Jerusalem, 1882, Albany, NY

Gordon, William H.: (F) Member Ineffable and Sublime Grand Lodge of Perfection, 1882, Albany, NY

Gorham, George E.: (F) Member Masters Lodge, No. 5, 1900, Albany, NY

Gould, G. Hudson: (F) Member Lowville Lodge No. 134, F. & A. M.,

1929, Lowville, NY, (CO) Lewis, (JD) Feb. 3, 1892

Gould, Milton M.: (F) Member Lowville Chapter No. 223, R. A. M., 1929, Lowville, NY, (CO) Lewis, (JD) Dec. 6, 1910

Goutremout, James E.: (F) Member Lowville Lodge No. 134, F. & A. M., 1929, Lowville, NY, (CO) Lewis, (JD) May 14, 1906

Gove, Charles L.: (F) Member Temple Lodge, No. 14, 1900, Albany, NY, (CEN) 1880, 9$^{th}$ Ward, Albany Albany CO., NY, Listed with Leonard Gove, 57, VT, Farmer, Lucy, 52, Henry C., 29, Milk Peddler, Lora A., 25, Chas L., 20.

Gove, Henry C.: (F) Member Temple Lodge, No. 14, 1900, Albany, NY, (CMTS) Life Member, (CEN) 1880, 9th Ward, Albany Albany Co., NY, Listed with Leonard Gove, 57, VT, Farmer, Lucy, 52, Henry C., 29, Milk Peddler, Lora A., 25, Chas L., 20.

Grafstein, Albert: (F) Member Arcana Lodge, No. 246, F. & A. M., 1934, New York, NY, (JD) Jun. 28, 1932

Grafstein, Jos.: (F) Member Arcana Lodge, No. 246, F. & A. M., 1934, New York, NY, (JD) Mar. 31, 1919

Graham, David R.: (F) Member Lowville Lodge No. 134, F. & A. M., 1929, Lowville, NY, (CO) Lewis, (JD) Jun. 11, 1926

Graham, R.: (F) Member Long Island Lodge, No. 382, F. &. A. M. 1874, NY

Graham, William J.: (F) Member Lowville Lodge No. 134, F. & A. M., 1929, Lowville, NY, (CO) Lewis, (JD) Dec. 13, 1895, (CEN) 1880 New Bremen, Lewis Co., NY Listed with John Graham, 35, Ireland, Celestia, 31, William, 11, Mary, 3

Granger, Mrs. J. A.: (F) Member Daughters of Temperances, Hope of the Fallen Union, Martinsburgh, NY, Jan. 9, 1851, (CO) Lewis

Grant, Gordon: (F) Member Arcana Lodge, No. 246, F. & A. M., 1934, New York, NY, (JD) Jun. 9, 1925

Grant, V.: (F) Member Long Island Lodge, No. 382, F. &. A. M., 1874, NY

Grantgegein, Miss Carrie: (F) Member Mispah Circle, 1888, Brooklyn, (I) *"Brooklyn Eagle,"* Dec. 12, 1888. Mentioned in an article about a fair raising funds for a Home for the Blind

Grau, Louis C.: (F) Member Lowville Lodge No. 134, F. & A. M., 1929, Lowville, NY, (CO) Lewis, (JD) Jull. 1, 1927

Graves, Harry E.: (F) Member Lowville Lodge No. 134, F. & A. M., 1929, Lowville, NY, (CO) Lewis, (JD) Apr. 7, 1922

Graves, Leon F.: (F) Member Lowville Chapter No. 223, R. A. M., 1929, Lowville, NY, (CO) Lewis, (JD) May 5, 1908

Gray, Alonzo: (F) Member Astromical Society, Brooklyn Observatory, Mar. 16, 1850, Brooklyn, NY, (I) *"Brooklyn Eagle,"* Mar. 21, 1853

Greb, Henry C.: (F) Member Temple Lodge, No. 14, 1900, Albany, NY, (CEN) 1$^{st}$ Ward, Albany, Albany Co., NY, Listed with Christian Greb, 46, Keeps Grocery, Hesse Darmstadt, Margaret, 48, Hesse,

Catharine, 21, Henry W. C., Anna H. Pflantz , 1 granddaughter
Green, Burdett S.: (F) Member Lowville Lodge No. 134, F. & A. M.,
   1929, Lowville, NY, (CO) Lewis, (CMTS) Past Master 1919, 1920
Green, Burdett S.: (F) Member Lowville Chapter No. 223, R. A. M.,
   1929, Lowville, NY, (CO) Lewis, (JD) Mar. 25, 1910
Green, Burdette S.: (F) Member Lowville Lodge No. 134, F. & A. M.,
   1929, Lowville, NY, (CO) Lewis, (JD) Apr. 7, 1911
Green, Harry B.: (F) Member Lowville Chapter No. 223, R. A. M.,
   1929, Lowville, NY, (CO) Lewis, (JD) Apr. 17, 1923
Green, Henry: (F) Member Arcana Lodge, No. 246, F. & A. M., 1934,
   New York, NY, (JD) May 8, 1928
Green, Isidore: (F) Member Arcana Lodge, No. 246, F. & A. M., 1934,
   New York, NY, (JD) Feb. 20, 1922
Green, Jacob: (F) Member Arcana Lodge, No. 246, F. & A. M., 1934,
   New York, NY, (JD) Nov. 7, 1921
Green, R. J.: (F) Member Lowville Lodge No. 134, F. & A. M., 1929, \
   Lowville, NY, (CO) Lewis, (JD) Mar. 5, 1920
Green, Ralph W.: (F) Member Temple Lodge, No. 14, 1900, Albany, NY
Greenbaum, Cooper: (F) Member Arcana Lodge, No. 246,F. & A. M.,
   1934, New York, NY, (JD) May 1, 1911
Greenberg, Alex.: (F) Member Arcana Lodge, No. 246, F. & A. M., 1934,
   New York, NY, (JD) Feb. 2, 1925
Greenberg, Geo.: (F) Member Arcana Lodge, No. 246, F. & A. M., 1934,
   New York, NY, (JD) Feb. 19, 1912
Greenberg, Jacob V.: (F) Member Arcana Lodge, No. 246, F. & A. M.,
   1934, New York, NY, (JD) Aug. 6, 1918
Greenberg, Samuel: (F) Member Arcana Lodge, No. 246, F. & A. M.,
   1934, New York, NY, (JD) May 17, 1915
Greene, J. Warren: (F) Member Brooklyn Revenue Reform Club, 1886,
   (I)*"Brooklyn Eagle,"* Jan. ,27 1886, Attendees at a dinner
Greene, Oscar: (OBIT*)* *"Journal News,"* Friday, Mar. 9, 2001. Oscar J.
   Greene, 92,resident of New Rochelle, died Wednesday March 7,
   2001 at The Guild Home in Yonkers, NY. Admitted to the Bar of
   the State of New York in 1939, Mr. Greene engaged in the general
   practice of law. and was a partner in the law firm of Block and
   Greene. He was past president of the New Rochelle Bar
   Association, Kiwanis Club of New Rochelle, and the New
   Rochelle High School scholarship Fund Corp. Until recently he
   was a dedicated volunteer for the Friends of New Rochelle Public
   Libraary. For over sixty years he was a member of Siwandy and
   John Jay Lodges of the Free and Accepted Masons. He attained the
   positions of District Deputy Grand Master, Grand Standard Bearer,
   Grand Junior Deacon and Trustee Emeritus of the Masonic Home
   and Hall Grand Lodge of the State of New York. He attained the
   rank of 33rd degree Mason. He was the devoted husband of Sara
   Block Greene and is survived by his daughter, Susan. He was

predeceased by his sister Blanche and brother Leonard. Services will be held at George T. Davis Funeral Home on Friday at 11:30AM. Interment to follow at Glenville Cemetery.

Greene, William H.: (F) Member Mount Vernon Lodge, No. 3, 1900, Albany, NY

Greenfield, Bernard L.: (F) Member Arcana Lodge, No. 246, F. & A. M., 1934, New York, NY, (JD) Apr. 26, 1929

Greenhalgh, William L.: (F) Member Temple Lodge, No. 14, 1900, Albany, NY

Greer, Leonard K.: (F) Member Lowville Lodge No. 134, F. & A. M., 1929, Lowville, NY, (CO) Lewis, (JD) Nov. 2, 1923

Gregory, G. F.: (F) Member Long Island Lodge, No. 382, F. &. A. M. 1874, NY

Gregory, J. E.: (F) Member Long Island Lodge, No. 382, F. &. A. M. 1874, NY

Gregory, Martha: (F) Member Mispah Circle, 1888, Brooklyn, (I) *"Brooklyn Eagle,"* Dec. 12, 1888. Mentioned in an article about a fair raising funds for a Home for the Blind

Gregory, W.: (F) Member Long Island Lodge, No. 382, F. &. A. M. 1874, NY

Greifer, Benjamin: (F) Member Arcana Lodge, No. 246, F. & A. M., 1934, New York, NY, (JD) Nov. 26, 1929

Greifer, Samuel: (F) Member Arcana Lodge, No. 246, F. & A. M., 1934, New York, NY, (JD) Mar. 27, 1928

Greiff, Lionel W. K.: (F) Member Lowville Lodge No. 134, F. & A. M., 1929, Lowville, NY, (CO) Lewis, (JD) Jun. 22, 1925

Gresham, Alfred E.: (F) Member Temple Lodge, No. 14, 1900, Albany, NY

Grey, Henry A.: (F) Member Temple Lodge, No. 14, 1900, Albany, NY

Grey, William W.: (F) Member Temple Lodge, No. 14, 1900, Albany, NY

Grierson, S. W.: (F) Member Brooklyn Revenue Reform Club, 1886, (I) *"Brooklyn Eagle,"* Jan. ,27 1886, Attendees at a dinner

Griesman, Frderick V.: (F) Member Temple Lodge, No. 14, 1900, Albany, NY

Griffith, William H.: (F) Member Masters Lodge, No. 5, 1900, Albany, NY

Griffiths, W. G.: (F) Member Long Island Lodge, No. 382, F. &. A. M. 1874, NY

Grimes, Lester A.: (F) Member Society of American Magicians, Apr., 1931, New York, (RES) Montclair, NJ

Grinden, Miss: (F) Member Nativity Sewing Society, 1900, Brooklyn, (I) *"Brooklyn Eagle,"* Feb. 3, 1900. Article regarding raising money to buy clothing for the poor.

Griswold, Aaron: (F) Member Clyde Lodge No. 341, F. A. M., 1905, Clyde, NY, (CO) Wayne, (CMTS) Past Master 1858, 1859, 1860

Gross, Charles E.: (F) Member Temple Lodge, No. 14, 1900, Albany, NY

Gross, James H.: (F) Member Grand Council of the Princes of Jerusalem, 1882, Albany, NY

Gross, James H.: (F) Member Ineffable and Sublime Grand Lodge of Perfection, 1882, Albany, NY

Grover, Mrs. Leonard: (F) Member Nativity Sewing Society, 1900, Brooklyn, (I) *"Brooklyn Eagle,"* Feb. 3, 1900. Article regarding raising money to buy clothing for the poor.

Gruss, L. Gruss (sic): (F) Member Arcana Lodge, No. 246, F. & A. M., 1934, New York, NY, (JD) Feb. 9, 1932

Guardineer, George H.: (F) Member Temple Lodge, No. 14, 1900, Albany, NY

Guhring, J. M.: (F) Member Herber Lodge, No. 698,1898, F. & A. M., New York, NY, Greenpoint area, (RES) New York City

Guide, G.: (F) Member Herber Lodge, No. 698,1898, F. & A. M., New York, NY, Greenpoint area, (RES) Brooklyn

Guion, S. S.: (F) Member Long Island Lodge, No. 382, F. &. A. M. 1874, NY

Gunhouse, H.: (F) Member Long Island Lodge, No. 382, F. &. A. M. 1874, NY

Gunnison, Herbert: (F) Member Friendly Sons of St. Patrick, 1893, Brooklyn, (CMTS)*"Brooklyn Eagle,"* May 18, 1893, Article Regarding the election of Andrew T. Sullivan as postmaster. In the article it mentioned that there were only 50 members in this Society., Guest. It is unknown if a member of the Society.

Gutherie, Alfred A.: (F) Member Temple Lodge, No. 14, 1900, Albany, NY, (CMTS) Master

Guttenberg, Julius H.: (F) Member Arcana Lodge, No. 246, F. & A. M., 1934, New York, NY, (JD) May 1, 1911

Guttzeit, F. P.: (F) Member National Union, Brooklyn No. 375, 1900, (I) *"Brooklyn Eagle,"* Feb. 3, 1900. Meeting Notice., (CMTS)
- President

Hach, J.: (F) Member Herber Lodge, No. 698,1898, F. & A. M., New York, NY, Greenpoint area, (RES) New York City

Hackett, William S.: (F) Member Masters Lodge, No. 5, 1900, Albany, NY, (CMTS) Master

Haehnlen, Jr., J. F.: (F) Member Long Island Lodge, No. 382, F. &. A. M. 1874, NY

Haesloop, D.: (F) Member Herber Lodge, No. 698,1898, F. & A. M., New York, NY, Greenpoint area, (RES) New York City

Hagan, Francis: (F) Member Temple Lodge, No. 14, 1900, Albany, NY, (CEN) 1880, 12$^{th}$ Ward, Albany. Albany Co., NY, Listed with Joseph Hagan, 46, Brick Mason, Mary, 40, Francis, 11, Catherine, 6.

Hagen, Winston H.: (F) Member Sons of New England, New England

Society of the City of Brooklyn, 1890, (CMTS)*"Brooklyn Eagle,"* Dec. 21, 1890, 11th Annual Dinner, Attendees

Haggerty, Judge: (F) Member Friendly Sons of St. Patrick, 1893, Brooklyn, (CMTS)*"Brooklyn Eagle,"* May 18, 1893, Article regardingthe election of Andrew T. Sullivan as postmaster. In the article it mentioned that there were only 50 members in this Society., Guest. It is unknown if a member of the Society.

Hagoort, Jan Ludoplh: (F) Member Society of American Magicians, Apr., 1931, New York, (RES) New York City

Hagy, Jr., John: (F) Member Temple Lodge, No. 14, 1900, Albany, NY, (CEN) 1880, 13$^{th}$ Ward, Albany, Albany Co., NY, List with John Hagy, Sr., 44, Swiss, Painter, Marhgaret, 36, Germany, John, NY, Bookkeeper, Frederick, 16, Painter, Anna, 14, Mary, 11, Maggie, 5, William, 3

Hahn, Chas. F.: (F) Member Herber Lodge, No. 698,1898, F. & A. M., New York, NY, Greenpoint area, (RES) New York City

Haight, Horace DeR.: (F) Member Masters Lodge, No. 5, 1900, Albany, NY

Hailes, Charles J.: (F) Member Temple Lodge, No. 14, 1900, Albany, NY, (CEN) 1880, 14$^{th}$ Ward, Albany, Albany Co., Listed with William Hailes, 55, England, Inventor, Ellen, 57, William, 30, Physician, Charles J., 26, Lawyer, Eva E., 21, Frderich A., 17.

Hailes, Theodore C.: (F) Member Temple Lodge, No. 14, 1900, Albany, NY, (CEN) 1880, 5$^{th}$ Ward, Albany, Albany Co., NY, 27, Drawing Professor, Elizabeth, 25, Lizzie, 4, Kate, 2.

Haiss, Eugene J.: (F) Member Temple Lodge, No. 14, 1900, Albany, NY

Halahran, Mrs.: (F) Member Nativity Sewing Society, 1900, Brooklyn, (I) *"Brooklyn Eagle,"* Feb. 3, 1900. Article regarding raising money to buy clothing for the poor.

Hall, Almon: (F) Member Mispah Circle, 1888, Brooklyn, (I) *"Brooklyn Eagle,"* Dec. 12, 1888. Mentioned in an article about a fair raising funds for a Home for the Blind

Hall, Alonzo: (F) Member Temple Lodge, No. 14, 1900, Albany, NY

Hall, Benjamin J.: (F) Member Friendly Sons of St. Patrick, 1893, Brooklyn, (CMTS)*"Brooklyn Eagle,"* May 18, 1893, Article regarding the election of Andrew T. Sullivan as postmaster. In the article it mentioned that there were only 50 members in this Society., Guest. It is unknown if a member of the Society.

Hall, C. W. G.: (F) Member Long Island Lodge, No. 382, F. &. A. M. 1874, NY

Hall, Charles J.: (F) Member Long Island Lodge, No. 382, F. &. A. M. 1874, NY

Hall, D. Harold: (F) Member Lowville Lodge No. 134, F. & A. M., 1929, Lowville, NY, (CO) Lewis, (CMTS) Past Master 1908, 1909

Hall, D. Harold: (F) Member Lowville Lodge No. 134, F. & A. M., 1929, Lowville, NY, (CO) Lewis, (JD) Feb. 9, 1900

Hall, D. Harold: (F) Member Lowville Chapter No. 223, R. A. M., 1929, Lowville, NY, (CO) Lewis, (JD) Apr. 21, 1908

Hall, Herman L.: (F) Member Lowville Lodge No. 134, F. & A. M., 1929, Lowville, NY, (CO) Lewis, (JD) Mar. 10, 1899

Hall, W. T.: (F) Member Long Island Lodge, No. 382, F. &. A. M., 1874, NY

Hallee, J. S.: (I) *"Brooklyn Eagle,"* Dec. 7, 1896. 12th Annual Memorial Services, Plymouth Church, Brooklyn Lodge No. 22, B. F. O. Elks, Roll Call of the dead. Address made by Maryland Senator George L. Wellington. , (CMTS) Name called.

Hallenbeck, G.: (F) Member Long Island Lodge, No. 382, F. &. A. M., 1874, NY

Hallis, H. C.: (F) Member Long Island Lodge, No. 382, F. &. A. M., 1874, NY

Halm, Joseph A.: (F) Member Temple Lodge, No. 14, 1900, Albany, NY

Halsey, Mrs. Dr.: (F) Member Ladies ' Willing Aid Society, 1888, Brooklyn, (I) *"Brooklyn Eagle,"* Dec. 12, 1888. Article regarding Societies aiding churches., (CMTS) Helping Green Avenue Presbyterian Church, Treasurer

Halstead, S. C. F.: (F) Member Brooklyn Revenue Reform Club, 1886, (I)*"Brooklyn Eagle,"* Jan. ,27 1886, Attendees at a dinner

Haltstead, Murat: (F) Member Sons of New England, New England Society of the City of Brooklyn, 1890, (CMTS)*"Brooklyn Eagle,"* Dec. 21, 1890, 11th Annual Dinner, Attendees

Ham, Fred C.: (F) Member Masters Lodge, No. 5, 1900, Albany, NY, (CEN) 1880, 16$^{th}$ ward, Albany, Albany Co., NY, Listed with Robert C. Ham, 54, Jane, 47, Fred C., 25, Lawyer, Thomas H., 22, Lawyer, Ada M., 13

Ham, John: (F) Member Mount Vernon Lodge, No. 3, 1900, Albany, NY

Hamblin, Mrs. James A.: (F) Member Lenox Ladies Aid Society of Lenox Road M. E. Church, Brooklyn, 1900, (CMTS) *"Brooklyn Eagle,"* Mar. 13, 1900. Meeting Notice, President

Hamblin, Mrs. Joshua M.: (F) Member Lenox Ladies Aid Society of Lenox Road M. E. Church, Brooklyn, 1900, (CMTS) *"Brooklyn Eagle,"* Mar. 13, 1900. Meeting Notice, Board of Managers

Hamilton, C. J.: (F) Member Murray Lodge, No. 380, F. & A. M., 1906, Holley, Orleans, Co., NY

Hamilton, C.H.: (F) Member Clyde Lodge No. 341, F. A. M., 1905, Clyde, NY, (CO) Wayne, (CMTS) Past Master 1887

Hamilton, Hamilton R.: (OBIT) *"The Hancock Herald"* Thursday, October 28, 1937. Hamilton Renwick Holcomb, aged 78, died at his home, 142 Murray street, Binghamton, Oct. 12. He was born near Cedarville, Herkimer county, in 1859. The early part of his life was spent at Trout Brook, Town of Hancock, where he and other members of the family were engaged in the lumber and acid business. He was a brother of the late Albert Holcomb, once supervisor of the Town of Fremont. In 1897 "Ren", as he was familiarly known, went to Binghamton and entered the insurance business which he carried on for many years. He was a member of the Masonic fraternity and of Christ Church in Binghamton. He is survived by his widow, Anna M. Holcomb; three daughters, Mrs. Charles E. Allen of Baldwinsville; Miss Grace F. Holcomb of Binghamton and Mrs. C. S. Luitwieler, Jr. of Westchester, Mass.; a son, Charles A. of Reading, Mass.; a sister, Mrs. William H. Snyder of Mileses.

Hamilton, Henry N.: (F) Member Temple Lodge, No. 14, 1900, Albany, NY

Hamilton, John A.: (F) Member Temple Lodge, No. 14, 1900, Albany, NY

Hammond, Charles D.: (F) Member Temple Lodge, No. 14, 1900, Albany, NY

Hampshire, Gertrude: (F) Member Hope Rebekah Lodge No. 10, 1949-1950, Brockport, NY, (CO) Monroe

Hanauer, J.: (F) Member Herber Lodge, No. 698,1898, F. & A. M., New York, NY, Greenpoint area, (RES) New York City

Hancock, C. J.: (F) Member Long Island Lodge, No. 382, F. &. A. M. 1874, NY

Hancock, G. B.: (F) Member Long Island Lodge, No. 382, F. &. A. M. 1874, NY

Hancock, L.: (F) Member Long Island Lodge, No. 382, F. &. A. M., 1874, NY

Hanes, Edward L.: (F) Member Masters Lodge, No. 5, 1900, Albany, NY

Hanson, Henry: (F) Member Mount Vernon Lodge, No. 3, 1900, Albany, NY

Hanson, Herbert D.: (F) Member Lowville Lodge No. 134, F. & A. M., 1929, Lowville, NY, (CO) Lewis, (JD) Sep. 21, 1928

Happel, William H.: (F) Member Temple Lodge, No. 14, 1900, Albany, NY

Hard, Jr., William B.: (F) Member Sons of New England, New England Society of the City of Brooklyn, 1890, (CMTS) *"Brooklyn Eagle,"* Dec. 21, 1890, 11th Annual Dinner, Attendees

Hardeen, Theo.: (F) Member Society of American Magicians, Apr., 1931, New York, (RES) Brooklyn, NY

Hardick, W. Clemishire: (F) Member Masters Lodge, No. 5, 1900, Albany, NY

Hardy, Jay C.: (F) Member Lowville Lodge No. 134, F. & A. M., 1929, Lowville, NY, (CO) Lewis, (JD) Feb. 21, 1913, (B) 1873, (D) 1942, (C) Beeches Bridge Cemetery, Lewis Co., NY

Hardy, Lyle V.: (F) Member Lowville Lodge No. 134, F. & A. M., 1929, Lowville, NY, (CO) Lewis, (JD) Jan. 15, 1926, (B) 1897, (D) 1953, (C) Beeches Bridge Cemetery, Lewis Co., NY

Hardy, Orlando: (F) Member Murray Lodge, No. 380, F. & A. M., 1906, Holley, Orleans, Co., NY, (CMTS) Past Master, Deceased as of 1906

Harf, Arthur: (F) Member Arcana Lodge, No. 246, F. & A. M., 1934, New York, NY, (JD) Jan. 21, 1924

Harkness, W.: (F) Member Long Island Lodge, No. 382, F. &. A. M. 1874, NY

Harlow, Hans H.: (F) Member Mount Vernon Lodge, No. 3, 1900, Albany, NY

Harper, Walter J.: (F) Member Brooklyn Choral Society, 1889, (CMTS) *"Brooklyn Eagle,"* Oct. 2, 1889, (CMTS) Librarian

Harppinger, Frank: (F) Member Mount Vernon Lodge, No. 3, 1900, Albany, NY

Harreys, O. W.: (F) Member Brooklyn Dental Society, 1877, Brooklyn, NY, (CMTS) *"Brooklyn Eagle,"* Dec. 15, 1877. Celebration of 10th Anniversary. Society established Dec. 14, 1867, (CMTS) Membership Committee

Harrington, Linn J.: (F) Member Temple Lodge, No. 14, 1900, Albany, NY

Harris, Charles B.: (F) Member Temple Lodge, No. 14, 1900, Albany, NY

Harris, Chas. B.: (F) Member Society of American Magicians, Apr., 1931, New York, (RES) New York City

Harris, Frank S.: (F) Member Masters Lodge, No. 5, 1900, Albany, NY

Harris, Julius F.: (F) Member Temple Lodge, No. 14, 1900, Albany, NY

Harris, Russell W.: (F) Member Lowville Lodge No. 134, F. & A. M., 1929, Lowville, NY, (CO) Lewis, (JD) Sep. 12, 1918

Harris, Russell W.: (F) Member Lowville Chapter No. 223, R. A. M., 1929, Lowville, NY, (CO) Lewis, (JD) Nov. 23, 1920

Harris, Stewart J.: (F) Member Lowville Lodge No. 134, F. & A. M., 1929, Lowville, NY, (CO) Lewis, (CMTS) Past Master 1928

Harris, Stuart J.: (F) Member Lowville Lodge No. 134, F. & A. M., 1929, Lowville, NY, (CO) Lewis, (JD) Feb. 24, 1922

Harris, Stuart J.: (F) Member Lowville Chapter No. 223, R. A. M., 1929, Lowville, NY, (CO) Lewis, (JD) Apr. 10, 1923

Harrison, A.: (I) *"Brooklyn Eagle,"* Feb. 19, 1902. Funeral Services at the Club House of the Brooklyn Lodge, No. 22, B. P. O. Elks for Wm. H. West. Elk services were first then masonic services by New York Lodge No. 330, F. A. & M., (CMTS) Secretary

Harrison, Charles M.: (F) Member Arcana Lodge, No. 246, F. & A. M., 1934, New York, NY, (JD) Jul. 17, 1911

Harrison, Charles W.: (F) Member Lowville Lodge No. 134, F. & A. M., 1929, Lowville, NY, (CO) Lewis, (JD) Jun. 21, 1907

Harrison, Lee: (I) *"Brooklyn Eagle,"* Feb. 19, 1902. Funeral Services at the Club House of the Brooklyn Lodge, No. 22, B. P. O. Elks for Wm. H. West. Elk services were first then masonic services by New York Lodge No. 330, F. A. & M., (CMTS) Pallbearer

Harrison, Mrs. A. : (F) Member Nativity Sewing Society, 1900, Brooklyn, (I) *"Brooklyn Eagle,"* Feb. 3, 1900. Article regarding

raising money to buy clothing for the poor.

Harrison, R. C.: (F) Member Long Island Lodge, No. 382, F. &. A. M. 1874, NY

Harrison, T. E.: (F) Member Long Island Lodge, No. 382, F. &. A. M. 1874, NY

Harrje, H.: (F) Member Herber Lodge, No. 698,1898, F. & A. M., New York, NY, Greenpoint area, (RES) New York City

Harrje, O.: (F) Member Herber Lodge, No. 698,1898, F. & A. M., New York, NY, Greenpoint area, (RES) New York City

Harrold, T.: (F) Member Long Island Lodge, No. 382, F. &. A. M., 1874, NY

Harse, Wm. H.: (F) Member Arcana Lodge, No. 246, F. & A. M., 1934, New York, NY, (JD) Mar. 21, 1910

Hart, Arthur: (F) Member Arcana Lodge, No. 246, F. & A. M., 1934, New York, NY, (JD) Jun. 17, 1918

Hart, C.: (F) Member Long Island Lodge, No. 382, F. &. A. M. 1874, NY

Hart, George W.: (F) Member Temple Lodge, No. 14, 1900, Albany, NY

Hart, Leo J.: (F) Member Arcana Lodge, No. 246, F. & A. M., 1934, New York, NY, (JD) Mar. 16, 1925

Hart, William S.: (F) Member Lowville Chapter No. 223, R. A. M., 1929, Lowville, NY, (CO) Lewis, (JD) May 14, 1895

Harteau, H.: (F) Member Long Island Lodge, No. 382, F. &. A. M., 1874, NY

Hartley, J.: (F) Member Long Island Lodge, No. 382, F. &. A. M., 1874, NY

Hartley, D.D.S., Lionel: (F) Member Society of American Magicians, Apr., 1931, New York, (RES) New York City

Hartner, L.: (F) Member Herber Lodge, No. 698,1898, F. & A. M., New York, NY, Greenpoint area, (RES) New York City

Harvey, D.: (F) Member Long Island Lodge, No. 382, F. &. A. M. 1874, NY

Haskell, Clayton K.: (F) Member Masters Lodge, No. 5, 1900, Albany, NY

Haskell, Henry C.: (F) Member Grand Council of the Princes of Jerusalem, 1882, Albany, NY

Haskell, Henry C.: (F) Member Ineffable and Sublime Grand Lodge of Perfection, 1882, Albany, NY

Haskell, Sandford R.: (F) Member Masters Lodge, No. 5, 1900, Albany, NY

Haskell, William H.: (F) Member Grand Council of the Princes of Jerusalem, 1882, Albany, NY

Haskell, William H.: (F) Member Ineffable and Sublime Grand Lodge of Perfection, 1882, Albany, NY

Haskell, 2d (sic), Clayton K.: (F) Member Masters Lodge, No. 5, 1900, Albany, NY

Haslam, J. K.: (F) Member Long Island Lodge, No. 382, F. &. A. M.

1874, NY
Haslam, William: (F) Member Brooklyn Revenue Reform Club, 1886, (I)*"Brooklyn Eagle,"* Jan. ,27 1886, Attendees at a dinner
Hastings, John W.: (F) Member Long Island Lodge, No. 382, F. &. A. M. 1874, NY
Haswell, George: (F) Member Temple Lodge, No. 14, 1900, Albany, NY, (CEN) 1880, $5^{th}$ Ward, Albany, Albany Co., NY, Listed with Justus, 61, Merchant, N. Louise, 55, Hiram W., 22, Post Office Clerk, Wm. Henry, 26, Grocer, Justus, 20, Clerk, George, 18, Sophia L. Davis, 30, daughter, Justus D. Davis, 8, grandson, Eliza Davis, 6, granddaughter, John Keyes Davis, 4, grandson
Haswell, William H.: (F) Member Temple Lodge, No. 14, 1900, Albany, NY (CEN) 1880, $5^{th}$ Ward, Albany, Albany Co., NY, Listed with Justus, 61, Merchant, N. Louise, 55, Hiram W., 22, Post Office Clerk, Wm. Henry, 26, Grocer, Justus, 20, Clerk, George, 18, Sophia L. Davis, 30, daughter, Justus D. Davis, 8, grandson, Eliza Davis, 6, granddaughter, John Keyes Davis, 4, grandson
Hatch, H. Lynden: (F) Member Monticello Lodge, No. 532, F. & A. M., (CO) Sullivan Co., NY, (CMTS) Past Master 1903, 1904, 1905
Hatch, W. T.: (F) Member Sons of New England, New England Society of the City of Brooklyn, 1887, (CMTS)*"Brooklyn Eagle,"* Dec. 22, 1887, Annual Dinner, Attendees
Hauenstein, Wm: (F) Member Society of American Magicians, Apr., 1931, New York, (RES) New York City
Haven, Alvin A.: (F) Member Society of American Magicians, Apr., 1931, New York, (RES) Brooklyn, NY
Havens, Morton: (F) Member Mount Vernon Lodge, No. 3, 1900, Albany, NY, (CEN) 1880, $14^{th}$ Ward, Albany, Albany Co., NY, Listed with Hamilton M., 41, Elizabeth W.,
Hawken, Wm. H.: (F) Member Murray Lodge, No. 380, F. & A. M., 1906, Holley, Orleans, Co., NY
Hawkins, John P.: (F) Member Long Island Lodge, No. 382, F. &. A. M. 1874, NY
Hawkins, Leslie: (F) Member Hope Rebekah Lodge No. 10, 1949-1950, Brockport, NY, (CO) Monroe, (CMTS Property Committee
Hawkins, Robert W.: (F) Member First Suffolk District, Stirling Chapter, No. 216, 1923, Greenport, NY, (CMTS) Patron, (RES) Greeport
Hawley, Henry E.: (F) Member Masters Lodge, No. 5, 1900, Albany, NY
Hawn, Orra G.: (F) Member Temple Lodge, No. 14, 1900, Albany, NY
Hayden, C. C.: (F) Member Murray Lodge, No. 380, F. & A. M., 1906, Holley, Orleans, Co., NY
Hayden, Harry E.: (F) Member Society of American Magicians, Apr., 1931, New York
Hayden, Henry I.: (F) Member Sons of New England, New England

Society of the City of Brooklyn, 1890, (CMTS) *"Brooklyn Eagle,"* Dec. 21, 1890, 11th Annual Dinner, Attendees

Hayden, Thomas T.: (I) *"Brooklyn Eagle,"* Feb. 19, 1902. Funeral Services at the Club House of the Brooklyn Lodge, No. 22, B. P. O. Elks for Wm. H. West. Elk services were first then masonic services by New York Lodge No. 330, F. A. & M., (CMTS) Lecturing Knight

Hayes, P. : (F) Member Friendly Sons of St. Patrick, 1893, Brooklyn, (CMTS)*"Brooklyn Eagle,"* May 18, 1893, Article regarding the election of Andrew T. Sullivan as postmaster. In the article it mentioned that there were only 50 members in this Society., Guest. It is unknown if a member of the Society.

Hayes, Paul N.: (F) Member Masters Lodge, No. 5, 1900, Albany, NY

Haynes, Alvina: (F) Member Hope Rebekah Lodge No. 10, 1949-1950, Brockport, NY, (CO) Monroe, (CMTS) Press

Haynes, Vina: (F) Member Hope Rebekah Lodge No. 10, 1949-1950, Brockport, NY, (CO) Monroe

Hazard, Miss: (F) Member Nativity Sewing Society, 1900, Brooklyn, (I) *"Brooklyn Eagle,"* Feb. 3, 1900. Article regarding raising money to buy clothing for the poor.

Hazard, William: (F) Member Friendly Sons of St. Patrick, 1893, Brooklyn, (CMTS)*"Brooklyn Eagle,"* May 18, 1893, Article regarding the election of Andrew T. Sullivan as postmaster. In the article it mentioned that there were only 50 members in this Society., Guest. It is unknown if a member of the Society.

Hazen, Henry: (F) Member Lowville Lodge No. 134, F. & A. M., 1929, Lowville, NY, (CO) Lewis, (CMTS) Past Master 1853

Healey, Richard: (F) Member Friendly Sons of St. Patrick, 1893, Brooklyn, (CMTS)*"Brooklyn Eagle,"* May 18, 1893, Article Regarding the election of Andrew T. Sullivan as postmaster. In the article it mentioned that there were only 50 members in this Society., Guest. It is unknown if a member of the Society.

Healty, Harry: (F) Member Brooklyn Revenue Reform Club, 1886, (I)*"Brooklyn Eagle,"* Jan. ,27 1886, Attendees at a dinner

Healy, A. A.: (F) Member Brooklyn Revenue Reform Club, 1886, (I)*"Brooklyn Eagle,"* Jan. ,27 1886, Attendees at a dinner

Healy, Aaron: (F) Member Brooklyn Revenue Reform Club, 1886, (I)*"Brooklyn Eagle,"* Jan. ,27 1886, Attendees at a dinner, (CEN) 1880, Brooklyn, Kings Co., NY, 65, Hide/Leather Dealer, Elizabeth, 63, Lizzie, 26.

Heaney, W.: (F) Member Long Island Lodge, No. 382, F. &. A. M. 1874, NY

Heath, Mrs. E.: (F) Member Lenox Ladies Aid Society of Lenox Road M. E. Church, Brooklyn, 1900, (CMTS) *"Brooklyn Eagle,"* Mar. 13, 1900. Meeting Notice, Board of Managers

Heath, Royal: (F) Member Society of American Magicians,

Apr., 1931, New York
Heath, Thomas D.: (F) Member Temple Lodge, No. 14, 1900, Albany, NY, (CEN) 1880, 10thward, Albany, Albany Co., NY, Listed with Alonzo Heath, 34, Butcher, Mary, 34, Mary E., 13, Lawrence P., 7, Thomas, 4
Hebberd, Robert W.: (F) Member Masters Lodge, No. 5, 1900, Albany, NY
Hebeler, H.: (F) Member Herber Lodge, No. 698,1898, F. & A. M., New York, NY, Greenpoint area, (RES) New York City
Heckel, Charles J.: (F) Member Society of American Magicians, Apr., 1931, New York, (RES) Jamaica, L.I., NY
Hedden, Amos K.: (F) Member Lowville Lodge No. 134, F. & A. M., 1929, Lowville, NY, (CO) Lewis, (CMTS) Past Master 1860, 1864, 1865
Hedden, Clarence R.: (F) Member Lowville Chapter No. 223, R. A. M., 1929, Lowville, NY, (CO) Lewis, (JD) Feb. 13, 1923
Hedger, Wm: (F) Member Long Island Lodge, No. 382, F. &. A. M. 1874, NY
Hedlam, William: (F) Member Mount Vernon Lodge, No. 3, 1900, Albany, NY
Heermance, Orville L.: (F) Member Temple Lodge, No. 14, 1900, Albany, NY, (B) Sep. 15, 1863, (D) May 10, 1938, (PRTS) Joseph Orville Heermance and Margaret Gertrude Smith
Hegeman, J. E.: (F) Member Long Island Lodge, No. 382, F. &. A. M. 1874, NY
Hegeman, John R.: (F) Member Sons of New England, New England Society of the City of Brooklyn, 1887, (CMTS) *"Brooklyn Eagle,"* Dec. 22, 1887, Annual Dinner, Attendees, (B) 1840, (D) 1929, (AKA) John Rogers Hegeman, (PRTS) John Hegeman
Hegeman, Joseph K.: (F) Member Sons of New England, New England Society of the City of Brooklyn, 1887, (CMTS) *"Brooklyn Eagle,"* Dec. 22, 1887, Annual Dinner, Attendees
Heineman, Abraham: (F) Member Mount Vernon Lodge, No. 3, 1900, Albany, NY
Heineman, J. C.: (F) Member Long Island Lodge, No. 382, F. &. A. M. 1874, NY, (CMTS) Past Master
Heinerfield, Benj.: (F) Member Arcana Lodge, No. 246, F. & A. M., 1934, New York, NY, (JD) Apr. 7, 1919
Heller, Henry M.: (F) Member Grand Council of the Princes of Jerusalem, 1882, Albany, NY
Heller, Henry M.: (F) Member Ineffable and Sublime Grand Lodge of Perfection, 1882, Albany, NY, (CEN) 1880, 7$^{th}$ Ward, Albany, Albany Co., NY, 42, Wholesale Milenary, Mary L., 35, Charlie R., 16, Carrie R., 15, Theodore L., 10, Ralph R., 4.
Heller, Hyman: (F) Member Arcana Lodge, No. 246, F. & A. M., 1934, New York, NY, (JD) Dec. 1, 1913

Heller, L.: (F) Member Long Island Lodge, No. 382, F. &. A. M. 1874, NY

Heller, Louis: (F) Member Arcana Lodge, No. 246, F. & A. M., 1934, New York, NY, (JD) Dec. 8, 1925

Heller, Mrs. Violenda R.: (F) Member Society of American Magicians, Apr., 1931, New York, (RES) New York City, NY

Hellman, George S.: (F) Member Society of American Magicians, Apr., 1931, New York, (RES) New York City, NY

Helms, Bert: (F) Member Arcana Lodge, No. 246, F. & A. M., 1934, New York, NY, (JD) Jan. 7, 1901, Life Member

Hembury, James: (F) Member Long Island Lodge, No. 382, F. &. A. M. 1874, NY

Hemma, Mrs. T. J.: (F) Member Ladies Aid Society of Flatbush, Brooklyn, 1888, (CMTS) *"Brooklyn Eagle,"* Oct. 7, 1888, Meeting Notice, President

Hendrickson, J. E.: (F) Member Long Island Lodge, No. 382, F. &. A. M. 1874, NY

Hendrix, Joseph C.: (F) Member Friendly Sons of St. Patrick,1893, Brooklyn, (CMTS)*"Brooklyn Eagle,"* May 18, 1893, Article Regarding the election of Andrew T. Sullivan as postmaster. In the article it mentioned that there were only 50 members in this Society., Guest. It is unknown if a member of the Society.

Henig, Abraham: (F) Member Arcana Lodge, No. 246, F. & A. M., 1934, New York, NY, (JD) Dec. 8, 1925

Henig, David: (F) Member Arcana Lodge, No. 246, F. & A. M., 1934, New York, NY, (JD) Mar. 16, 1925

Henig, Reuben: (F) Member Arcana Lodge, No. 246, F. & A. M., 1934, New York, NY, (JD) Mar. 28, 1933

Henry, John F.: (F) Member Sons of New England, New England Society of the City of Brooklyn, 1890, (CMTS)*"Brooklyn Eagle,"* Dec. 21, 1890, 11th Annual Dinner, Attendees

Henshaw, John V.: (F) Member Temple Lodge, No. 14, 1900, Albany, NY

Hentz, Jacob: (F) Member Friendly Sons of St. Patrick,1893, Brooklyn, (CMTS)*"Brooklyn Eagle,"* May 18, 1893, Article Regarding the election of Andrew T. Sullivan as postmaster. In the article it mentioned that there were only 50 members in this Society., Guest. It is unknown if a member of the Society.

Hepworth, Paul: (F) Member Arcana Lodge, No. 246, F. & A. M., 1934, New York, NY, (JD) May 7, 1917

Herbst, A.: (F) Member Long Island Lodge, No. 382, F. &. A. M. 1874, NY

Hering, Peter E.: (F) Member Temple Lodge, No. 14, 1900, Albany, NY

Herman, M. Robert: (F) Member Society of American Magicians, Apr., 1931, New York, (RES) Cedarhurst, L.I., NY

Herrick, Avery: (F) Member Grand Council of the Princes of Jerusalem,

1882, Albany, NY
Herrick, Avery: (F) Member Ineffable and Sublime Grand Lodge of Perfection, 1882, Albany, NY
Herrick, Avery: (F) Member Mount Vernon Lodge, No. 3, 1900, Albany, NY
Herries, William: (F) Member National Provident Union, Lafayette No. 28, 1900, Brooklyn, (I) *"Brooklyn Eagle,"* Feb. 3, 1900. Meeting Notice., (CMTS) President
Herrmann, Mme. Adelaide: (F) Member Society of American Magicians, Apr., 1931, New York, (RES) New York City, NY
Herrscher, H.: (F) Member Herber Lodge, No. 698,1898, F. & A. M., New York, NY, Greenpoint area, (RES) New York City
Herschberger, H. I.: (F) Member Washington Lodge, No. 85, 1900, Albany, NY, (CMTS) Past Members
Hersey, I. E.: (F) Member Long Island Lodge, No. 382, F. &. A. M. 1874, NY
Herson, Samuel: (F) Member Arcana Lodge, No. 246, F. & A. M., 1934, New York, NY, (JD) Jun. 8, 1926
Herzog, Jacob H.: (F) Member Masters Lodge, No. 5, 1900, Albany, NY
Hess, Charles H.: (F) Member Lowville Lodge No. 134, F. & A. M., 1929, Lowville, NY, (CO) Lewis, (JD) Jun. 7, 1912
Hess, Charles H.: (F) Member Lowville Chapter No. 223, R. A. M., 1929, Lowville, NY, (CO) Lewis, (JD) Mar. 17, 1914
Hess, J. Raymond: (F) Member Lowville Lodge No. 134, F. & A. M., 1929, Lowville, NY, (CO) Lewis, (JD) Mar. 20, 1914
Hess, John H.: (F) Member Monticello Lodge, No. 532, F. & A. M., (CO) Sullivan Co., NY, (CMTS) Past Master 1916, 1917
Hesser, Phillip C.: (F) Member Foresters of America, Fort Greene No. 23, 1900, Brooklyn, (I) *"Brooklyn Eagle,"* Feb. 3, 1900. Meeting Notice., (CMTS) Treasurer
Hester, William: (F) Member Sons of New England, New England Society of the City of Brooklyn, 1890, (CMTS)*"Brooklyn Eagle,"* Dec. 21, 1890, 11th Annual Dinner, Attendees
Hetrick, M.D., J. A. Werner: (F) Member Society of American Magicians, Apr., 1931, New York, (RES) New York City, NY
Hetrick, M.D., Llewellyn E.: (F) Member Society of American Magicians, Apr., 1931, New York, (RES) New York City, NY
Hettinger, William: (F) Member Temple Lodge, No. 14, 1900, Albany, NY
Hewitt, Mrs. L.: (F) Member Ladies Aid Society of Flatbush, Brooklyn, 1888, (CMTS) *"Brooklyn Eagle,"* Oct. 7, 1888, Meeting Notice, Vice President
Hewitt, William J.: (F) Member Society of American Magicians, Apr., 1931, New York, (RES) Hoboken, NJ
Hewlett, Don A.: (F) Member Brooklyn Revenue Reform Club, 1886,

(I)*"Brooklyn Eagle,"* Jan. ,27 1886, Attendees at a dinner
Heyman, H.: (F) Member Herber Lodge, No. 698,1898, F. & A. M., New York, NY, Greenpoint area, (RES) New York City
Hicks, Bengie R.: (F) Member Acanthus Lodge No. 719, F. A. M., (CMTS) Meeting Notes, *"Brooklyn Eagle,"* Mar. 13, 1887, Closed the meeting.
Hicks, John J.: (F) Member Masters Lodge, No. 5, 1900, Albany, NY
Higbie, S.: (F) Member Long Island Lodge, No. 382, F. &. A. M. 1874, NY
Higginbotham, Miss: (F) Member Nativity Sewing Society, 1900, Brooklyn, (I) *"Brooklyn Eagle,"* Feb. 3, 1900. Article regarding raising money to buy clothing for the poor.
Higgins, Algernon S.: (F) Member Sons of New England, New England Society of the City of Brooklyn, 1890, (CMTS)*"Brooklyn Eagle,"* Dec. 21, 1890, 11th Annual Dinner, Attendees
Hill, Cornelius: (F) Member Temple Lodge, No. 14, 1900, Albany, NY
Hill, Erastus C.: (F) Member Temple Lodge, No. 14, 1900, Albany, NY
Hill, Francis C.: (F) Member Society of American Magicians, Apr., 1931, New York
Hill, Francis F.: (F) Member Society of American Magicians, Apr., 1931, New York
Hill, George C.: (F) Member Temple Lodge, No. 14, 1900, Albany, NY
Hill, James H.: (F) Member Temple Lodge, No. 14, 1900, Albany, NY
Hill, L. J.: (F) Member Murray Lodge, No. 380, F. & A. M., 1906, Holley, Orleans, Co., NY
Hill, O. E.: (F) Member Brooklyn Dental Society, 1877, Brooklyn, NY, (CMTS) *"Brooklyn Eagle,"* Dec. 15, 1877. Celebration of 10th Anniversary. Society established Dec. 14, 1867, (CMTS) President
Hill, Robert: (F) Member Temple Lodge, No. 14, 1900, Albany, NY, (CEN) 1880, 3$^{rd}$ Ward, Albany, Albany CO., NY, 41, England, Laborer, Mary A., 28, wife, Margaret, 8, William, 7, Mary, 5, Emma, 4, Alice, 2, Robert, 6 months.
Hill, Warren E.: (F) Member Sons of New England, New England Society of the City of Brooklyn, 1887, (CMTS)*"Brooklyn Eagle,"* Dec. 22, 1887, Annual Dinner, Attendees
Hill, William H.: (F) Member Sons of New England, New England Society of the City of Brooklyn, 1890, (CMTS)*"Brooklyn Eagle,"* Dec. 21, 1890, 11th Annual Dinner, Attendees
Hill, William J. M.: (F) Member Temple Lodge, No. 14, 1900, Albany, NY
Hill, William W.: (F) Member Grand Council of the Princes of Jerusalem, 1882, Albany, NY
Hill, William W.: (F) Member Ineffable and Sublime Grand Lodge of Perfection, 1882, Albany, NY
Hilton, Charles: (F) Member Grand Council of the Princes of Jerusalem, 1882, Albany, NY, (CEN) 1880, 4$^{th}$ Ward, Albany, Albany Co.,

NY, 35, Boiler Maker, Sarah, 30, Sarah, 6, Bessie, 4, Annie, 1

Hilton, Charles: (F) Member Ineffable and Sublime Grand Lodge of Perfection, 1882, Albany, NY

Hilton, James H.: (F) Member Temple Lodge, No. 14, 1900, Albany, NY, (CEN) 1880, Guilderland, Albany Co., NY, 44, Farmer, Nancy, 38, Julia H., 15, Frederick L., 13, Avery C., 8, Nicholas Severson, Father-in-law, 67, Melissa Severson, 46, sister-in-law, Philip H. Livingston, Uncle, 67, Retired Farmer

Hilts, Stephen: (F) Member Lowville Lodge No. 134, F. & A. M., 1929, Lowville, NY, (CO) Lewis, (JD) Mar. 20, 1925

Hiltz, W. S.: (F) Member Long Island Lodge, No. 382, F. &. A. M., 1874, NY

Hinckel, Fredrick: (F) Member Temple Lodge, No. 14, 1900, Albany, NY, (CMTS) Life Member

Hinds, F. N.: (F) Member Murray Lodge, No. 380, F. & A. M., 1906, Holley, Orleans, Co., NY

Hine, James W.: (F) Member Temple Lodge, No. 14, 1900, Albany, NY

Hinq, Edward P.: (F) Member Temple Lodge, No. 14, 1900, Albany, NY, (CMTS) Life Member

Hinrichs, C. F. A.: (F) Member Brooklyn Revenue Reform Club, 1886, (I)*"Brooklyn Eagle,"* Jan. ,27 1886, Attendees at a dinner

Hinrichs, Frederick W.: (F) Member Brooklyn Revenue Reform Club, 1886, (I)*"Brooklyn Eagle,"* Jan. ,27 1886, Attendees at a dinner

Hinrichs, J. W.: (F) Member Brooklyn Revenue Reform Club, 1886, (I)*"Brooklyn Eagle,"* Jan. ,27 1886, Attendees at a dinner

Hirsch, J.: (F) Member Herber Lodge, No. 698,1898, F. & A. M., New York, NY, Greenpoint area, (RES) New York City

Hirsch, L.: (F) Member Long Island Lodge, No. 382, F. &. A. M. 1874, NY

Hirsch, M.: (F) Member Long Island Lodge, No. 382, F. &. A. M. 1874, NY

Hirschfield, Herman: (F) Member Arcana Lodge, No. 246, F. & A. M., 1934, New York, NY, (JD) Feb. 14, 1928

Hirschfield, Louis: (F) Member Arcana Lodge, No. 246, F. & A. M., 1934, New York, NY, (JD) Jun. 9, 1925

Hirschfield, Morris S.: (F) Member Arcana Lodge, No. 246, F. & A. M., 1934, New York, NY, (JD) Jun. 26, 1928

Hitch, E. A.: (F) Member Brooklyn Revenue Reform Club, 1886, (I)*"Brooklyn Eagle,"* Jan. ,27 1886, Attendees at a dinner

Hitchcock, Frank P.: (F) Member Temple Lodge, No. 14, 1900, Albany, NY

Hoag, John D.: (F) Member Temple Lodge, No. 14, 1900, Albany, NY

Hoag, John S.: (F) Member Mount Vernon Lodge, No. 3, 1900, Albany, NY

Hoagland, C. N.: (F) Member Sons of New England, New England

Society of the City of Brooklyn, 1890, (CMTS) *"Brooklyn Eagle,"* Dec. 21, 1890, 11th Annual Dinner, Attendees

Hoawrd, J. C.: (F) Member Murray Lodge, No. 380, F. & A. M., 1906, Holley, Orleans, Co., NY

Hobbs, George W.: (F) Member Masters Lodge, No. 5, 1900, Albany, NY, (Spouse) Frances Louise Gibbs, (CEN) 1880, 16th Ward, Albany, Albany CO., NY, 36, Store Clerk, Lousie, 34, Edward R., 9, Grace L., 7, Edith, 2.

Hodges, E. F.: (F) Member Long Island Lodge, No. 382, F. &. A. M. 1874, NY

Hodgkins, George R.: (F) Member Temple Lodge, No. 14, 1900, Albany, NY, (CMTS) Past Master 1888, (CEN) 1880, 15th Ward, Albany, Albany Co., 30, Elizabeth, 29, George, 1

Hodgkins, Stephen C.: (F) Member Temple Lodge, No. 14, 1900, Albany, NY

Hodgson, George R.: (F) Member Temple Lodge, No. 14, 1900, Albany, NY

Hoffman, George A.: (F) Member Temple Lodge, No. 14, 1900, Albany, NY

Hoffman, Karl R.: (F) Member Masters Lodge, No. 5, 1900, Albany, NY

Hoffman, Paul W.: (F) Member Masters Lodge, No. 5, 1900, Albany, NY

Hoffman, William: (F) Member Mount Vernon Lodge, No. 3, 1900, Albany, NY

Hoit, David: (F) Member Ineffable and Sublime Grand Lodge of Perfection, 1882, Albany, NY

Hoit, Judson: (F) Member Mount Vernon Lodge, No. 3, 1900, Albany, NY

Hoit, William W.: (F) Member Masters Lodge, No. 5, 1900, Albany, NY

Holahran, Mrs. G.: (F) Member Nativity Sewing Society, 1900, Brooklyn, (I) *"Brooklyn Eagle,"* Feb. 3, 1900. Article regarding raising money to buy clothing for the poor.

Holbohm, B.: (F) Member Herber Lodge, No. 698,1898, F. & A. M., New York, NY, Greenpoint area, (RES) New York City

Holden, Max: (F) Member Society of American Magicians, Apr., 1931, New York, (RES) New York City

Holland, Almon: (F) Member Masters Lodge, No. 5, 1900, Albany, NY

Hollender, F.: (F) Member Long Island Lodge, No. 382, F. &. A. M. 1874, NY

Holly, Ferdinand L.: (F) Member Society of American Magicians, Apr., 1931, New York, (RES) Brooklyn, NY

Holmes, Lewis H.: (F) Member Mount Vernon Lodge, No. 3, 1900, Albany, NY

Holmes, Miss Kittie: (F) Member Mispah Circle, 1888, Brooklyn, (I) *"Brooklyn Eagle,"* Dec. 12, 1888. Mentioned in an article about a fair raising funds for a Home for the Blind

Holt, David : (F) Member Grand Council of the Princes of Jerusalem,

1882, Albany, NY
Holt, Howard D.: (F) Member Lowville Lodge No. 134, F. & A. M.,
    1929, Lowville, NY, (CO) Lewis, (JD) Jan. 16, 1920
Holt, Howard D.: (F) Member Lowville Chapter No. 223, R. A. M.,
    1929, Lowville, NY, (CO) Lewis, (JD) May 23, 1922
Holt, Milton W.: (F) Member Lowville Lodge No. 134, F. & A. M.,
    1929, Lowville, NY, (CO) Lewis, (JD) Jan. 11, 1920
Holzman, Morton E.: (F) Member Arcana Lodge, No. 246,
    F. & A. M., 1934, New York, NY, (JD) Jun. 7, 1920
Homan, C. E.: (F) Member Long Island Lodge, No. 382, F. &. A. M.
    1874, NY
Homer, Eugene M.: (F) Member Society of American Magicians,
    Apr., 1931, New York, (RES) New York City
Hood, John T.: (F) Member Arcana Lodge, No. 246, F. & A. M., 1934,
    New York, NY, (JD) Jun. 6, 1910
Hooker, Samuel C.: (F) Member Society of American Magicians,
    Apr., 1931, New York, (RES) Brooklyn, NY
Hooper, F. W.: (F) Member Brooklyn Revenue Reform Club, 1886,
    (I)*"Brooklyn Eagle,"* Jan. ,27 1886, Attendees at a dinner
Horn, Hubert: (F) Member Brooklyn Revenue Reform Club, 1886,
    (I)*"Brooklyn Eagle,"* Jan. ,27 1886, Attendees at a dinner
Hornstein, Isador J.: (F) Member Arcana Lodge, No. 246, F. & A. M.,
    1934, New York, NY, (JD) Oct. 21, 1918
Hornstein, Samuel L.: (F) Member Arcana Lodge, No. 246, F. & A. M.,
    1934, New York, NY, (JD) Mar. 19, 1914
Horr, Marcus M.: (F) Member Temple Lodge, No. 14, 1900, Albany, NY
Horton, Frederick: (F) Member Temple Lodge, No. 14, 1900, Albany, NY
Hoskins, Charles M.: (F) Member Temple Lodge, No. 14, 1900,
    Albany, NY
Hotaling, Charles E.: (F) Member Washington Lodge, No. 85, 1900,
    Albany, NY, (CMTS) Past Members
Hotaling, William R.: (F) Member Mount Vernon Lodge, No. 3, 1900,
    Albany, NY, (CMTS) Past Master 1882
Hotchkiss, Henry D.: (F) Member Sons of New England, New England
    Society of the City of Brooklyn, 1890, (CMTS)*"Brooklyn Eagle,"*
    Dec. 21, 1890, 11th Annual Dinner, Attendees
Houdini, Mrs. Beatrice: (F) Member Society of American Magicians,
    Apr., 1931, New York, (RES) New York City
Hough, F. B.: (F) Member Society for the Acquistion of Useful
    Knowledge, Apr. 26, 1843, (CO) Lewis
Houghkerk, Silas H.: (F) Member Temple Lodge, No. 14, 1900,
    Albany, NY
Houghtee, O. E.: (F) Member Brooklyn Dental Society, 1877, Brooklyn,
    NY, (CMTS) *"Brooklyn Eagle,"* Dec. 15, 1877. Celebration of
    10th Anniversary. Society established Dec. 14, 1867, (CMTS)
    Subjects Committee

Houghton, Dr. George H.: (I) *"Brooklyn Eagle,"* Jun. 2, 1879, Dedication of the burial plot of the Order of Elks in Evergreen Cemetery, (CMTS) Present in attendance. Pastor of the Church of Transfiguration also known as the "Little Church Around the Corner."

Houghton, George H.: (F) Member Mount Vernon Lodge, No. 3, 1900, Albany, NY

Houghton, P.: (F) Member Long Island Lodge, No. 382, F. &. A. M. 1874, NY

Hourigan, William F.: (F) Member Temple Lodge, No. 14, 1900, Albany, NY

House, Adam: (F) Member Lowville Lodge No. 134, F. & A. M., 1929, Lowville, NY, (CO) Lewis, (JD) Dec, 23, 1912

House, Joseph S.: (F) Member Masters Lodge, No. 5, 1900, Albany, NY

Housel, W. S.: (F) Member Murray Lodge, No. 380, F. & A. M., 1906, Holley, Orleans, Co., NY

Hovey, Bertha: (F) Member Hope Rebekah Lodge No. 10, 1949-1950, Brockport, NY, (CO) Monroe

How, John L.: (F) Member Sons of New England, New England Society of the City of Brooklyn, 1887, (CMTS)*"Brooklyn Eagle,"* Dec. 22, 1887, Annual Dinner, Attendees

Howard, General O. : (F) Member Sons of New England, New England Society of the City of Brooklyn, 1890, (CMTS)*"Brooklyn Eagle,"* Dec. 21, 1890, 11th Annual Dinner, Attendees

Howard, Samuel E.: (F) Member Sons of New England, New England Society of the City of Brooklyn, 1890, (CMTS)*"Brooklyn Eagle,"* Dec. 21, 1890, 11th Annual Dinner, Attendees

Howard, W. E.: (F) Member Murray Lodge, No. 380, F. & A. M., 1906, Holley, Orleans, Co., NY, (CMTS) Past Master

Howell, Mrs. G.: (F) Member Nativity Sewing Society, 1900, Brooklyn, (I) *"Brooklyn Eagle,"* Feb. 3, 1900. Article regarding raising money to buy clothing for the poor.

Howell, Ruth: (F) Member Hope Rebekah Lodge No. 10, 1949-1950, Brockport, NY, (CO) Monroe, (CMTS) Finance Committee

Hower, F.: (F) Member Long Island Lodge, No. 382, F. &. A. M. 1874, NY

Hoxie, Charles A.: (F) Member Temple Lodge, No. 14, 1900, Albany, NY

Hubbard, Leo W.: (F) Member Lowville Lodge No. 134, F. & A. M., 1929, Lowville, NY, (CO) Lewis, (JD) Jun. 4, 1915

Huber, Otto: (F) Member Friendly Sons of St. Patrick,1893, Brooklyn, (CMTS)*"Brooklyn Eagle,"* May 18,1893, Article regardingthe election of Andrew T. Sullivan as postmaster. In the article it mentioned that there were only 50 members in this Society., Guest. It is unknown if a member of the Society.

Hudson, J. B.: (F) Member Murray Lodge, No. 380, F. & A. M., 1906, Holley, Orleans, Co., NY

Hufnagel, Ph.: (F) Member Herber Lodge, No. 698,1898, F. & A. M.,
    New York, NY, Greenpoint area, (RES) New York City
Hufnagel, R.: (F) Member Herber Lodge, No. 698,1898, F. & A. M.,
    New York, NY, Greenpoint area, (RES) New York City
Hughes, S. A.: (F) Member Long Island Lodge, No. 382, F. &. A. M.
    1874, NY
Hughs, Dr. Peter: (F) Member Friendly Sons of St. Patrick,1893,
    Brooklyn, (CMTS) *"Brooklyn Eagle,"* May 18,1893,
    Article regardingthe election of Andrew T. Sullivan as postmaster.
    In the article it mentioned that there were only 50 members in this
    Society., Guest. It is unknown if a member of the Society.
Hulbert, Ernest: (F) Member Lowville Lodge No. 134, F. & A. M., 1929,
    Lowville, NY, (CO) Lewis, (JD) Apr. 19, 1907
Hull, W. W.: (F) Member Long Island Lodge, No. 382, F. &. A. M.,
    1874, NY
Humphrey, Gorrel: (F) Member Grand Council of the Princes of
    Jerusalem, 1882, Albany, NY
Humphrey, Harvey W.: (F) Member Lowville Lodge No. 134, F. & A. M.,
    1929, Lowville, NY, (CO) Lewis, (JD) Oct. 31, 1913
Humphrey, Harvey W.: (F) Member Lowville Chapter No. 223, R. A. M.,
    1929, Lowville, NY, (CO) Lewis, (JD) Nov. 3, 1913
Humstone, W. C.: (F) Member Anglo Saxon Lodge No. 137, F. A. M.,
    (CMTS) Meeting Notes, *"Brooklyn Eagle,"* Mar. 23, 1887,
    Presiding Master
Hungerford, Martin L.: (F) Member Lowville Chapter No. 223, R. A. M.,
    1929, Lowville, NY, (CO) Lewis, (JD) Jun. 6, 1893
Hunt, Arthur S.: (F) Member Society of American Magicians,
    Apr., 1931, New York, (RES) Brooklyn, NY
Hunt, Burton T.: (F) Member Lowville Lodge No. 134, F. & A. M.,
    1929, Lowville, NY, (CO) Lewis, (CMTS) Past Master 1913, 1914
Hunt, Burton T.: (F) Member Lowville Lodge No. 134, F. & A. M.,
    1929, Lowville, NY, (CO) Lewis, (JD) Mar. 16, 1906
Hunt, Burton T.: (F) Member Lowville Chapter No. 223, R. A. M.,
    1929, Lowville, NY, (CO) Lewis, (JD) Nov. 20, 1906
Hunt, H. W.: (F) Member Sons of New England, New England Society of
    the City of Brooklyn, 1890, (CMTS) *"Brooklyn Eagle,"*
    Dec. 21, 1890, 11th Annual Dinner, Attendees
Hunt , Edward T.: (F) Member Sons of New England, New England
    Society of the City of Brooklyn, 1887, (CMTS) *"Brooklyn Eagle,"*
    Dec. 22, 1887, Annual Dinner, Attendees
Hunter, John W.: (F) Member Sons of New England, New England
    Society of the City of Brooklyn, 1887, (CMTS) *"Brooklyn Eagle,"*
    Dec. 22, 1887, Annual Dinner, Attendees
Hunting, Edwin F.: (F) Member Mount Vernon Lodge, No. 3, 1900,
    Albany, NY
Huntington, Samuel C.: (F) Member Ineffable and Sublime Grand Lodge

of Perfection, 1882, Albany, NY

Huntington, Samuel H.: (F) Member Grand Council of the Princes of Jerusalem, 1882, Albany, NY

Huntley, Ava: (F) Member Temple Lodge, No. 14, 1900, Albany, NY

Hurcomb, Walter F.: (F) Member Ineffable and Sublime Grand Lodge of Perfection, 1882, Albany, NY

Hurd, James K.: (F) Member Murray Lodge, No. 380, F. & A. M., 1906, Holley, Orleans, Co., NY

Husted, Alfred B.: (F) Member Temple Lodge, No. 14, 1900, Albany, NY

Hutchins, George M.: (F) Member Lowville Lodge No. 134, F. & A. M., 1929, Lowville, NY, (CO) Lewis, (JD) Jul. 4, 1890

Hutchinson, D. R. W.: (F) Member Ineffable and Sublime Grand Lodge of Perfection, 1882, Albany, NY

Hutchinson, G. S.: (F) Member Sons of New England, New England Society of the City of Brooklyn, 1890, (CMTS) *"Brooklyn Eagle,"* Dec. 21, 1890, 11th Annual Dinner, Attendees

Hutchinson, R. M.: (F) Akron Lodge No. 527, F. A. & M., Akron, NY, (CMTS) Signer as Secretary on Member card no. 29 for Robert R. Brandt, dated Dec. 31, 1966.

Hyde, J. W.: (F) Member Sons of New England, New England Society of the City of Brooklyn, 1890, (CMTS) *"Brooklyn Eagle,"* Dec. 21, 1890, 11th Annual Dinner, Attendees

Hyde, Joel W.: (F) Member Sons of New England, New England Society of the City of Brooklyn, 1887, (CMTS) *"Brooklyn Eagle,"* Dec. 22, 1887, Annual Dinner, Attendees

Hyder, Frank G.: (F) Member Independent Order of Good Templars, Westhampton Lodge No. 885, instituted Apr. 16, 1889, New Officers installed Feb. 16, 1900, (CMTS) Meeting Notes, *"Brooklyn Eagle,"* Feb. 18, 1900, Chief Templar

Hyman, Abraham E.: (F) Member Arcana Lodge, No. 246, F. & A. M., 1934, New York, NY, (JD) Apr. 1, 1907, Life Member

Ide, Almon H.: (F) Member Lowville Lodge No. 134, F. & A. M., 1929, Lowville, NY, (CO) Lewis, (JD) Dec. 3, 1902, (CEN) 1880 Shelby, Oleans Co., NY Listed with Nathan Ide 53, Farmer, NY, Hannah, 50, Almon, 13, Minnie 10

Ide, Beryl B.: (F) Member Lowville Lodge No. 134, F. & A. M., 1929, Lowville, NY, (CO) Lewis, (JD) May 21, 1920

Ide, Charles W.: (F) Member Sons of New England, New England Society of the City of Brooklyn, 1887, (CMTS) *"Brooklyn Eagle,"* Dec. 22, 1887, Annual Dinner, Attendees

Iles, E. F.: (F) Member Long Island Lodge, No. 382, F. &. A. M. 1874, NY

Illch, William: (F) Member Mount Vernon Lodge, No. 3, 1900, Albany, NY

Indig, Edward: (F) Member Long Island Lodge, No. 382, F. &. A. M.

1874, NY

Ingenthron, Frank: (F) Member Temple Lodge, No. 14, 1900, Albany, NY

Inglis, Thomas: (F) Member Arcana Lodge, No. 246, F. & A. M., 1934, New York, NY, (JD) Mar. 7, 1910

Ingraham, G.: (F) Member Long Island Lodge, No. 382, F. &. A. M. 1874, NY

Ingraham, Jarvis S.: (F) Member Temple Lodge, No. 14, 1900, Albany, NY

Ireland, Arthur J.: (F) Member Temple Lodge, No. 14, 1900, Albany, NY, (CEN) 1880, 11$^{th}$ Ward, Albany, Albany Co., NY, Julis D., 35, Bookkeeper at Printing House, Jenny, 38, Edwin D., 13, Arthur J., 8, Harry, 5, Walter,I., 1

Ireland, Edwin D.: (F) Member Temple Lodge, No. 14, 1900, Albany, NY (CEN)1880, 11$^{th}$ Ward, Albany, Albany Co., NY, Julis D., 35, Bookkeeper at Printing House, Jenny, 38, Edwin D., 13, Arthur J., 8, Harry, 5, Walter,I., 1

Ireland, Harry D.: (F) Member Temple Lodge, No. 14, 1900, Albany, NY, (CEN) 1880, 11$^{th}$ Ward, Albany, Albany Co., NY, Julis D., 35, Bookkeeper at Printing House, Jenny, 38, Edwin D., 13, Arthur J., 8, Harry, 5, Walter,I., 1

Ireland, Julius D.: (F) Member Temple Lodge, No. 14, 1900, Albany, NY, (CMTS) Past Master 1890, Life Member, (CEN) 1880, 11$^{th}$ Ward, Albany, Albany Co., NY, Julis D., 35, Bookkeeper at Printing House, Jenny, 38, Edwin D., 13, Arthur J., 8, Harry, 5, Walter,I., 1, (B) Nov. 12, 1844, (D) Dec. 2, 1934, (AKA) Augustus Drake Ireland, (PRTS) Daniel Ireland and Augusta Drake, (MD) Jul. 5, 1866, (Spouse) Sara Jane Willard

Irons, Sadie: (F) Member Ladies Loyal Orange Legion, Princess of Orange No. 6, 1900, Brooklyn, (I) *"Brooklyn Eagle,"* Feb. 3, 1900. Meeting Notice., (CMTS) Recording Secretary

Irving, Jean: (F) Member Society of American Magicians, Apr., 1931, New York, (RES) Jersey City, NJ

Irwin, James: (F) Member Long Island Lodge, No. 382, F. &. A. M., 1874, NY

Israel, David: (F) Member Arcana Lodge, No. 246, F. & A. M., 1934, New York, NY, (JD) Sep. 15, 1913

Israel, Max M.: (F) Member Arcana Lodge, No. 246, F. & A. M., 1934, New York, NY, (JD) Nov. 29, 1920

Israelson, Abraham: (F) Member Society of American Magicians, Apr., 1931, New York, (RES) Brooklyn, NY

Jackman, Mrs. Kate: (F) Member First District Suffolk, Jepthah's Daughter, No. 187, 1923, Huntington, NY, (CMTS) Matron, (RES) Huntington

Jackson, Charles: (F) Member Long Island Lodge, No. 382, F. &. A. M.,

1874, NY
Jackson, Lewis D.: (F) Member Lowville Chapter No. 223, R. A. M., 1929, Lowville, NY, (CO) Lewis, (JD) Feb. 24, 1925
Jackson, Miss Maggie: (F) Member Mispah Circle, 1888, Brooklyn, (I) *"Brooklyn Eagle,"* Dec. 12, 1888. Mentioned in an article about a fair raising funds for a Home for the Blind
Jacob, Henry: (F) Member Arcana Lodge, No. 246, F. & A. M., 1934, New York, NY, (JD) Feb. 14, 1928
Jacobs, Myer C.: (F) Member Washington Lodge, No. 85, 1900, Albany, NY, (CMTS) Master
Jacques, Charles E.: (F) Member Lowville Lodge No. 134, F. & A. M., 1929, Lowville, NY, (CO) Lewis, (JD) Jan. 31, 1896
Jacques, Charles E.: (F) Member Lowville Chapter No. 223, R. A. M., 1929, Lowville, NY, (CO) Lewis, (JD) Apr. 17, 1923
Jacques, Fred C.: (F) Member Lowville Lodge No. 134, F. & A. M., 1929, Lowville, NY, (CO) Lewis, (JD) Nov. 7, 1919
Jacques, Fred C.: (F) Member Lowville Chapter No. 223, R. A. M., 1929, Lowville, NY, (CO) Lewis, (JD) Apr. 17, 1923
Jacques, Harold B.: (F) Member Lowville Lodge No. 134, F. & A. M., 1929, Lowville, NY, (CO) Lewis, (JD) Feb. 1, 1924
Jacques, W. L.: (F) Member Long Island Lodge, No. 382, F. &. A. M., 1874, NY
Jagger, George C.: (F) Member Independent Order of Good Templars, Westhampton Lodge No. 885, instituted Apr. 16, 1889, New Officers installed Feb. 16, 1900, (CMTS) Meeting Notes, *"Brooklyn Eagle,"* Feb. 18, 1900, Past Chief Templar
James, G. S.: (F) Member Long Island Lodge, No. 382, F. &. A. M. 1874, NY
James, J. R. W.: (F) Member Long Island Lodge, No. 382, F. &. A. M. 1874, NY
James, John S.: (F) Member Sons of New England, New England Society of the City of Brooklyn, 1890, (CMTS)*"Brooklyn Eagle,"* Dec. 21, 1890, 11th Annual Dinner, Attendees
James, M. A.: (F) Member Murray Lodge, No. 380, F. & A. M., 1906, Holley, Orleans, Co., NY
Jamison, Walter W.: (F) Member Lowville Chapter No. 223, R. A. M., 1929, Lowville, NY, (CO) Lewis, (JD) Aug. 1, 1893
Janes, Franklin H.: (F) Member Temple Lodge, No. 14, 1900, Albany, NY
Janes, J. Edward: (F) Member Temple Lodge, No. 14, 1900, Albany, NY
Janes, William G.: (F) Member Temple Lodge, No. 14, 1900, Albany, NY, (CMTS) Past Master 1881
Jarrett, Arthur R.: (F) Member Sons of New England, New England Society of the City of Brooklyn, 1890, (CMTS)*"Brooklyn Eagle,"* Dec. 21, 1890, 11th Annual Dinner, Attendees
Jarvie, Wm.: (F) Member Brooklyn Dental Society, 1877, Brooklyn, NY,

(CMTS) *"Brooklyn Eagle,"* Dec. 15, 1877. Celebration of 10th Anniversary. Society established Dec. 14, 1867, (CMTS) Membership Committee

Jeannin, Lewis J.: (F) Member Temple Lodge, No. 14, 1900, Albany, NY

Jeannott, A. A.: (F) Member Long Island Lodge, No. 382, F. &. A. M. 1874, NY

Jenkins, George: (F) Member Grand Council of the Princes of Jerusalem, 1882, Albany, NY

Jenkins, George H.: (F) Member Ineffable and Sublime Grand Lodge of Perfection, 1882, Albany, NY

Jenkins, Mrs. J. E.: (F) Member Mispah Circle, 1888, Brooklyn, (I) *"Brooklyn Eagle,"* Dec. 12, 1888. Mentioned in an article about a fair raising funds for a Home for the Blind

Jlodge, Jr., Barington: (F) Member Temple Lodge, No. 14, 1900, Albany, NY, (CMTS) Life Member

Joffe, Philip: (F) Member Arcana Lodge, No. 246, F. & A. M., 1934, New York, NY, (JD) Nov. 7, 1921

Johnson, A. H.: (F) Member Long Island Lodge, No. 382, F. &. A. M., 1874, NY

Johnson, Eugene C.: (F) Member Masters Lodge, No. 5, 1900, Albany, NY

Johnson, Frank J.: (F) Member Friendly Sons of St. Patrick,1893, Brooklyn, (CMTS)*"Brooklyn Eagle,"* May 18,1893, Article regarding the election of Andrew T. Sullivan as postmaster. In the article it mentioned that there were only 50 members in this Society., Guest. It is unknown if a member of the Society.

Johnson, Jesse: (F) Member Sons of New England, New England Society of the City of Brooklyn, 1890, (CMTS)*"Brooklyn Eagle,"* Dec. 21, 1890, 11th Annual Dinner, Attendees

Johnson, Jessee: (F) Member Sons of New England, New England Society of the City of Brooklyn, 1887, (CMTS)*"Brooklyn Eagle,"* Dec. 22, 1887, Annual Dinner, Attendees

Johnson, John L.: (F) Member Lowville Lodge No. 134, F. & A. M., 1929, Lowville, NY, (CO) Lewis, (JD) Feb. 25, 1898

Johnson, John L.: (F) Member Lowville Chapter No. 223, R. A. M., 1929, Lowville, NY, (CO) Lewis, (JD) Dec. 19, 1899

Johnson, John M.: (F) Member Temple Lodge, No. 14, 1900, Albany, NY

Johnson, John T.: (F) Member Temple Lodge, No. 14, 1900, Albany, NY

Johnson, R.: (F) Member Long Island Lodge, No. 382, F. &. A. M. 1874, NY

Johnson, S.: (F) Member Long Island Lodge, No. 382, F. &. A. M. 1874, NY

Johnson, Samuel W.: (F) Member Society for the Acquistion of Useful Knowledge, Apr. 26, 1843, (CO) Lewis

Johnson, William: (F) Member Temple Lodge, No. 14, 1900, Albany, NY

Johnston, Augusta: (F) Member Hope Rebekah Lodge No. 10, 1949-1950, Brockport, NY, (CO) Monroe

Johnston, Russell M.: (F) Member Masters Lodge, No. 5, 1900, Albany, NY

Jones, Charles E.: (F) Member Ineffable and Sublime Grand Lodge of Perfection, 1882, Albany, NY

Jones, Edward R.: (F) Member Lowville Lodge No. 134, F. & A. M., 1929, Lowville, NY, (CO) Lewis, (JD) Mar. 6, 1908

Jones, Erasmus D.: (F) Member Grand Council of the Princes of Jerusalem, 1882, Albany, NY

Jones, Erasmus D.: (F) Member Ineffable and Sublime Grand Lodge of Perfection, 1882, Albany, NY

Jones, Everett E.: (F) Member Lowville Lodge No. 134, F. & A. M., 1929, Lowville, NY, (CO) Lewis, (JD) May 1, 1925

Jones, F. Edward: (F) Member Lowville Lodge No. 134, F. & A. M., 1929, Lowville, NY, (CO) Lewis, (JD) Dec. 7, 1906

Jones, Harry O.: (F) Member Murray Lodge, No. 380, F. & A. M., 1906, Holley, Orleans, Co., NY, (CMTS) Past Master

Jones, Lottie: (F) Member Hope Rebekah Lodge No. 10, 1949-1950, Brockport, NY, (CO) Monroe

Jones, R.: (F) Member Long Island Lodge, No. 382, F. &. A. M., 1874, NY

Jones, Roger G.: (F) Member Lowville Lodge No. 134, F. & A. M., 1929, Lowville, NY, (CO) Lewis, (JD) Mar. 17, 1920

Jones, Wellington S.: (F) Member Lowville Lodge No. 134, F. & A. M., 1929, Lowville, NY, (CO) Lewis, (JD) Jul. 1, 1904

Jones, Wellington S.: (F) Member Lowville Chapter No. 223, R. A. M., 1929, Lowville, NY, (CO) Lewis, (JD) Mar. 3, 1908

Jones, Wm. M.: (F) Member Long Island Lodge, No. 382, F. &. A. M., 1874, NY

Jorn, H.: (F) Member Herber Lodge, No. 698,1898, F. & A. M., New York, NY, Greenpoint area, (RES) Brooklyn

Jorn, J.: (F) Member Herber Lodge, No. 698,1898, F. & A. M., New York, NY, Greenpoint area, (RES) Brooklyn

Joseph, Michael: (F) Member Arcana Lodge, No. 246, F. & A. M., 1934, New York, NY, (JD) Oct. 20, 1913

Joseph, Myer: (F) Member Lowville Lodge No. 134, F. & A. M., 1929, Lowville, NY, (CO) Lewis, (JD) May 27, 1904

Joslyn, Frank G.: (F) Member Anglo Saxon Lodge No. 137, F. A. M., (CMTS) Meeting Notes, *"Brooklyn Eagle,"* Mar. 13, 1887, Entered the Apprentice Degree by W. M. Jerome E. Morse, (CEN) 1880, Brooklyn, Kings Co., NY, Frank Joslin, 30, VT, Dry Goods Merchant, Caroline, 33, PA, wife, Francis Joslin, 61, VT, Father, David, 28, Brother, Dry Goods Clerk, Amos

Joslin, 26, VT, Dry Goods Clerk
Joslyn, H. B.: (F) Member Murray Lodge, No. 380, F. & A. M., 1906, Holley, Orleans, Co., NY
Joslyn, Hiram H.: (F) Member Murray Lodge, No. 380, F. & A. M., 1906, Holley, Orleans, Co., NY, (CMTS) Past Master
Judd, George W.: (F) Member Lowville Lodge No. 134, F. & A. M., 1929, Lowville, NY, (CO) Lewis, (CMTS) Past Master 1859
Judson, Albert C.: (F) Member Albany Conclave, No. 8, Red Cross of Constantine, 1882, Albany, NY
Judson, Albert C.: (F) Member Ineffable and Sublime Grand Lodge of Perfection, 1882, Albany, NY
Judson, Albert L.: (F) Member Masters Lodge, No. 5, 1900, Albany, NY
Judson, Edmund L.: (F) Member Albany Conclave, No. 8, Red Cross of Constantine, 1882, Albany, NY
Judson, Edmund L.: (F) Member Grand Council of the Princes of Jerusalem, 1882, Albany, NY
Judson, Edmund L.: (F) Member Ineffable and Sublime Grand Lodge of Perfection, 1882, Albany, NY
Just, Martin F.: (F) Member Lowville Lodge No. 134, F. & A. M., 1929, Lowville, NY, (CO) Lewis, (JD) Nov. 26, 1926
Kaack, Henry: (F) Member Temple Lodge, No. 14, 1900, Albany, NY
Kaiser, John: (F) Member Temple Lodge, No. 14, 1900, Albany, NY
Kaley, John R.: (F) Member Masters Lodge, No. 5, 1900, Albany, NY
Kallmann, Chas.: (F) Member Herber Lodge, No. 698,1898, F. & A. M., New York, NY, Greenpoint area, (RES) New York City
Kamps, Wm.: (F) Member Herber Lodge, No. 698,1898, F. & A. M., New York, NY, Greenpoint area, (RES) New York City
Kanzelmyer, J. Chas.: (F) Member Mount Vernon Lodge, No. 3, 1900, Albany, NY
Kapfer, Frank M.: (F) Member Lowville Chapter No. 223, R. A. M., 1929, Lowville, NY, (CO) Lewis, (JD) Oct. 27, 1920
Kaplan, David: (F) Member Arcana Lodge, No. 246, F. & A. M., 1934, New York, NY, (JD) Mar. 16, 1925
Kaplan, Harry E.: (F) Member Arcana Lodge, No. 246, F. & A. M., 1934, New York, NY, (JD) Jun. 17, 1918
Karp, David: (F) Member Arcana Lodge, No. 246, F. & A. M., 1934, New York, NY, (JD) Jun. 4, 1923
Karp, Morris M.: (F) Member Shakespeare Lodge, No. 750, F. & A. M., Aug. 1, 1956, New York City, NY, (Raised) 1954
Karp, Philip: (F) Member Arcana Lodge, No. 246, F. & A. M., 1934, New York, NY, (JD) Mar. 6, 1922
Karroll, Morris S.: (F) Member Arcana Lodge, No. 246, F. & A. M., 1934, New York, NY, (JD) Mar. 7, 1921
Kasher, Irving: (F) Member Shakespeare Lodge, No. 750, F. & A. M., Aug. 1, 1956, New York City, NY, (Raised) 1949, (RES)

Brooklyn
Kasher, Leonard S.: (F) Member Shakespeare Lodge, No. 750,
F. & A. M., Aug. 1, 1956, New York City, NY, (Raised) 1952,
(RES) Brooklyn
Kaskawitz, Irwin: (F) Member Shakespeare Lodge, No. 750, F. & A. M.,
Aug. 1, 1956, New York City, NY, (Raised) 1949, (RES)
Brooklyn
Kass, Joseph: (F) Member Arcana Lodge, No. 246, F. & A. M., 1934,
New York, NY, (JD) May 2, 1921, No. 1, (sic)
Kass, Joseph: (F) Member Arcana Lodge, No. 246, F. & A. M., 1934,
New York, NY, (JD) Jun. 11, 1929, No. 2, (sic)
Kass, Meyer: (F) Member Shakespeare Lodge, No. 750, F. & A. M.,
Aug. 1, 1956, New York City, NY, (Raised) 1953, (RES)
Brooklyn
Kass, Samuel: (F) Member Arcana Lodge, No. 246, F. & A. M., 1934,
New York, NY, (JD) Jun. 11, 1929
Kastenbaum, Sidney B.: (F) Member Shakespeare Lodge, No. 750,
F. & A. M., Aug. 1, 1956, New York City, NY, (Raised) 1948,
(RES) Forest Hills
Kastner, Max: (F) Member Arcana Lodge, No. 246, F. & A. M., 1934,
New York, NY, (JD) Dec. 31, 1916
Katoff, Laurice: (F) Member Society of American Magicians,
Apr., 1931, New York, (RES) Brooklyn, NY
Katyza, A.: (F) Member Herber Lodge, No. 698,1898, F. & A. M.,
New York, NY, Greenpoint area, (RES) New York City
Katz, Herman A.: (F) Member Shakespeare Lodge, No. 750, F. & A. M.,
Aug. 1, 1956, New York City, NY, (Raised) 1925, Life Member,
(RES) Brooklyn
Katz, Hyman J.: (F) Member Shakespeare Lodge, No. 750, F. & A. M.,
Aug. 1, 1956, New York City, NY, (Raised) 1924, Life Member
Katz, Isaac: (F) Member Arcana Lodge, No. 246, F. & A. M., 1934, New
York, NY, (JD) May 7, 1900, Life Member
Katz, Louis: (F) Member Shakespeare Lodge, No. 750, F. & A. M.,
Aug. 1, 1956, New York City, NY, (Raised) 1921, Life Member,
(RES) Caldwell
Katz, Maxwell C.: (F) Member Shakespeare Lodge, No. 750, F. & A. M.,
Aug. 1, 1956, New York City, NY, (Raised) 1923, Life Member,
(RES) Kings Point
Katz, Paul: (F) Member Shakespeare Lodge, No. 750, F. & A. M.,
Aug. 1, 1956, New York City, NY, (Raised) 1950, (RES) Brooklyn
Katz, Ralph: (F) Member Shakespeare Lodge, No. 750, F. & A. M.,
Aug. 1, 1956, New York City, NY, (Raised) 1953, (RES) Brooklyn
Katz, Samuel: (F) Member Arcana Lodge, No. 246, F. & A. M., 1934,
New York, NY, (JD) Sep. 15, 1919
Katz, Samuel : (F) Member Shakespeare Lodge, No. 750, F. & A. M.,
Aug. 1, 1956, New York City, NY ., (Raised) 1916, Life Member

Kaufman, Albert: (F) Member Arcana Lodge, No. 246, F. & A. M., 1934, New York, NY, (JD) Apr. 7, 1919

Kaufman, Clement: (F) Member Arcana Lodge, No. 246, F. & A. M., 1934, New York, NY, (JD) Jul. 17, 1911

Kaufman, Gerld L.: (F) Member Society of American Magicians, Apr., 1931, New York, (RES) Brooklyn, NY

Kaufman, Herman: (F) Member Arcana Lodge, No. 246, F. & A. M., 1934, New York, NY, (JD) Jan. 19, 1920

Kaufman, Joseph: (F) Member Arcana Lodge, No. 246, F. & A. M., 1934, New York, NY, (JD) Sep. 15, 1913, No. 1, (sic)

Kaufman, Joseph: (F) Member Arcana Lodge, No. 246, F. & A. M., 1934, New York, NY, (JD) Jun. 11, 1929, No. 2, (sic)

Kaufman, Levi H.: (F) Member Mount Vernon Lodge, No. 3, 1900, Albany, NY, (CMTS) Past Master 1878

Kaufman, Mr.: (F) Member Mispah Circle, 1888, Brooklyn, (I) *"Brooklyn Eagle,"* Dec. 12, 1888. Mentioned in an article about a fair raising funds for a Home for the Blind

Kaufman, Mrs.: (F) Member Mispah Circle, 1888, Brooklyn, (I) *"Brooklyn Eagle,"* Dec. 12, 1888. Mentioned in an article about a fair raising funds for a Home for the Blind

Kavanaugh, William: (F) Member Mount Vernon Lodge, No. 3, 1900, Albany, NY

Kay, Howard A.: (F) Member Shakespeare Lodge, No. 750, F. & A. M., Aug. 1, 1956, New York City, NY, (Raised) 1930, Life Member, (RES) Brooklyn, (B) Aug. 20, 1904

Kay, Jack: (F) Member Shakespeare Lodge, No. 750, F. & A. M., Aug. 1, 1956, New York City, NY, (Raised) 1949, (RES) Brooklyn

Kaye, Max B.: (F) Member Shakespeare Lodge, No. 750, F. & A. M., Aug. 1, 1956, New York City, NY, (Rasied) 1942, (RES) Brooklyn

Keating, Fred: (F) Member Society of American Magicians, Apr., 1931, New York, (RES) New York City

Keays, Edward: (F) Member Temple Lodge, No. 14, 1900, Albany, NY

Keefer, David H.: (F) Member Temple Lodge, No. 14, 1900, Albany, NY

Keeler, Frederick H.: (F) Member Temple Lodge, No. 14, 1900, Albany, NY

Keeler, John: (F) Member Temple Lodge, No. 14, 1900, Albany, NY

Keenan, Mrs. J.: (F) Member Nativity Sewing Society, 1900, Brooklyn, (I) *"Brooklyn Eagle,"* Feb. 3, 1900. Article regarding raising money to buy clothing for the poor.

Keenholts, James C.: (F) Member Temple Lodge, No. 14, 1900, Albany, NY

Keenholts, Walter S.: (F) Member Temple Lodge, No. 14, 1900, Albany, NY

Keens, Joseph W.: (F) Member Mount Vernon Lodge, No. 3, 1900, Albany, NY

Kellar, Willard O.: (F) Member Lowville Chapter No. 223, R. A. M., 1929, Lowville, NY, (CO) Lewis, (JD) Nov. 9, 1920

Kellar, Williard O.: (F) Member Lowville Lodge No. 134, F. & A. M., 1929, Lowville, NY, (CO) Lewis, (JD) Nov. 17, 1916

Kellener, Eugene J.: (F) Member Shakespeare Lodge, No. 750, F. & A. M., Aug. 1, 1956, New York City, NY, (Raised) 1923, Life Member

Keller, George A.: (F) Member Masters Lodge, No. 5, 1900, Albany, NY

Kellogg, E. H.: (F) Member Sons of New England, New England Society of the City of Brooklyn, 1890, (CMTS)*"Brooklyn Eagle,"* Dec. 21, 1890, 11th Annual Dinner, Attendees

Kellogg, Woodward: (F) Member Society of American Magicians, Apr., 1931, New York, (RES) Elizabeth, NJ

Kelly, Erroll J.: (F) Member Lowville Lodge No. 134, F. & A. M., 1929, Lowville, NY, (CO) Lewis, (JD) May 21, 1917

Kelly, Fred J.: (F) Member Lowville Lodge No. 134, F. & A. M., 1929, Lowville, NY, (CO) Lewis, (JD) Mar. 15, 1907

Kelly, Fred J.: (F) Member Lowville Chapter No. 223, R. A. M., 1929, Lowville, NY, (CO) Lewis, (JD) Dec. 3, 1912

Kelly, Hoyt D.: (F) Member Lowville Lodge No. 134, F. & A. M., 1929, Lowville, NY, (CO) Lewis, (JD) Jun. 30, 1916

Kelly, J. H.: (F) Member Long Island Lodge, No. 382, F. &. A. M., 1874, NY

Kelly, James A.: (F) Member Arcana Lodge, No. 246, F. & A. M., 1934, New York, NY, (JD) Sep. 21, 1891

Kelly, James H.: (F) Member Grand Council of the Princes of Jerusalem, 1882, Albany, NY

Kelly, James H.: (F) Member Ineffable and Sublime Grand Lodge of Perfection, 1882, Albany, NY

Kelly, John C.: (F) Member Friendly Sons of St. Patrick,1893, Brooklyn, (CMTS)*"Brooklyn Eagle,"* May 18,1893, Article regarding the election of Andrew T. Sullivan as postmaster. In the article it mentioned that there were only 50 members in this Society., Guest. It is unknown if a member of the Society.

Kelly, John T.: (I) *"Brooklyn Eagle,"* Feb. 19, 1902. Funeral Services at the Club House of the Brooklyn Lodge, No. 22, B. P. O. Elks for Wm. H. West. Elk services were first then masonic services by New York Lodge No. 330, F. A. & M., (CMTS) Pallbearer

Kelly, Miss Kate: (F) Member Nativity Sewing Society, 1900, Brooklyn, (I) *"Brooklyn Eagle,"* Feb. 3, 1900. Article regarding raising money to buy clothing for the poor.

Kelly, Miss Lucy: (F) Member Nativity Sewing Society, 1900, Brooklyn, (I) *"Brooklyn Eagle,"* Feb. 3, 1900. Article regarding raising money to buy clothing for the poor.

Kelly, Mrs. J. H.: (F) Member Nativity Sewing Society, 1900,

Brooklyn, (I) *"Brooklyn Eagle,"* Feb. 3, 1900. Article regarding raising money to buy clothing for the poor.

Kelly, P. R.: (F) Member Long Island Lodge, No. 382, F. &. A. M., 1874, NY

Kelly, Shirley: (OBIT) *"News Journal,"* Thursday, Sep. 6, 2001. Shirley Kelly of Yonkers, died September 5, 2001. Born on June 22, 1932 to Charles and Anna Wissman Hegenauer in Linthicum Heights, MD. She graduated from Hastings High School in 1950. She attended the Art Students League in New York City. Shirley married Donald P. Kelly in 1952. He predeceased her in 1982. She was active in Women's Masonic organizations. A past Queen of the Triangle Girls, past matron of the Eastern Star, past High Priestess of the Lady Shriners, past Directress and past Royal Directress of the Royal Order of Jesteretts. She was the arts and crafts chairman of the Community Hospital at Dobbs Ferry Auxiliary. Shirley was a parishioner of Sacred Heart Church in Dobbs Ferry and a member of the Sodality. Survivors include two sons, Bruce of Yorktown Heights and Chuck of Ansonia, CT; three grandsons, one granddaughter, her brother Charles of Sandy Hook, CT and several nieces and nephews. She was predeceased by her sister, June Giroux on August 20, of this year.

Kelton, Charles R.: (F) Member Monticello Lodge, No. 532, F. & A. M., (CO) Sullivan Co., NY, (CMTS) Past Master 1871

Kemble, Miss: (F) Member Mispah Circle, 1888, Brooklyn, (I) *"Brooklyn Eagle,"* Dec. 12, 1888. Mentioned in an article about a fair raising funds for a Home for the Blind

Kemble, Mrs. William: (F) Member Mispah Circle, 1888, Brooklyn, (I) *"Brooklyn Eagle,"* Dec. 12, 1888. Mentioned in an article about a fair raising funds for a Home for the Blind

Kemp, Mrs. Henry: (F) Member Mispah Circle, 1888, Brooklyn, (I) *"Brooklyn Eagle,"* Dec. 12, 1888. Mentioned in an article about a fair raising funds for a Home for the Blind

Kempler, Edward: (F) Member Shakespeare Lodge, No. 750, F. & A. M., Aug. 1, 1956, New York City, NY, (Raised) 1946

Kempler, Joseph M.: (F) Member Shakespeare Lodge, No. 750, F. & A. M., Aug. 1, 1956, New York City, NY, (Raised) 1916, Life Member

Kempner, Samuel M.: (F) Member Society of American Magicians, Apr., 1931, New York, (RES) New York City

Kendrick, Fred M. H.: (F) Member Masters Lodge, No. 5, 1900, Albany, NY

Kennedy, E. R.: (F) Member Sons of New England, New England Society of the City of Brooklyn, 1887, (CMTS) *"Brooklyn Eagle,"* Dec. 22, 1887, Annual Dinner, Attendees

Kennedy, Frank I.: (F) Member Temple Lodge, No. 14, 1900, Albany, NY

Kennedy, Harry: (I) *"Brooklyn Eagle,"* Dec. 7, 1896. 12th Annual

Memorial Services, Plymouth Church, Brooklyn Lodge No. 22, B. F. O. Elks, Roll Call of the dead. Address made by Maryland Senator George L. Wellington. , (CMTS) Name called.

Kennedy, Hugh H.: (I) *"Brooklyn Eagle,"* Feb. 19, 1902. Funeral Services at the Club House of the Brooklyn Lodge, No. 22, B. P. O. Elks for Wm. H. West. Elk services were first then masonic services by New York Lodge No. 330, F. A. & M., (CMTS) Member of Metropolitian Male Quartet. Member of the Elks

Kenyon, George W.: (F) Member Sons of New England, New England Society of the City of Brooklyn, 1890, (CMTS)*"Brooklyn Eagle,"* Dec. 21, 1890, 11th Annual Dinner, Attendees

Kerschner, E.: (F) Member Long Island Lodge, No. 382, F. &. A. M. 1874, NY

Kerstain, Herman S.: (F) Member Shakespeare Lodge, No. 750, F. & A. M., Aug. 1, 1956, New York City, NY, (Raised) 1953

Kerster, Joseph : (F) Member Shakespeare Lodge, No. 750, F. & A. M., Aug. 1, 1956, New York City, NY, (Raised) 1950, (RES) Brooklyn

Kesler, Geo. C.: (F) Member Murray Lodge, No. 380, F. & A. M., 1906, Holley, Orleans, Co., NY

Kessel, Louis: (F) Member Long Island Lodge, No. 382, F. &. A. M., 1874, NY

Kessler, Milton R.: (F) Member Arcana Lodge, No. 246, F. & A. M., 1934, New York, NY, (JD) Oct. 15, 1923

Kestenbaum, Ignatz: (F) Member Shakespeare Lodge, No. 750, F. & A. M., Aug. 1, 1956, New York City, NY, (Raised) 1908, Life Member, (RES) Newark

Keyes, Addison A.: (F) Member Grand Council of the Princes of Jerusalem, 1882, Albany, NY, (CEN) 37, IL, Editor, Mary A., 39, Edward, 14, Molly, 12, Jeltie, 9, Annie, 7, (B) Oct. 3, 1842, (BP) Elgin, IL, (MD) Jul. 27, 1860, (Spouse) Mary Agnes Bradley, (PRTS) Eber Keyes (b. Jan. 15, 1799, bp. Nefane, VT, md. Jun. 23, 1831) and Clarinda J. Gray (b. Sep. 20, 1839, d. Oct. 24, 1845). (SIB)Lidya Kidder, Eber Keyes parents were Ashley Keyes and Anna Williard. Clarinda Gray's parents were Elijah Gray (b. Mar. 12, 1764) and Sarah Raymond. Elijah Gray's Parents were Nathaniel Gray (b. Mar. 17, 1736, d. Jun. 24, 1810, md. Feb. 15, 1763) and Deborah Lothrop.

Keyes, Addison A.: (F) Member Ineffable and Sublime Grand Lodge of Perfection, 1882, Albany, NY

Keys, Berton: (F) Member Murray Lodge, No. 380, F. & A. M., 1906, Holley, Orleans, Co., NY, (CMTS) Past Master

Keyser, Edward: (F) Member Temple Lodge, No. 14, 1900, Albany, NY

Khouri, N. A.: (F) Member Arcana Lodge, No. 246, F. & A. M., 1934, New York, NY, (JD) Oct. 16, 1922

Kiby, Joseph: (F) Member Herber Lodge, No. 698,1898, F. & A. M.,

New York, NY, Greenpoint area, (RES) Hoboken, NJ
Kidder, C. G.: (F) Member Brooklyn Revenue Reform Club, 1886,
(I)*"Brooklyn Eagle,"* Jan. ,27 1886, Attendees at a dinner
Kidger, Miss: (F) Member Mispah Circle, 1888, Brooklyn, (I) *"Brooklyn Eagle,"* Dec. 12, 1888. Mentioned in an article about a fair raising funds for a Home for the Blind
Kidney, Richard: (F) Member Ineffable and Sublime Grand Lodge of Perfection, 1882, Albany, NY
Kidney, Richard V.: (F) Member Grand Council of the Princes of Jerusalem, 1882, Albany, NY
Kiely, Rev. John M.: (F) Member Friendly Sons of St. Patrick,1893, Brooklyn, (CMTS)*"Brooklyn Eagle,"* May 18,1893,
Article regardingthe election of Andrew T. Sullivan as postmaster. In the article it mentioned that there were only 50 members in this Society., Guest. It is unknown if a member of the Society.
Kiernan, Charles B.: (F) Member Temple Lodge, No. 14, 1900, Albany, NY
Kieselstein, Fred: (F) Member Arcana Lodge, No. 246, F. & A. M., 1934, New York, NY, (JD) Oct. 20, 1919
Kieselstein, Sol.: (F) Member Arcana Lodge, No. 246, F. & A. M., 1934, New York, NY, (JD) Sep. 20, 1909
Kilbourne, James B.: (F) Member Mount Vernon Lodge, No. 3, 1900, Albany, NY
Kilburn, William E.: (F) Member Lowville Lodge No. 134, F. & A. M., 1929, Lowville, NY, (CO) Lewis, (JD) May 14, 1928
Kimmey, Edson: (F) Member Masters Lodge, No. 5, 1900, Albany, NY
King, A. B.: (F) Member Brooklyn Revenue Reform Club, 1886,
(I)*"Brooklyn Eagle,"* Jan. ,27 1886, Attendees at a dinner
King, C. P.: (F) Member Murray Lodge, No. 380, F. & A. M., 1906, Holley, Orleans, Co., NY, (CMTS) Past Master
Kinglesy, Dr. N. W.: (F) Member Brooklyn Dental Society, 1877, Brooklyn, NY, (CMTS) *"Brooklyn Eagle,"* Dec. 15, 1877. Celebration of 10th Anniversary. Society established Dec. 14, 1867, (CMTS) Present from New York
Kirschner, Harold: (F) Member Shakespeare Lodge, No. 750, F. & A. M., Aug. 1, 1956, New York City, NY, (Raised) 1942, (RES) Brooklyn
Kirschner, Jacob M.: (F) Member Shakespeare Lodge, No. 750, F. & A. M., Aug. 1, 1956, New York City, NY, (Raised) 1923, Life Member, (RES) Pelham Manor
Kirschner, Julius J.: (F) Member Shakespeare Lodge, No. 750, F. & A. M., Aug. 1, 1956, New York City, NY, (Raised) 1931, Life Member, (RES) Brooklyn
Kirschner, Paul: (F) Member Shakespeare Lodge, No. 750, F. & A. M., Aug. 1, 1956, New York City, NY, (Raised) 1954, (RES) Kew Gardens Hills

Kirschner, Sol L.: (F) Member Shakespeare Lodge, No. 750, F. & A. M., Aug. 1, 1956, New York City, NY, (Raised), Life Member, (RES) Brooklyn

Kissel, Fred: (F) Member Arcana Lodge, No. 246, F. & A. M., 1934, New York, NY, (JD) May 7, 1906, Life Member

Kissel, Martin S.: (F) Member Arcana Lodge, No. 246, F. & A. M., 1934, New York, NY, (JD) Jun. 15, 1921

Klarman, Jacob : (F) Member Shakespeare Lodge, No. 750, F. & A. M., Aug. 1, 1956, New York City, NY, (Raised) 1921, Life Member, (RES) Mt. Vernon

Klarman, Stanley : (F) Member Shakespeare Lodge, No. 750, F. & A. M., Aug. 1, 1956, New York City, NY, (Raised) 1946, (RES) White Plains

Kleiman, Sol L.: (F) Member Shakespeare Lodge, No. 750, F. & A. M., Aug. 1, 1956, New York City, NY, (Raised) 1916, Life Member

Klein, Armin: (F) Member Arcana Lodge, No. 246, F. & A. M., 1934, New York, NY, (JD) Nov. 17,1919

Klein, George H.: (F) Member Shakespeare Lodge, No. 750, F. & A. M., Aug. 1, 1956, New York City, NY, (Raised) 1923, Life Member

Klein, Harry: (F) Member Arcana Lodge, No. 246, F. & A. M., 1934, New York, NY, (JD) Dec. 3, 1917

Klein, Harry D.: (F) Member Shakespeare Lodge, No. 750, F. & A. M., Aug. 1, 1956, New York City, NY, (Raised) 1916, (RES) Greenfield, MA

Klein, V.: (F) Member Herber Lodge, No. 698,1898, F. & A. M., New York, NY, Greenpoint area, (RES) Brooklyn

Kleinschnitz, K.: (F) Member Herber Lodge, No. 698,1898, F. & A. M., New York, NY, Greenpoint area, (RES) New York City

Klepner, Henry M.: (F) Member Arcana Lodge, No. 246, F. & A. M., 1934, New York, NY, (JD) Nov. 20, 1922

Klepner, Irving: (F) Member Arcana Lodge, No. 246, F. & A. M., 1934, New York, NY, (JD) Nov. 20, 1922

Klepper, Paul: (F) Member Arcana Lodge, No. 246, F. & A. M., 1934, New York, NY, (JD) Jun. 23, 1931

Klett, Emil: (F) Member Lowville Lodge No. 134, F. & A. M., 1929, Lowville, NY, (CO) Lewis, (JD) Mar. 20, 1908

Klett, Jr., Philip P.: (F) Member Lowville Lodge No. 134, F. & A. M., 1929, Lowville, NY, (CO) Lewis, (JD) Dec. 16, 1916

Knapp, George B.: (F) Member Temple Lodge, No. 14, 1900, Albany, NY

Knapp, Ira G.: (F) Member Temple Lodge, No. 14, 1900, Albany, NY

Knapp, Joseph F.: (F) Member Sons of New England, New England Society of the City of Brooklyn, 1887, (CMTS) *"Brooklyn Eagle,"* Dec. 22, 1887, Annual Dinner, Attendees

Knight, Charles F.: (F) Member Temple Lodge, No. 14, 1900, Albany, NY

Knight, Frederick A.: (F) Member Life Apollo Comandery No. 15,

Knights, Templar, Troy, NY, 1901
Knighton, M.D., Willis S.: (F) Member Society of American Magicians, Apr., 1931, New York, (RES) New York City
Knoop, John: (F) Member Long Island Lodge, No. 382, F. &. A. M., 1874, NY
Knowles, George E.: (F) Member Temple Lodge, No. 14, 1900, Albany, NY
Knowlton, E. F.: (F) Member Sons of New England, New England Society of the City of Brooklyn, 1890, (CMTS)*"Brooklyn Eagle,"* Dec. 21, 1890, 11th Annual Dinner, Attendees
Knowlton, E. F.: (F) Member Sons of New England, New England Society of the City of Brooklyn, 1887, (CMTS)*"Brooklyn Eagle,"* Dec. 22, 1887, Annual Dinner, Attendees
Knowlton, E. J.: (F) Member Sons of New England, New England Society of the City of Brooklyn, 1890, (CMTS)*"Brooklyn Eagle,"* Dec. 21, 1890, 11th Annual Dinner, Attendees
Knox, James L.: (F) Member Lowville Lodge No. 134, F. & A. M., 1929, Lowville, NY, (CO) Lewis, (CMTS) Past Master 1873-1874
Knox, James L.: (F) Member Lowville Lodge No. 134, F. & A. M., 1929, Lowville, NY, (CO) Lewis, (CMTS) D. D. G. M. 1874, 1875
Knox, Mrs.: (F) Member Mispah Circle, 1888, Brooklyn, (I) *"Brooklyn Eagle,"* Dec. 12, 1888. Mentioned in an article about a fair raising funds for a Home for the Blind
Knox, Samuel J.: (F) Member Temple Lodge, No. 14, 1900, Albany, NY, (CEN) 1$^{st}$ Ward, Albany, Albany Co., NY, 46, Ireland, Laborer, Elizabeth, 44, Racheal J., 20, John, 16, Charles H., 9, Isabella, 5.
Kochkeller, Ed. E.: (F) Member Arcana Lodge, No. 246, F. & A. M., 1934, New York, NY, (JD) Feb. 3, 1908, Life Member
Koenig, Albert: (F) Member Arcana Lodge, No. 246, F. & A. M., 1934, New York, NY, (JD) Jun. 13, 1933
Koenig, Fred.: (F) Member American Legion of Honor, Stella Lodge No. 400, 1900, Brooklyn, (I) *"Brooklyn Eagle,"* Feb. 3, 1900. Meeting Notice., (CMTS) Collector
Koenig, J. Charles: (F) Member Arcana Lodge, No. 246, F. & A. M., 1934, New York, NY, (JD) Jun. 28, 1932
Koeppel, Isadore S.: (F) Member Shakespeare Lodge, No. 750, F. & A. M., Aug. 1, 1956, New York City, NY, (Raised) 1915, Life Member, (RES) Brooklyn
Koff, Tabby M.: (F) Member Shakespeare Lodge, No. 750, F. & A. M., Aug. 1, 1956, New York City, NY, (Raised) 1952, (RES) Mt. Vernon
Kohen, Stanley G.: (F) Member Shakespeare Lodge, No. 750, F. & A. M., Aug. 1, 1956, New York City, NY, (Raised) 1952
Kohler, John L.: (F) Member Lowville Lodge No. 134, F. & A. M., 1929, Lowville, NY, (CO) Lewis, (JD) Jun. 1, 1923
Kohler, Theodore S.: (F) Member Lowville Lodge No. 134, F. & A. M.,

1929, Lowville, NY, (CO) Lewis, (JD) Dec. 28, 1911
Koonz, Edward C.: (F) Member Grand Council of the Princes of
Jerusalem, 1882, Albany, NY
Koonz, Edward C.: (F) Member Ineffable and Sublime Grand Lodge of
Perfection, 1882, Albany, NY
Koplowitz, S.: (F) Member Herber Lodge, No. 698,1898, F. & A. M.,
New York, NY, Greenpoint area, (RES) Brooklyn
Koppel, Jacob: (F) Member Shakespeare Lodge, No. 750, F. & A. M.,
Aug. 1, 1956, New York City, NY, (Raised) 119, Life Member
Kopper, A. G.: (F) Member Herber Lodge, No. 698,1898, F. & A. M.,
New York, NY, Greenpoint area, (RES) New York City
Korff, W.: (F) Member Long Island Lodge, No. 382, F. &. A. M.,
1874, NY
Koster, Charles: (F) Member Arcana Lodge, No. 246, F. & A. M., 1934,
New York, NY, (JD) May 20, 1901, Life Member
Koster, George E.: (F) Member Lowville Chapter No. 223, R. A. M.,
1929, Lowville, NY, (CO) Lewis, (JD) Mar. 7, 1905
Kovats, Adolph: (F) Member Arcana Lodge, No. 246, F. & A. M., 1934,
New York, NY, (JD) Oct. 21, 1918
Kovats, Stephen: (F) Member Arcana Lodge, No. 246, F. & A. M., 1934,
New York, NY, (JD) Mar. 16, 1925
Kovitz, Bernard: (F) Member Shakespeare Lodge, No. 750, F. & A. M.,
Aug. 1, 1956, New York City, NY, (Raised) 1950, (RES) Brooklyn
Kovitz, Joel: (F) Member Shakespeare Lodge, No. 750, F. & A. M.,
Aug. 1, 1956, New York City, NY, (Raised) 1948
Kovitz, Max: (F) Member Shakespeare Lodge, No. 750, F. & A. M.,
Aug. 1, 1956, New York City, NY, (Raised) 1927, Life Member
Kramer, Aaron R.: (F) Member Shakespeare Lodge, No. 750, F. & A. M.,
Aug. 1, 1956, New York City, NY, (Raised) 1956
Kramer, Abraham L.: (F) Member Shakespeare Lodge, No. 750,
F. & A. M., Aug. 1, 1956, New York City, NY, (Raised) 1922,
Life Member
Kramer, Benjamin F.: (F) Member Shakespeare Lodge, No. 750,
F. & A. M., Aug. 1, 1956, New York City, NY, (Raised) 1932,
(RES) San Francisco
Kramer, Harold B.: (F) Member Shakespeare Lodge, No. 750, F. & A. M.,
Aug. 1, 1956, New York City, NY, (Raised) 1946, Brooklyn
Kramer, Israel: (F) Member Arcana Lodge, No. 246, F. & A. M., 1934,
New York, NY, (JD) Nov. 19, 1923
Kramer, Leroy A.: (F) Member Shakespeare Lodge, No. 750, F. & A. M.,
Aug. 1, 1956, New York City, NY, (Raised) 1946, Brooklyn
Kramrath, Alexander: (F) Member Temple Lodge, No. 14, 1900,
Albany, NY, (CEN) 1880, 6th Ward, Albany, Albany Co., NY,
Listed with Martin Kramrath, Carpet Store, 56, Prussia, Catherine,
51, Kate, 20, Henry, 13, Alexander, 7.
Kramrath, Henry M.: (F) Member Temple Lodge, No. 14, 1900,

Albany, NY (CEN) 1880, 6th Ward, Albany, Albany Co., NY,
Listed with Martin Kramrath, Carpet Store, 56, Prussia, Catherine,
51, Kate, 20, Henry, 13, Alexander, 7.

Krankenberg, H.: (F) Member Herber Lodge, No. 698,1898, F. & A. M.,
New York, NY, Greenpoint area, (RES) New York City

Krapkoff, Charles : (F) Member Arcana Lodge, No. 246,
F. & A. M., 1934, New York, NY, (JD) Oct. 11, 1927

Krass, Dr. Rev. Nathan: (F) Member Society of American Magicians,
Apr., 1931, New York, (RES) New York City

Kratz, Conrad: (F) Member Temple Lodge, No. 14, 1900, Albany, NY,
(CEN) 1880, 10th Ward, Albany, Albany Co., NY Listed with
Henry Kratz, 52, Hesse, Retail Grocer, Catherine, 54, Conrad, 20,
Carpenter, Henry, 17,

Kraus, George: (F) Member Shakespeare Lodge, No. 750, F. & A. M.,
Aug. 1, 1956, New York City, NY, (Raised) 1894, (RES)
Hollywood, FL

Kraus, Herman L.: (F) Member Shakespeare Lodge, No. 750, F. & A. M.,
Aug. 1, 1956, New York City, NY, (Raised) 1931, Life Member,
(RES) Brooklyn

Kraus, Milton: (F) Member Shakespeare Lodge, No. 750, F. & A. M.,
Aug. 1, 1956, New York City, NY, (Raised) 1953, (RES)
Kew Gardens

Krause, Sylvan B.: (F) Member Arcana Lodge, No. 246, F. & A. M.,
1934, New York, NY, (JD) May 11, 1926

Kraushaar, C. C.: (F) Member Long Island Lodge, No. 382, F. &. A. M.,
1874, NY

Kraushaar, P. Fred.: (F) Member Long Island Lodge, No. 382,
F. &. A. M., 1874, NY

Kretzschmar, Dr. L. H.: (F) Member Brooklyn Revenue Reform Club,
1886, (I)*"Brooklyn Eagle,"* Jan. ,27 1886, Attendees at a dinner

Kretzschmar, Dr. Paul H.: (F) Member Brooklyn Revenue Reform Club,
1886, (I)*"Brooklyn Eagle,"* Jan. ,27 1886, Attendees at a dinner

Kretzschmar, M. D., P. H.: (F) Member Sons of New England, New
England Society of the City of Brooklyn, 1890, (CMTS)*"Brooklyn
Eagle,"* Dec. 21, 1890, 11th Annual Dinner, Attendees

Krieger, Louis I.: (F) Member Shakespeare Lodge, No. 750, F. & A. M.,
Aug. 1, 1956, New York City, NY, (Raised) 1915, Life Member

Krigel, Harry G.: (F) Member Shakespeare Lodge, No. 750, F. & A. M.,
Aug. 1, 1956, New York City, NY, (Raised) 917, Life Member

Kroll, Charles G.: (F) Member Shakespeare Lodge, No. 750, F. & A. M.,
Aug. 1, 1956, New York City, NY, (Raised) 1918, Life Member

Krom, Chas.: (F) Member Arcana Lodge, No. 246,F. & A. M., 1934,
New York, NY, (JD) Nov. 6,1893, Life Member

Kropp, F.: (F) Member Herber Lodge, No. 698,1898, F. & A. M.,
New York, NY, Greenpoint area, (RES) New York City

Krueger, August F.: (F) Member Lowville Lodge No. 134, F. & A. M.,

1929, Lowville, NY, (CO) Lewis, (JD) Mar. 2, 1923

Krueger, August F.: (F) Member Lowville Chapter No. 223, R. A. M., 1929, Lowville, NY, (CO) Lewis, (JD) May 27, 1924

Krulik, Herbert A.: (F) Member Shakespeare Lodge, No. 750, F. & A. M., Aug. 1, 1956, New York City, NY, (Raised) 1951, (RES) Levittown, PA

Krulik, Stephen E.: (F) Member Shakespeare Lodge, No. 750, F. & A. M., Aug. 1, 1956, New York City, NY, (Raised) 1954

Kullman, Augustus: (F) Member Temple Lodge, No. 14, 1900, Albany, NY (CEN) 1880, $2^{nd}$ Ward, Albany, Albany Co., NY, 25, Grocery Owner, Louise, 26, wife

Kullman, Theodore C.: (F) Member Temple Lodge, No. 14, 1900, Albany, NY,.(CEN) 1880, $2^{nd}$ Ward, Albany, Albany Co., NY, Listed with Frederick C., 54, Cabinet Maker, Rosa, 53, Ferdinand, 23, Cutter in Shoe Shop, Pauline, 21, Works in Millnery, Theodore, 19, Apprentice Wagon Maker, Adolph, 14, Works in Grocery

Kunkel, Martin: (F) Member Temple Lodge, No. 14, 1900, Albany, NY

Kuntz, J.: (F) Member Herber Lodge, No. 698,1898, F. & A. M., New York, NY, Greenpoint area, (RES) New York City

Kupferberg, Benjamin S.: (F) Member Shakespeare Lodge, No. 750, F. & A. M., Aug. 1, 1956, New York City, NY, (Raised) 1930, (RES) Jersey City

Kurz, L.: (F) Member Herber Lodge, No. 698,1898, F. & A. M., New York, NY, Greenpoint area, (RES) Brooklyn

Kurzrok, Benjamin: (F) Member Arcana Lodge, No. 246, F. & A. M., 1934, New York, NY, (JD) Mar. 31, 1924

Kurzweil, Charles G.: (F) Member Shakespeare Lodge, No. 750, F. & A. M., Aug. 1, 1956, New York City, NY, (Raised) 1915, Life Member, (RES) Brooklyn

Kyle, Arthur C.: (F) Member Monticello Lodge, No. 532, F. & A. M., (CO) Sullivan Co., NY, (CMTS) Past Master 1910, 1911

Ladden, William: (F) Member Arcana Lodge, No. 246, F. & A. M., 1934, New York, NY, (JD) May 12, 1931

Lafferty, J. H.: (F) Member Long Island Lodge, No. 382, F. &. A. M., 1874, NY

Lahah, Arthur H.: (F) Member Lowville Chapter No. 223, R. A. M., 1929, Lowville, NY, (CO) Lewis, (JD) Nov. 13, 1923

Laighton, George J.: (F) Member Sons of New England, New England Society of the City of Brooklyn, 1890, (CMTS) *"Brooklyn Eagle,"* Dec. 21, 1890, 11th Annual Dinner, Attendees

Laike, Alex.: (F) Member Arcana Lodge, No. 246, F. & A. M., 1934, New York, NY, (JD) May 19, 1924

Laird, James L.: (F) Member Knights and Ladies of Honor, 1900, Brooklyn, (I) *"Brooklyn Eagle,"* Feb. 3, 1900. Meeting Notice., (CMTS) Secretary

Laird, W.: (F) Member Long Island Lodge, No. 382, F. &. A. M., 1874, NY

Lake, Elmer P.: (F) Member Lowville Chapter No. 223, R. A. M., 1929, Lowville, NY, (CO) Lewis, (JD) Jan. 5, 1892

Lamb, A. E.: (F) Member Sons of New England, New England Society of the City of Brooklyn, 1890, (CMTS)*"Brooklyn Eagle,"* Dec. 21, 1890, 11th Annual Dinner, Attendees

Lamb, Charles W.: (F) Member Temple Lodge, No. 14, 1900, Albany, NY

Lambert, Lewis A.: (F) Member Murray Lodge, No. 380, F. & A. M., 1906, Holley, Orleans, Co., NY

Lambert, S.: (F) Member Herber Lodge, No. 698,1898, F. & A. M., New York, NY, Greenpoint area, (RES) Brooklyn

Lamp, Michael: (F) Member Temple Lodge, No. 14, 1900, Albany, NY

Lampert, Herman: (F) Member Shakespeare Lodge, No. 750, F. & A. M., Aug. 1, 1956, New York City, NY, (Raised) 1946, (RES) Brooklyn

Lampman, John J.: (F) Member Lowville Lodge No. 134, F. & A. M., 1929, Lowville, NY, (CO) Lewis, (JD) Oct., 1926

Lampman, John J.: (F) Member Lowville Chapter No. 223, R. A. M., 1929, Lowville, NY, (CO) Lewis, (JD) Feb. 26, 1924

Lanagan, Elmer D.: (F) Member Temple Lodge, No. 14, 1900, Albany, NY

Landres, Arnold G.: (F) Member Shakespeare Lodge, No. 750, F. & A. M., Aug. 1, 1956, New York City, NY, (Raised) 1918, Life Member

Landweber, M. Martin: (F) Member Shakespeare Lodge, No. 750, F. & A. M., Aug. 1, 1956, New York City, NY, (Raised) 1946

Lane, Charles B.: (F) Member Masters Lodge, No. 5, 1900, Albany, NY

Lane, D. Webster: (F) Member Lowville Lodge No. 134, F. & A. M., 1929, Lowville, NY, (CO) Lewis, (CMTS) Past Master 1877, 1879

Lang, Charles M.: (F) Member Temple Lodge, No. 14, 1900, Albany, NY

Lang, William: (I) *"Brooklyn Eagle,"* Dec. 7, 1896. 12th Annual Memorial Services, Plymouth Church, Brooklyn Lodge No. 22, B. F. O. Elks, Roll Call of the dead. Address made by Maryland Senator George L. Wellington. , (CMTS) Name called.

Langdon, Loomis L.: (F) Member Sons of New England, New England Society of the City of Brooklyn, 1890, (CMTS)*"Brooklyn Eagle,"* Dec. 21, 1890, 11th Annual Dinner, Attendees

Lanpher, A. M.: (F) Member Lowville Lodge No. 134, F. & A. M., 1929, Lowville, NY, (CO) Lewis, (CMTS) Past Master 1875-1876

Lanpher, Harry M.: (F) Member Lowville Lodge No. 134, F. & A. M., 1929, Lowville, NY, (CO) Lewis, (JD) Mar. 16, 1896

Lansing, Andrew D.: (F) Member Grand Council of the Princes of Jerusalem, 1882, Albany, NY

Lansing, Charles E.: (F) Member Temple Lodge, No. 14, 1900, Albany, NY

Lansing, Henry: (F) Member Grand Council of the Princes of Jerusalem, 1882, Albany, NY

Laraway, Frank J.: (F) Member Temple Lodge, No. 14, 1900, Albany, NY

Larraway, John W.: (F) Member Temple Lodge, No. 14, 1900, Albany, NY, (CMTS) Life Member

Larsdrager, Henry: (F) Member Long Island Lodge, No. 382, F. &. A. M., 1874, NY

Larwood, Thomas W.: (F) Member Masters Lodge, No. 5, 1900, Albany, NY, (CEN) 1880, 14$^{th}$ Ward, Albany, Albany Co., NY, 41, Clerk Insurance Dept., Jane C., 42, Thos. W., 17, Marion E., 13

Latham, George E.: (F) Member Temple Lodge, No. 14, 1900, Albany, NY

Lathrop, Augustus H.: (F) Member Temple Lodge, No. 14, 1900, Albany, NY

Latter, Harry: (F) Member Arcana Lodge, No. 246, F. & A. M., 1934, New York, NY, (JD) Mar. 27, 1928

Latz, Harry L.: (F) Member Society of American Magicians, Apr., 1931, New York, (RES) New York City

Lauber, Joseph E.: (F) Member Arcana Lodge, No. 246, F. & A. M., 1934, New York, NY, (JD) Nov. 18, 1912

Lauder, Peter C.: (F) Member Grand Council of the Princes of Jerusalem, 1882, Albany, NY

Lauder, Peter C.: (F) Member Ineffable and Sublime Grand Lodge of Perfection, 1882, Albany, NY

Laulicht, Daniel: (F) Member Shakespeare Lodge, No. 750, F. & A. M., Aug. 1, 1956, New York City, NY, (Raised) 1955, (RES) Kew Gardens

Laureyns, Gustave G.: (F) Member Society of American Magicians, Apr., 1931, New York, (RES) Bllomfield, NJ

Lavine, Maximilam: (F) Member Shakespeare Lodge, No. 750, F. & A. M., Aug. 1, 1956, New York City, NY, (Raised) 1924, Life Member, (RES) Brooklyn

Lawner, Isadore: (F) Member Shakespeare Lodge, No. 750, F. & A. M., Aug. 1, 1956, New York City, NY, (Raised) 1930, Life Member, (RES) Brooklyn

Lawrence, Charles E.: (F) Member Temple Lodge, No. 14, 1900, Albany, NY

Lawrence, Fred J.: (F) Member Ineffable and Sublime Grand Lodge of Perfection, 1882, Albany, NY

Lawrence, Fred J.: (F) Member Temple Lodge, No. 14, 1900, Albany, NY

Lawrence, Jerome K.: (F) Member Shakespeare Lodge, No. 750, F. & A. M., Aug. 1, 1956, New York City, NY, (Raised) 1947, (RES) Brooklyn

Lawson, Joseph A.: (F) Member Masters Lodge, No. 5, 1900, Albany, NY, (CMTS) Past Master

Lawtenslager, Albert: (F) Member Masters Lodge, No. 5, 1900,

Albany, NY
Lawtenslager, Joseph J.: (F) Member Masters Lodge, No. 5, 1900, Albany, NY
Lawton, George: (F) Member Mount Vernon Lodge, No. 3, 1900, Albany, NY
Lawton, George: (F) Member Temple Lodge, No. 14, 1900, Albany, NY
Lawton, Reugene E.: (F) Member Murray Lodge, No. 380, F. & A. M., 1906, Holley, Orleans, Co., NY
Lawyer, Abraham L.: (F) Member Mount Vernon Lodge, No. 3, 1900, Albany, NY, (CEN) 1880, 15th Ward, Albany, Albany Co., NY, 40, Harness Maker, Helen, 46, Clarence, 14, Jenny, 12, Abraham L., Annie M., 8, Helen, 7, Alphonso, 5, Augusta, 3.
Lawyer, Abram S.: (F) Member Washington Lodge, No. 85, 1900, Albany, NY, (CMTS) Past Members
Lawyer, George: (F) Member Temple Lodge, No. 14, 1900, Albany, NY
Lazarus, J. Louis: (F) Member Shakespeare Lodge, No. 750, F. & A. M., Aug. 1, 1956, New York City, NY, (Raised) 1928, Life Member, (RES) Lake Success, NY
Lazarus, Robt. A.: (F) Member Arcana Lodge, No. 246, F. & A. M., 1934, New York, NY, (JD) Nov. 18, 1912
Lazarus, Sol: (F) Member Shakespeare Lodge, No. 750, F. & A. M., Aug. 1, 1956, New York City, NY, (Raised) 1910, Life Member, (RES) Miami Beach
Le Boeuf, Randall J.: (F) Member Masters Lodge, No. 5, 1900, Albany, NY
Le Brun, Louis : (F) Member Masters Lodge, No. 5, 1900, Albany, NY
Le Fevre, Claude B.: (F) Member Masters Lodge, No. 5, 1900, Albany, NY
Leach, Hosea K.: (F) Member Temple Lodge, No. 14, 1900, Albany, NY, (CEN) 1880, 7th Ward, Albany Albany Co., NY, Listed with Edwin Leach, 55, Teamster, Catherine, 56, Hosea, 34, Painter, George, 19, Teamster
Leavitt, J. M.: (F) Member Sons of New England, New England Society of the City of Brooklyn, 1890, (CMTS)*"Brooklyn Eagle,"* Dec. 21, 1890, 11th Annual Dinner, Attendees
Leavitt, Joseph: (F) Member Arcana Lodge, No. 246, F. & A. M., 1934, New York, NY, (JD) Apr. 2, 1923
Leavitt, Saul M.: (F) Member Shakespeare Lodge, No. 750, F. & A. M., Aug. 1, 1956, New York City, NY, (Raised) 1947, (RES) Brooklyn
Leckie, Miss Florence: (F) Member Mispah Circle, 1888, Brooklyn, (I) *"Brooklyn Eagle,"* Dec. 12, 1888. Mentioned in an article about a fair raising funds for a Home for the Blind
Lederer, C.: (F) Member Herber Lodge, No. 698, 1898, F. & A. M., New York, NY, Greenpoint area, (RES) California
Lederer, Mortimer: (F) Member Shakespeare Lodge, No. 750, F. & A. M., Aug. 1, 1956, New York City, NY, (Raised) 1919, Life Member

Lederkramer, Harry: (F) Member Arcana Lodge, No. 246, F. & A. M., 1934, New York, NY, (JD) Jan. 21, 1924

Lee, F. R.: (F) Member Brooklyn Revenue Reform Club, 1886, (I)*"Brooklyn Eagle,"* Jan. ,27 1886, Attendees at a dinner

Lee, J.: (F) Member Long Island Lodge, No. 382, F. &. A. M., 1874, NY

Leeds, Monroe: (F) Member Shakespeare Lodge, No. 750, F. & A. M., Aug. 1, 1956, New York City, NY, (Raised) 1926, Life Member, (RES) Lynbrook

LeFevre, Arthur N.: (F) Member Temple Lodge, No. 14, 1900, Albany, NY

LeFevre, DeWitt C.: (F) Member Lowville Lodge No. 134, F. & A. M., 1929, Lowville, NY, (CO) Lewis, (JD) Nov. 18, 1927

LeFevre, Harold M. S.: (F) Member Lowville Lodge No. 134, F. & A. M., 1929, Lowville, NY, (CO) Lewis, (JD) Feb. 19, 1926

LeFevre, Howard I.: (F) Member Lowville Lodge No. 134, F. & A. M., 1929, Lowville, NY, (CO) Lewis, (JD) Jun. 1, 1926

LeFevre, Sherwood: (F) Member Temple Lodge, No. 14, 1900, Albany, NY

Leff, Harold A.: (F) Member Shakespeare Lodge, No. 750, F. & A. M., Aug. 1, 1956, New York City, NY, (Raised) 1946, (RES) Jackson Heights

Leff, Hilton A.: (F) Member Shakespeare Lodge, No. 750, F. & A. M., Aug. 1, 1956, New York City, NY, (Raised) 1931, Life Member, (RES) Norwalk

Leffler, Henry: (F) Member Arcana Lodge, No. 246, F. & A. M., 1934, New York, NY, (JD) Oct. 11, 1927

Leffler, Otto: (F) Member Arcana Lodge, No. 246, F. & A. M., 1934, New York, NY, (JD) May 19, 1924

Lehing, Wm. F.: (F) Member Herber Lodge, No. 698,1898, F. & A. M., New York, NY, Greenpoint area, (RES) New York City

Lehnert, A.: (F) Member Herber Lodge, No. 698,1898, F. & A. M., New York, NY, Greenpoint area, (RES) New York City

Lehr, Benjamin: (F) Member Shakespeare Lodge, No. 750, F. & A. M., Aug. 1, 1956, New York City, NY, (Raised) 1923

Lehr, George M.: (F) Member Shakespeare Lodge, No. 750, F. & A. M., Aug. 1, 1956, New York City, NY, (Raised) 1953, (RES) Rosyln Heights

Lehr, Harry: (F) Member Shakespeare Lodge, No. 750, F. & A. M., Aug. 1, 1956, New York City, NY, (Raised) 1923, Life Member

Lehr, Lewis: (F) Member Shakespeare Lodge, No. 750, F. & A. M., Aug. 1, 1956, New York City, NY, (Raised) 1953, (RES) Rosyln Heights

Leibfried, J.: (F) Member Herber Lodge, No. 698,1898, F. & A. M., New York, NY, Greenpoint area, (RES) New York City

Leidesdorf, Arthur D.: (F) Member Shakespeare Lodge, No. 750,

F. & A. M., Aug. 1, 1956, New York City, NY, (Raised) 1946, (RES) Jackson Heights

Leiter, Hazel: (F) Member Hope Rebekah Lodge No. 10, 1949-1950, Brockport, NY, (CO) Monroe, (CMTS) Sick Committee

Leland, Charles E.: (F) Member Grand Council of the Princes of Jerusalem, 1882, Albany, NY

Leland, Charles E.: (F) Member Ineffable and Sublime Grand Lodge of Perfection, 1882, Albany, NY

Leland, Charles E.: (F) Member Masters Lodge, No. 5, 1900, Albany, NY

Lenkowsky, Nathan: (F) Member Arcana Lodge, No. 246, F. & A. M., 1934, New York, NY, (JD) Apr. 2, 1923

Lentz, George E.: (F) Member Arcana Lodge, No. 246, F. & A. M., 1934, New York, NY, (JD) Feb. 8, 1927

Leonard, Gardner C.: (F) Member Masters Lodge, No. 5, 1900, Albany, NY

Leonard, Jesse Hoyt: (F) Member Temple Lodge, No. 14, 1900, Albany, NY

Leonard, Stephen: (F) Member Lewis County Bible Society, 1812, Charter Officers, (CMTS) Treasurer

Leonard, William B.: (F) Member Sons of New England, New England Society of the City of Brooklyn, 1887, (CMTS) *"Brooklyn Eagle,"* Dec. 22, 1887, Annual Dinner, Attendees

Leonforte, Andrew W.: (F) Member Arcana Lodge, No. 246, F. & A. M., 1934, New York, NY, (JD) Apr. 2, 1923

Lerman, Charles: (F) Member Shakespeare Lodge, No. 750, F. & A. M., Aug. 1, 1956, New York City, NY, (Raised) 1918, Life Member

Leserman, Jr., Philip: (F) Member Society of American Magicians, Apr., 1931, New York, (RES) New York City

Leslie, Harry W.: (F) Member Temple Lodge, No. 14, 1900, Albany, NY

Leverich, J. D.: (F) Member Long Island Lodge, No. 382, F. &. A. M., 1874, NY

Levin, David: (F) Member Arcana Lodge, No. 246, F. & A. M., 1934, New York, NY, (JD) Jun. 28, 1927

Levin, Mitchell J.: (F) Member Shakespeare Lodge, No. 750, F. & A. M., Aug. 1, 1956, New York City, NY, (Raised) 1924, Life Member

Levin, Paul: (F) Member Shakespeare Lodge, No. 750, F. & A. M., Aug. 1, 1956, New York City, NY, (Raised) 1924, Life Member

Levine, Abram: (F) Member Arcana Lodge, No. 246, F. & A. M., 1934, New York, NY, (JD) May 19, 1924

Levine, Abram H.: (F) Member Arcana Lodge, No. 246, F. & A. M., 1934, New York, NY, (JD) Jan. 19, 1920

Levine, David: (F) Member Arcana Lodge, No. 246, F. & A. M., 1934, New York, NY, (JD) Dec. 5, 1921

Levine, Harry G.: (F) Member Shakespeare Lodge, No. 750, F. & A. M., Aug. 1, 1956, New York City, NY, (Raised) 1918, Life Member

Levine, Julius: (F) Member Shakespeare Lodge, No. 750, F. & A. M., Aug. 1, 1956, New York City, NY, (Raised) 1909, Life Member, (RES) Richmond Hill

Levings, Amos W.: (F) Member Temple Lodge, No. 14, 1900, Albany, NY

Levinson, David: (F) Member Shakespeare Lodge, No. 750, F. & A. M., Aug. 1, 1956, New York City, NY, (Raised) 1954

Levinson, Samuel: (F) Member Arcana Lodge, No. 246, F. & A. M., 1934, New York, NY, (JS) Mar. 1, 1909, Life Member

Levy, Bernard: (F) Member Arcana Lodge, No. 246, F. & A. M., 1934, New York, NY, (JD) Mar. 15, 1912

Levy, Bernard: (F) Member Shakespeare Lodge, No. 750, F. & A. M., Aug. 1, 1956, New York City, NY, (Raised) 1956

Levy, C.: (F) Member Long Island Lodge, No. 382, F. &. A. M., 1874, NY

Levy, Chas.: (F) Member Herber Lodge, No. 698,1898, F. & A. M., New York, NY, Greenpoint area, (RES) New York City

Levy, David D.: (F) Member Shakespeare Lodge, No. 750, F. & A. M., Aug. 1, 1956, New York City, NY, (Raised) 1945, (RES) Mt. Vernon

Levy, Edward H.: (F) Member Arcana Lodge, No. 246, F. & A. M., 1934, New York, NY, (JD) Apr. 15, 1912

Levy, M.: (F) Member Long Island Lodge, No. 382, F. &. A. M., 1874, NY

Levy, Marvin: (F) Member Shakespeare Lodge, No. 750, F. & A. M., Aug. 1, 1956, New York City, NY, (Raised) 1956

Levy, Norman: (F) Member Shakespeare Lodge, No. 750, F. & A. M., Aug. 1, 1956, New York City, NY, (Raised) 1949, (RES) Flushing

Levy, Stephen H.: (F) Member Shakespeare Lodge, No. 750, F. & A. M., Aug. 1, 1956, New York City, NY, (Raised) 1939

Lewald, Siegfried: (F) Member Shakespeare Lodge, No. 750, F. & A. M., Aug. 1, 1956, New York City, NY, (Raised) 1912, Life

Lewis, Daniel F.: (F) Member Sons of New England, New England Society of the City of Brooklyn, 1890, (CMTS) *"Brooklyn Eagle,"* Dec. 21, 1890, 11th Annual Dinner, Attendees

Lewis, Isadore: (F) Member Mount Vernon Lodge, No. 3, 1900, Albany, NY

Lewis, L.: (F) Member Long Island Lodge, No. 382, F. &. A. M., 1874, NY

Lewis, L. A.: (F) Member Long Island Lodge, No. 382, F. &. A. M., 1874, NY

Lewis, Mrs. Hannah J.: (F) Member First District Suffolk, Adah Chapter. No. 52, 1923, Northport, NY, (CMTS) Secretary, (RES) Northport

Lewis, Philip A.: (F) Member Lowville Lodge No. 134, F. & A. M., 1929, Lowville, NY, (CO) Lewis, (JD) Jun. 30, 1916

Lewis, Philip A.: (F) Member Lowville Chapter No. 223, R. A. M.,

1929, Lowville, NY, (CO) Lewis, (JD) May 10, 1921
Lewis, T.: (F) Member Long Island Lodge, No. 382, F. &. A. M., 1874, NY
Lewis, William A.: (F) Member Temple Lodge, No. 14, 1900, Albany, NY
Lewitz, Oscar: (F) Member Shakespeare Lodge, No. 750, F. & A. M., Aug. 1, 1956, New York City, NY, (Raised) 1953, (RES) Brooklyn
Lewy, M. Julius: (F) Member Shakespeare Lodge, No. 750, F. & A. M., Aug. 1, 1956, New York City, NY, (Raised) 1921, Life Member
Lewy, Morris L.: (F) Member Shakespeare Lodge, No. 750, F. & A. M., Aug. 1, 1956, New York City, NY, (Raised) 1923, Life Member, (RES) Cedarhurst
Leyrer, Ralph G.: (F) Member First Suffolk District, Meridan Chapter, No. 336, 1923, Islip, NY, (CMTS) Patron, (RES) Bay Shore, Long Island
Libby, Clarence E.: (F) Member Lowville Lodge No. 134, F. & A. M., 1929, Lowville, NY, (CO) Lewis, (JD) Nov. 18, 1927
Liberman, Jacob I.: (F) Member Shakespeare Lodge, No. 750, F. & A. M., Aug. 1, 1956, New York City, NY, (Raised) 1953, (RES) Jersey City
Lichtenstein, Isidor: (F) Member Shakespeare Lodge, No. 750, F. & A. M., Aug. 1, 1956, New York City, NY, (Raised) 1923, Life Member
Lichtenstein, Meyer L.: (F) Member Shakespeare Lodge, No. 750, F. & A. M., Aug. 1, 1956, New York City, NY, (Raised) 1931, Life Member, (RES) Brooklyn
Lieberman, Solomon: (F) Member Arcana Lodge, No. 246, F. & A. M., 1934, New York, NY, (JD) Mar. 9, 1926
Liebmann, Herman: (F) Member Brooklyn Revenue Reform Club, 1886, (I) *"Brooklyn Eagle,"* Jan. ,27 1886, Attendees at a dinner, (B) Jul. 20, 1871, (BP) Brooklyn, Kings Co., NY, (PRTS) Charles Liebmann and Sophia Beavers
Liebmann, Louis: (F) Member Brooklyn Revenue Reform Club, 1886, (I) *"Brooklyn Eagle,"* Jan. ,27 1886, Attendees at a dinner
Lifschey, Samuel: (F) Member Shakespeare Lodge, No. 750, F. & A. M., Aug. 1, 1956, New York City, NY, (Raised) 1917, Life Member, (RES) Philadelphia
Lifsey, Oscar: (F) Member Shakespeare Lodge, No. 750, F. & A. M., Aug. 1, 1956, New York City, NY, (Raised) 1924, Life Member, (RES) Brooklyn
Linaberry, Harry B.: (F) Member Society of American Magicians, Apr., 1931, New York, (RES) New York City
Lincoln, William: (F) Member Mount Vernon Lodge, No. 3, 1900, Albany, NY
Linder, Nicholas C.: (F) Member Temple Lodge, No. 14, 1900, Albany, NY

Lindsay, J. Hally: (F) Member Temple Lodge, No. 14, 1900, Albany, NY

Ling, Edward C.: (F) Member Lowville Lodge No. 134, F. & A. M., 1929, Lowville, NY, (CO) Lewis, (JD) Dec. 6, 1918, (B) Dec. 28, 1883, (BP) Lowville, Lewis Co., NY, (PRTS) Walter Ling and Helen Rice, (MD) Nov. 17, 1905, (Spouse) Maud Tiffany

Linn, George C.: (F) Member Shakespeare Lodge, No. 750, F. & A. M., Aug. 1, 1956, New York City, NY, (Raised) 1945, (RES) Mt. Vernon

Linstruth, Charles A.: (F) Member Lowville Lodge No. 134, F. & A. M., 1929, Lowville, NY, (CO) Lewis, (JD) Jun. 20, 1924

Linstruth, Glen F.: (F) Member Lowville Lodge No. 134, F. & A. M., 1929, Lowville, NY, (CO) Lewis, (JD) Feb. 1, 1924

Linto, Frank P.: (F) Member Friendly Sons of St. Patrick,1893, Brooklyn, (CMTS)*"Brooklyn Eagle,"* May 18,1893, Article regarding the election of Andrew T. Sullivan as postmaster. In the article it mentioned that there were only 50 members in this Society., Guest. It is unknown if a member of the Society. Assistant District Attorney

Lipman, Jacob: (F) Member Arcana Lodge, No. 246, F. & A. M., 1934, New York, NY, (JD) Nov. 19, 1906, Life Member

Lippincott, Wilmot: (F) Member Society of American Magicians, Apr., 1931, New York, (RES) New York City

Liss, Bernard: (F) Member Shakespeare Lodge, No. 750, F. & A. M., Aug. 1, 1956, New York City, NY, (Raised) 1956

Liss, Carl: (F) Member Shakespeare Lodge, No. 750, F. & A. M., Aug. 1, 1956, New York City, NY, (Raised) 1953, (RES) Flushing

Liss, Joseph M.: (F) Member Shakespeare Lodge, No. 750, F. & A. M., Aug. 1, 1956, New York City, NY, (Raised) 1954, (RES) West Englewood

Liss, Meyer C.: (F) Member Shakespeare Lodge, No. 750, F. & A. M., Aug. 1, 1956, New York City, NY, (Raised) 1946, (RES) Teaneck

Litchfield, E. H.: (F) Member Sons of New England, New England Society of the City of Brooklyn, 1887, (CMTS)*"Brooklyn Eagle,"* Dec. 22, 1887, Annual Dinner, Attendees

Litchult, W. H.: (F) Member Long Island Lodge, No. 382, F. &. A. M., 1874, NY

Little, Fred H.: (F) Member Society of American Magicians, Apr., 1931, New York, (RES) Yonkers, NY

Little, George I.: (F) Member Lowville Lodge No. 134, F. & A. M., 1929, Lowville, NY, (CO) Lewis, (JD) May 14, 1928

Littlefield, G. Oliver: (F) Member Lowville Chapter No. 223, R. A. M., 1929, Lowville, NY, (CO) Lewis, (JD) May 10, 1921

Littlefield, Henry C.: (F) Member Albany Conclave, No. 8, Red Cross of Constantine, 1882, Albany, NY

Littlefield, Henry C.: (F) Member Grand Council of the Princes of

Jerusalem, 1882, Albany, NY
Littlefield, Henry C.: (F) Member Ineffable and Sublime Grand Lodge of Perfection, 1882, Albany, NY
Littlefield, Henry C.: (F) Member Masters Lodge, No. 5, 1900, Albany, NY, (PRTS) Dennis C. Littlefield and Sarah Jane Brown
Littman, Samuel: (F) Member Shakespeare Lodge, No. 750, F. & A. M., Aug. 1, 1956, New York City, NY, (Raised) 1942, (RES) Brooklyn
Livingston, Anson E.: (F) Member Lowville Lodge No. 134, F. & A. M., 1929, Lowville, NY, (CO) Lewis, (JD) Jan. 15, 1926
Livingston, John: (F) Member Murray Lodge, No. 380, F. & A. M., 1906, Holley, Orleans, Co., NY, (CMTS) Past Master , (CEN) 1880, Holley, Oreleans Co., NY, 38, Carriage Maker, Mary 36, Francis, 13, Minnie, 12, Joseph, 10, Kate, 8, Julia, 4, Mary Miller, 59, Mother-in-law
Lloyd, D.: (F) Member Long Island Lodge, No. 382, F. &. A. M., 1874, NY
Lloyd, William G.: (F) Member Grand Council of the Princes of Jerusalem, 1882, Albany, NY
Lloyd, William G.: (F) Member Ineffable and Sublime Grand Lodge of Perfection, 1882, Albany, NY
Lloyd, William L.: (F) Member Mount Vernon Lodge, No. 3, 1900, Albany, NY, (CMTS) Life Member
Lobenstein, J.: (F) Member Herber Lodge, No. 698,1898, F. & A. M., New York, NY, Greenpoint area, (RES) Brooklyn
Lochner, G. Emory: (F) Member Masters Lodge, No. 5, 1900, Albany, NY
Lochner, Jacob L.: (F) Member Mount Vernon Lodge, No. 3, 1900, Albany, NY
Lock, Charles O.: (F) Member Temple Lodge, No. 14, 1900, Albany, NY
Lock, James B.: (F) Member Mount Vernon Lodge, No. 3, 1900, Albany, NY
Lockwood, DeForest: (F) Member Murray Lodge, No. 380, F. & A. M., 1906, Holley, Orleans, Co., NY
Lockwood, H. C.: (F) Member Murray Lodge, No. 380, F. & A. M., 1906, Holley, Orleans, Co., NY
Loeb, Harry M.: (F) Member Arcana Lodge, No. 246, F. & A. M., 1934, New York, NY, (JD) Jun. 12, 1912
Loeb, James H.: (F) Member Arcana Lodge, No. 246, F. & A. M., 1934, New York, NY, (JD) Mar. 9, 1926
Loerner, Jacob: (F) Member Arcana Lodge, No. 246, F. & A. M., 1934, New York, NY, (JD) Nov. 19, 1923
Loesch, A.: (F) Member Herber Lodge, No. 698,1898, F. & A. M., New York, NY, Greenpoint area, (RES) New York City
Loewenthal, Herbert: (F) Member Shakespeare Lodge, No. 750, F. & A. M., Aug. 1, 1956, New York City, NY, (Raised) 1942
Loewer, Henry: (F) Member Arcana Lodge, No. 246, F. & A. M., 1934,

New York, NY, (JD) Mar, 18, 1901, Life Member
Loftus, Helen: (F) Member Hope Rebekah Lodge No. 10, 1949-1950, Brockport, NY, (CO) Monroe
Logan, Geoge: (F) Member Mount Vernon Lodge, No. 3, 1900, Albany, NY, (CEN) 1880, 17th Ward, Albany, Albany CO., NY, 30, Scotland, Carpenter, Mary 24, Jennie, 6, Rosanna, 4, Mary 3, Grace, 10 months
Logan, J.: (F) Member Long Island Lodge, No. 382, F. &. A. M., 1874, NY
Logan, Walter S.: (F) Member Sons of New England, New England Society of the City of Brooklyn, 1890, (CMTS) *"Brooklyn Eagle,"* Dec. 21, 1890, 11th Annual Dinner, Attendees
Loiselle, Guy L.: (F) Member Lowville Lodge No. 134, F. & A. M., 1929, Lowville, NY, (CO) Lewis, (JD) Jan. 16, 1920
Loiselle, Samuel A.: (F) Member Lowville Lodge No. 134, F. & A. M., 1929, Lowville, NY, (CO) Lewis, (JD) Nov. 5, 1897
Loiselle, Samuel A.: (F) Member Lowville Chapter No. 223, R. A. M., 1929, Lowville, NY, (CO) Lewis, (JD) Mar. 29, 1898
Lokietz, Moe: (F) Member Arcana Lodge, No. 246, F. & A. M., 1934, New York, NY, (JD) May 8, 1928
Lomax, John: (F) Member Mount Vernon Lodge, No. 3, 1900, Albany, NY, (CMTS) Past Master 1870
Long, Leroy Y.: (F) Member Temple Lodge, No. 14, 1900, Albany, NY
Long, Merril D.: (F) Member Lowville Lodge No. 134, F. & A. M., 1929, Lowville, NY, (CO) Lewis, (JD) Dec. 19, 1915
Loran, Frank: (F) Member Temple Lodge, No. 14, 1900, Albany, NY
Lord, Dr. Benjamin: (F) Member Brooklyn Dental Society, 1877, Brooklyn, NY, (CMTS) *"Brooklyn Eagle,"* Dec. 15, 1877. Celebration of 10th Anniversary. Society established Dec. 14, 1867, (CMTS) Present from New York, (CEN) 1880, Manhattan, NY, 60, Dentist, Julia, 45, CT, (B) Aug., 21, 1819, (Spouse1) Amanda Potter, (MD1) May 23, 1843, (Spouse2) Julia Fowler, (MD2) Dec. 6, 1871, (PRTS) Benjamin Lord, b. Jan. 1, 1785, d. May 27, 1854, md. Apr. 19, 1807, and Lurainda Child, b. May 27, 1789, d. Jan. 9, 1871. Benjamin Lord's Parents were John Lord and Abgail Gray
Lothridge, William E.: (F) Member Temple Lodge, No. 14, 1900, Albany, NY
Lott, A.: (F) Member Long Island Lodge, No. 382, F. &. A. M., 1874, NY
Lotterle, F. H.: (F) Member Herber Lodge, No. 698,1898, F. & A. M., New York, NY, Greenpoint area, (RES) New York City
Lotz, Wm. H.: (F) Member Herber Lodge, No. 698,1898, F. & A. M., New York, NY, Greenpoint area, (RES) Union Hill
Loucks, Lloyd A.: (F) Member Lowville Lodge No. 134, F. & A. M., 1929, Lowville, NY, (CO) Lewis, (JD) Apr. 16, 1920

Loud, John: (F) Member Denmark Ecclesiastical Society, Sep. 21, 1810, (CO) Lewis, (CMTS) Trustee, (Spouse) Susannah Shaw

Loughran, Michael: (F) Member Friendly Sons of St. Patrick,1893, Brooklyn, (CMTS)*"Brooklyn Eagle,"* May 18,1893, Article regarding the election of Andrew T. Sullivan as postmaster. In the article it mentioned that there were only 50 members in this Society., Guest. It is unknown if a member of the Society. Ex-Judge

Lovell, F. H.: (F) Member Sons of New England, New England Society of the City of Brooklyn, 1890, (CMTS)*"Brooklyn Eagle,"* Dec. 21, 1890, 11th Annual Dinner, Attendees

Low, Nathan S.: (F) Member Arcana Lodge, No. 246, F. & A. M., 1934, New York, NY, (JD) May 5, 1913

Lowell, S. V.: (F) Member Brooklyn Revenue Reform Club, 1886, (I)*"Brooklyn Eagle,"* Jan. ,27 1886, Attendees at a dinner

Lowenthal, Ferd. M.: (F) Member Arcana Lodge, No. 246, F. & A. M., 1934, New York, NY, (JD) Apr. 7, 1919

Lowrey, Charles J.: (F) Member Sons of New England, New England Society of the City of Brooklyn, 1887, (CMTS)*"Brooklyn Eagle,"* Dec. 22, 1887, Annual Dinner, Attendees

Lowrey, Seth: (F) Member Sons of New England, New England Society of the City of Brooklyn, 1887, (CMTS)*"Brooklyn Eagle,"* Dec. 22, 1887, Annual Dinner, Attendees

Lubben, J. H.: (F) Member Long Island Lodge, No. 382, F. &. A. M., 1874, NY

Lublin, Emil: (F) Member Arcana Lodge, No. 246, F. & A. M., 1934, New York, NY, (JD) Oct. 13, 1925

Luck, William H.: (F) Member Mount Vernon Lodge, No. 3, 1900, Albany, NY, (CEN) 1880, 6$^{th}$ Ward, Albany, Albany Co., NY, Listed with Christopher Luck, 37, Merchant, Philena S., 38, Charles H., 18, Printer, William H., 15, Store Clerk, Elizabeth Underhill, sister-in-law, 44, Edgar A. Hunt, 25, Store Clerk, Cousin.

Lucy, James: (F) Member Temple Lodge, No. 14, 1900, Albany, NY

Luddington, Charles H.: (F) Member Masters Lodge, No. 5, 1900, Albany, NY

Luddington, James S.: (F) Member Temple Lodge, No. 14, 1900, Albany, NY

Ludelof, Ida: (F) Member Mispah Circle, 1888, Brooklyn, (I) *"Brooklyn Eagle,"* Dec. 12, 1888. Mentioned in an article about a fair raising funds for a Home for the Blind

Ludington, Geo. W.: (F) Member Murray Lodge, No. 380, F. & A. M., 1906, Holley, Orleans, Co., NY

Ludington, Mrs. John : (F) Member Hope Rebekah Lodge No. 10, 1949-1950, Brockport, NY, (CO) Monroe

Ludington, V. D.: (F) Member Murray Lodge, No. 380, F. & A. M.,

1906, Holley, Orleans, Co., NY

Ludlum, Richard T.: (F) Member Temple Lodge, No. 14, 1900, Albany, NY

Luetke, O.: (F) Member Herber Lodge, No. 698,1898, F. & A. M., New York, NY, Greenpoint area, (RES) Brooklyn

Luhrs, F. H.: (F) Member Herber Lodge, No. 698,1898, F. & A. M., New York, NY, Greenpoint area, (RES) New York City

Luhrs, J. W.: (F) Member Herber Lodge, No. 698,1898, F. & A. M., New York, NY, Greenpoint area, (RES) New York City

Lusk, Jacob L.: (F) Member Arcana Lodge, No. 246, F. & A. M., 1934, New York, NY, (JD) Apr. 2, 1923

Lustig, Albert A.: (F) Member Arcana Lodge, No. 246, F. & A. M., 1934, New York, NY, (JD) Feb. 21, 1910

Luther, M.: (F) Member Long Island Lodge, No. 382, F. &. A. M., 1874, NY

Lydenburg, Harry M.: (F) Member Society of American Magicians, Apr., 1931, New York, (RES) New York City

Lyman, Myron M.: (F) Member Lowville Lodge No. 134, F. & A. M., 1929, Lowville, NY, (CO) Lewis, (JD) Apr. 30, 1920

Lyman, Varner M.: (F) Member Lowville Lodge No. 134, F. & A. M., 1929, Lowville, NY, (CO) Lewis, (JD) Jul. 2, 1920

Lyon, C. C.: (F) Member Long Island Lodge, No. 382, F. &. A. M., 1874, NY

Lyon, Richard B.: (F) Member Lowville Lodge No. 134, F. & A. M., 1929, Lowville, NY, (CO) Lewis, (JD) Jan. 18, 1929

Lyon, William H.: (F) Member Sons of New England, New England Society of the City of Brooklyn, 1890, (CMTS) *"Brooklyn Eagle,"* Dec. 21, 1890, 11th Annual Dinner, Attendees

Lyons, Edward: (F) Member Mount Vernon Lodge, No. 3, 1900, Albany, NY

Lyons, George R.: (I) *"Brooklyn Eagle,"* Dec. 7, 1896. 12th Annual Memorial Services, Plymouth Church, Brooklyn Lodge No. 22, B. F. O. Elks, Roll Call of the dead. Address made by Maryland Senator George L. Wellington. , (CMTS) Name called.

Lyons, Irving: (F) Member Arcana Lodge, No. 246, F. & A. M., 1934, New York, NY, (JD) Mar. 6, 1922

MacDonald, George H.: (F) Member Temple Lodge, No. 14, 1900, Albany, NY

MacDonald, Pirie (sic): (F) Member Temple Lodge, No. 14, 1900, Albany, NY

MacFadgen, J. L.: (F) Member Temple Lodge, No. 14, 1900, Albany, NY

Machalske, F. J.: (F) Member Herber Lodge, No. 698,1898, F. & A. M., New York, NY, Greenpoint area, (RES) New York City

MacHarg, Martin: (F) Member Masters Lodge, No. 5, 1900, Albany, NY

Mack, S. S.: (F) Member Arcana Lodge, No. 246, F. & A. M., 1934, New York, NY, (JD) Mar. 6, 1905, Life Member

MacKenzie, Arthur C.: (F) Member Lowville Chapter No. 223, R. A. M., 1929, Lowville, NY, (CO) Lewis, (JD) Nov. 27, 1928

Mackey, Samuel J.: (F) Member Temple Lodge, No. 14, 1900, Albany, NY

Maddock, Henry: (F) Member Brooklyn Revenue Reform Club, 1886, (I)*"Brooklyn Eagle,"* Jan. ,27 1886, Attendees at a dinner

Maddock, W. B.: (F) Member Brooklyn Revenue Reform Club, 1886, (I)*"Brooklyn Eagle,"* Jan. ,27 1886, Attendees at a dinner

Maddox, William S.: (F) Member Young Peoples' Society of Christian Endeavor, 1888, Brooklyn, (I) *"Brooklyn Eagle,"* Dec. 12, 1888. Article regarding Societies aiding churches., (CMTS) Helping Green Avenue Presbyterian Church, President

Magid, Harry: (F) Member Arcana Lodge, No. 246, F. & A. M., 1934, New York, NY, (JD) Sep. 20, 1920

Magid, Samuel: (F) Member Arcana Lodge, No. 246, F. & A. M., 1934, New York, NY, (JD) Sep. 20, 1920

Magner, Edward L. J.: (F) Member Society of American Magicians, Apr., 1931, New York, (RES) New York City

Magner, Thomas F.: (F) Member Friendly Sons of St. Patrick,1893, Brooklyn, (CMTS)*"Brooklyn Eagle,"* May 18,1893, Article regarding the election of Andrew T. Sullivan as postmaster. In the article it mentioned that there were only 50 members in this Society., Guest. It is unknown if a member of the Society.

Magoun, Edward P.: (F) Member Grand Council of the Princes of Jerusalem, 1882, Albany, NY

Magoun, Edward P.: (F) Member Ineffable and Sublime Grand Lodge of Perfection, 1882, Albany, NY

Magrath, George B.: (F) Member Friendly Sons of St. Patrick,1893, Brooklyn, (CMTS)*"Brooklyn Eagle,"* May 18,1893, Article regarding the election of Andrew T. Sullivan as postmaster. In the article it mentioned that there were only 50 members in this Society., Guest. It is unknown if a member of the Society.

Magrath, James W.: (F) Member Friendly Sons of St. Patrick,1893, Brooklyn, (CMTS)*"Brooklyn Eagle,"* May 18,1893, Article regarding the election of Andrew T. Sullivan as postmaster. In the article it mentioned that there were only 50 members in this Society., Guest. It is unknown if a member of the Society.

Magrath, Joseph S.: (F) Member Friendly Sons of St. Patrick,1893, Brooklyn, (CMTS)*"Brooklyn Eagle,"* May 18,1893, Article regarding the election of Andrew T. Sullivan as postmaster. In the article it mentioned that there were only 50 members in this Society., Guest. It is unknown if a member of the Society.

Maguire, John C.: (F) Member Sons of New England, New England Society of the City of Brooklyn, 1890, (CMTS)*"Brooklyn Eagle,"* Dec. 21, 1890, 11th Annual Dinner, Attendees, President of the St. Patrick Society

Maguire, Leon: (F) Member Society of American Magicians,
 Apr., 1931, New York, (RES) Brooklyn, NY
Maguire, Mrs. Charles J.: (F) Member Nativity Sewing Society, 1900,
 Brooklyn, (I) *"Brooklyn Eagle,"* Feb. 3, 1900. Article regarding
 raising money to buy clothing for the poor.
Mahler, Jacob P.: (F) Member Temple Lodge, No. 14, 1900, Albany, NY,
 (CEN) 1880, 13th Ward, Albany, Albany CO., NY, Listed with
 Julia Mahler, 44, widow, Rosa, 24, Jacob, 22, Bookkeeper, Kate,
 20, Louisa, 18, Lena, 16, John, 14
Mahnken, J. L.: (F) Member Long Island Lodge, No. 382, F. &. A. M.,
 1874, NY
Male, W. H.: (F) Member Sons of New England, New England
 Society of the City of Brooklyn, 1890, (CMTS)*"Brooklyn Eagle,"*
 Dec. 21, 1890, 11th Annual Dinner, Attendees
Mall, Charles: (F) Member Brooklyn Revenue Reform Club, 1886, (I)
 *"Brooklyn Eagle,"* Jan. ,27 1886, Attendees at a dinner , (CEN)
 Brooklyn, Kings CO., NY, 45, Book Binding, Barbara, 44,
 Charles, 10, Frank, 7.
Manchester, Charles N.: (F) Member Sons of New England, New England
 Society of the City of Brooklyn, 1890, (CMTS)*"Brooklyn Eagle,"*
 Dec. 21, 1890, 11th Annual Dinner, Attendees, (CEN) 1880,
 Brooklyn, Kings Co., NY, 34, Agent White Lead Co., Fannie, 32,
 Charles, 10.
Mandel, Benj. E.: (F) Member Arcana Lodge, No. 246, F. & A. M., 1934,
 New York, NY, (JD) Oct. 15, 1923
Mandel, Sampson D.: (F) Member Arcana Lodge, No. 246, F. & A. M.,
 1934, New York, NY, (JD) May 19, 1924
Mandeville, Robert P.: (F) Member Mount Vernon Lodge, No. 3, 1900,
 Albany, NY
Mandeville, William G.: (F) Member Lowville Lodge No. 134,
 F. & A. M., 1929, Lowville, NY, (CO) Lewis, (JD) Mar. 5, 1920
Mandlebaum, Milton R.: (F) Member Arcana Lodge, No. 246,
 F. & A. M., 1934, New York, NY, (JD) Jun. 16, 1919
Manly, S. F.: (F) Member Murray Lodge, No. 380, F. & A. M., 1906,
 Holley, Orleans, Co., NY
Mann, Joseph L.: (F) Member Murray Lodge, No. 380, F. & A. M.,
 1906, Holley, Orleans, Co., NY
Manning, David F.: (F) Member Friendly Sons of St. Patrick,1893,
 Brooklyn, (CMTS)*"Brooklyn Eagle,"* May 18,1893,
 Article regarding the election of Andrew T. Sullivan as postmaster.
 In the article it mentioned that there were only 50 members in this
 Society., Guest. It is unknown if a member of the Society.
Manning, G.: (F) Member Long Island Lodge, No. 382, F. &. A. M.,
 1874, NY
Manning, Henry S.: (F) Member Sons of New England, New England

Society of the City of Brooklyn, 1890, (CMTS) *"Brooklyn Eagle,"*
Dec. 21, 1890, 11th Annual Dinner, Attendees
Manning, James H.: (F) Member Temple Lodge, No. 14, 1900,
Albany, NY
Manning, Jerry C.: (F) Member Lowville Lodge No. 134, F. & A. M.,
1929, Lowville, NY, (CO) Lewis, (JD) Mar. 2, 1928
Manning, Mrs.: (F) Member Mispah Circle, 1888, Brooklyn, (I)
*"Brooklyn Eagle,"* Dec. 12, 1888. Mentioned in an article about a
fair raising funds for a Home for the Blind
Manning, Mrs. E. M.: (F) Member Mispah Circle, 1888, Brooklyn, (I)
*"Brooklyn Eagle,"* Dec. 12, 1888. Mentioned in an article about a
fair raising funds for a Home for the Blind
Manning, Samuel W.: (F) Member Masters Lodge, No. 5, 1900,
Albany, NY
Manning, William S.: (F) Member Masters Lodge, No. 5, 1900, Albany,
NY
Mansfield, ParkerR.: (F) Member Murray Lodge, No. 380, F. & A. M.,
1906, Holley, Orleans, Co., NY
Marchell, Charles: (F) Member Masters Lodge, No. 5, 1900, Albany, NY
Marcher, Ben: (F) Member Arcana Lodge, No. 246, F. & A. M., 1934,
New York, NY, (JD) Sep. 15, 1919
Marean, Josiah T.: (F) Member Sons of New England, New England
Society of the City of Brooklyn, 1890, (CMTS) *"Brooklyn Eagle,"*
Dec. 21, 1890, 11th Annual Dinner, Attendees
Margules, Sam.: (F) Member Society of American Magicians, Apr., 1931,
New York, (RES) Brooklyn, NY
Marion, Frank: (F) Member Arcana Lodge, No. 246, F. & A. M., 1934,
New York, NY, (JD) Jun. 10, 1930
Mark, Isidor: (F) Member Arcana Lodge, No. 246, F. & A. M., 1934,
New York, NY, (JD) Apr. 26, 1932
Markell, Mrs.: (F) Member Ladies' Home and Foreign Mission Society,
1888, Brooklyn, (I) *"Brooklyn Eagle,"* Dec. 12, 1888. Article
regarding Societies aiding churches., (CMTS) Helping Green
Avenue Presbyterian Church, Treasurer
Markham, Earl S.: (F) Member Lowville Chapter No. 223, R. A. M.,
1929, Lowville, NY, (CO) Lewis, (JD) Dec. 18, 1922
Markowitz, Osias: (F) Member Arcana Lodge, No. 246, F. & A. M., 1934,
New York, NY, (JD) Sep. 15, 1913
Marks, Frances: (F) Member Hope Rebekah Lodge No. 10, 1949-1950,
Brockport, NY, (CO) Monroe, (CMTS) Frances Marks
Marks, Joseph: (F) Member Arcana Lodge, No. 246, F. & A. M., 1934,
New York, NY, (JD) Oct. 13, 1925
Marks, Ted D.: (I) *"Brooklyn Eagle,"* Feb. 19, 1902. Funeral Services
at the Club House of the Brooklyn Lodge, No. 22, B. P. O. Elks for
Wm. H. West. Elk services were first then masonic services by
New York Lodge No. 330, F. A. & M., (CMTS) Made a floral gift.

Marlowe, Herman: (F) Member Arcana Lodge, No. 246, F. & A. M., 1934, New York, NY, (JD) Jun. 28, 1927'

Marr, Wm. M.: (F) Member Society of American Magicians, Apr., 1931, New York, (RES) Union City, NJ

Marriott, B.N.: (F) Member Clyde Lodge No. 341, F. A. M., 1905, Clyde, NY, (CO) Wayne, (CMTS) Past Master 1897, 1898, 1899

Marsh, John B.: (F) Member Grand Council of the Princes of Jerusalem, 1882, Albany, NY

Marsh, John B.: (F) Member Ineffable and Sublime Grand Lodge of Perfection, 1882, Albany, NY

Marsh, John B.: (F) Member Masters Lodge, No. 5, 1900, Albany, NY

Marshall, Chauncey: (F) Member Sons of New England, New England Society of the City of Brooklyn, 1890, (CMTS) *"Brooklyn Eagle,"* Dec. 21, 1890, 11th Annual Dinner, Attendees

Marshall, Chauncy: (F) Member Brooklyn Revenue Reform Club, 1886, (I) *"Brooklyn Eagle,"* Jan. ,27 1886, Attendees at a dinner

Marshall, Eleanor: (F) Member Hope Rebekah Lodge No. 10, 1949-1950, Brockport, NY, (CO) Monroe

Marshall, Mrs. Grace E.: (F) Member First Suffolk District, Meridan Chapter, No. 336, 1923, Islip, NY, (CMTS) Matron, (RES) Islip

Marshall, William: (F) Member Brooklyn Revenue Reform Club, 1886, (I) *"Brooklyn Eagle,"* Jan. ,27 1886, Attendees at a dinner

Martin, Charles A.: (F) Member Long Island Lodge, No. 382, F. &. A. M., 1874, NY

Martin, George W.: (F) Member Long Island Lodge, No. 382, F. &. A. M., 1874, NY

Martin, James B.: (F) Member Mount Vernon Lodge, No. 3, 1900, Albany, NY

Martin, John: (F) Member Ineffable and Sublime Grand Lodge of Perfection, 1882, Albany, NY

Martin, Kathleen: (F) Member Hope Rebekah Lodge No. 10, 1949-1950, Brockport, NY, (CO) Monroe, (CMTS) Left Escort

Martin, William L.: (F) Member Masters Lodge, No. 5, 1900, Albany, NY

Marvin, Charles D.: (F) Member Sons of New England, New England Society of the City of Brooklyn, 1890, (CMTS) *"Brooklyn Eagle,"* Dec. 21, 1890, 11th Annual Dinner, Attendees

Marvin, Jr., Selden E.: (F) Member Masters Lodge, No. 5, 1900, Albany, NY

Marwill, Harris: (F) Member Temple Lodge, No. 14, 1900, Albany, NY

Mascord, Brother: (F) Member Anglo Saxon Lodge No. 137, F. A. M., (CMTS) Meeting Notes, *"Brooklyn Eagle,"* Mar. 23, 1887, Presided at the meeting, of Altair Lodge No. 601

Mascord, E. W.: (F) Member Acanthus Lodge No. 719, F. A. M., (CMTS) Meeting Notes, *"Brooklyn Eagle,"* Mar. 13, 1887, of Altair

Mason, Frank J.: (F) Member Temple Lodge, No. 14, 1900, Albany, NY

Mason, G. L.: (F) Member Brooklyn Dental Society, 1877, Brooklyn, NY, (CMTS) *"Brooklyn Eagle,"* Dec. 15, 1877. Celebration of 10th Anniversary. Society established Dec. 14, 1867, (CMTS) Clinics Committee

Mason, H. B.: (F) Member Murray Lodge, No. 380, F. & A. M., 1906, Holley, Orleans, Co., NY

Mason, W. A.: (F) Member Murray Lodge, No. 380, F. & A. M., 1906, Holley, Orleans, Co., NY

Masten, Edson W.: (F) Member Temple Lodge, No. 14, 1900, Albany, NY

Matheson, Dr. A.: (F) Member Brooklyn Revenue Reform Club, 1886, (I)*"Brooklyn Eagle,"* Jan. ,27 1886, Attendees at a dinner

Mathews, John: (F) Member Long Island Lodge, No. 382, F. &. A. M., 1874, NY

Matik, George E.: (F) Member Arcana Lodge, No. 246, F. & A. M., 1934, New York, NY, (JD) Mar. 26, 1929

Matson, T. D.: (F) Member Murray Lodge, No. 380, F. & A. M., 1906, Holley, Orleans, Co., NY

Matt, Albert O.: (F) Member Society of American Magicians, Apr., 1931, New York, (RES) Glenridge, NJ

Mattson, Arthur W.: (F) Member Lowville Lodge No. 134, F. & A. M., 1929, Lowville, NY, (CO) Lewis, (JD) Sep. 2, 1912

Mattson, Arthur W.: (F) Member Lowville Chapter No. 223, R. A. M., 1929, Lowville, NY, (CO) Lewis, (JD) Mar. 17, 1914

Matty, Charles H.: (F) Member Lowville Chapter No. 223, R. A. M., 1929, Lowville, NY, (CO) Lewis, (JD) Mar. 19, 1907

Matty, Hoyt D.: (F) Member Lowville Chapter No. 223, R. A. M., 1929, Lowville, NY, (CO) Lewis, (JD) Mar. 19, 1907

Maune, Oswald: (F) Member Catholic Knights of Amercia, 1900, Brooklyn, (I) *"Brooklyn Eagle,"* Feb. 3, 1900. Meeting Notice., (CMTS) State President

Maus, Gerald E.: "(OBIT) *"The River Reporter,"* Aug. 23, 2001. Gerald E. Maus of Roscoe, a retired heavy equipment operator and lifelong area resident, died Wednesday, August 15, 2001 at home. He was 78. Son of the late John and Bessie Kinne Maus, he was born January 31, 1923 in Acidalia. He had been an employee of the Town of Rockland Highway Department and had served as the Town Highway Superintendent. He was a veteran of the US Army during World War II and was a member of the Harold Wood VFW Post #5911 in Roscoe and the Floyd Keener American Legion Post #315 in Roscoe. He was a member of the Karan's Hunting Club and a long time member of the NRA. Survivors include his wife, Mildred Soules Maus, at home; two daughters, Linda Buck of Roscoe and Betty Dole of Parksville; a son, Roy of Roscoe; a brother, Walter of Roscoe; a sister, Bernice Mann of Liberty; two sisters-in-law, Laverna of Roscoe and Rita of Jeffersonville; grandchildren, great-grandchildren; nieces and nephews. Services were held at the Harris Funeral Home in Roscoe. The Rev. Theo Lynne Hoffman officiated. Burial was in Riverview Cemetery in Roscoe.

Mauser, Chr.: (F) Member Herber Lodge, No. 698,1898, F. & A. M., New York, NY, Greenpoint area, (RES) Brooklyn, (Spouse) Mary Sceller

Mauser, J.: (F) Member Herber Lodge, No. 698,1898, F. & A. M., New York, NY, Greenpoint area, (RES) Brooklyn

Maxon, David N.: (I) *"Brooklyn Eagle,"* Feb. 19, 1902. Funeral Services at the Club House of the Brooklyn Lodge, No. 22, B. P. O. Elks for Wm. H. West. Elk services were first then masonic services by New York Lodge No. 330, F. A. & M., (CMTS) Member of Metropolitian Male Quartet. Member of the Elks

Maxwell, Blanche: (F) Member Mispah Circle, 1888, Brooklyn, (I) *"Brooklyn Eagle,"* Dec. 12, 1888. Mentioned in an article about a fair raising funds for a Home for the Blind

Maxwell, Eugene L.: (F) Member Sons of New England, New England Society of the City of Brooklyn, 1890, (CMTS) *"Brooklyn Eagle,"* Dec. 21, 1890, 11th Annual Dinner, Attendees

Maxwell, Henry W.: (F) Member Sons of New England, New England Society of the City of Brooklyn, 1890, (CMTS) *"Brooklyn Eagle,"* Dec. 21, 1890, 11th Annual Dinner, Attendees

May, A.: (F) Member Long Island Lodge, No. 382, F. &. A. M., 1874, NY

May, Daniel: (F) Member Arcana Lodge, No. 246, F. & A. M., 1934, New York, NY, (JD) Dec. 1, 1913

Mayell, Ten Broeck: (F) Member Temple Lodge, No. 14, 1900, Albany, NY, (CEN) 1880, 15$^{th}$ Ward, Albany, Albany Co., NY, Listed with Henry Mayell, rubber goods, 55, NJ, Elizabeth, 54, Ten Broeck, 28, Store Clerk, James H., 25, Clerk & Partner, Sarah E., 22, Bella T., 15

Mayer, Asher: (F) Member Arcana Lodge, No. 246, F. & A. M., 1934, New York, NY, (JD) May 20, 1907, Life Member

Mayer, J.: (F) Member Herber Lodge, No. 698,1898, F. & A. M., New York, NY, Greenpoint area, (RES) New York City

Mayer, Josh W.: (F) Member Society of American Magicians, Apr., 1931, New York, (RES) New York City

Mayer, Louis L.: (F) Member Arcana Lodge, No. 246, F. & A. M., 1934, New York, NY, (JD) Dec. 5, 1921

Mayer, Wm.: (F) Member Herber Lodge, No. 698,1898, F. & A. M., New York, NY, Greenpoint area, (RES) New York City

Mayer, Wm. C.: (F) Member Arcana Lodge, No. 246, F. & A. M., 1934, New York, NY, (JD) Apr 17, 1922

Mayette, Mrs.: (F) Member Ladies' Willing Aid Society, 1888, Brooklyn, (I) *"Brooklyn Eagle,"* Dec. 12, 1888. Article regarding

Societies aiding churches., (CMTS) Helping Green Avenue Presbyterian Church, President
Mayette, Mrs.: (F) Member Ladies' Home and Foreign Mission Society, 1888, Brooklyn, (I) *"Brooklyn Eagle,"* Dec. 12, 1888. Article regarding Societies aiding churches., (CMTS) Helping Green Avenue Presbyterian Church, President
Mayhew, David P.: (F) Member Educational Society of Lewis Co., NY, Nov. 14, 1845, (CMTS) President
Maylock, Philip: (F) Member Arcana Lodge, No. 246, F. & A. M., 1934, New York, NY, (JD) Jun. 9, 1925
Maynard, Rev. Dr. N.: (F) Member Sons of New England, New England Society of the City of Brooklyn, 1887, (CMTS) *"Brooklyn Eagle,"* Dec. 22, 1887, Annual Dinner, Attendees
McAdam, Graham: (F) Member Brooklyn Revenue Reform Club, 1886, (I) *"Brooklyn Eagle,"* Jan. ,27 1886, Attendees at a dinner, (MD) Jun. 20, 1872, (Spouse) Mary S. Cone, (CEN) 1880, $16^{th}$ Ward, $11^{th}$ District, Manhattan, NY, 32, Journalist, Mrs.McAdam, 30, Harry G., 7, Edw. W., 6, Florence, 3, Lucius R., 2, Rodge, 1 month
McAleary, Mrs. S.: (F) Member Ladies ' Willing Aid Society, 1888, Brooklyn, (I) *"Brooklyn Eagle,"* Dec. 12, 1888. Article regarding Societies aiding churches., (CMTS) Helping Green Avenue Presbyterian Church, Second Directress
McAleer, Miss D.: (F) Member Nativity Sewing Society, 1900, Brooklyn, (I) *"Brooklyn Eagle,"* Feb. 3, 1900. Article regarding raising money to buy clothing for the poor.
McAleer, Mrs. H.: (F) Member Nativity Sewing Society, 1900, Brooklyn, (I) *"Brooklyn Eagle,"* Feb. 3, 1900. Article regarding raising money to buy clothing for the poor.
McAlphine, William J.: (F) Member Grand Council of the Princes of Jerusalem, 1882, Albany, NY
McAlphine, William J.: (F) Member Ineffable and Sublime Grand Lodge Of Perfection, 1882, Albany, NY
McAvenue, Owen F.: (F) Member Temple Lodge, No. 14, 1900, Albany, NY
McCabe, John: (F) Member Arcana Lodge, No. 246, F. & A. M., 1934, New York, NY, (JD) Mar. 1, 1897, Life Member
McCabe, Mrs. D. F.: (F) Member Nativity Sewing Society, 1900, Brooklyn, (I) *"Brooklyn Eagle,"* Feb. 3, 1900. Article regarding raising money to buy clothing for the poor.
McCall, Henry S.: (F) Member Masters Lodge, No. 5, 1900, Albany, NY
McCammon, Edward: (F) Member Grand Council of the Princes of Jerusalem, 1882, Albany, NY
McCammon, Edward: (F) Member Ineffable and Sublime Grand Lodge of Perfection, 1882, Albany, NY

McCarren, Senator P. H. M.: (F) Member Friendly Sons of St. Patrick, 1893, Brooklyn, (CMTS)*"Brooklyn Eagle,"* May 18,1893, Article regarding the election of Andrew T. Sullivan as postmaster. In the article it mentioned that there were only 50 members in this Society., Guest. It is unknown if a member of the Society.

McCarthy, Rev. D. J.: (F) Member Nativity Sewing Society, 1900, Brooklyn, (I) *"Brooklyn Eagle,"* Feb. 3, 1900. Article regarding raising money to buy clothing for the poor.

McCaughan, James B.: (F) Member Mount Vernon Lodge, No. 3, 1900, Albany, NY

McCauley, Robert J.: (F) Member Temple Lodge, No. 14, 1900, Albany, NY

McChesney, George: (F) Member Acanthus Lodge No. 719, F. A. M., (CMTS) Meeting Notes, *"Brooklyn Eagle,"* Mar. 13, 1887, Acting Chaplain

McClellan, George W.: (F) Member Temple Lodge, No. 14, 1900, Albany, NY

McClure, James H.: (F) Member Masters Lodge, No. 5, 1900, Albany, NY

McCollister, John: (F) Member Lewis County Bible Society, 1812, Charter Officers, (CMTS) Committee

McConnell, Elyde E.: (F) Member Lowville Lodge No. 134, F. & A. M., 1929, Lowville, NY, (CO) Lewis, (JD) Apr. 4, 1924

McCooey, John H.: (F) Member Friendly Sons of St. Patrick, 1899, Brooklyn, (CMTS)*"Brooklyn Eagle,"* Dec. 9, 1899, Article Regarding the election of officers for 1900, (CMTS) Treasurer

McCormick, Carl C.: (F) Member Lowville Lodge No. 134, F. & A. M., 1929, Lowville, NY, (CO) Lewis, (JD) Apr. 19, 1904

McCormick, Carl C.: (F) Member Lowville Chapter No. 223, R. A. M., 1929, Lowville, NY, (CO) Lewis, (JD) Apr. 3, 1906

McCormick, M.: (F) Member Friendly Sons of St. Patrick,1893, Brooklyn, (CMTS)*"Brooklyn Eagle,"* May 18,1893, Article regarding the election of Andrew T. Sullivan as postmaster. In the article it mentioned that there were only 50 members in this Society., Guest. It is unknown if a member of the Society.

McCovey, John H.: (F) Member Friendly Sons of St. Patrick,1893, Brooklyn, (CMTS)*"Brooklyn Eagle,"* May 18,1893, Article regarding the election of Andrew T. Sullivan as postmaster. In the article it mentioned that there were only 50 members in this Society., Guest. It is unknown if a member of the Society.

McCrea, James: (F) Member Long Island Lodge, No. 382, F. &. A. M., 1874, NY

McCrillis, Chas. M.: (F) Member Murray Lodge, No. 380, F. & A. M., 1906, Holley, Orleans, Co., NY

McCrillis, M. M.: (F) Member Murray Lodge, No. 380, F. & A. M., 1906, Holley, Orleans, Co., NY

McCue, L. Rae: (F) Member Lowville Lodge No. 134, F. & A. M., 1929, Lowville, NY, (CO) Lewis, (JD) Jun. 4, 1915

McCumber, George A.: (F) Member Temple Lodge, No. 14, 1900, Albany, NY

McCune, Dr. W. E.: (F) Member The Plymouth League, 1888, Brooklyn, (I) *"Brooklyn Eagle,"* Dec. 12, 1888. Article regarding Societies aiding churches., (CMTS) Helping Plymouth Church, Secretary

McDonald, A.: (F) Member Long Island Lodge, No. 382, F. &. A. M., 1874, NY

McDonald, Albert G.: (F) Member Sons of New England, New England Society of the City of Brooklyn, 1887, (CMTS)*"Brooklyn Eagle,"* Dec. 22, 1887, Annual Dinner, Attendees

McDonald, Alton P.: (F) Member Temple Lodge, No. 14, 1900, Albany, NY

McDonald, Donald: (F) Member Masters Lodge, No. 5, 1900, Albany, NY

McDonald, George D.: (F) Member Grand Council of the Princes of Jerusalem, 1882, Albany, NY

McDonald, George D.: (F) Member Ineffable and Sublime Grand Lodge Of Perfection, 1882, Albany, NY

McDonald, Mrs. C.: (F) Member Mispah Circle, 1888, Brooklyn, (I) *"Brooklyn Eagle,"* Dec. 12, 1888. Mentioned in an article about a fair raising funds for a Home for the Blind

McDonald, William: (F) Member Temple Lodge, No. 14, 1900, Albany, NY

McDowell, Robert P.: (F) Member Mount Vernon Lodge, No. 3, 1900, Albany, NY

McElvane, James F.: (F) Member Friendly Sons of St. Patrick,1893, Brooklyn, (CMTS)*"Brooklyn Eagle,"* May 18,1893, Article regarding the election of Andrew T. Sullivan as postmaster. In the article it mentioned that there were only 50 members in this Society., Guest. It is unknown if a member of the Society.

McEntree, Charles S.: (F) Member Grand Council of the Princes of Jerusalem, 1882, Albany, NY

McEvoy, Philip J.: (F) Member Murray Lodge, No. 380, F. & A. M., 1906, Holley, Orleans, Co., NY

McEwan, Alex. M.: (F) Member Temple Lodge, No. 14, 1900, Albany, NY

McEwan, James B.: (F) Member Temple Lodge, No. 14, 1900, Albany, NY, (CMTS) Past Master 1892

McEwan, John P.: (F) Member Temple Lodge, No. 14, 1900, Albany, NY

McEwan, John S.: (F) Member Temple Lodge, No. 14, 1900, Albany, NY

McEwan, Walter: (F) Member Temple Lodge, No. 14, 1900,

Albany, NY, (CMTS) Life Member
McEwan, Walter S.: (F) Member Temple Lodge, No. 14, 1900, Albany, NY
McEwan, William: (F) Member Temple Lodge, No. 14, 1900, Albany, NY, (CMTS) Life Member
McEwan, Jr., John S.: (F) Member Temple Lodge, No. 14, 1900, Albany, NY
McFadden, Jas.: (F) Member Arcana Lodge, No. 246, F. & A. M., 1934, New York, NY, (JD) Oct. 2, 1905, Life Member
McFarlane, Mrs.: (F) Member Nativity Sewing Society, 1900, Brooklyn, (I) *"Brooklyn Eagle,"* Feb. 3, 1900. Article regarding raising money to buy clothing for the poor.
McGaughlin, Miss: (F) Member Nativity Sewing Society, 1900, Brooklyn, (I) *"Brooklyn Eagle,"* Feb. 3, 1900. Article regarding raising money to buy clothing for the poor.
McGee, James F.: (F) Member Friendly Sons of St. Patrick, 1899, Brooklyn, (CMTS)*"Brooklyn Eagle,"* Dec. 9, 1899, Article regarding the election of officers for 1900, (CMTS) Secretary
McGee, James F.: (F) Member Friendly Sons of St. Patrick,1893, Brooklyn, (CMTS)*"Brooklyn Eagle,"* May 18,1893, Article regarding the election of Andrew T. Sullivan as postmaster. In the article it mentioned that there were only 50 members in this Society., Guest. It is unknown if a member of the Society.
McGeorge, C. D.: (F) Member Home Circle, 1900, Brooklyn, (I) *"Brooklyn Eagle,"* Feb. 3, 1900. Meeting Notice., (CMTS) Leader
McGinnis, Alonzo: (F) Member Friendly Sons of St. Patrick,1893, Brooklyn, (CMTS)*"Brooklyn Eagle,"* May 18,1893, Article regarding the election of Andrew T. Sullivan as postmaster. In the article it mentioned that there were only 50 members in this Society., Guest. It is unknown if a member of the Society.
McGovern, Frank W.: (F) Member Lowville Lodge No. 134, F. & A. M., 1929, Lowville, NY, (CO) Lewis, (JD) Jul. 1, 1887
McGovern, Frank W.: (F) Member Lowville Chapter No. 223, R. A. M., 1929, Lowville, NY, (CO) Lewis, (JD) Apr. 26, 1889
McGowan, James: (I) *"Brooklyn Eagle,"* Dec. 7, 1896. 12th Annual Memorial Services, Plymouth Church, Brooklyn Lodge No. 22, B. F. O. Elks, Roll Call of the dead. Address made by Maryland Senator George L. Wellington. , (CMTS) Name called.
McGrath, Edward: (I) *"Brooklyn Eagle,"* Feb. 19, 1902. Funeral Services at the Club House of the Brooklyn Lodge, No. 22, B. P. O. Elks for Wm. H. West. Elk services were first then masonic services by New York Lodge No. 330, F. A. & M., (CMTS) Chaplain
McHaffle, Robert : (F) Member Temple Lodge, No. 14, 1900, Albany, NY
McIntyre, Archibald: (F) Member Temple Lodge, No. 14, 1900, Albany, NY

McIntyre, Charles A.: (F) Member Temple Lodge, No. 14, 1900, Albany, NY

McIntyre, Peter C.: (F) Member Temple Lodge, No. 14, 1900, Albany, NY

McKay, J. W.: (F) Member Long Island Lodge, No. 382, F. &. A. M., 1874, NY

McKean, Robt. A.: (F) Member Arcana Lodge, No. 246, F. & A. M., 1934, New York, NY, (JD) Dec. 1, 1913

McKelway, St. Clair: (F) Member Friendly Sons of St. Patrick,1893, Brooklyn, (CMTS)*"Brooklyn Eagle,"* May 18,1893, Article regarding the election of Andrew T. Sullivan as postmaster. In the article it mentioned that there were only 50 members in this Society., Guest. It is unknown if a member of the Society.

McKenzie, Arthur C.: (F) Member Lowville Lodge No. 134, F. & A. M., 1929, Lowville, NY, (CO) Lewis, (JD) Feb. 17, 1922

McKnight, Wm. G.: (F) Member Temple Lodge, No. 14, 1900, Albany, NY, (CMTS) Past Master 1872

McLaughlin, M. J.: (F) Member Friendly Sons of St. Patrick,1893, Brooklyn, (CMTS)*"Brooklyn Eagle,"* May 18,1893, Article regarding the election of Andrew T. Sullivan as postmaster. In the article it mentioned that there were only 50 members in this Society., Guest. It is unknown if a member of the Society.

McLean, F. St. George: (F) Member Masters Lodge, No. 5, 1900, Albany, NY

McLean, Hugh B.: (F) Member Masters Lodge, No. 5, 1900, Albany, NY

McMahon, J.: (F) Member Long Island Lodge, No. 382, F. &. A. M., 1874, NY

McManus, Charles: (I) *"Brooklyn Eagle,"* Dec. 7, 1896. 12th Annual Memorial Services, Plymouth Church, Brooklyn Lodge No. 22, B. F. O. Elks, Roll Call of the dead. Address made by Maryland Senator George L. Wellington. , (CMTS) Name called.

McNamee, John: (F) Member Friendly Sons of St. Patrick,1893, Brooklyn, (CMTS)*"Brooklyn Eagle,"* May 18,1893, Article regarding the election of Andrew T. Sullivan as postmaster. In the article it mentioned that there were only 50 members in this Society., Vice President

McNamee, Mrs. J. : (F) Member Nativity Sewing Society, 1900, Brooklyn, (I) *"Brooklyn Eagle,"* Feb. 3, 1900. Article regarding raising money to buy clothing for the poor.

McNear, Mrs. S. A.: (F) Member Ladies Auxilary to Foreign Missions, 1888, Brooklyn, (I) *"Brooklyn Eagle,"* Dec. 12, 1888. Article regarding Societies aiding churches., (CMTS) Helping St. John's Methodist Episcopal Church. President

McNear, Mrs. S. A.: (F) Member Ladies Social and Benvolent Circle, 1888, Brooklyn, (I) *"Brooklyn Eagle,"* Dec. 12, 1888. Article regarding Societies aiding churches., (CMTS) Helping St. John's Methodist Episcopal Church. President

McNear, Mrs. S. A.: (F) Member Young Ladies' Mission Circle, 1888, Brooklyn, (I) *"Brooklyn Eagle,"* Dec. 12, 1888. Article regarding Societies aiding churches., (CMTS) Helping St. John's Methodist Episcopal Church. President

McNickle, Robert: (F) Member Monticello Lodge, No. 532, F. & A. M., (CO) Sullivan Co., NY, (CMTS) Past Master 1891, 1898, 1901

McNulty, Peter: (F) Member Brooklyn Revenue Reform Club, 1886, (I)*"Brooklyn Eagle,"* Jan. ,27 1886, Attendees at a dinner

McQuade, Miss: (F) Member Nativity Sewing Society, 1900, Brooklyn, (I) *"Brooklyn Eagle,"* Feb. 3, 1900. Article regarding raising money to buy clothing for the poor.

McQuillan, Professor: (F) Member Brooklyn Dental Society, 1877, Brooklyn, NY, (CMTS) *"Brooklyn Eagle,"* Dec. 15, 1877. Celebration of 10th Anniversary. Society established Dec. 14, 1867, (CMTS) Present from Philadelphia

McQuire, Miss: (F) Member Nativity Sewing Society, 1900, Brooklyn, (I) *"Brooklyn Eagle,"* Feb. 3, 1900. Article regarding raising money to buy clothing for the poor.

McRae, Roderick: (F) Member Lowville Lodge No. 134, F. & A. M., 1929, Lowville, NY, (CO) Lewis, (JD) Jun. 10, 1892

McRae, Roderick: (F) Member Lowville Chapter No. 223, R. A. M., 1929, Lowville, NY, (CO) Lewis, (JD) Feb. 8, 1898

McSherry, Miss P.: (F) Member Nativity Sewing Society, 1900, Brooklyn, (I) *"Brooklyn Eagle,"* Feb. 3, 1900. Article regarding raising money to buy clothing for the poor.

Mead, Charles W.: (F) Member Temple Lodge, No. 14, 1900, Albany, NY, (CMTS) Past Master 1886

Mead, Charles W.: (F) Member Temple Lodge, No. 14, 1900, Albany, NY, (CMTS) Life Member

Mead, Eugene: (F) Member Temple Lodge, No. 14, 1900, Albany, NY

Mearns, John S.: (F) Member Monticello Lodge, No. 532, F. & A. M., (CO) Sullivan Co., NY, (CMTS) Past Master 1920

Meiggs, Mrs. C. H.: (F) Member Nativity Sewing Society, 1900, Brooklyn, (I) *"Brooklyn Eagle,"* Feb. 3, 1900. Article regarding raising money to buy clothing for the poor.

Meigs, Mrs.: (F) Member Nativity Sewing Society, 1900, Brooklyn, (I) *"Brooklyn Eagle,"* Feb. 3, 1900. Article regarding raising money to buy clothing for the poor.

Meinhardt, Elise L.: (F) Member Hope Rebekah Lodge No. 10, 1949-1950, Brockport, NY, (CO) Monroe

Meister, David S.: (F) Member Society of American Magicians, Apr., 1931, New York, (RES) New York City

Melick, James H.: (F) Member Temple Lodge, No. 14, 1900, Albany, NY

Mellins, David J.: (F) Member Arcana Lodge, No. 246,
F. & A. M., 1934, New York, NY, (JD) Jun. 8, 1926

Mencher, Harry: (F) Member Arcana Lodge, No. 246,
F. & A. M., 1934, New York, NY, (JD) Aug. 31, 1918

Mencher, Irving: (F) Member Arcana Lodge, No. 246,
F. & A. M., 1934, New York, NY, (JD) Feb. 2, 19125

Mendelsohn, Charles S.: (F) Member Society of American Magicians,
Apr., 1931, New York, (RES) New York City

Mensch, C. E.: (F) Member Brooklyn Dental Society, 1877, Brooklyn,
NY, (CMTS) *"Brooklyn Eagle,"* Dec. 15, 1877. Celebration of
10th Anniversary. Society established Dec. 14, 1867, (CMTS)
Librarian

Mensch, C. E.: (F) Member Brooklyn Dental Society, 1877, Brooklyn,
NY, (CMTS) *"Brooklyn Eagle,"* Dec. 15, 1877. Celebration of
10th Anniversary. Society established Dec. 14, 1867, (CMTS)
Ethics Committee

Mereness, Charles S.: (F) Member Lowville Lodge No. 134, F. & A. M.,
1929, Lowville, NY, (CO) Lewis, (CMTS) Past Master 1880, 1881

Meriam, Lee A.: (F) Member Young People's Association, 1888,
Brooklyn, (I) *"Brooklyn Eagle,"* Dec. 12, 1888. Article regarding
Societies aiding churches., (CMTS) Helping St. John's Methodist
Episcopal Church. President

Merkens, P. H.: (F) Member Herber Lodge, No. 698,1898, F. & A. M.,
New York, NY, Greenpoint area, (RES) New York City

Merrell, Edgar S. K.: (F) Member Lowville Lodge No. 134, F. & A. M.,
1929, Lowville, NY, (CO) Lewis, (JD) May 2, 1888

Merrell, Nathaniel E.: (F) Member Lowville Lodge No. 134, F. & A. M.,
1929, Lowville, NY, (CO) Lewis, (JD) Dec. 1, 1922

Merrihew, Mrs. Edna Adelle: (F) Member First District Suffolk, Adah
Chapter. No. 52, 1923, Northport, NY, (CMTS) Matron, (RES)
Northport

Merrihew, Rufus: (F) Member Mount Vernon Lodge, No. 3, 1900,
Albany, NY

Merrill, Cyrus S.: (F) Member Masters Lodge, No. 5, 1900,
Albany, NY

Merrill, George P.: (F) Member Sons of New England, New England
Society of the City of Brooklyn, 1890, (CMTS)*"Brooklyn Eagle,"*
Dec. 21, 1890, 11th Annual Dinner, Attendees

Merritt, William: (I) *"Brooklyn Eagle,"* Dec. 7, 1896. 12th Annual
Memorial Services, Plymouth Church, Brooklyn Lodge No. 22,
B. F. O. Elks, Roll Call of the dead. Address made by Maryland
Senator George L. Wellington. , (CMTS) Name called.

Mesick, Charles E.: (F) Member Mount Vernon Lodge, No. 3, 1900,
Albany, NY

Mestel, Aaron A.: (F) Member Arcana Lodge, No. 246, F. & A. M., 1934,
New York, NY, (JD) Oct. 21, 1918

Mestel, Nathan: (F) Member Arcana Lodge, No. 246, F. & A. M., 1934, New York, NY, (JD) Jun. 22, 1926

Metcalf, Edward B.: (F) Member Temple Lodge, No. 14, 1900, Albany, NY

Metzer, Barnett: (F) Member Arcana Lodge, No. 246, F. & A. M., 1934, New York, NY, (JD) Mar. 26, 1929

Metzger, August F.: (F) Member Lowville Lodge No. 134, F. & A. M., 1929, Lowville, NY, (CO) Lewis, (JD) Feb. 10, 1909

Meyenberg, William: (F) Member Society of American Magicians, Apr., 1931, New York, (RES) East Orange, NJ

Meyer, Alvin J.: (F) Member Arcana Lodge, No. 246, F. & A. M., 1934, New York, NY, (JD) Nov. 17, 1924

Meyer, C.: (F) Member Herber Lodge, No. 698,1898, F. & A. M., New York, NY, Greenpoint area, (RES) New York City

Meyer, Herbert: (F) Member Society of American Magicians, Apr., 1931, New York, (RES) Brooklyn, NY

Meyer, John: (F) Member Mount Vernon Lodge, No. 3, 1900, Albany, NY

Meyer, John E.: (F) Member Arcana Lodge, No. 246, F. & A. M., 1934, New York, NY, (JD) Apr. 4, 1904, Life Member

Meyer, Oscar A.: (F) Member Temple Lodge, No. 14, 1900, Albany, NY

Meyer, Otto L.: (F) Member Arcana Lodge, No. 246, F. & A. M., 1934, New York, NY, (JD) Nov. 17, 1924

Meyer, Samuel G.: (F) Member Arcana Lodge, No. 246, F. & A. M., 1934, New York, NY, (JD) Nov. 17, 1924

Meyerowitz, Benj.: (F) Member Arcana Lodge, No. 246, F. & A. M., 1934, New York, NY, (JD) Jun. 17, 1912

Meyers, W.: (F) Member Long Island Lodge, No. 382, F. &. A. M., 1874, NY

Meyerson, A. Irving: (F) Member Arcana Lodge, No. 246, F. & A. M., 1934, New York, NY, (JD) May 12, 1931

Michael, Anthony M.: (F) Member Mount Vernon Lodge, No. 3, 1900, Albany, NY

Michaelis, Gustavus: (F) Member Masters Lodge, No. 5, 1900, Albany, NY

Mickel, Augustus: (F) Member Temple Lodge, No. 14, 1900, Albany, NY

Micklejohn, George : (F) Member Arcana Lodge, No. 246, F. & A. M., 1934, New York, NY, (JD_ May 16, 1921

Midford, John C.: (F) Member Grand Council of the Princes of Jerusalem, 1882, Albany, NY

Miggael, Edward: (F) Member Grand Council of the Princes of Jerusalem, 1882, Albany, NY

Miggael, Edward: (F) Member Ineffable and Sublime Grand Lodge of Perfection, 1882, Albany, NY

Mihalyi, Stephen S.: (F) Member Lowville Chapter No. 223, R. A. M.,

1929, Lowville, NY, (CO) Lewis, (JD) May 10, 1921
Miles, William A.: (F) Member Grand Council of the Princes of
    Jerusalem, 1882, Albany, NY
Miles, William A/: (F) Member Ineffable and Sublime Grand Lodge of
    Perfection, 1882, Albany, NY
Miles, William T.: (F) Member Grand Council of the Princes of
    Jerusalem, 1882, Albany, NY
Millard, Everett F.: (F) Member Lowville Lodge No. 134, F. & A. M.,
    1929, Lowville, NY, (CO) Lewis, (JD) May 2, 1919
Millener, W. S.: (F) Member Murray Lodge, No. 380, F. & A. M., 1906,
    Holley, Orleans, Co., NY
Miller, A.: (F) Member Long Island Lodge, No. 382, F. &. A. M.,
    1874, NY
Miller, Albert T.: (F) Member Temple Lodge, No. 14, 1900, Albany, NY
Miller, Ernest L.: (F) Member Masters Lodge, No. 5, 1900, Albany, NY
Miller, Harry S.: (F) Member Masters Lodge, No. 5, 1900, Albany, NY
Miller, J. H.: (F) Member Long Island Lodge, No. 382, F. &. A. M.,
    1874, NY
Miller, John H.: (F) Member Temple Lodge, No. 14, 1900, Albany, NY
Miller, Leon S.: (F) Member Lowville Lodge No. 134, F. & A. M., 1929,
    Lowville, NY, (CO) Lewis, (JD) Mar. 30, 1906
Miller, Leon S.: (F) Member Lowville Chapter No. 223, R. A. M., 1929,
    Lowville, NY, (CO) Lewis, (JD) May 29, 1900
Miller, Lyman E.: (F) Member Mount Vernon Lodge, No. 3, 1900,
    Albany, NY
Miller, Mrs. J.: (F) Member Nativity Sewing Society, 1900, Brooklyn, (I)
    "*Brooklyn Eagle,*" Feb. 3, 1900. Article regarding raising money
    to buy clothing for the poor.
Miller, S.: (F) Member Long Island Lodge, No. 382, F. &. A. M., 1874,
    NY
Miller, Stanley B.: (F) Member Lowville Lodge No. 134, F. & A. M.,
    1929, Lowville, NY, (CO) Lewis, (JD) Mar. 3, 1916
Miller, Stanley B.: (F) Member Lowville Chapter No. 223, R. A. M.,
    1929, Lowville, NY, (CO) Lewis, (JD) Nov. 23, 1920
Miller, W. E.: (F) Member Long Island Lodge, No. 382, F. &. A. M.,
    1874, NY
Miller, William C.: (F) Member Masters Lodge, No. 5, 1900, Albany, NY
Milles, William T.: (F) Member Ineffable and Sublime Grand Lodge of
    Perfection, 1882, Albany, NY
Milligan, C. Harry: (F) Member Lowville Lodge No. 134, F. & A. M.,
    1929, Lowville, NY, (CO) Lewis, (JD) Oct. 16, 1914
Milligan, C. Harry: (F) Member Lowville Chapter No. 223, R. A. M.,
    1929, Lowville, NY, (CO) Lewis, (JD) Mar. 16, 1915
Milligan, William J.: (F) Member Lowville Lodge No. 134, F. & A. M.,
    1929, Lowville, NY, (CO) Lewis, (CMTS) Past Master 1896, 1897
Milligan, William J.: (F) Member Lowville Chapter No. 223, R. A. M.,

1929, Lowville, NY, (CO) Lewis, (JD) Oct. 4, 1892
Milligan, William J.: (F) Member Lowville Lodge No. 134, F. & A. M., 1929, Lowville, NY, (CO) Lewis, (JD) Mar. 14, 1890
Milliken, F. A.: (F) Member Murray Lodge, No. 380, F. & A. M., 1906, Holley, Orleans, Co., NY
Milliman, Frank: (F) Member Temple Lodge, No. 14, 1900, Albany, NY
Mills, Charles A.: (F) Member Lowville Lodge No. 134, F. & A. M., 1929, Lowville, NY, (CO) Lewis, (JD) May 7, 1886
Mills, Charles H.: (F) Member Temple Lodge, No. 14, 1900, Albany, NY
Mills, G. A.: (F) Member Brooklyn Dental Society, 1877, Brooklyn, NY, (CMTS) *"Brooklyn Eagle,"* Dec. 15, 1877. Celebration of 10th Anniversary. Society established Dec. 14, 1867, (CMTS) Ethics Committee
Mirick, Dr. H. G.: (F) Member Brooklyn Dental Society, 1877, Brooklyn, NY, (CMTS) *"Brooklyn Eagle,"* Dec. 15, 1877. Celebration of 10th Anniversary. Society established Dec. 14, 1867, (CMTS) Clinics Committee
Mix, Frederick L.: (F) Member Temple Lodge, No. 14, 1900, Albany, NY, (CMTS) Life Member
Mnione, Rev. Slyvester: (F) Member Friendly Sons of St. Patrick, 1899, Brooklyn, (CMTS) *"Brooklyn Eagle,"* Dec. 9, 1899, Article Regarding the election of officers for 1900, (CMTS) Chaplain
Moak, John M.: (F) Member Temple Lodge, No. 14, 1900, Albany, NY, (AKA) John Mosher Moak, (B) May 18, 1842, (BP) Westerlo, NY, (D) Jan. 14, 1911, (DP) Westerlo, NY, (PRTS) Henry Moak and Polly Stewart, (Spouse) Julie Wideman, (CEN) 1880, Westerlo, Albany Co., NY, 38, Farmer, Julia Ett, 40, Almeta, 17, Henry J., 15, Willie G., 13, Manly, 10, Bertha, 6, Levi, 3
Moffatt, R. B.: (F) Member Brooklyn Revenue Reform Club, 1886, (I) *"Brooklyn Eagle,"* Jan. ,27 1886, Attendees at a dinner
Moliari, J. A.: (F) Member Long Island Lodge, No. 382, F. &. A. M., 1874, NY
Molter, Wm.: (F) Member Herber Lodge, No. 698,1898, F. & A. M., New York, NY, Greenpoint area, (RES) New York City
Moody, Arthur E.: (F) Member Lowville Lodge No. 134, F. & A. M., 1929, Lowville, NY, (CO) Lewis, (JD) Dec. 30, 1921
Mooneles, A.: (F) Member Herber Lodge, No. 698,1898, F. & A. M., New York, NY, Greenpoint area, (RES) Brooklyn
Moore, C. W.: (F) Member Murray Lodge, No. 380, F. & A. M., 1906, Holley, Orleans, Co., NY
Moore, Charles A.: (F) Member Sons of New England, New England Society of the City of Brooklyn, 1890, (CMTS) *"Brooklyn Eagle,"* Dec. 21, 1890, 11th Annual Dinner, Attendees
Moore, Charles D.: (F) Member Lowville Lodge No. 134, F. & A. M.,

1929, Lowville, NY, (CO) Lewis, (CMTS) Past Master 1882, 1883, 1884, 1886

Moore, H.: (F) Member Long Island Lodge, No. 382, F. &. A. M., 1874, NY

Moore, H. B.: (F) Member Sons of New England, New England Society of the City of Brooklyn, 1890, (CMTS)*"Brooklyn Eagle,"* Dec. 21, 1890, 11th Annual Dinner, Attendees

Moore, Ira H.: (I) *"Brooklyn Eagle,"* Dec. 7, 1896. 12th Annual Memorial Services, Plymouth Church, Brooklyn Lodge No. 22, B. F. O. Elks, Roll Call of the dead. Address made by Maryland Senator George L. Wellington. , (CMTS) Name called.

Moore, J. Yale: (F) Member Lowville Lodge No. 134, F. & A. M., 1929, Lowville, NY, (CO) Lewis, (JD) Mar. 20, 1908

Moore, James N.: (F) Member Masters Lodge, No. 5, 1900, Albany, NY

Moore, LaverneG.: (F) Member Lowville Lodge No. 134, F. & A. M., 1929, Lowville, NY, (CO) Lewis, (JD) Nov. 17, 1916

Moore, Miss A.: (F) Member Nativity Sewing Society, 1900, Brooklyn, (I) *"Brooklyn Eagle,"* Feb. 3, 1900. Article regarding raising money to buy clothing for the poor.

Moore, Miss J. E.: (F) Member Mispah Circle, 1888, Brooklyn, (I) *"Brooklyn Eagle,"* Dec. 12, 1888. Mentioned in an article about a fair raising funds for a Home for the Blind

Moore, Mrs. Charles J.: (F) Member Nativity Sewing Society, 1900, Brooklyn, (I) *"Brooklyn Eagle,"* Feb. 3, 1900. Article regarding raising money to buy clothing for the poor.

Moore, Thomas S.: (F) Member Sons of New England, New England Society of the City of Brooklyn, 1890, (CMTS)*"Brooklyn Eagle,"* Dec. 21, 1890, 11th Annual Dinner, Attendees

Moore, Thomas S.: (F) Member Sons of New England, New England Society of the City of Brooklyn, 1887, (CMTS)*"Brooklyn Eagle,"* Dec. 22, 1887, Annual Dinner, Attendees

Moorehead, John: (F) Member Temple Lodge, No. 14, 1900, Albany, NY

Moquin, William C.: (F) Member Brooklyn Revenue Reform Club, 1886, (I)*"Brooklyn Eagle,"* Jan. ,27 1886, Attendees at a dinner

Moran, Miller B.: (F) Member Lowville Lodge No. 134, F. & A. M., 1929, Lowville, NY, (CO) Lewis, (JD) Apr. 22, 1921

Moran, Rev. M. J.: (F) Member Nativity Sewing Society, 1900, Brooklyn, (I) *"Brooklyn Eagle,"* Feb. 3, 1900. Article regarding raising money to buy clothing for the poor.

Moran, Rev. M. J.: (F) Member Nativity Sewing Society, 1900, Brooklyn, (I) *"Brooklyn Eagle,"* Feb. 3, 1900. Article regarding raising money to buy clothing for the poor.

Morange, J. W.: (F) Member Masters Lodge, No. 5, 1900, Albany, NY

Morange, James W.: (F) Member Grand Council of the Princes of Jerusalem, 1882, Albany, NY

Morange, James W.: (F) Member Ineffable and Sublime Grand Lodge of

Perfection, 1882, Albany, NY
Morgan, Charles A.: (F) Member Masters Lodge, No. 5, 1900, Albany, NY
Morgan, Herbert: (F) Member Lowville Chapter No. 223, R. A. M., 1929, Lowville, NY, (CO) Lewis, (JD) Oct. 27, 1920
Morgan, Otto G.: (F) Member Society of American Magicians, Apr., 1931, New York, (RES) Station, NY
Morgan, W. S.: (F) Member Mount Vernon Lodge, No. 3, 1900, Albany, NY
Morgan, Jr., James L.: (F) Member Sons of New England, New England Society of the City of Brooklyn, 1890, (CMTS) *"Brooklyn Eagle,"* Dec. 21, 1890, 11th Annual Dinner, Attendees
Morrill, John R.: (F) Member Temple Lodge, No. 14, 1900, Albany, NY
Morris, Edward H.: (F) Member Society of American Magicians, Apr., 1931, New York, (RES) New York City
Morris, Henry: (F) Member Grand Council of the Princes of Jerusalem, 1882, Albany, NY
Morris, Henry: (F) Member Ineffable and Sublime Grand Lodge of Perfection, 1882, Albany, NY
Morris, J.: (F) Member Long Island Lodge, No. 382, F. &. A. M., 1874, NY
Morris, Mrs.: (F) Member Nativity Sewing Society, 1900, Brooklyn, (I) *"Brooklyn Eagle,"* Feb. 3, 1900. Article regarding raising money to buy clothing for the poor.
Morris, T. C.: (F) Member Long Island Lodge, No. 382, F. &. A. M., 1874, NY
Morrison, James P.: (F) Member Arcana Lodge, No. 246, F. & A. M., 1934, New York, NY, (JD) Mar. 3, 1913
Morrison, W. A.: (F) Member Long Island Lodge, No. 382, F. &. A. M., 1874, NY
Morrison, William H.: (F) Member Lowville Lodge No. 134, F. & A. M., 1929, Lowville, NY, (CO) Lewis, (CMTS) Past Master 1887
Morrow, Emory L.: (F) Member Lowville Lodge No. 134, F. & A. M., 1929, Lowville, NY, (CO) Lewis, (JD) May 20, 1920
Morse, Daniel P.: (F) Member Sons of New England, New England Society of the City of Brooklyn, 1890, (CMTS) *"Brooklyn Eagle,"* Dec. 21, 1890, 11th Annual Dinner, Attendees
Morse, Fred B.: (F) Member Lowville Chapter No. 223, R. A. M., 1929, Lowville, NY, (CO) Lewis, (JD) Nov. 15, 1892
Morse, Fred B.: (F) Member Lowville Lodge No. 134, F. & A. M., 1929, Lowville, NY, (CO) Lewis, (JD) Mar. 25, 1892
Morse, R. G.: (F) Member Anglo Saxon Lodge No. 137, F. A. M., (CMTS) Meeting Notes, *"Brooklyn Eagle,"* Mar. 23, 1887, Predestrian at the meeting
Mortimer, M.D., W. Golden: (F) Member Society of American Magicians, Apr., 1931, New York, (RES) New York City

Morton, D. M.: (F) Member Murray Lodge, No. 380, F. & A. M., 1906, Holley, Orleans, Co., NY

Moschcowitz, M.D., Eli: (F) Member Society of American Magicians, Apr., 1931, New York, (RES) New York City

Moseley, Frank E.: (F) Member Temple Lodge, No. 14, 1900, Albany, NY

Moses, Leonard: (F) Member Arcana Lodge, No. 246, F. & A. M., 1934, New York, NY, (JD) Oct. 6, 1924

Moses, Nathan: (F) Member Arcana Lodge, No. 246, F. & A. M., 1934, New York, NY, (JD) Sep. 15, 1919

Moses, Wm. C.: (F) Member Arcana Lodge, No. 246, F. & A. M., 1934, New York, NY, (JD) Oct. 16, 1922

Mosher, Hattie: (F) Member Hope Rebekah Lodge No. 10, 1949-1950, Brockport, NY, (CO) Monroe

Moskovitz, A. Otto: (F) Member Arcana Lodge, No. 246, F. & A. M., 1934, New York, NY, (JD) Jan. 26, 1932

Moss, Abram B.: (F) Member Arcana Lodge, No. 246, F. & A. M., 1934, New York, NY, (JD) Dec. 1, 1919

Moston, George T.: (F) Member Temple Lodge, No. 14, 1900, Albany, NY

Mott, Thomas B.: (I) *"Brooklyn Eagle,"* Dec. 7, 1896. 12th Annual Memorial Services, Plymouth Church, Brooklyn Lodge No. 22, B. F. O. Elks, Roll Call of the dead. Address made by Maryland Senator George L. Wellington. , (CMTS) Name called.

Mowers, Gretchen: (F) Member Hope Rebekah Lodge No. 10, 1949-1950, Brockport, NY, (CO) Monroe, (CMTS) Inside Guardian

Moyer, J. William: (F) Member Lowville Chapter No. 223, R. A. M., 1929, Lowville, NY, (CO) Lewis, (JD) Jul. 19, 1904

Mudge, A. E.: (F) Member Sons of New England, New England Society of the City of Brooklyn, 1890, (CMTS)*"Brooklyn Eagle,"* Dec. 21, 1890, 11th Annual Dinner, Attendees

Mueller, A.: (F) Member Herber Lodge, No. 698,1898, F. & A. M., New York, NY, Greenpoint area, (RES) New York City

Mulholland, John: (F) Member Society of American Magicians, Apr., 1931, New York, (RES) New York City

Mull, Abram M.: (F) Member Washington Lodge, No. 85, 1900, Albany, NY, (CMTS) Past Members

Mull, Leonard M.: (F) Member Washington Lodge, No. 85, 1900, Albany, NY, (CMTS) Past Members

Mullaney, James F.: (F) Member Arcana Lodge, No. 246, F. & A. M., 1934, New York, NY, (JD) Oct. 4, 1907, Life Member

Mulledy, Miss: (F) Member Nativity Sewing Society, 1900, Brooklyn, (I) *"Brooklyn Eagle,"* Feb. 3, 1900. Article regarding raising money to buy clothing for the poor.

Mullen, George W.: (F) Member Lowville Lodge No. 134, F. & A. M., 1929, Lowville, NY, (CO) Lewis, (JD) May 1, 1925

Muller, Abraham: (F) Member Arcana Lodge, No. 246,
F. & A. M., 1934, New York, NY, (JD) Jun. 11, 1929

Muller, Charles: (F) Member Arcana Lodge, No. 246,
F. & A. M., 1934, New York, NY, (JD) May 18, 1908, Life Member

Mullin, Wade H.: (F) Member Lowville Lodge No. 134, F. & A. M., 1929, Lowville, NY, (CO) Lewis, (JD) Dec. 7, 1906

Mullings, J. B.: (F) Member Long Island Lodge, No. 382, F. &. A. M., 1874, NY

Mullins, John C.: (F) Member Star of Bethlem No. 322, F. A. M., 1900, Brooklyn, (I) *"Brooklyn Eagle,"* Feb. 3, 1900. Meeting Notice., (CMTS) Secretary

Munson, George S.: (F) Member Masters Lodge, No. 5, 1900, Albany, NY

Munson, Samuel L.: (F) Member Masters Lodge, No. 5, 1900, Albany, NY

Murdock, Rev. James: (F) Member Lewis County Bible Society, 1812, Charter Officers, (CMTS) President

Murkey, Mrs. R. : (F) Member Nativity Sewing Society, 1900, Brooklyn, (I) *"Brooklyn Eagle,"* Feb. 3, 1900. Article regarding raising money to buy clothing for the poor.

Murphey, John: (F) Member Friendly Sons of St. Patrick,1893, Brooklyn, (CMTS)*"Brooklyn Eagle,"* May 18,1893, Article regarding the election of Andrew T. Sullivan as postmaster. In the article it mentioned that there were only 50 members in this Society., Member of the Dinner Committee

Murphey, Mrs. C. O.: (F) Member Nativity Sewing Society, 1900, Brooklyn, (I) *"Brooklyn Eagle,"* Feb. 3, 1900. Article regarding raising money to buy clothing for the poor.

Murphey, Peter M.: (F) Member Grand Council of the Princes of Jerusalem, 1882, Albany, NY

Murphy, Henry C.: (F) Member St. Nicholas Society of Nassau Island, 1861, (CMTS)"Brooklyn Eag;e," Dec. 11, 1861, Article regarding the Anniversary Dinner, Guest, ex-minister to the Hague

Murphy, James B.: (F) Member Mount Vernon Lodge, No. 3, 1900, Albany, NY

Murphy, John D.: (F) Member Friendly Sons of St. Patrick, 1899, Brooklyn, (CMTS)*"Brooklyn Eagle,"* Dec. 9, 1899, Article Regarding the election of officers for 1900, (CMTS) Vice Present

Murphy, John F.: (F) Member Friendly Sons of St. Patrick,1893, Brooklyn, (CMTS)*"Brooklyn Eagle,"* May 18,1893, Article regarding the election of Andrew T. Sullivan as postmaster. In the article it mentioned that there were only 50 members in this Society., Guest It is unknown if a member of the Society.

Murphy, Patrick: (I) *"Brooklyn Eagle,"* Dec. 7, 1896. 12th Annual

Memorial Services, Plymouth Church, Brooklyn Lodge No. 22, B. F. O. Elks, Roll Call of the dead. Address made by Maryland Senator George L. Wellington. , (CMTS) Name called.

Murphy, Peter M.: (F) Member Ineffable and Sublime Grand Lodge of Perfection, 1882, Albany, NY

Murphy, Thomas D.: (F) Member Friendly Sons of St. Patrick,1893, Brooklyn, (CMTS)*"Brooklyn Eagle,"* May 18,1893, Article regarding the election of Andrew T. Sullivan as postmaster. In the article it mentioned that there were only 50 members in this Society., Secretary

Murphy, Thomas S.: (F) Member Temple Lodge, No. 14, 1900, Albany, NY

Murray, Clinton J.: (F) Member Lowville Lodge No. 134, F. & A. M., 1929, Lowville, NY, (CO) Lewis, (JD) Feb. 15, 1895

Mushlin, Chas.: (F) Member Arcana Lodge, No. 246, F. & A. M., 1934, New York, NY, (JD) Oct. 6, 1924

Mussey, J. Barows: (F) Member Society of American Magicians, Apr., 1931, New York, (RES) New York City

Mutari, Rosario: (F) Member Mount Vernon Lodge, No. 3, 1900, Albany, NY

Myers, Jr., John: (F) Member Mount Vernon Lodge, No. 3, 1900, Albany, NY

Nadell, H. Joseph: (F) Member Arcana Lodge, No. 246, F. & A. M., 1934, New York, NY, (JD) Mar. 28, 1933

Nadelstein, Adolph: (F) Member Arcana Lodge, No. 246, F. & A. M., 1934, New York, NY, (JD) Dec. 5, 1921

Naegeley, Jr., John: (F) Member Mount Vernon Lodge, No. 3, 1900, Albany, NY

Nagel, Charles: (F) Member Society of American Magicians, Apr., 1931, New York, (RES) New York City

Nash, V. W.: (F) Member Long Island Lodge, No. 382, F. &. A. M., 1874, NY

Nassu, Joseph: (F) Member Arcana Lodge, No. 246, F. & A. M., 1934, New York, NY, (JD) Jun. 17, 1918

Nathan, Philip : (I) *"Brooklyn Eagle,"* Dec. 7, 1896. 12th Annual Memorial Services, Plymouth Church, Brooklyn Lodge No. 22, B. F. O. Elks, Roll Call of the dead. Address made by Maryland Senator George L. Wellington. , (CMTS) Name called.

Naughton, J. W.: (F) Member Friendly Sons of St. Patrick,1893, Brooklyn, (CMTS)*"Brooklyn Eagle,"* May 18,1893, Article regarding the election of Andrew T. Sullivan as postmaster. In the article it mentioned that there were only 50 members in this Society., Guest. It is unknown if a member of the Society.

Naumer, F.: (F) Member Long Island Lodge, No. 382, F. &. A. M., 1874, NY

Needham, George J.: (F) Member Temple Lodge, No. 14, 1900,

Albany, NY
Neely, Herman: (F) Member Lexington Lodge, 310, F. A. & M., 1900, Brooklyn, (I) *"Brooklyn Eagle,"* Feb. 3, 1900. Meeting Notice., (CMTS) Junior Warden
Neely, Jr., David G.: (F) Member Lowville Lodge No. 134, F. & A. M., 1929, Lowville, NY, (CO) Lewis
Neff, Samuel J.: (F) Member Lowville Chapter No. 223, R. A. M., 1929, Lowville, NY, (CO) Lewis, (JD) Mar. 29, 1898
Nefsey, James: (F) Member Lowville Chapter No. 223, R. A. M., 1929, Lowville, NY, (CO) Lewis, (JD) Apr. 12, 1923
Nefsey, James E.: (F) Member Lowville Lodge No. 134, F. & A. M., 1929, Lowville, NY, (CO) Lewis, (JD) May 31, 1901
Nellis, William J.: (F) Member Masters Lodge, No. 5, 1900, Albany, NY
Nelson, Mark: (F) Member Arcana Lodge, No. 246, F. & A. M., 1934, New York, NY, (JD) May 18, 1908. Life Member
Nelson, Miss: (F) Member Nativity Sewing Society, 1900, Brooklyn, (I) *"Brooklyn Eagle,"* Feb. 3, 1900. Article regarding raising money to buy clothing for the poor.
Nelson, Ralph G.: (F) Member Arcana Lodge, No. 246, F. & A. M., 1934, New York, NY, (JD) Jun. 29, 1908, Life Member
Nelson, Jr., Thomas: (F) Member Sons of New England, New England Society of the City of Brooklyn, 1890, (CMTS)*"Brooklyn Eagle,"* Dec. 21, 1890, 11th Annual Dinner, Attendees
Nesmith, Jr., H. E.: (F) Member Brooklyn Revenue Reform Club, 1886, (I)*"Brooklyn Eagle,"* Jan. ,27 1886, Attendees at a dinner
Neson, Henry S.: (F) Member Temple Lodge, No. 14, 1900, Albany, NY
Neudorf, Jr., Frederick: (F) Member Masters Lodge, No. 5, 1900, Albany, NY
Nevins, Thomas E.: (F) Member Friendly Sons of St. Patrick,1893, Brooklyn, (CMTS)*"Brooklyn Eagle,"* May 18,1893, Article regarding the election of Andrew T. Sullivan as postmaster. In the article it mentioned that there were only 50 members in this Society., Guest. It is unknown if a member of the Society.
Newburger, Morton J.: (F) Member Society of American Magicians, Apr., 1931, New York, (RES) New York City
Newcomb, F. J.: (F) Member Long Island Lodge, No. 382, F. &. A. M., 1874, NY
Newcomb, Grant: (F) Member Washington Lodge, No. 85, 1900, Albany, NY, (CMTS) Past Members
Newell, John: (F) Member Temple Lodge, No. 14, 1900, Albany, NY
Newell, Nathaniel: (F) Member Foresters of America, Fort Greene No. 23, 1900, Brooklyn, (I) *"Brooklyn Eagle,"* Feb. 3, 1900. Meeting Notice., (CMTS) C. R.

Newins, C. M.: (I) *"Brooklyn Eagle,"* Dec. 7, 1896. 12th Annual Memorial Services, Plymouth Church, Brooklyn Lodge No. 22, B. F. O. Elks, Roll Call of the dead. Address made by Maryland Senator George L. Wellington. , (CMTS) Exalted Rulers. Opened the memorial services.

Newman, Charles: (F) Member Masters Lodge, No. 5, 1900, Albany, NY

Newman, Frederick W.: (F) Member Temple Lodge, No. 14, 1900, Albany, NY

Newton, Aaron L.: (F) Member Temple Lodge, No. 14, 1900, Albany, NY

Newton, H. G.: (F) Member Murray Lodge, No. 380, F. & A. M., 1906, Holley, Orleans, Co., NY

Newton, Henry A.: (F) Member Temple Lodge, No. 14, 1900, Albany, NY

Newton, Thomas C.: (F) Member Temple Lodge, No. 14, 1900, Albany, NY

Newton, Walter M.: (F) Member Masters Lodge, No. 5, 1900, Albany, NY

Nichols, George M.: (F) Member Sons of New England, New England Society of the City of Brooklyn, 1890, (CMTS)*"Brooklyn Eagle,"* Dec. 21, 1890, 11th Annual Dinner, Attendees

Nichols, George M.: (F) Member Brooklyn Revenue Reform Club, 1886, (I)*"Brooklyn Eagle,"* Jan. ,27 1886, Attendees at a dinner

Nichols, William A.: (F) Member Lowville Lodge No. 134, F. & A. M., 1929, Lowville, NY, (CO) Lewis, (JD) Apr. 18, 1892

Nigro, A.: (F) Member Long Island Lodge, No. 382, F. &. A. M., 1874, NY

Niven, William B.: (F) Member Monticello Lodge, No. 532, F. & A. M., (CO) Sullivan Co., NY, (CMTS) Past Master 1873, 1874, 1875, 1882, 1883, 1885, 1889, 1890, 1892, 1893

Noble, Edward B.: (F) Member Temple Lodge, No. 14, 1900, Albany, NY

Noble, James E.: (F) Member Temple Lodge, No. 14, 1900, Albany, NY

Nocks, Daniel E.: (F) Member Arcana Lodge, No. 246, F. & A. M., 1934, New York, NY, (JD) Jun. 4, 1923

Noland, M. W.: (F) Member Friendly Sons of St. Patrick,1893, Brooklyn, (CMTS)*"Brooklyn Eagle,"* May 18,1893, Article regarding the election of Andrew T. Sullivan as postmaster. In the article it mentioned that there were only 50 members in this Society., Guest. It is unknown if a member of the Society.

Noon, J. H.: (F) Member Murray Lodge, No. 380, F. & A. M., 1906, Holley, Orleans, Co., NY

Norcross, T. R.: (F) Member Long Island Lodge, No. 382, F. &. A. M., 1874, NY

Nordstron, Miss Julia: (F) Member Mispah Circle, 1888, Brooklyn, (I)

*"Brooklyn Eagle,"* Dec. 12, 1888. Mentioned in an article about a fair raising funds for a Home for the Blind

Norris, Mrs.: (F) Member Nativity Sewing Society, 1900, Brooklyn, (I) *"Brooklyn Eagle,"* Feb. 3, 1900. Article regarding raising money to buy clothing for the poor.

Northrop, Millington E.: (F) Member Temple Lodge, No. 14, 1900, Albany, NY

Northup, D. L.: (F) Member Sons of New England, New England Society of the City of Brooklyn, 1890, (CMTS)*"Brooklyn Eagle,"* Dec. 21, 1890, 11th Annual Dinner, Attendees

Norton, Thomas J.: (F) Member Arcana Lodge, No. 246, F. & A. M., 1934, New York, NY, (JD) May 29, 1911

Nortz, Henry N.: (F) Member Lowville Lodge No. 134, F. & A. M., 1929, Lowville, NY, (CO) Lewis, (JD) Apr. 21, 1922

Nortz, Henry N.: (F) Member Lowville Chapter No. 223, R. A. M., 1929, Lowville, NY, (CO) Lewis, (JD) Jun. 12, 1923

Norworth, Jack: (F) Member Society of American Magicians, Apr., 1931, New York, (RES) Kew Gardens, L, Long Island, NY

Noy, Francis: (F) Member Clyde Lodge No. 341, F. A. M., 1905, Clyde, NY, (CO) Wayne, (CMTS) Past Master 1881

Nozilia, A.: (F) Member Long Island Lodge, No. 382, F. &. A. M., 1874, NY, (CMTS) Past Master

Nuhn, M.: (F) Member Herber Lodge, No. 698,1898, F. & A. M., New York, NY, Greenpoint area, (RES) Brooklyn

Nuspliger, Earl J.: (F) Member Lowville Lodge No. 134, F. & A. M., 1929, Lowville, NY, (CO) Lewis, (JD) Feb. 6, 1925

Nuspliger, Ernest S.: (F) Member Lowville Lodge No. 134, F. & A. M., 1929, Lowville, NY, (CO) Lewis, (JD) Jun. 4, 1926

Nutt, Mrs. Kate W.: (F) Member The Ladies Sewing Society, 1888, Brooklyn, (I) *"Brooklyn Eagle,"* Dec. 12, 1888. Article regarding Societies aiding churches., (CMTS) Helping Plymouth Church, Vice President

Oakley, H.: (F) Member Long Island Lodge, No. 382, F. &. A. M., 1874, NY

Oaks, Charles J.: (F) Member Masters Lodge, No. 5, 1900, Albany, NY

Oatman, Mrs. E. B.: (F) Member Mispah Circle, 1888, Brooklyn, (I) *"Brooklyn Eagle,"* Dec. 12, 1888. Mentioned in an article about a fair raising funds for a Home for the Blind

O'Brien, P. Lothwell: (F) Member Friendly Sons of St. Patrick,1893, Brooklyn, (CMTS)*"Brooklyn Eagle,"* May 18,1893, Article regarding the election of Andrew T. Sullivan as postmaster. In the article it mentioned that there were only 50 members in this Society., Guest. It is unknown if a member of the Society.

O'Conner, Miss: (F) Member Nativity Sewing Society, 1900, Brooklyn, (I) *"Brooklyn Eagle,"* Feb. 3, 1900. Article regarding raising money to buy clothing for the poor.

O'Connor, Eugene : (F) Member Sons of New England, New England
Society of the City of Brooklyn, 1887, (CMTS)*"Brooklyn Eagle,"*
Dec. 22, 1887, Annual Dinner, Attendees

O'Connor, T. B.: (F) Member Friendly Sons of St. Patrick,1893,
Brooklyn, (CMTS)*"Brooklyn Eagle,"* May 18,1893,
Article regarding the election of Andrew T. Sullivan as postmaster.
In the article it mentioned that there were only 50 members in this
Society., Member of the Dinner Committee

O'Donnell, Miss: (F) Member Nativity Sewing Society, 1900,
Brooklyn, (I) *"Brooklyn Eagle,"* Feb. 3, 1900. Article regarding
raising money to buy clothing for the poor.

O'Donohue, Robert E.: (F) Member First Suffolk District, Meridan
Chapter, No. 336, 1923, Islip, NY, (CMTS) Secretary, (RES)
Central Islip

Odze, Louis G.: (F) Member Arcana Lodge, No. 246, F. & A. M., 1934,
New York, NY, (JD) Mar. 31, 1919

Oesterle, Adolph G.: (F) Member Arcana Lodge, No. 246,
F. & A. M., 1934, New York, NY, (JD) Nov. 17, 1919

O'Harn, Mrs. J.: (F) Member Nativity Sewing Society, 1900,
Brooklyn, (I) *"Brooklyn Eagle,"* Feb. 3, 1900. Article regarding
raising money to buy clothing for the poor.

O'Keefe, Miss Regina: (F) Member Nativity Sewing Society, 1900,
Brooklyn, (I) *"Brooklyn Eagle,"* Feb. 3, 1900. Article regarding
raising money to buy clothing for the poor.

O'Keefe, Mrs. P. : (F) Member Nativity Sewing Society, 1900,
Brooklyn, (I) *"Brooklyn Eagle,"* Feb. 3, 1900. Article regarding
raising money to buy clothing for the poor.

Olcott, Chauncey: (I) *"Brooklyn Eagle,"* Feb. 19, 1902. Funeral Services
at the Club House of the Brooklyn Lodge, No. 22, B. P. O. Elks for
Wm. H. West. Elk services were first then masonic services by
New York Lodge No. 330, F. A. & M., (CMTS) Made a floral gift.

Olcutt, D. D., Cornelius: (F) Member Sons of New England, New England
Society of the City of Brooklyn, 1890, (CMTS)*"Brooklyn Eagle,"*
Dec. 21, 1890, 11th Annual Dinner, Attendees

Oldham, Wm.: (F) Member Long Island Lodge, No. 382, F. &. A. M.,
1874, NY

Olds, George D.: (F) Member Masters Lodge, No. 5, 1900, Albany, NY

Oliver, George E.: (F) Member Mount Vernon Lodge, No. 3, 1900,
Albany, NY

Oliver, Harry I.: (OBIT) *"The Post Standard,"* Syracuse, NY, Sunday,
August 31, 1924. Dr. Oliver Services To Be Held At Home In
Redfield Place - Funeral services for Dr. Harry I. Oliver, 48, who
died early yesterday morning, will take place at the home, 118
Redfield Place, at 2:30 O'clock tomorrow afternoon. Burial will be
at Oakhurst Cemetery. Dr. Oliver was for many years one of the
leading dental surgeons in Central New York. He had been ill

several months. An autopsy at the county morgue showed death was due to tumor of the lungs. Besides his widow, Mrs. Bessie P. Oliver, he is survived by a daughter Miss Betty Oliver; a sister, Mrs. W. D. Moore of Binghamton and a brother Silas D. Oliver of Andes. Dr. Oliver was born at Andes and received his professional training at the College of Dental Surgery, University of Pennsylvania. For some time he was associated with Dr. S. C. Dayan of this city, and later became a member of the staff of Syracuse Memorial Hospital. Dr. Oliver was a member of the Chamber of Commerce, of the Bellevue Country club, and was affiliated with several Masonic Clubs. The dinner planned by Mr. and Mrs. DeWitt Stillwell in honor of Mr. and Mrs. Giles Heath Silwell last evening, was postponed on account of the death of Dr. H. I. Oliver, brother-in-law of Mrs. DeWitt Stillwell

O'Mahoney, Edward: (F) Member Friendly Sons of St. Patrick,1893, Brooklyn, (CMTS)*"Brooklyn Eagle,"* May 18,1893, Article regarding the election of Andrew T. Sullivan as postmaster. In the article it mentioned that there were only 50 members in this Society., Guest. It is unknown if a member of the Society.

Onativia, Jr., Jose V.: (F) Member Society of American Magicians, Apr., 1931, New York, (RES) New York City

Opie, Richard: (F) Member Mount Vernon Lodge, No. 3, 1900, Albany, NY

Oppenheim, Wm. L.: (F) Member Mount Vernon Lodge, No. 3, 1900, Albany, NY

Opper, J.: (F) Member Herber Lodge, No. 698,1898, F. & A. M., New York, NY, Greenpoint area, (RES) New York City

Orf, Andrew: (F) Member Long Island Lodge, No. 382, F. &. A. M., 1874, NY

Orr, A. E.: (F) Member Sons of New England, New England Society of the City of Brooklyn, 1887, (CMTS)*"Brooklyn Eagle,"* Dec. 22, 1887, Annual Dinner, Attendees

Orton, Darius S.: (F) Member Ineffable and Sublime Grand Lodge of Perfection, 1882, Albany, NY

Osborn, Morris A.: (F) Member Society of American Magicians, Apr., 1931, New York, (RES) Brooklyn, NY

Osborne, J. G.: (F) Member Long Island Lodge, No. 382, F. &. A. M., 1874, NY

Ostrau, Louis: (F) Member Arcana Lodge, No. 246, F. & A. M., 1934, New York, NY, (JD) Mar. 26, 1929

Otis, H. J.: (F) Member Long Island Lodge, No. 382, F. &. A. M., 1874, NY

Otis, PhD., Arthur S.: (F) Member Society of American Magicians, Apr., 1931, New York, (RES) Yonkers, NY

O'Toole, Mrs. Margaret: (F) Member Ladies Catholic Benevolent Association, St. Augustines No. 214, 1900, Brooklyn, (I)

*"Brooklyn Eagle,"* Feb. 3, 1900. Meeting Notice., (CMTS) President

Oursler, Chas. F.: (F) Member Society of American Magicians, Apr., 1931, New York, (RES) New York City

Overocker, Wm. F.: (F) Member Long Island Lodge, No. 382, F. &. A. M., 1874, NY

Owens, Abraham L.: (F) Member Temple Lodge, No. 14, 1900, Albany, NY

Owens, Horace A.: (F) Member Lowville Lodge No. 134, F. & A. M., 1929, Lowville, NY, (CO) Lewis, (JD) May 21, 1920

Owings, Col. J. F.: (F) Member Sons of New England, New England Society of the City of Brooklyn, 1887, (CMTS) *"Brooklyn Eagle,"* Dec. 22, 1887, Annual Dinner, Attendees

Pabst, William: (F) Member Mount Vernon Lodge, No. 3, 1900, Albany, NY

Packard, E. H.: (F) Member Sons of New England, New England Society of the City of Brooklyn, 1890, (CMTS) *"Brooklyn Eagle,"* Dec. 21, 1890, 11th Annual Dinner, Attendees

Packer, Israel: (F) Member Arcana Lodge, No. 246, F. & A. M., 1934, New York, NY, (JD) Oct. 9, 1928

Packer, Joseph: (F) Member Arcana Lodge, No. 246, F. & A. M., 1934, New York, NY, (JD) Apr. 22, 1930

Packer, Milton R.: (F) Member Arcana Lodge, No. 246, F. & A. M., 1934, New York, NY, (JD) Nov. 10, 1931

Packer, Wolf: (F) Member Arcana Lodge, No. 246, F. & A. M., 1934, New York, NY, (JD) Jan. 13, 1931

Paddock, Edward: (F) Member Temple Lodge, No. 14, 1900, Albany, NY

Paddock, William G.: (F) Member Masters Lodge, No. 5, 1900, Albany, NY

Page, E. F.: (F) Member Long Island Lodge, No. 382, F. &. A. M., 1874, NY

Page, Frederick G.: (F) Member Temple Lodge, No. 14, 1900, Albany, NY

Paige, Joseph Yates: (F) Member Masters Lodge, No. 5, 1900, Albany, NY

Pakula, Hyman: (F) Member Arcana Lodge, No. 246, F. & A. M., 1934, New York, NY, (JD) Nov. 20, 1922

Palmer, Edwin: (F) Member Temple Lodge, No. 14, 1900, Albany, NY

Palmer, Frank R.: (F) Member Masters Lodge, No. 5, 1900, Albany, NY

Palmer, Grant M.: (F) Member Murray Lodge, No. 380, F. & A. M., 1906, Holley, Orleans, Co., NY , (CEN) 1880, Murray, Orleans Co., NY, Listed with M. C., 47, Farmer, Jennie, 48, Harry R., 11, Grant M., 9, Coolidge C., 7.

Palmer, John: (F) Member Washington Lodge, No. 85, 1900, Albany, NY, (CMTS) Past Members

Palmer, Louis G.: (F) Member Temple Lodge, No. 14, 1900, Albany, NY

Palmer, Lowell W.: (F) Member Sons of New England, New England Society of the City of Brooklyn, 1887, (CMTS) *"Brooklyn Eagle,"* Dec. 22, 1887, Annual Dinner, Attendees

Pangburn, William C.: (F) Member Temple Lodge, No. 14, 1900, Albany, NY

Pape, George: (F) Member Long Island Lodge, No. 382, F. &. A. M., 1874, NY

Parenti, Oscar: (F) Member Society of American Magicians, Apr., 1931, New York, (RES) Bronx, NY

Paresell, Rev. Henry V. A.: (F) Member Society of American Magicians, Apr., 1931, New York, (RES) New York City

Park, Paul: (F) Member Arcana Lodge, No. 246, F. & A. M., 1934, New York, NY, (JD) Jun. 11, 1929

Park , Grace: (F) Member Hope Rebekah Lodge No. 10, 1949-1950, Brockport, NY, (CO) Monroe, (CMTS) Right Escort

Parker, A. W.: (F) Member Long Island Lodge, No. 382, F. &. A. M., 1874, NY

Parker, Fay L.: (F) Member Lowville Lodge No. 134, F. & A. M., 1929, Lowville, NY, (CO) Lewis, (JD) Mar. 16, 1906

Parker, Fay L.: (F) Member Lowville Chapter No. 223, R. A. M., 1929, Lowville, NY, (CO) Lewis, (JD) Nov. 20, 1906

Parker, Frederick b.: (F) Member Lowville Lodge No. 134, F. & A. M., 1929, Lowville, NY, (CO) Lewis

Parker, Frederick S.: (F) Member Sons of New England, New England Society of the City of Brooklyn, 1890, (CMTS) *"Brooklyn Eagle,"* Dec. 21, 1890, 11th Annual Dinner, Attendees

Parker, Lester B.: (F) Member Lowville Lodge No. 134, F. & A. M., 1929, Lowville, NY, (CO) Lewis, (JD) Mar 29, 1878

Parker, Lester B.: (F) Member Lowville Chapter No. 223, R. A. M., 1929, Lowville, NY, (CO) Lewis, (JD) Feb. 23, 1892

Parker, Lynn B.: (F) Member Lowville Lodge No. 134, F. & A. M., 1929, Lowville, NY, (CO) Lewis, (JD) Nov. 7, 1919

Parker, Miss Lillie: (F) Member Mispah Circle, 1888, Brooklyn, (I) *"Brooklyn Eagle,"* Dec. 12, 1888. Mentioned in an article about a fair raising funds for a Home for the Blind

Parker, Mrs. Edward M.: (F) Member Lenox Ladies Aid Society of Lenox Road M. E. Church, Brooklyn, 1900, (CMTS) *"Brooklyn Eagle,"* Mar. 13, 1900. Meeting Notice, Treasurer

Parker, Rev. Lindsay: (I) *"Brooklyn Eagle,"* Feb. 19, 1902. Funeral Services at the Club House of the Brooklyn Lodge, No. 22, B. P. O. Elks for Wm. H. West. Elk services were first then masonic services by New York Lodge No. 330, F. A. & M., (CMTS) Rector of St. Peter's Church read the committal service.

Parker, Wm.: (F) Member Long Island Lodge, No. 382, F. &. A. M., 1874, NY

Parker, Lewis R.: (F) Member Masters Lodge, No. 5, 1900, Albany, NY

Parker, Jr., Amasa J.: (F) Member Masters Lodge, No. 5, 1900, Albany, NY

Parrish, Homer E.: (F) Member Lowville Chapter No. 223, R. A. M., 1929, Lowville, NY, (CO) Lewis, (JD) Feb. 24, 1925

Parsons, Charles H.: (F) Member Sons of New England, New England Society of the City of Brooklyn, 1890, (CMTS) *"Brooklyn Eagle,"* Dec. 21, 1890, 11th Annual Dinner, Attendees

Parsons, Henry C.: (F) Member Temple Lodge, No. 14, 1900, Albany, NY

Parsons, Jr., John D.: (F) Member Masters Lodge, No. 5, 1900, Albany, NY

Partridge, E. F.: (F) Member Long Island Lodge, No. 382, F. &. A. M., 1874, NY

Passage, George M.: (F) Member Mount Vernon Lodge, No. 3, 1900, Albany, NY

Pastor, Mrs. Tony: (I) *"Brooklyn Eagle,"* Feb. 19, 1902. Funeral Services at the Club House of the Brooklyn Lodge, No. 22, B. P. O. Elks for Wm. H. West. Elk services were first then masonic services by New York Lodge No. 330, F. A. & M., (CMTS) Made a floral gift.

Pastor, Tony: (I) *"Brooklyn Eagle,"* Feb. 19, 1902. Funeral Services at the Club House of the Brooklyn Lodge, No. 22, B. P. O. Elks for Wm. H. West. Elk services were first then masonic services by New York Lodge No. 330, F. A. & M., (CMTS) Made a floral gift.

Patten, W. Frank: (F) Member Lowville Lodge No. 134, F. & A. M., 1929, Lowville, NY, (CO) Lewis, (JD) Jun. 11, 1926

Patterson, Charles J.: (F) Member Sons of New England, New England Society of the City of Brooklyn, 1890, (CMTS) *"Brooklyn Eagle,"* Dec. 21, 1890, 11th Annual Dinner, Attendees

Patterson, John: (F) Member Temple Lodge, No. 14, 1900, Albany, NY

Patterson, Judge: (F) Member Friendly Sons of St. Patrick,1893, Brooklyn, (CMTS) *"Brooklyn Eagle,"* May 18,1893, Article regarding the election of Andrew T. Sullivan as postmaster. In the article it mentioned that there were only 50 members in this Society., Guest. It is unknown if a member of the Society.

Patterson, W. E.: (F) Member Friendly Sons of St. Patrick,1893, Brooklyn, (CMTS) *"Brooklyn Eagle,"* May 18,1893, Article regarding the election of Andrew T. Sullivan as postmaster. In the article it mentioned that there were only 50 members in this Society., Guest. It is unknown if a member of the Society.

Payne, Wm.: (F) Member Murray Lodge, No. 380, F. & A. M., 1906, Holley, Orleans, Co., NY

Peabody, George F.: (F) Member Sons of New England, New England

Society of the City of Brooklyn, 1887, (CMTS) *"Brooklyn Eagle,"* Dec. 22, 1887, Annual Dinner, Attendees

Pearl, John J.: (F) Member Temple Lodge, No. 14, 1900, Albany, NY

Pearsall, Thomas W.: (F) Member Sons of New England, New England Society of the City of Brooklyn, 1887, (CMTS) *"Brooklyn Eagle,"* Dec. 22, 1887, Annual Dinner, Attendees

Pease, Alpheus D.: (F) Member Educational Society of Lewis Co., NY, Nov. 14, 1845, (CMTS) Second Vice President, (B) Aug. 20, 1815, (BP) Martinsburg, Lewis Co., NY, (D) Nov. 10, 1914, (MD1) Jun. 3, 1840, (Spouse1) Nancy Miller, (MD2) Mar. 5, 1849, (Spouse2) Susan Miller, (MD3) Jun. 22, 1870, (Spouse3) Chloe ????, (PRTS) Jabez Pease and Fanny Dewey, (md. Oct. 18, 1809, bp. Lewis Co., NY)

Pease, George L.: (F) Member Sons of New England, New England Society of the City of Brooklyn, 1887, (CMTS) *"Brooklyn Eagle,"* Dec. 22, 1887, Annual Dinner, Attendees

Pease, Howard A.: (F) Member Lowville Lodge No. 134, F. & A. M., 1929, Lowville, NY, (CO) Lewis, (JD) Jun. 11, 1886, (CEN) 1880 Constableville, Lewis Co., NY, Clerk, 20, NY

Pease, Howard A.: (F) Member Lowville Chapter No. 223, R. A. M., 1929, Lowville, NY, (CO) Lewis, (JD) Apr. 8, 1890

Peasell, Carman: *"Daily Star,"* Jul. 7, 1898. Former Greenpointers, Now of Freeport, Had a Celebration on Monday. Many people of Greenpoint will remember Mr. and Mrs. Carman Peasell, who lived in the Seventeenth Ward a good many years ago. Mr. Peasell was at one time a leading mechant here. He is a brother of our respected fellow citizen, Mr. H. Peasell. Mr. and Mrs. Carman Peasell have lived in Freeport about a dozen years. They went there long before it became famous as an annex to Greenpoint. Well, to cut a long story short, Mr. and Mrs. Carman Peasell celebrated their golden wedding anniversary in Freeport on Monday evening. Mr. Peasell comes of the old Long Island family of that name. He was born at Lynbrook in 1827, then know as Pearsall's Corner. His parents were Mr. and Mrs. William Peasell, now dead. Carman and his wife were married in 1848 in New York by the Rev. Mr. Seeley, pastor of the Sixth Street Baptist Church. Harriet A. Earle, his wife was the daughter of Mr. and Mrs. Thomas Earle, of New Jersey. She was born in Durham, N.J. In 1886 Mr. and Mrs. Peasell moved to Freeport. They are members of the Methodist Episcopal Church of that place; he is also a member of the Official Board. He has been a Mason for years, and was a charter member of the Seawanhaka Lodge of Greenpoint. Mr. and Mrs. Peasell have but one living child, George W. Peasell who is married and has three children.

Pech, Robert M.: (F) Member Arcana Lodge, No. 246, F. & A. M., 1934,

New York, NY, (JD)Oct. 11, 1927
Peck, Edward A.: (F) Member Mount Vernon Lodge, No. 3, 1900, Albany, NY
Peck, James H.: (F) Member Mount Vernon Lodge, No. 3, 1900, Albany, NY
Peckham, Floyd F.: (F) Member Lowville Lodge No. 134, F. & A. M., 1929, Lowville, NY, (CO) Lewis, (JD) May 18, 1917
Peckham, Frank A.: (F) Member Lowville Lodge No. 134, F. & A. M., 1929, Lowville, NY, (CO) Lewis, (JD) Apr. 2, 1915
Peckham, Russell R.: (F) Member Lowville Lodge No. 134, F. & A. M., 1929, Lowville, NY, (CO) Lewis, (JD) Jun. 20, 1919
Peckham, W. H.: (F) Member Brooklyn Consistory No. 24, A. A. S. R., (CMTS) Meeting Notes, *"Brooklyn Eagle,"* Mar. 13, 1887, Grand Commander giving an address
Peebles, C. Eugene: (F) Member Lowville Lodge No. 134, F. & A. M., 1929, Lowville, NY, (CO) Lewis, (JD) May 2, 1913
Peebles, C. Eugene: (F) Member Lowville Chapter No. 223, R. A. M., 1929, Lowville, NY, (CO) Lewis, (JD) Mar. 8, 1921
Peet, Fred T.: (F) Member Astromical Society, Brooklyn Observatory, Mar. 16, 1850, Brooklyn, NY, (I) *"Brooklyn Eagle,"* Mar. 21, 1851
Peete, W.: (F) Member Long Island Lodge, No. 382, F. &. A. M., 1874, NY
Pelton, Daniel C.: (F) Member Monticello Lodge, No. 532, F. & A. M., (CO) Sullivan Co., NY, (CMTS) Past Master 1884
Pelton, Edward A.: (F) Member Lowville Lodge No. 134, F. & A. M., 1929, Lowville, NY, (CO) Lewis, (JD) Mar. 20, 1925
Pelton, Edward R.: (F) Member Long Island Lodge, No. 382, F. &. A. M., 1874, NY
Pelton, George D.: (F) Member Monticello Lodge, No. 532, F. & A. M., (CO) Sullivan Co., NY, (CMTS) Past Master 1912, 1913
Pelton, Leonard D.: (F) Member Lowville Lodge No. 134, F. & A. M., 1929, Lowville, NY, (CO) Lewis, (JD) Apr. 30m 1920
Pelton, Leonard D.: (F) Member Lowville Chapter No. 223, R. A. M., 1929, Lowville, NY, (CO) Lewis, (JD) Nov. 9, 1920
Peltzman, Henry: (F) Member Arcana Lodge, No. 246,F. & A. M., 1934, New York, NY, (JD) Nov. 29, 1920
Penders, Ester: (F) Member Hope Rebekah Lodge No. 10, 1949-1950, Brockport, NY, (CO) Monroe, (CMTS) Vice Grand
Pendlebury, J.: (F) Member Long Island Lodge, No. 382, F. &. A. M., 1874, NY
Percival, H. E. A.: (F) Member Society of American Magicians, Apr., 1931, New York, (RES) Jersey City, NJ
Percy, William E.: (F) Member Temple Lodge, No. 14, 1900, Albany, NY
Perlmmutter, Benjamin: (F) Member Arcana Lodge, No. 246, F. & A. M.,

1934, New York, NY, (JD) Oct. 16, 1922
Perlmmutter, Harry: (F) Member Arcana Lodge, No. 246, F. & A. M., 1934, New York, NY, (JD) Nov, 7, 1921
Perlmmutter, Louis: (F) Member Arcana Lodge, No. 246, F. & A. M., 1934, New York, NY, (JD) Jun. 9, 1925
Perrigo , B. J.: (F) Member Murray Lodge, No. 380, F. & A. M., 1906, Holley, Orleans, Co., NY, (CMTS) Past Master, Deceased as of 1906
Perrigo, Jr., Simri: (F) Member Murray Lodge, No. 380, F. & A. M., 1906, Holley, Orleans, Co., NY, (CMTS) Past Master, Deceased as of 1906
Perry, A. J.: (F) Member Sons of New England, New England Society of the City of Brooklyn, 1890, (CMTS) *"Brooklyn Eagle,"* Dec. 21, 1890, 11th Annual Dinner, Attendees
Perry, Dr. S. G.: (F) Member Brooklyn Dental Society, 1877, Brooklyn, NY, (CMTS) *"Brooklyn Eagle,"* Dec. 15, 1877. Celebration of 10th Anniversary. Society established Dec. 14, 1867, (CMTS) Present from New York
Perry, Thornton K.: (F) Member Temple Lodge, No. 14, 1900, Albany, NY
Perry, Wm. M.: (F) Member Long Island Lodge, No. 382, F. &. A. M., 1874, NY
Peterkin, Mrs.: (F) Member Nativity Sewing Society, 1900, Brooklyn, (I) *"Brooklyn Eagle,"* Feb. 3, 1900. Article regarding raising money to buy clothing for the poor.
Peterkin, Walter G.: (F) Member Society of American Magicians, Apr., 1931, New York, (RES) Amityville, Long Island, NY
Peterman, Jefferson: (F) Member Grand Council of the Princes of Jerusalem, 1882, Albany, NY
Peters, Thomas P.: (F) Member Young Men's Lyccum, 1888, Brooklyn, (I) *"Brooklyn Eagle,"* Dec. 12, 1888. Article regarding Societies aiding churches., (CMTS) Helping All Souls Universalist Church, President
Peterson, Bernard: (F) Member Friendly Sons of St. Patrick,1893, Brooklyn, (CMTS) *"Brooklyn Eagle,"* May 18,1893, Article regarding the election of Andrew T. Sullivan as postmaster. In the article it mentioned that there were only 50 members in this Society., Guest. It is unknown if a member of the Society.
Peterson, George: (F) Member Lowville Chapter No. 223, R. A. M., 1929, Lowville, NY, (CO) Lewis, (JD) Nov. 13, 1923
Peterson, J. H.: (F) Member Long Island Lodge, No. 382, F. &. A. M., 1874, NY
Peterson, Mrs. Lillian: (F) Member First District Suffolk, Jepthah's Daughter, No. 187, 1923, Huntington, NY, (CMTS) Associate Matron, (RES) Huntington
Peterson, T. E.: (F) Member Herber Lodge, No. 698,1898, F. & A. M.,

New York, NY, Greenpoint area, (RES) New York City
Peterson, William J.: (F) Member Temple Lodge, No. 14, 1900, Albany, NY
Petrie, Lansing G..: (F) Member Lowville Chapter No. 223, R. A. M., 1929, Lowville, NY, (CO) Lewis, (JD) Feb. 24, 1925
Pett, Philip S.: (F) Member Arcana Lodge, No. 246, F. & A. M., 1934, New York, NY, (JD) Dec. 7, 1910
Pettengill, W. T.: (F) Member Murray Lodge, No. 380, F. & A. M., 1906, Holley, Orleans, Co., NY
Petterson, F. E.: (I) *"Brooklyn Eagle,"* Feb. 19, 1902. Funeral Services at the Club House of the Brooklyn Lodge, No. 22, B. P. O. Elks for Wm. H. West. Elk services were first then masonic services by New York Lodge No. 330, F. A. & M., (CMTS) Made a floral gift.
Pettit, Jr., Skidmore: (F) Member American Legion of Honor, Stella Lodge No. 400, 1900, Brooklyn, (I) *"Brooklyn Eagle,"* Feb. 3, 1900. Meeting Notice., (CMTS) Secretary
Pfaff, Samuel : (F) Member Lowville Lodge No. 134, F. & A. M., 1929, Lowville, NY, (CO) Lewis, (JD) Jun. 9, 1928
Pfister, Fay B.: (F) Member Lowville Lodge No. 134, F. & A. M., 1929, Lowville, NY, (CO) Lewis, (JD) Nov. 16, 1917
Phillips, John M.: (F) Member Murray Lodge, No. 380, F. & A. M., 1906, Holley, Orleans, Co., NY
Phillips, Samuel W.: (F) Member Arcana Lodge, No. 246, F. & A. M., 1934, New York, NY, (JD) Oct. 16, 1922
Phillips, Sherman: (F) Member Lowville Lodge No. 134, F. & A. M., 1929, Lowville, NY, (CO) Lewis, (CMTS) Past Master 1861, (CEN) 1880 Lowville, Lewis Co., NY Census, 55, Life Insurance Agent, NY, Harriet, 58, wife, NY, Francis H., 22, Clerk Milliner, Ella M., 20, James L. Phillips. Brother, traveling Jeweler
Phippard, W. T.: (F) Member Long Island Lodge, No. 382, F. &. A. M., 1874, NY
Pierrepont, Henry E.: (F) Member Sons of New England, New England Society of the City of Brooklyn, 1887, (CMTS)*"Brooklyn Eagle,"* Dec. 22, 1887, Annual Dinner, Attendees
Pinco, M. D., Moses L.: (F) Member Society of American Magicians, Apr., 1931, New York, (RES) New York City
Pincus, Kalman: (F) Member Arcana Lodge, No. 246, F. & A. M., 1934, New York, NY, (JD) Jan. 21, 1924
Pine, William S.: (F) Member Lowville Lodge No. 134, F. & A. M., 1929, Lowville, NY, (CO) Lewis, (JD) May 19, 1916
Pine, William S.: (F) Member Lowville Chapter No. 223, R. A. M., 1929, Lowville, NY, (CO) Lewis, (JD) Mar. 8, 1921
Piretti, F. J.: (F) Member Knights of Columbus, Columbus Council No. 126, 1900, Brooklyn, (I) *"Brooklyn Eagle,"* Feb. 3, 1900. Meeting Notice., (CMTS) Recording Secretary
Pitt, W.: (F) Member Long Island Lodge, No. 382, F. &. A. M.,

1874, NY

Pladwell, John: (F) Member Grand Council of the Princes of Jerusalem, 1882, Albany, NY

Pladwell, John: (F) Member Ineffable and Sublime Grand Lodge of Perfection, 1882, Albany, NY

Pladwell, John: (F) Member Temple Lodge, No. 14, 1900, Albany, NY

Platt, Andrew: (F) Member Mount Vernon Lodge, No. 3, 1900, Albany, NY

Platt, J. H.: (F) Member Long Island Lodge, No. 382, F. &. A. M., 1874, NY

Podell, David L.: (F) Member Society of American Magicians, Apr., 1931, New York, (RES) New York City

Podlesney, Andrew G.: (F) Member Lowville Lodge No. 134, F. & A. M., 1929, Lowville, NY, (CO) Lewis, (JD) Jun. 20, 1924

Podolsky, Isudor: (F) Member Arcana Lodge, No. 246, F. & A. M., 1934, New York, NY, (JD) Mar. 3, 1924

Polhemus, H. D.: (F) Member Sons of New England, New England Society of the City of Brooklyn, 1887, (CMTS)*"Brooklyn Eagle,"* Dec. 22, 1887, Annual Dinner, Attendees

Poling, Okey J.: (F) Member Arcana Lodge, No. 246, F. & A. M., 1934, New York, NY, (JD) Jun. 21, 1912

Pollack, Samuel B.: (F) Member Arcana Lodge, No. 246, F. & A. M., 1934, New York, NY, (JD) Nov. 7, 1921

Pollak, Alfred W.: (F) Member Arcana Lodge, No. 246, F. & A. M., 1934, New York, NY, (JD) May 16, 1910

Pollard, Walter H.: (F) Member Anglo Saxon Lodge No. 137, F. A. M., (CMTS) Meeting Notes, *"Brooklyn Eagle,"* Mar. 13, 1887, Entered the Apprentice Degree by W. M. Jerome E. Morse

Poole, Edward A.: (F) Member Temple Lodge, No. 14, 1900, Albany, NY

Porter, General Horace: (F) Member Sons of New England, New England Society of the City of Brooklyn, 1887, (CMTS)*"Brooklyn Eagle,"* Dec. 22, 1887, Annual Dinner, Attendees

Porter, Rev. Dr.: (F) Member St. Nicholas Society of Nassau Island, 1861, (CMTS) *"Brooklyn Eagle,"* Dec. 11, 1861, Article regarding the Anniversary Dinner, Guest

Posner, Morris: (F) Member Arcana Lodge, No. 246, F. & A. M., 1934, New York, NY, (JD) May 5, 1913

Post, William M.: (F) Member Long Island Lodge, No. 382, F. &. A. M., 1874, NY, (CMTS) Past Master

Potter, A. M.: (F) Member Murray Lodge, No. 380, F. & A. M., 1906, Holley, Orleans, Co., NY, (CMTS) Past Master

Potter, Eugene L.: (F) Member Masters Lodge, No. 5, 1900, Albany, NY

Potter, F. T.: (F) Member Murray Lodge, No. 380, F. & A. M., 1906, Holley, Orleans, Co., NY

Potter, Julius: (F) Member Arcana Lodge, No. 246, F. & A. M., 1934, New York, NY, (JD) Nov. 20, 1922

Potter, R. M. Earl: (F) Member Lowville Chapter No. 223, R. A. M., 1929, Lowville, NY, (CO) Lewis, (JD) Jun. 12, 1917

Potter, William C.: (F) Member Temple Lodge, No. 14, 1900, Albany, NY

Pottick, Benj.: (F) Member Arcana Lodge, No. 246, F. & A. M., 1934, New York, NY, (JD) Jan. 26, 1932

Potts, Mrs.: (F) Member Mispah Circle, 1888, Brooklyn, (I) *"Brooklyn Eagle,"* Dec. 12, 1888. Mentioned in an article about a fair raising funds for a Home for the Blind

Potts, William: (F) Member Sons of New England, New England Society of the City of Brooklyn, 1890, (CMTS)*"Brooklyn Eagle,"* Dec. 21, 1890, 11th Annual Dinner, Attendees

Pouch, Frank E.: (F) Member Lexington Lodge, 310, F. A. & M., 1900, Brooklyn, (I) *"Brooklyn Eagle,"* Feb. 3, 1900. Meeting Notice., (CMTS) Master

Praeger, Louis: (F) Member Sons of New England, New England Society of the City of Brooklyn, 1890, (CMTS)*"Brooklyn Eagle,"* Dec. 21, 1890, 11th Annual Dinner, Attendees

Pratt, C.: (F) Member Sons of New England, New England Society of the City of Brooklyn, 1890, (CMTS)*"Brooklyn Eagle,"* Dec. 21, 1890, 11th Annual Dinner, Attendees

Pratt, C. M.: (F) Member Sons of New England, New England Society of the City of Brooklyn, 1890, (CMTS)*"Brooklyn Eagle,"* Dec. 21, 1890, 11th Annual Dinner, Attendees

Pratt, C. M.: (F) Member Sons of New England, New England Society of the City of Brooklyn, 1887, (CMTS)*"Brooklyn Eagle,"* Dec. 22, 1887, Annual Dinner, Attendees

Pratt, Charles: (F) Member Sons of New England, New England Society of the City of Brooklyn, 1887, (CMTS)*"Brooklyn Eagle,"* Dec. 22, 1887, Annual Dinner, Attendees

Pratt, E. A.: (F) Member Brooklyn Revenue Reform Club, 1886, (I)*"Brooklyn Eagle,"* Jan. ,27 1886, Attendees at a dinner

Pratt, F. B.: (F) Member Sons of New England, New England Society of the City of Brooklyn, 1890, (CMTS)*"Brooklyn Eagle,"* Dec. 21, 1890, 11th Annual Dinner, Attendees

Pratt, F. B.: (F) Member Sons of New England, New England Society of the City of Brooklyn, 1887, (CMTS)*"Brooklyn Eagle,"* Dec. 22, 1887, Annual Dinner, Attendees

Pratt, J. T.: (F) Member Sons of New England, New England Society of the City of Brooklyn, 1890, (CMTS)*"Brooklyn Eagle,"* Dec. 21, 1890, 11th Annual Dinner, Attendees

Pratt, Judge Calvin E.: (F) Member Sons of New England, New England Society of the City of Brooklyn, 1890, (CMTS)*"Brooklyn Eagle,"* Dec. 21, 1890, 11th Annual Dinner, Attendees

Pratt, Mrs. Frances L.: (F) Member The Ladies Sewing Society, 1888, Brooklyn, (I) *"Brooklyn Eagle,"* Dec. 12, 1888. Article regarding Societies aiding churches., (CMTS) Helping Plymouth Church, Treasurer

Pratt, W. H. B.: (F) Member Sons of New England, New England Society of the City of Brooklyn, 1887, (CMTS) *"Brooklyn Eagle,"* Dec. 22, 1887, Annual Dinner, Attendees

Pratt, W. O.: (F) Member Sons of New England, New England Society of the City of Brooklyn, 1887, (CMTS) *"Brooklyn Eagle,"* Dec. 22, 1887, Annual Dinner, Attendees

Preece, Geo. Donald: (F) Member Arcana Lodge, No. 246, F. & A. M., 1934, New York, NY, (JD) Mar. 6, 1922

Preece, Geo. W.: (F) Member Arcana Lodge, No. 246, F. & A. M., 1934, New York, NY, (JD) Jan. 15, 1906, Life Member

Prentiss, George H.: (F) Member Sons of New England, New England Society of the City of Brooklyn, 1890, (CMTS) *"Brooklyn Eagle,"* Dec. 21, 1890, 11th Annual Dinner, Attendees

Pressman, D.D.S., Benj. J.: (F) Member Society of American Magicians, Apr., 1931, New York, (RES) New York City

Prest, George M.: (F) Member Temple Lodge, No. 14, 1900, Albany, NY

Prest, John B.: (F) Member Temple Lodge, No. 14, 1900, Albany, NY

Price, Mrs. Irene Price: (F) Member First Suffolk District, Stirling Chapter, No. 216, 1923, Greenport, NY, (CMTS) Matron, (RES) Greenport

Price , M. O.: (F) Member National Union, Brooklyn No. 375, 1900, (I) *"Brooklyn Eagle,"* Feb. 3, 1900. Meeting Notice., (CMTS) Secretary

Primrose, Al: (I) *"Brooklyn Eagle,"* Feb. 19, 1902. Funeral Services at the Club House of the Brooklyn Lodge, No. 22, B. P. O. Elks for Wm. H. West. Elk services were first then masonic services by New York Lodge No. 330, F. A. & M., (CMTS) Made a floral gift.

Primrose, George H.: (I) *"Brooklyn Eagle,"* Feb. 19, 1902. Funeral Services at the Club House of the Brooklyn Lodge, No. 22, B. P. O. Elks for Wm. H. West. Elk services were first then masonic services by New York Lodge No. 330, F. A. & M., (CMTS) Made a floral gift.

Primrose, Mrs. George H.: (I) *"Brooklyn Eagle,"* Feb. 19, 1902. Funeral Services at the Club House of the Brooklyn Lodge, No. 22, B. P. O. Elks for Wm. H. West. Elk services were first then masonic services by New York Lodge No. 330, F. A. & M., (CMTS) Made a floral gift.

Prince, Walter G.: (F) Member Monticello Lodge, No. 532, F. & A. M., (CO) Sullivan Co., NY, (CMTS) Past Master 1906, 1907

Pring, Emilo: (F) Member Friendly Sons of St. Patrick,1893, Brooklyn, (CMTS) *"Brooklyn Eagle,"* May 18,1893,

Article regarding the election of Andrew T. Sullivan as postmaster. In the article it mentioned that there were only 50 members in this Society., Guest. It is unknown if a member of the Society.
Prochaska, M.: (F) Member Long Island Lodge, No. 382, F. &. A. M., 1874, NY
Proctor, Albert H.: (F) Member Temple Lodge, No. 14, 1900, Albany, NY, (CMTS) Life Member
Proddow, Robert: (F) Member Sons of New England, New England Society of the City of Brooklyn, 1890, (CMTS) *"Brooklyn Eagle,"* Dec. 21, 1890, 11th Annual Dinner, Attendees
Prokocimer, William: (F) Member Arcana Lodge, No. 246, F. & A. M., 1934, New York, NY, (JD) Jan. 19, 1920
Proskauer, Julien J.: (F) Member Society of American Magicians, Apr., 1931, New York, (RES) New York City
Proujansky, Leonard: (F) Member Arcana Lodge, No. 246, F. & A. M., 1934, New York, NY, (JD) Jun. 3, 1918
Pruyn, Robert H.: (F) Member Grand Council of the Princes of Jerusalem, 1882, Albany, NY
Pruyn, Robert H.: (F) Member Ineffable and Sublime Grand Lodge of Perfection, 1882, Albany, NY
Pulver, Abraham: (F) Member Arcana Lodge, No. 246, F. & A. M., 1934, New York, NY, (JD) Jun. 13, 1933
Pumpelly, John H.: (F) Member Masters Lodge, No. 5, 1900, Albany, NY
Putnam, Etta: (F) Member Mispah Circle, 1888, Brooklyn, (I) *"Brooklyn Eagle,"* Dec. 12, 1888. Mentioned in an article about a fair raising funds for a Home for the Blind
Putnam, Harrington: (F) Member Sons of New England, New England Society of the City of Brooklyn, 1890, (CMTS) *"Brooklyn Eagle,"* Dec. 21, 1890, 11th Annual Dinner, Attendees
Pyburn, Miss: (F) Member Nativity Sewing Society, 1900, Brooklyn, (I) *"Brooklyn Eagle,"* Feb. 3, 1900. Article regarding raising money to buy clothing for the poor.
Pyrke, Henry W.: (F) Member Temple Lodge, No. 14, 1900, Albany, NY
Quailer, Alex. .: (F) Member Arcana Lodge, No. 246, F. & A. M., 1934, New York, NY, (JD) Mar. 3, 1919
Quakenbush, Mrs. Cark: (F) Member Hope Rebekah Lodge No. 10, 1949-1950, Brockport, NY, (CO) Monroe
Quary, Miss: (F) Member Nativity Sewing Society, 1900, Brooklyn, (I) *"Brooklyn Eagle,"* Feb. 3, 1900. Article regarding raising money to buy clothing for the poor.
Quay, William A.: (F) Member Temple Lodge, No. 14, 1900, Albany, NY
Quayle, Oliver A.: (F) Member Temple Lodge, No. 14, 1900, Albany, NY
Quee, Miss Maggie: (F) Member Mispah Circle, 1888, Brooklyn, (I)

*"Brooklyn Eagle,"* Dec. 12, 1888. Mentioned in an article about a fair raising funds for a Home for the Blind

Quimby, David S.: (F) Member American Legion of Honor, Stella Lodge No. 400, 1900, Brooklyn, (I) *"Brooklyn Eagle,"* Feb. 3, 1900. Meeting Notice., (CMTS) Commander

Quimby, PhD., Shirley L.: (F) Member Society of American Magicians, Apr., 1931, New York, (RES) New York City

Quinby, Franklin: (F) Member Sons of New England, New England Society of the City of Brooklyn, 1890, (CMTS)*"Brooklyn Eagle,"* Dec. 21, 1890, 11th Annual Dinner, Attendees

Quinby, John H.: (F) Member Grand Council of the Princes of Jerusalem, 1882, Albany, NY

Quinby, John H.: (F) Member Ineffable and Sublime Grand Lodge of Perfection, 1882, Albany, NY

Quinby, John H.: (F) Member Masters Lodge, No. 5, 1900, Albany, NY, (CMTS) Past Master

Quinby, Stanley F.: (F) Member Sons of New England, New England Society of the City of Brooklyn, 1890, (CMTS)*"Brooklyn Eagle,"* Dec. 21, 1890, 11th Annual Dinner, Attendees

Rab, Edward O.: (F) Member Arcana Lodge, No. 246, F. & A. M., 1934, New York, NY, (JD) Jan. 19, 1920

Rab, Fed J.: (F) Member Arcana Lodge, No. 246, F. & A. M., 1934, New York, NY, (JD) Jan. 1, 1919

Race, J. H.: (F) Member Brooklyn Dental Society, 1877, Brooklyn, NY, (CMTS) *"Brooklyn Eagle,"* Dec. 15, 1877. Celebration of 10th Anniversary. Society established Dec. 14, 1867, (CMTS) Membership Committee

Radcliff, William S.: (F) Member Lewis County Bible Society, 1812, Charter Officers, (CMTS) Committee

Radcliffe, Miss Belle: (F) Member Mispah Circle, 1888, Brooklyn, (I) *"Brooklyn Eagle,"* Dec. 12, 1888. Mentioned in an article about a fair raising funds for a Home for the Blind

Rafferty, John W.: (F) Member Friendly Sons of St. Patrick,1893, Brooklyn, (CMTS)*"Brooklyn Eagle,"* May 18,1893, Article regarding the election of Andrew T. Sullivan as postmaster. In the article it mentioned that there were only 50 members in this Society., Guest. It is unknown if a member of the Society.

Ramage, Lawson: (F) Member Lowville Lodge No. 134, F. & A. M., 1929, Lowville, NY, (CO) Lewis, (JD) Jul. 12, 1924

Ramsey, Charles G.: (F) Member Lowville Lodge No. 134, F. & A. M., 1929, Lowville, NY, (CO) Lewis, (JD) Dec. 4, 1890

Ramsey, Milton W,: (F) Member Lowville Lodge No. 134, F. & A. M., 1929, Lowville, NY, (CO) Lewis, (JD) Feb. 12, 1925

Randall, F. E.: (F) Member Long Island Lodge, No. 382, F. &. A. M., 1874, NY

Randall, George H.: (F) Member Friendly Sons of St. Patrick,1893,

Brooklyn, (CMTS)*"Brooklyn Eagle,"* May 18,1893,
Article regarding the election of Andrew T. Sullivan as postmaster. In the article it mentioned that there were only 50 members in this Society., Guest. It is unknown if a member of the Society.

Randall, Howard S.: (F) Member Sons of New England, New England Society of the City of Brooklyn, 1890, (CMTS)*"Brooklyn Eagle,"* Dec. 21, 1890, 11th Annual Dinner, Attendees

Randall, Thomas J.: (F) Member Mount Vernon Lodge, No. 3, 1900, Albany, NY

Ranken, John M.: (F) Member Friendly Sons of St. Patrick,1893, Brooklyn, (CMTS)*"Brooklyn Eagle,"* May 18,1893,
Article regarding the election of Andrew T. Sullivan as postmaster. In the article it mentioned that there were only 50 members in this Society., Guest. It is unknown if a member of the Society.

Ransom, Elmer P.: (F) Member Society of American Magicians, Apr., 1931, New York, (RES) New York City

Ransom, William A.: (F) Member Society of American Magicians, Apr., 1931, New York, (RES) Rahway, NJ

Rapalee, Evelyn: (F) Member Hope Rebekah Lodge No. 10, 1949-1950, Brockport, NY, (CO) Monroe

Rapelyea, James P.: (F) Member Friendly Sons of St. Patrick,1893, Brooklyn, (CMTS)*"Brooklyn Eagle,"* May 18,1893,
Article regarding the election of Andrew T. Sullivan as postmaster. In the article it mentioned that there were only 50 members in this Society., Guest. It is unknown if a member of the Society.

Raphael, R. H.: (I) *"Brooklyn Eagle,"* Dec. 7, 1896. 12th Annual Memorial Services, Plymouth Church, Brooklyn Lodge No. 22, B. F. O. Elks, Roll Call of the dead. Address made by Maryland Senator George L. Wellington. , (CMTS) Name called.

Rasechdorf, R.: (F) Member Herber Lodge, No. 698,1898, F. & A. M., New York, NY, Greenpoint area, (RES) New York City

Rathbone, Charles D.: (F) Member Grand Council of the Princes of Jerusalem, 1882, Albany, NY

Rathbone, Charles D.: (F) Member Ineffable and Sublime Grand Lodge of Perfection, 1882, Albany, NY

Rathbone, Charles D.: (F) Member Masters Lodge, No. 5, 1900, Albany, NY

Rathbone, Clarence: (F) Member Grand Council of the Princes of Jerusalem, 1882, Albany, NY

Rathbone, Clarence: (F) Member Ineffable and Sublime Grand Lodge of Perfection, 1882, Albany, NY

Rathbone, Clarence: (F) Member Masters Lodge, No. 5, 1900, Albany, NY, (CMTS) Past Master

Rathbone, John F.: (F) Member Masters Lodge, No. 5, 1900, Albany, NY

Rathbone, Solomon: (F) Member Daughters of Temperances, Hope of the

Fallen Union, Martinsburgh, NY, Jan. 9, 1851, (CO) Lewis
Rathbone, William F.: (F) Member Masters Lodge, No. 5, 1900, Albany, NY
Rathbone, Jr., C. D.: (F) Member Masters Lodge, No. 5, 1900, Albany, NY
Raymond, Dr. R. W.: (F) Member The Plymouth League, 1888, Brooklyn, (I) *"Brooklyn Eagle,"* Dec. 12, 1888. Article regarding Societies aiding churches., (CMTS) Helping Plymouth Church, V Vice President
Raynor, Miss Ida: (F) Member Independent Order of Good Templars, Westhampton Lodge No. 885, instituted Apr. 16, 1889, New Officers installed Feb. 16, 1900, (CMTS) Meeting Notes, *"Brooklyn Eagle,"* Feb. 18, 1900, Chaplain
Raynor, Thurston H.: (F) Member Independent Order of Good Templars, Westhampton Lodge No. 885, instituted Apr. 16, 1889, New Officers installed Feb. 16, 1900, (CMTS) Meeting Notes, *"Brooklyn Eagle,"* Feb. 18, 1900, Secretary
Raynor, Jr., John G.: (F) Member Independent Order of Good Templars, Westhampton Lodge No. 885, instituted Apr. 16, 1889, New Officers installed Feb. 16, 1900, (CMTS) Meeting Notes, *"Brooklyn Eagle,"* Feb. 18, 1900, Lodge Deputy
Raynsford, George W.: (F) Member Temple Lodge, No. 14, 1900, Albany, NY
Rea, Robert H.: (F) Member Lowville Chapter No. 223, R. A. M., 1929, Lowville, NY, (CO) Lewis, (JD) Nov. 11, 1924
Read, Daniel P.: (F) Member Temple Lodge, No. 14, 1900, Albany, NY
Read, Harmon P.: (F) Member Masters Lodge, No. 5, 1900, Albany, NY
Read, J. Meredith: (F) Member Masters Lodge, No. 5, 1900, Albany, NY
Read, John J.: (I) *"Brooklyn Eagle,"* Dec. 7, 1896. 12th Annual Memorial Services, Plymouth Church, Brooklyn Lodge No. 22, B. F. O. Elks, Roll Call of the dead. Address made by Maryland Senator George L. Wellington. , (CMTS) Name called.
Read, John Meredith: (F) Member Grand Council of the Princes of Jerusalem, 1882, Albany, NY
Read, John Meredith: (F) Member Ineffable and Sublime Grand Lodge of Perfection, 1882, Albany, NY
Read, Mrs. G.: (F) Member Nativity Sewing Society, 1900, Brooklyn, (I) *"Brooklyn Eagle,"* Feb. 3, 1900. Article regarding raising money to buy clothing for the poor.
Reagan, F. A.: (F) Member Friendly Sons of St. Patrick,1893, Brooklyn, (CMTS) *"Brooklyn Eagle,"* May 18,1893, Article regarding the election of Andrew T. Sullivan as postmaster.

In the article it mentioned that there were only 50 members in this Society., Guest. It is unknown if a member of the Society.

Reams, Alfred: (F) Member National Provident Union, Lafayette No. 28, 1900, Brooklyn, (I) *"Brooklyn Eagle,"* Feb. 3, 1900. Meeting Notice.

Rebb, Homer DeW.: (F) Member Lowville Lodge No. 134, F. & A. M., 1929, Lowville, NY, (CO) Lewis, (JD) May 1, 1925

Rebhun, Charles A.: (F) Member Temple Lodge, No. 14, 1900, Albany, NY

Rechenberg, John H.: (F) Member Temple Lodge, No. 14, 1900, Albany, NY

Redhun, Daniel C.: (F) Member Temple Lodge, No. 14, 1900, Albany, NY

Redway, George H.: (F) Member Masters Lodge, No. 5, 1900, Albany, NY

Reed, George S.: (F) Member Lowville Lodge No. 134, F. & A. M., 1929, Lowville, NY, (CO) Lewis, (JD) Mar. 16, 1906

Reed, Jesse R.: (F) Member Lowville Lodge No. 134, F. & A. M., 1929, Lowville, NY, (CO) Lewis, (JD) Apr. 19, 1907

Reed, Jesse R.: (F) Member Lowville Chapter No. 223, R. A. M., 1929, Lowville, NY, (CO) Lewis, (JD) Mar. 9, 1920

Reed, Joseph P.: (F) Member Temple Lodge, No. 14, 1900, Albany, NY

Reeve, H.: (F) Member Long Island Lodge, No. 382, F. &. A. M., 1874, NY

Reigelman, Chas.: (F) Member Arcana Lodge, No. 246, F. & A. M., 1934, New York, NY, (JD) Dec. 19, 1910

Reinhardt, F.: (F) Member Long Island Lodge, No. 382, F. &. A. M., 1874, NY

Reinhart, Robert: (F) Member Society of American Magicians, Apr., 1931, New York, (RES) New York City

Reipley, Joseph: (F) Member Astromical Society, Brooklyn Observatory, Mar. 16, 1850, Brooklyn, NY, (I) *"Brooklyn Eagle,"* Mar. 21, 1854

Reiser, A.: (F) Member Herber Lodge, No. 698,1898, F. & A. M., New York, NY, Greenpoint area, (RES) Staten Island

Reisner, Herman: (F) Member Arcana Lodge, No. 246, F. & A. M., 1934, New York, NY, (JD) Jun. 17, 1918

Relyea, Lewis L.: (F) Member Mount Vernon Lodge, No. 3, 1900, Albany, NY

Renner, C. A.: (F) Member Herber Lodge, No. 698,1898, F. & A. M., New York, NY, Greenpoint area, (RES) New York City

Rennie, Thomas: (F) Member Lowville Lodge No. 134, F. & A. M., 1929, Lowville, NY, (CO) Lewis , (JD) Dec. 18, 1896

Reock, George: (I) *"Brooklyn Eagle,"* Dec. 7, 1896. 12th Annual

Memorial Services, Plymouth Church, Brooklyn Lodge No. 22, B. F. O. Elks, Roll Call of the dead. Address made by Maryland Senator George L. Wellington. , (CMTS) Name called.

Resnick, Max: (F) Member Arcana Lodge, No. 246, F. & A. M., 1934, New York, NY, (JD)Feb. 2, 1925

Resseguie, James E.: (F) Member Temple Lodge, No. 14, 1900, Albany, NY

Retzky, Harold: (F) Member Arcana Lodge, No. 246, F. & A. M., 1934, New York, NY, (JD) Jun. 26, 1928

Reynders, John C.: (F) Member Temple Lodge, No. 14, 1900, Albany, NY

Reynolds, Frank: (F) Member Arcana Lodge, No. 246, F. & A. M., 1934, New York, NY, (JD) May 20, 1901, Life Member

Reynolds, George G.: (F) Member Sons of New England, New England Society of the City of Brooklyn, 1890, (CMTS) *"Brooklyn Eagle,"* Dec. 21, 1890, 11th Annual Dinner, Attendees

Reynolds, George G.: (F) Member Sons of New England, New England Society of the City of Brooklyn, 1887, (CMTS) *"Brooklyn Eagle,"* Dec. 22, 1887, Annual Dinner, Attendees

Reynolds, John H.: (F) Member Masters Lodge, No. 5, 1900, Albany, NY

Reynolds, M. J.: (I) *"Brooklyn Eagle,"* Dec. 7, 1896. 12th Annual Memorial Services, Plymouth Church, Brooklyn Lodge No. 22, B. F. O. Elks, Roll Call of the dead. Address made by Maryland Senator George L. Wellington. , (CMTS) Name called.

Reynolds, William A.: (F) Member Mount Vernon Lodge, No. 3, 1900, Albany, NY

Reynolds, William H.: (I) *"Brooklyn Eagle,"* Feb. 19, 1902. Funeral Services at the Club House of the Brooklyn Lodge, No. 22, B. P. O. Elks for Wm. H. West. Elk services were first then masonic services by New York Lodge No. 330, F. A. & M., (CMTS) Made a floral gift.

Ricaby, Sandford: (I) *"Brooklyn Eagle,"* Feb. 19, 1902. Funeral Services at the Club House of the Brooklyn Lodge, No. 22, B. P. O. Elks for Wm. H. West. Elk services were first then masonic services by New York Lodge No. 330, F. A. & M., (CMTS) Made a floral gift.

Rice, Charles J.: (F) Member Lowville Lodge No. 134, F. & A. M., 1929, Lowville, NY, (CO) Lewis, (JD) Apr. 16, 1920

Rice, Ernest A.: (F) Member Lowville Lodge No. 134, F. & A. M., 1929, Lowville, NY, (CO) Lewis, (CMTS) Past Master 1921, 1922

Rice, Ernest A.: (F) Member Lowville Lodge No. 134, F. & A. M., 1929, Lowville, NY, (CO) Lewis, (JD) Apr. 2, 1915

Rice, Ernest A.: (F) Member Lowville Chapter No. 223, R. A. M., 1929, Lowville, NY, (CO) Lewis, (JD) Jan. 23, 1917

Rice, Frederick H.: (F) Member Temple Lodge, No. 14, 1900, Albany, NY

Rice, George M.: (F) Member Lowville Lodge No. 134, F. & A. M., 1929, Lowville, NY, (CO) Lewis, (CMTS) Past Master 1915, 1916

Rice, George M.: (F) Member Lowville Lodge No. 134, F. & A. M., 1929, Lowville, NY, (CO) Lewis, (JD) Jan. 8, 1904

Rice, George M.: (F) Member Lowville Chapter No. 223, R. A. M., 1929, Lowville, NY, (CO) Lewis, (JD) Jul. 19, 1904

Rice, James D.: (F) Member Temple Lodge, No. 14, 1900, Albany, NY

Rich, Dr. John B.: (F) Member Brooklyn Dental Society, 1877, Brooklyn, NY, (CMTS) *"Brooklyn Eagle,"* Dec. 15, 1877. Celebration of 10th Anniversary. Society established Dec. 14, 1867, (CMTS) Present from New York

Rich, Henry C.: (F) Member Lowville Lodge No. 134, F. & A. M., 1929, Lowville, NY, (CO) Lewis, (JD) Mar. 3,1923

Richards, A. E.: (I) *"Brooklyn Eagle,"* Dec. 7, 1896. 12th Annual Memorial Services, Plymouth Church, Brooklyn Lodge No. 22, B. F. O. Elks, Roll Call of the dead. Address made by Maryland Senator George L. Wellington. , (CMTS) Name called.

Richards, Brother: (F) Member Acanthus Lodge No. 719, F. A. M., (CMTS) Meeting Notes, *"Brooklyn Eagle,"* Mar. 13, 1887, of Tyrain

Richards, Charles R.: (F) Member Sons of New England, New England Society of the City of Brooklyn, 1890, (CMTS)*"Brooklyn Eagle,"* Dec. 21, 1890, 11th Annual Dinner, Attendees

Richards, Walter Scott: (F) Member Temple Lodge, No. 14, 1900, Albany, NY

Richardson, Frank: (F) Member Temple Lodge, No. 14, 1900, Albany, NY

Richardson, Harold J.: (F) Member Lowville Lodge No. 134, F. & A. M., 1929, Lowville, NY, (CO) Lewis, (CMTS) Past Master 1912

Richardson, Harold J.: (F) Member Lowville Lodge No. 134, F. & A. M., 1929, Lowville, NY, (CO) Lewis, (JD) Nov. 3, 1905

Richardson, Harold J.: (F) Member Lowville Chapter No. 223, R. A. M., 1929, Lowville, NY, (CO) Lewis, (JD) Nov. 20, 1906

Richardson, Raymond S.: (F) Member Lowville Lodge No. 134, F. & A. M., 1929, Lowville, NY, (CO) Lewis, (JD) Nov. 20, 1908

Richardson, Raymond S.: (F) Member Lowville Chapter No. 223, R. A. M., 1929, Lowville, NY, (CO) Lewis, (JD) Mar. 16, 1915

Richardson, S. Brown: (F) Member Lowville Lodge No. 134, F. & A. M., 1929, Lowville, NY, (CO) Lewis, (CMTS) Past Master 1888, 1889, 1890

Richardson, William J.: (F) Member Sons of New England, New England Society of the City of Brooklyn, 1890, (CMTS)*"Brooklyn Eagle,"* Dec. 21, 1890, 11th Annual Dinner, Attendees

Richer, Grant J.: (F) Member Lowville Chapter No. 223, R. A. M., 1929, Lowville, NY, (CO) Lewis, (JD) Mar. 27, 1928

Rickert, George C.: (F) Member Temple Lodge, No. 14, 1900, Albany, NY

Ridgway, James W.: (F) Member Sons of New England, New England Society of the City of Brooklyn, 1890, (CMTS)*"Brooklyn Eagle,"* Dec. 21, 1890, 11th Annual Dinner, Attendees

Rieck, Ernest W.: (F) Member Mount Vernon Lodge, No. 3, 1900, Albany, NY

Rigney, Miss: (F) Member Nativity Sewing Society, 1900, Brooklyn, (I) *"Brooklyn Eagle,"* Feb. 3, 1900. Article regarding raising money to buy clothing for the poor.

Ring, Caryle C.: (F) Member Lowville Lodge No. 134, F. & A. M., 1929, Lowville, NY, (CO) Lewis, (JD) May 16, 1924

Rink, Niccholas: (F) Member Temple Lodge, No. 14, 1900, Albany, NY

Rinn, Joseh F.: (F) Member Society of American Magicians, Apr., 1931, New York, (RES) New York City

Rinolda, S.: (F) Member Long Island Lodge, No. 382, F. &. A. M., 1874, NY

Ripley, George H.: (F) Member Sons of New England, New England Society of the City of Brooklyn, 1890, (CMTS)*"Brooklyn Eagle,"* Dec. 21, 1890, 11th Annual Dinner, Attendees

Rippier, Miss Maud: (F) Member Childrens's Mission Band, 1888, Brooklyn, (I) *"Brooklyn Eagle,"* Dec. 12, 1888. Article regarding Societies aiding churches., (CMTS) Helping St. John's Methodist Episcopal Church. President

Rippier, Mrs. R. D.: (F) Member Ladies Auxilary to Foregin Missions, 1888, Brooklyn, (I) *"Brooklyn Eagle,"* Dec. 12, 1888. Article regarding Societies aiding churches., (CMTS) Helping St. John's Methodist Episcopal Church, Secretary

Riskin, S. Irving: (F) Member Arcana Lodge, No. 246, F. & A. M., 1934, New York, NY, (JD) May12, 1931

Ritter, Albert F.: (F) Member Arcana Lodge, No. 246, F. & A. M., 1934, New York, NY, (JD) Nov. 17, 1919

Ritterbusch, Wm.: (F) Member Herber Lodge, No. 698,1898, F. & A. M., New York, NY, Greenpoint area, (RES) Brooklyn

Rittis, Charles: (F) Member Lowville Lodge No. 134, F. & A. M., 1929, Lowville, NY, (CO) Lewis, (JD) Mar. 5, 1920

Rittis, Edward E.: (F) Member Lowville Lodge No. 134, F. & A. M., 1929, Lowville, NY, (CO) Lewis, (JD) Nov. 18, 1927

Rivenburgh, Clarence H.: (F) Member Temple Lodge, No. 14, 1900, Albany, NY

Rivenburgh, James: (F) Member Temple Lodge, No. 14, 1900, Albany, NY

Robbins, Levi: (F) Member Harrisburgh Ecclesiastical Society, Jul. 9, 1805, (CO) Lewis

Robbins, Rowland A.: (F) Member Friendly Sons of St. Patrick,1893,

Brooklyn, (CMTS)*"Brooklyn Eagle,"* May 18,1893, Article regarding the election of Andrew T. Sullivan as postmaster. In the article it mentioned that there were only 50 members in this Society., Guest. It is unknown if a member of the Society.

Roberts, Charles A.: (F) Member Lowville Lodge No. 134, F. & A. M., 1929, Lowville, NY, (CO) Lewis, (JD) May 16, 1880

Roberts, Charles A.: (F) Member Lowville Chapter No. 223, R. A. M., 1929, Lowville, NY, (CO) Lewis, (JD) Mar. 31, 1891

Roberts, David S.: (F) Member Lowville Lodge No. 134, F. & A. M., 1929, Lowville, NY, (CO) Lewis, (JD) Apr. 27, 1923

Roberts, Ernest W.: (F) Member Lowville Chapter No. 223, R. A. M., 1929, Lowville, NY, (CO) Lewis, (JD) May 8, 1923

Roberts, W. Burton: (F) Member Lowville Lodge No. 134, F. & A. M., 1929, Lowville, NY, (CO) Lewis, (JD) May 2, 1913

Roberts, W. Burton: (F) Member Lowville Chapter No. 223, R. A. M., 1929, Lowville, NY, (CO) Lewis, (JD) Nov. 23, 1920

Robinson, Fay S.: (F) Member Lowville Lodge No. 134, F. & A. M., 1929, Lowville, NY, (CO) Lewis, (JD) jan. 8, 1905

Robinson, George: (I) *"Brooklyn Eagle,"* Feb. 19, 1902. Funeral Services at the Club House of the Brooklyn Lodge, No. 22, B. P. O. Elks for Wm. H. West. Elk services were first then masonic services by New York Lodge No. 330, F. A. & M., (CMTS) Made a floral gift.

Robinson, George W.: (F) Member Temple Lodge, No. 14, 1900, Albany, NY, (CMTS) Life Member

Robinson, James E.: (F) Member Mount Vernon Lodge, No. 3, 1900, Albany, NY

Robinson, John C.: (F) Member Albany Conclave, No. 8, Red Cross of Constantine, 1882, Albany, NY

Robinson, M. W.: (F) Member Sons of New England, New England Society of the City of Brooklyn, 1887, (CMTS)*"Brooklyn Eagle,"* Dec. 22, 1887, Annual Dinner, Attendees

Robinson, Mrs. George: (I) *"Brooklyn Eagle,"* Feb. 19, 1902. Funeral Services at the Club House of the Brooklyn Lodge, No. 22, B. P. O. Elks for Wm. H. West. Elk services were first then masonic services by New York Lodge No. 330, F. A. & M., (CMTS) Made a floral gift.

Robinson, R. G.: (F) Member Mount Vernon Lodge, No. 3, 1900, Albany, NY

Robinson, W. B.: (F) Member Murray Lodge, No. 380, F. & A. M., 1906, Holley, Orleans, Co., NY

Robson, Peter R.: (F) Member Temple Lodge, No. 14, 1900, Albany, NY

Roche, David F.: (I) *"Brooklyn Eagle,"* Dec. 7, 1896. 12th Annual Memorial Services, Plymouth Church, Brooklyn Lodge No. 22, B. F. O. Elks, Roll Call of the dead. Address made by Maryland Senator George L. Wellington. , (CMTS) Name called.

Rocke, Hugo: (F) Member Arcana Lodge, No. 246, F. & A. M., 1934,

New York, NY, (JD) Mar. 3, 1924
Rockwell, Lewis H.: (F) Member Temple Lodge, No. 14, 1900, Albany, NY
Rockwell, Mrs. Fenton: (F) Member Ladies ' Willing Aid Society, 1888, Brooklyn, (I) *"Brooklyn Eagle,"* Dec. 12, 1888. Article regarding Societies aiding churches., (CMTS) Helping Green Avenue Presbyterian Church, President
Rodgers, Lemuel L.: (F) Member Mount Vernon Lodge, No. 3, 1900, Albany, NY
Rogers, Charles J.: (F) Member Lowville Chapter No. 223, R. A. M., 1929, Lowville, NY, (CO) Lewis, (JD) Sep. 1, 1908
Rogers, J. A.: (F) Member Murray Lodge, No. 380, F. & A. M., 1906, Holley, Orleans, Co., NY
Rogers, L. Albert: (F) Member Lowville Chapter No. 223, R. A. M., 1929, Lowville, NY, (CO) Lewis, (JD) Sep. 18, 1928
Rogers, Rufus L.: (F) Member Lowville Lodge No. 134, F. & A. M., 1929, Lowville, NY, (CO) Lewis, (CMTS) Past Master 1871
Rollings, C. H.: (F) Member Long Island Lodge, No. 382, F. &. A. M., 1874, NY
Rollings, J.: (F) Member Long Island Lodge, No. 382, F. &. A. M., 1874, NY
Rollins, Andrew M.: (F) Member Temple Lodge, No. 14, 1900, Albany, NY
Rooker, William H. A.: (F) Member Temple Lodge, No. 14, 1900, Albany, NY
Rooney, Miss C.: (F) Member Nativity Sewing Society, 1900, Brooklyn, (I) *"Brooklyn Eagle,"* Feb. 3, 1900. Article regarding raising money to buy clothing for the poor.
Roos, Charles J.: (I) *"Brooklyn Eagle,"* Feb. 19, 1902. Funeral Services at the Club House of the Brooklyn Lodge, No. 22, B. P. O. Elks for Wm. H. West. Elk services were first then masonic services by New York Lodge No. 330, F. A. & M., (CMTS) Made a floral gift.
Roos, Mrs. Charles J.: (I) *"Brooklyn Eagle,"* Feb. 19, 1902. Funeral Services at the Club House of the Brooklyn Lodge, No. 22, B. P. O. Elks for Wm. H. West. Elk services were first then masonic services by New York Lodge No. 330, F. A. & M., (CMTS) Made a floral gift.
Roossin, Isidor P.: (F) Member Arcana Lodge, No. 246, F. & A. M., 1934, New York, NY, (JD) Nov. 7, 1921
Roossin, Norman: (F) Member Arcana Lodge, No. 246, F. & A. M., 1934, New York, NY, (JD) Jun. 23, 1931
Root, Andrew J.: (F) Member Masters Lodge, No. 5, 1900, Albany, NY
Root, Arthur G.: (F) Member Masters Lodge, No. 5, 1900, Albany, NY
Root, Elihu: (F) Member Sons of New England, New England Society of the City of Brooklyn, 1890, (CMTS)*"Brooklyn Eagle,"*

Dec. 21, 1890, 11th Annual Dinner, Attendees, President New England Society of New York
Root, Wm. : (F) Member Denmark Ecclesiastical Society, Sep. 21, 1810, (CO) Lewis, (CMTS) Trustee
Ropes, Ripley: (F) Member Sons of New England, New England Society of the City of Brooklyn, 1887, (CMTS) *"Brooklyn Eagle,"* Dec. 22, 1887, Annual Dinner, Attendees
Rose, Miss: (F) Member Nativity Sewing Society, 1900, Brooklyn, (I) *"Brooklyn Eagle,"* Feb. 3, 1900. Article regarding raising money to buy clothing for the poor.
Rosebaum, Henry: (F) Member Arcana Lodge, No. 246, F. & A. M., 1934, New York, NY, (JD) Oct. 1, 1917
Rosenbaum, J.: (F) Member Herber Lodge, No. 698,1898, F. & A. M., New York, NY, Greenpoint area, (RES) New York City
Rosenbaum, M.: (F) Member Herber Lodge, No. 698,1898, F. & A. M., New York, NY, Greenpoint area, (RES) New York City
Rosenberg, Benj.: (F) Member Arcana Lodge, No. 246, F. & A. M., 1934, New York, NY, (JD) Jan. 29, 1923
Rosenblatt, B.: (F) Member Herber Lodge, No. 698,1898, F. & A. M., New York, NY, Greenpoint area, (RES) Pittsburg
Rosenblatt, Irving D.: (F) Member Arcana Lodge, No. 246, F. & A. M., 1934, New York, NY, (JD) Jun. 5, 1922
Rosenblatt, Joseph : (F) Member Arcana Lodge, No. 246, F. & A. M., 1934, New York, NY, (JD) Mar. 26, 1929
Rosenbluh, Edwin H.: (F) Member Society of American Magicians, Apr., 1931, New York, (RES) New York City
Rosenblum, William: (F) Member Arcana Lodge, No. 246, F. & A. M., 1934, New York, NY, (JD) Jun. 26, 1928
Rosendale, Simon W.: (F) Member Washington Lodge, No. 85, 1900, Albany, NY, (CMTS) Past Members
Rosenthal, Benj.: (F) Member Arcana Lodge, No. 246, F. & A. M., 1934, New York, NY, (JD) Jan. 29, 1923
Rosenthal, Rubin: (F) Member Arcana Lodge, No. 246, F. & A. M., 1934, New York, NY, (JD Mar. 3, 1924
Rosini, Carl D.: (F) Member Society of American Magicians, Apr., 1931, New York, (RES) Beechurst, Long Island, NY
Ross, Charles H.: (F) Member Temple Lodge, No. 14, 1900, Albany, NY
Ross, Charles J.: (I) *"Brooklyn Eagle,"* Feb. 19, 1902. Funeral Services at the Club House of the Brooklyn Lodge, No. 22, B. P. O. Elks for Wm. H. West. Elk services were first then masonic services by New York Lodge No. 330, F. A. & M., (CMTS) Actor. Member of the Elks, Read the Eulogy.
Ross, Charles J.: (I) *"Brooklyn Eagle,"* Feb. 19, 1902. Funeral Services at

the Club House of the Brooklyn Lodge, No. 22, B. P. O. Elks for Wm. H. West. Elk services were first then masonic services by New York Lodge No. 330, F. A. & M., (CMTS) Pallbearer

Ross, Miss Agnes G.: (F) Member Nativity Sewing Society, 1900, Brooklyn, (I) *"Brooklyn Eagle,"* Feb. 3, 1900. Article regarding raising money to buy clothing for the poor.

Ross, Miss Minnie: (F) Member Nativity Sewing Society, 1900, Brooklyn, (I) *"Brooklyn Eagle,"* Feb. 3, 1900. Article regarding raising money to buy clothing for the poor.

Ross, Orrin F.: (F) Member Lowville Lodge No. 134, F. & A. M., 1929, Lowville, NY, (CO) Lewis, (CMTS) Past Master 1923

Ross, Orrin F.: (F) Member Lowville Chapter No. 223, R. A. M., 1929, Lowville, NY, (CO) Lewis, (JD) Dec. 24, 1918

Rossbottom, J. J.: (F) Member Star of Bethlem No. 322, F. A. M., 1900, Brooklyn, (I) *"Brooklyn Eagle,"* Feb. 3, 1900. Meeting Notice., (CMTS) Senior Warden

Rossiter, William W.: (F) Member Sons of New England, New England Society of the City of Brooklyn, 1890, (CMTS) *"Brooklyn Eagle,"* Dec. 21, 1890, 11th Annual Dinner, Attendees

Rost, M.: (F) Member Long Island Lodge, No. 382, F. &. A. M., 1874, NY

Roth, Gabriel: (F) Member Arcana Lodge, No. 246, F. & A. M., 1934, New York, NY, (JD) Jun. 28, 1932

Roth, Jules: (F) Member Arcana Lodge, No. 246, F. & A. M., 1934, New York, NY, (JD) Apr. 6, 1903, Life Member

Roth, Julius L.: (F) Member Arcana Lodge, No. 246, F. & A. M., 1934, New York, NY, (JD) Oct. 11, 1927

Rotheberg, Jos. P.: (F) Member Arcana Lodge, No. 246, F. & A. M., 1934, New York, NY, (JD) Apr. 15, 1918

Rothenberg, Fred N.: (F) Member Society of American Magicians, Apr., 1931, New York, (RES) New York City

Rothgarn, Charles W.: (F) Member Lowville Chapter No. 223, R. A. M., 1929, Lowville, NY, (CO) Lewis, (JD) Dec. 15, 1925

Rothkopf, S. Irving: (F) Member Arcana Lodge, No. 246, F. & A. M., 1934, New York, NY, (JD) Jun. 15, 1903, Life Member

Rothschild, Leon D.: (F) Member Arcana Lodge, No. 246, F. & A. M., 1934, New York, NY, (JD) Jun. 9, 1925

Rothschild, Otto: (F) Member Arcana Lodge, No. 246, F. & A. M., 1934, New York, NY, (JD) Feb. 19, 1912

Rouclere, Harry: (F) Member Society of American Magicians, Apr., 1931, New York, (RES) Ridgewood, NJ

Rowe, George H.: (F) Member Friendly Sons of St. Patrick,1893, Brooklyn, (CMTS) *"Brooklyn Eagle,"* May 18,1893,
Article regarding the election of Andrew T. Sullivan as postmaster. In the article it mentioned that there were only 50 members in this Society., Guest. It is unknown if a member of the Society.

Roy, Miss Lizzie: (F) Member Young Peoples' Society of Christian Endeavor, 1888, Brooklyn, (I) *"Brooklyn Eagle,"* Dec. 12, 1888. Article regarding Societies aiding churches., (CMTS) Helping Green Avenue Presbyterian Church, Secretary

Roy, Robert H.: (F) Member Young Peoples' Society of Christian Endeavor, 1888, Brooklyn, (I) *"Brooklyn Eagle,"* Dec. 12, 1888. Article regarding Societies aiding churches., (CMTS) Helping Green Avenue Presbyterian Church, Vice President

Royce, Charles H.: (F) Member Monticello Lodge, No. 532, F. & A. M., (CO) Sullivan Co., NY, (CMTS) Past Master 1899

Rubin, Harry: (F) Member Arcana Lodge, No. 246, F. & A. M., 1934, New York, NY, (JD) Aug. 6, 1918

Rubin, Joseph: (F) Member Arcana Lodge, No. 246, F. & A. M., 1934, New York, NY, (JD) Feb. 9, 1932

Rudman, Marion: (F) Member Hope Rebekah Lodge No. 10, 1949-1950, Brockport, NY, (CO) Monroe

Rudolph, O.: (F) Member Herber Lodge, No. 698,1898, F. & A. M., New York, NY, Greenpoint area, (RES) Brooklyn

Ruf, John P.: (F) Member Clyde Lodge No. 341, F. A. M., 1905, Clyde, NY, (CO) Wayne, (CMTS) Past Master 1888

Ruger, Doris: (F) Member Hope Rebekah Lodge No. 10, 1949-1950, Brockport, NY, (CO) Monroe

Rullman, Leo: (F) Member Society of American Magicians, Apr., 1931, New York, (RES) New York City

Rumble, Charles A.: (F) Member Lowville Lodge No. 134, F. & A. M., 1929, Lowville, NY, (CO) Lewis, (JD) Nov. 22, 1895

Rumble, Charles A.: (F) Member Lowville Chapter No. 223, R. A. M., 1929, Lowville, NY, (CO) Lewis, (JD) Mar. 16, 1915

Runge, C. L.: (F) Member Long Island Lodge, No. 382, F. &. A. M., 1874, NY

Ruoff, M.: (F) Member Herber Lodge, No. 698,1898, F. & A. M., New York, NY, Greenpoint area, (RES) New York City

Rushmore, C.: (F) Member Long Island Lodge, No. 382, F. &. A. M., 1874, NY

Rushmore, G.: (F) Member Long Island Lodge, No. 382, F. &. A. M., 1874, NY

Rushmore, Mrs. Remson: (F) Member Lenox Ladies Aid Society of Lenox Road M. E. Church, Brooklyn, 1900, (CMTS) *"Brooklyn Eagle,"* Mar. 13, 1900. Meeting Notice, Board of Managers

Rushmore, R.: (F) Member Long Island Lodge, No. 382, F. &. A. M., 1874, NY

Ruso, Conrad: (F) Member Temple Lodge, No. 14, 1900, Albany, NY

Ruso, James M.: (F) Member Temple Lodge, No. 14, 1900, Albany, NY, (CMTS) Life Member

Russ, Alanson B.: (F) Member Temple Lodge, No. 14, 1900,

Albany, NY
Russ, Herman H.: (F) Member Albany Conclave, No. 8, Red Cross of Constantine, 1882, Albany, NY
Russ, Herman H.: (F) Member Grand Council of the Princes of Jerusalem, 1882, Albany, NY
Russ, Herman H.: (F) Member Ineffable and Sublime Grand Lodge of Perfection, 1882, Albany, NY
Russ, John: (F) Member Friendly Sons of St. Patrick,1893, Brooklyn, (CMTS)*"Brooklyn Eagle,"* May 18,1893, Article regarding the election of Andrew T. Sullivan as postmaster. In the article it mentioned that there were only 50 members in this Society., Guest. It is unknown if a member of the Society.
Russell, Robert B.: (F) Member Mount Vernon Lodge, No. 3, 1900, Albany, NY
Russll, C. H.: (F) Member Young People's Missionary Society, 1888, Brooklyn, (I) *"Brooklyn Eagle,"* Dec. 12, 1888. Article regarding Societies aiding churches., (CMTS) Helping All Souls Universalist Church, President
Ruthenberg, A.: (F) Member Herber Lodge, No. 698,1898, F. & A. M., New York, NY, Greenpoint area, (RES) New York City
Ruttblatt, Max: (F) Member Arcana Lodge, No. 246, F. & A. M., 1934, New York, NY, (JD) Feb. 9, 1932
Ruve, D.: (F) Member Long Island Lodge, No. 382, F. &. A. M., 1874, NY
Ryan, Charles H.: (F) Member Lowville Lodge No. 134, F. & A. M., 1929, Lowville, NY, (CO) Lewis, (JD) Jun. 12, 1896
Ryan, Charles H.: (F) Member Lowville Chapter No. 223, R. A. M., 1929, Lowville, NY, (CO) Lewis, (JD) Jan. 16, 1906
Ryan, Clarence B.: (F) Member Lowville Lodge No. 134, F. & A. M., 1929, Lowville, NY, (CO) Lewis, (JD) Mar. 29, 1912
Ryan, Clarence B.: (F) Member Lowville Chapter No. 223, R. A. M., 1929, Lowville, NY, (CO) Lewis, (JD) Jun. 4, 1912
Ryan, John F.: (F) Member Friendly Sons of St. Patrick,1893, Brooklyn, (CMTS)*"Brooklyn Eagle,"* May 18,1893, Article regarding the election of Andrew T. Sullivan as postmaster. In the article it mentioned that there were only 50 members in this Society., Member of the Dinner Committee
Ryan, John T.: (F) Member Friendly Sons of St. Patrick,1893, Brooklyn, (CMTS)*"Brooklyn Eagle,"* May 18,1893, Article regarding the election of Andrew T. Sullivan as postmaster. In the article it mentioned that there were only 50 members in this Society., Guest. It is unknown if a member of the Society.
Ryckman,Jr., R.: (F) Member Long Island Lodge, No. 382, F. &. A. M., 1874, NY
Ryder, S. G.: (F) Member Long Island Lodge, No. 382, F. &. A. M.,

Sabbagh, S. G.: (F) Member Arcana Lodge, No. 246, F. & A. M., 1934, New York, NY, (JD) Feb. 15, 1915
Sabin, G. D.: (F) Member Long Island Lodge, No. 382, F. &. A. M., 1874, NY
Saffen, Henry C.: (I) *"Brooklyn Eagle,"* Dec. 7, 1896. 12th Annual Memorial Services, Plymouth Church, Brooklyn Lodge No. 22, B. F. O. Elks, Roll Call of the dead. Address made by Maryland Senator George L. Wellington. , (CMTS) Name called.
Safranko, Abraham: (F) Member Arcana Lodge, No. 246, F. & A. M., 1934, New York, NY, (JD) Feb. 14, 1928
Safranko, Natalio B.: (F) Member Arcana Lodge, No. 246, F. & A. M., 1934, New York, NY, (JD) Jun. 8, 1926
Salinger, Robert E.: (F) Member Society of American Magicians, Apr., 1931, New York, (RES) New York City
Salisbury, Calvin O.: (F) Member Lowville Chapter No. 223, R. A. M., 1929, Lowville, NY, (CO) Lewis, (JD) May 27, 1890
Salisbury, Clavin O.: (F) Member Lowville Lodge No. 134, F. & A. M., 1929, Lowville, NY, (CO) Lewis, (JD) Apr. 6, 1883
Salisbury, George E.: (F) Member Lowville Lodge No. 134, F. & A. M., 1929, Lowville, NY, (CO) Lewis, (JD) Nov. 11, 1887
Salisbury, Walter S.: (F) Member Lowville Lodge No. 134, F. & A. M., 1929, Lowville, NY, (CO) Lewis, (JD) Jan. 23, 1891
Salisbury, Walter S.: (F) Member Lowville Chapter No. 223, R. A. M., 1929, Lowville, NY, (CO) Lewis, (JD) Mar. 2, 1897
Salladin, W. A.: (F) Member Lowville Lodge No. 134, F. & A. M., 1929, Lowville, NY, (CO) Lewis, (CMTS) Past Master1893, 1894
Sallee, Charles F.: (F) Member Lowville Lodge No. 134, F. & A. M., 1929, Lowville, NY, (CO) Lewis, (JD) Apr. 22, 1921
Sallee, Charles F.: (F) Member Lowville Chapter No. 223, R. A. M., 1929, Lowville, NY, (CO) Lewis, (JD) Nov. 28, 1922
Salmon, N. Wells: (F) Member Lowville Lodge No. 134, F. & A. M., 1929, Lowville, NY, (CO) Lewis, (JD) Apr. 7, 1922
Salvage, Mrs. W. : (F) Member Nativity Sewing Society, 1900, Brooklyn, (I) *"Brooklyn Eagle,"* Feb. 3, 1900. Article regarding raising money to buy clothing for the poor.
Sammis, E. Alden: (F) Member Lowville Chapter No. 223, R. A. M., 1929, Lowville, NY, (CO) Lewis, (JD) Nov. 27, 1928
Sammis, Edgar A.: (F) Member Lowville Lodge No. 134, F. & A. M., 1929, Lowville, NY, (CO) Lewis, (JD) Mar. 20, 1914
Sampson, Miss W.: (F) Member Nativity Sewing Society, 1900, Brooklyn, (I) *"Brooklyn Eagle,"* Feb. 3, 1900. Article regarding raising money to buy clothing for the poor.
Sanaders, Francis N.: (F) Member Temple Lodge, No. 14, 1900, Albany, NY

Sanders, Charles P.: (F) Member Grand Council of the Princes of
   Jerusalem, 1882, Albany, NY
Sanders, Charles P.: (F) Member Ineffable and Sublime Grand Lodge of
   Perfection, 1882, Albany, NY
Sanders, Eugene: (F) Member Temple Lodge, No. 14, 1900,
   Albany, NY
Sanders, William N. S.: (F) Member Masters Lodge, No. 5, 1900,
   Albany, NY
Sanderson, George: (F) Member Temple Lodge, No. 14, 1900,
   Albany, NY
Sanderson, Henry S.: (I) *"Brooklyn Eagle,"* Jun. 2, 1879, Dedication of
   the burial plot of the Order of Elks in Evergreen Cemetery,
   (CMTS) Esteemed Leading Knight
Sanford, M. F.: (F) Member Long Island Lodge, No. 382, F. &. A. M.,
   1874, NY
Sanger, Miss Anna P.: (I) *"Brooklyn Eagle,"* Jun. 2, 1879, Dedication of
   the burial plot of the Order of Elks in Evergreen Cemetery,
   (CMTS) Singer from Dr. Budington's Church
Sangmaster, Augustus: (F) Member Grand Council of the Princes of
   Jerusalem, 1882, Albany, NY, (CEN) 1880, $6^{th}$ Ward, Albany,
   Albany Co., NY, 51, Tailor, Hesse, Louise, 50, Maggie, 27,
   Mary M., 25, Augustus K., 23, Lillie G., 21, George C. Cook,
   23, nephew
Sangmaster, Augustus: (F) Member Ineffable and Sublime Grand Lodge
   Of Perfection, 1882, Albany, NY
Sann, Charles: (F) Member Temple Lodge, No. 14, 1900,
   Albany, NY
Sann, Fredrick: (F) Member Temple Lodge, No. 14, 1900, Albany, NY,
   (B) Oct. 22, 1871, (BAPT) Oct. 9, 1874, First Lutheran Church,
   Albany, NY
Sanxay, Charles S.: (F) Member Sons of New England, New England
   Society of the City of Brooklyn, 1890, (CMTS)*"Brooklyn Eagle,"*
   Dec. 21, 1890, 11th Annual Dinner, Attendees
Sargent, Mrs. Bertha L.: (F) Member Society of American Magicians,
   Apr., 1931, New York, (RES) New York City
Sautter, Jr., Louis: (F) Member Mount Vernon Lodge, No. 3, 1900,
   Albany, NY
Savas, John: (F) Member Lowville Lodge No. 134, F. & A. M., 1929,
   Lowville, NY, (CO) Lewis, (JD) Dec. 3, 1926
Sawtelle, H. C.: (F) Member Anglo Saxon Lodge No. 137, F. A. M.,
   (CMTS) Meeting Notes, *"Brooklyn Eagle,"* Mar. 23, 1887, Stood
   as guardian at the meeting
Sayles, James M.: (F) Member Temple Lodge, No. 14, 1900, Albany, NY,
   (CMTS) Past Maser 1869. (AKA) James Mason Sayles, (B)
   Mar. 1, 1837, (PRTS) John Sayles and Mary Ann Burton
Schaab, Henry H.: (F) Member Lowville Lodge No. 134, F. & A. M.,

1929, Lowville, NY, (CO) Lewis, (JD) Sep. 21, 1928

Schaefer, F.: (F) Member Herber Lodge, No. 698,1898, F. & A. M., New York, NY, Greenpoint area, (RES) New York City

Schaefer, H.: (F) Member Herber Lodge, No. 698,1898, F. & A. M., New York, NY, Greenpoint area, (RES) New York City

Schaefer, M.: (F) Member Herber Lodge, No. 698,1898, F. & A. M., New York, NY, Greenpoint area, (RES) New York City

Schafer, Henry: (F) Member Mount Vernon Lodge, No. 3, 1900, Albany, NY

Schaffer, Charles: (F) Member Long Island Lodge, No. 382, F. &. A. M., 1874, NY

Schaffer, Justus: (F) Member Long Island Lodge, No. 382, F. &. A. M., 1874, NY

Schaler, William: (F) Member Mount Vernon Lodge, No. 3, 1900, Albany, NY

Schantz, A. Arthur: (F) Member Lowville Lodge No. 134, F. & A. M., 1929, Lowville, NY, (CO) Lewis, (JD) Mar. 20, 1925

Schantz, Benjamin H,: (F) Member Lowville Chapter No. 223, R. A. M., 1929, Lowville, NY, (CO) Lewis, (JD) Mar. 9, 1920

Schantz, Benjamin H.: (F) Member Lowville Lodge No. 134, F. & A. M., 1929, Lowville, NY, (CO) Lewis, (JD) Mar. 5, 1920

Schantz, Leon H.: (F) Member Lowville Lodge No. 134, F. & A. M., 1929, Lowville, NY, (CO) Lewis, (JD) Oct. 15, 1920

Scharman, Henry J.: (I) *"Brooklyn Eagle,"* Dec. 7, 1896. 12th Annual Memorial Services, Plymouth Church, Brooklyn Lodge No. 22, B. F. O. Elks, Roll Call of the dead. Address made by Maryland Senator George L. Wellington. , (CMTS) Name called.

Schenck, W. V. B.: (F) Member Long Island Lodge, No. 382, F. &. A. M., 1874, NY

Scherer, Robert G.: (F) Member Temple Lodge, No. 14, 1900, Albany, NY

Schermerhorn, J. A.: (F) Member Temple Lodge, No. 14, 1900, Albany, NY

Schermerhorn, Mrs. Laura A.: (F) Member First Suffolk District, Meridan Chapter, No. 336, 1923, Islip, NY, (CMTS) Associate Matron, (RES) Islip

Schermerhorn, Wm. R.: (F) Member Temple Lodge, No. 14, 1900, Albany, NY

Scheurer, Charles T.: (F) Member Temple Lodge, No. 14, 1900, Albany, NY

Schifferdecker, Fred. A.: (F) Member Mount Vernon Lodge, No. 3, 1900, Albany, NY

Schifferdecker, Frederick: (F) Member Mount Vernon Lodge, No. 3, 1900, Albany, NY

Schimpf, Frank F.: (F) Member Mount Vernon Lodge, No. 3, 1900, Albany, NY

Schindler, John P.: (F) Member Lowville Lodge No. 134, F. & A. M., 1929, Lowville, NY, (CO) Lewis, (JD) Nov. 10, 1893

Schindler, John P.: (F) Member Lowville Chapter No. 223, R. A. M., 1929, Lowville, NY, (CO) Lewis, (JD) Feb. 9, 1898

Schlesinger, L.: (F) Member Herber Lodge, No. 698,1898, F. & A. M., New York, NY, Greenpoint area, (RES) Brooklyn

Schley, Evander M.: (F) Member Temple Lodge, No. 14, 1900, Albany, NY

Schlieder, Clarence A.: (F) Member Lowville Lodge No. 134, F. & A. M., 1929, Lowville, NY, (CO) Lewis, (JD) Mar. 21, 1919

Schlieper, Chas. F.: (F) Member Society of American Magicians, Apr., 1931, New York, (RES) Woodhaven, NY

Schmall, C.: (F) Member Long Island Lodge, No. 382, F. &. A. M., 1874, NY

Schmidt, Aug. A.: (F) Member Herber Lodge, No. 698,1898, F. & A. M., New York, NY, Greenpoint area, (RES) New York City

Schmidt, Brother: (F) Member Lessing Lodge No. 608, (CMTS) Meeting Notes, *"Brooklyn Eagle,"* Mar. 23, 1887, Past Master in attendance

Schmidt, Loretta: (F) Member Hope Rebekah Lodge No. 10, 1949-1950, Brockport, NY, (CO) Monroe, (CMTS) Chaplain

Schnebbe, Fred D.: (F) Member Society of American Magicians, Apr., 1931, New York, (RES) New York City

Schneider, Harry G.: (F) Member Knights and Ladies of Honor, 1900, Brooklyn, (I) *"Brooklyn Eagle,"* Feb. 3, 1900. Meeting Notice., (CMTS) Protector

Schneider, Hermon: (F) Member Knights and Ladies of Honor, 1900, Brooklyn, (I) *"Brooklyn Eagle,"* Feb. 3, 1900. Meeting Notice., (CMTS Treasurer

Schneider, J.: (F) Member Long Island Lodge, No. 382, F. &. A. M., 1874, NY

Schneider, Valentino: (F) Member Anglo Saxon Lodge No. 137, F. A. M., (CMTS) Meeting Notes, *"Brooklyn Eagle,"* Mar. 23, 1887, Member of New York Lodge No. 330 presented the working tools for the meeting

Schooping, Harvey W.: (F) Member Lowville Lodge No. 134, F. & A. M., 1929, Lowville, NY, (CO) Lewis, (JD) Nov. 18, 1927

Schorsch, M.: (F) Member Herber Lodge, No. 698,1898, F. & A. M., New York, NY, Greenpoint area, (RES) Brooklyn

Schreiber, M.D., Martin: (F) Member Society of American Magicians, Apr., 1931, New York, (RES) New York Ciry

Schroder, Mrs. Herman: (F) Member Mispah Circle, 1888, Brooklyn, (I) *"Brooklyn Eagle,"* Dec. 12, 1888. Mentioned in an article about a fair raising funds for a Home for the Blind

Schroeder, A.: (F) Member Herber Lodge, No. 698,1898, F. & A. M., New York, NY, Greenpoint area, (RES) New York City

Schultz, Andrew: (F) Member Independent Order of Good Templars, Westhampton Lodge No. 885, instituted Apr. 16, 1889, New Officers installed Feb. 16, 1900, (CMTS) Meeting Notes, *"Brooklyn Eagle,"* Feb. 18, 1900, Deputy Marshal

Schultz, F. G.: (F) Member Long Island Lodge, No. 382, F. &. A. M., 1874, NY

Schultz, H. F.: (F) Member Long Island Lodge, No. 382, F. &. A. M., 1874, NY

Schultz, Miss Etta: (F) Member Independent Order of Good Templars, Westhampton Lodge No. 885, instituted Apr. 16, 1889, New Officers installed Feb. 16, 1900, (CMTS) Meeting Notes, *"Brooklyn Eagle,"* Feb. 18, 1900, Vice Templar

Schumacher, Peter: (F) Member Temple Lodge, No. 14, 1900, Albany, NY

Schuman, F. C.: (F) Member Long Island Lodge, No. 382, F. &. A. M., 1874, NY

Schumann, Henry W.: (F) Member Temple Lodge, No. 14, 1900, Albany, NY

Schuster, Geo. D.: (F) Member Society of American Magicians, Apr., 1931, New York, (RES) Newark, NJ

Schwarz, C. F.: (F) Member Herber Lodge, No. 698,1898, F. & A. M., \ New York, NY, Greenpoint area, (RES) New York City

Scofield, Robert W.: (F) Member Temple Lodge, No. 14, 1900, Albany, NY

Scott, Daniel E.: (F) Member Temple Lodge, No. 14, 1900, Albany, NY

Scott, Louis A.: (F) Member Lowville Lodge No. 134, F. & A. M., 1929, Lowville, NY, (CO) Lewis, (CMTS) Past Master 1885

Scott, Rufus L.: (F) Member Sons of New England, New England Society of the City of Brooklyn, 1890, (CMTS)*"Brooklyn Eagle,"* Dec. 21, 1890, 11th Annual Dinner, Attendees

Scott, Warren L.: (F) Member Lowville Lodge No. 134, F. & A. M., 1929, Lowville, NY, (CO) Lewis, (CMTS) Past Master 1868

Scrimgeour, J.: (F) Member Long Island Lodge, No. 382, F. &. A. M., 1874, NY, (CMTS) Past Master

Seabury, Melvin: (F) Member Temple Lodge, No. 14, 1900, Albany, NY

Sealy, Glenn A.: (F) Member Lowville Chapter No. 223, R. A. M., 1929, Lowville, NY, (CO) Lewis, (JD) Jan. 18, 1927

Seaman, Frank W.: (F) Member Temple Lodge, No. 14, 1900, Albany, NY

Seaman, T. H.: (F) Member Long Island Lodge, No. 382, F. &. A. M., 1874, NY

Seaman, V. H.: (F) Member Brooklyn Revenue Reform Club, 1886, (I)*"Brooklyn Eagle,"* Jan. ,27 1886, Attendees at a dinner

Seaman, Jr., V. H.: (F) Member Brooklyn Revenue Reform Club,

1886, (I) *"Brooklyn Eagle,"* Jan. ,27 1886, Attendees at a dinner
Searl, Myron E.: (F) Member Lowville Lodge No. 134, F. & A. M., 1929, Lowville, NY, (CO) Lewis, (JD) Mar. 7, 1906
Searl, Myron E.: (F) Member Lowville Chapter No. 223, R. A. M., 1929, Lowville, NY, (CO) Lewis, (JD) Dec. 27, 1906
Seaver, H. G.: (F) Member Brooklyn Revenue Reform Club, 1886, (I) *"Brooklyn Eagle,"* Jan. ,27 1886, Attendees at a dinner
Sebast, Martin: (F) Member Temple Lodge, No. 14, 1900, Albany, NY
Secor, Benjamin M.: (F) Member Temple Lodge, No. 14, 1900, Albany, NY
Seeley, David W.: (F) Member Mount Vernon Lodge, No. 3, 1900, Albany, NY
Seimel, C.: (F) Member Herber Lodge, No. 698,1898, F. & A. M., New York, NY, Greenpoint area, (RES) New York City
Senrick, Charles M.: (F) Member Temple Lodge, No. 14, 1900, Albany, NY
Serviss, H. A.: (F) Member Long Island Lodge, No. 382, F. &. A. M., 1874, NY
Sewell, John: (F) Member Masters Lodge, No. 5, 1900, Albany, NY
Seyffert, J.: (F) Member Herber Lodge, No. 698,1898, F. & A. M., New York, NY, Greenpoint area, (RES) Brooklyn
Seymour, Frank: (F) Member Knights and Ladies of Honor, 1900, Brooklyn, (I) *"Brooklyn Eagle,"* Feb. 3, 1900. Meeting Notice., (CMTS) Financial Secretary
Shaffer, Calvin: (F) Member Mount Vernon Lodge, No. 3, 1900, Albany, NY
Shanks, Seth G.: (F) Member Mount Vernon Lodge, No. 3, 1900, Albany, NY
Sharp, A.: (F) Member Herber Lodge, No. 698,1898, F. & A. M., New York, NY, Greenpoint area, (RES) New York City
Sharp, George H.: (F) Member Mount Vernon Lodge, No. 3, 1900, Albany, NY
Shattuck, J. W. M.: (F) Member Temple Lodge, No. 14, 1900, Albany, NY
Shattuck, James A.: (F) Member Mount Vernon Lodge, No. 3, 1900, Albany, NY
Shaw, Edmond A.: (F) Member Lowville Lodge No. 134, F. & A. M., 1929, Lowville, NY, (CO) Lewis, (JD) Nov. 26, 1926
Shaw, John: (F) Member Sons of New England, New England Society of the City of Brooklyn, 1890, (CMTS) *"Brooklyn Eagle,"* Dec. 21, 1890, 11th Annual Dinner, Attendees
Shaw, John B.: (F) Member Temple Lodge, No. 14, 1900, Albany, NY
Shaw, O. R.: (F) Member Long Island Lodge, No. 382, F. &. A. M., 1874, NY
Shaxby, Charles J.: (F) Member Mount Vernon Lodge, No. 3, 1900,

Albany, NY

Shayne, Mrs. M. E.: (I) *"Brooklyn Eagle,"* Dec. 7, 1896. 12th Annual Memorial Services, Plymouth Church, Brooklyn Lodge No. 22, B. F. O. Elks, Roll Call of the dead. Address made by Maryland Senator George L. Wellington. , (CMTS) Sang a solo of "The Last Greeting"

Shea, Miss L. F.: (F) Member Nativity Sewing Society, 1900, Brooklyn, (I) *"Brooklyn Eagle,"* Feb. 3, 1900. Article regarding raising money to buy clothing for the poor.

Shearman, J. T.: (F) Member Brooklyn Revenue Reform Club, 1886, (I) *"Brooklyn Eagle,"* Jan. ,27 1886, Attendees at a dinner

Shearman, John A.: (F) Member Brooklyn Revenue Reform Club, 1886, (I) *"Brooklyn Eagle,"* Jan. ,27 1886, Attendees at a dinner

Sheely, Rev. Daniel: (F) Member Friendly Sons of St. Patrick,1893, Brooklyn, (CMTS)*"Brooklyn Eagle,"* May 18,1893, Article regarding the election of Andrew T. Sullivan as postmaster. In the article it mentioned that there were only 50 members in this Society., Guest. It is unknown if a member of the Society.

Sheffer, James H.: (F) Member Temple Lodge, No. 14, 1900, Albany, NY

Sheffield, G. H.: (F) Member Murray Lodge, No. 380, F. & A. M., 1906, Holley, Orleans, Co., NY, (CMTS) Past Master

Sheffield, G. Roland: (F) Member Murray Lodge, No. 380, F. & A. M., 1906, Holley, Orleans, Co., NY

Shelley, Charles E.: (F) Member Mount Vernon Lodge, No. 3, 1900, Albany, NY, (CMTS) Past Master 1885

Shelton, G. N.: (F) Member Long Island Lodge, No. 382, F. &. A. M., 1874, NY

Shepard, Dr. Charles H.: (F) Member Brooklyn Revenue Reform Club, 1886, (I)*"Brooklyn Eagle,"* Jan. ,27 1886, Attendees at a dinner

Shepard, Edward M.: (F) Member Brooklyn Revenue Reform Club, 1886, (I)*"Brooklyn Eagle,"* Jan. ,27 1886, Attendees at a dinner

Shepard, Frank A.: (F) Member Temple Lodge, No. 14, 1900, Albany, NY

Shepard, Frederic B.: (F) Member Society of American Magicians, Apr., 1931, New York, (RES) New York City

Shepard, George A.: (F) Member Lowville Lodge No. 134, F. & A. M., 1929, Lowville, NY, (CO) Lewis, (JD) Apr. 16, 1909

Shepard, K. M.: (F) Member Sons of New England, New England Society of the City of Brooklyn, 1887, (CMTS)*"Brooklyn Eagle,"* Dec. 22, 1887, Annual Dinner, Attendees

Shepard, Lewis F.: (F) Member Lowville Lodge No. 134, F. & A. M., 1929, Lowville, NY, (CO) Lewis, (JD) Apr. 6, 1883

Shepard, T. Mills: (F) Member Lowville Lodge No. 134, F. & A. M., 1929, Lowville, NY, (CO) Lewis, (JD) Jul. 5, 1918

Shepard, W. H.: (F) Member Brooklyn Revenue Reform Club, 1886,

(I)*"Brooklyn Eagle,"* Jan. ,27 1886, Attendees at a dinner
Shephard, George A.: (F) Member Lowville Chapter No. 223, R. A. M., 1929, Lowville, NY, (CO) Lewis, (JD) Jan. 17, 1911
Shephard, T. Mills: (F) Member Lowville Chapter No. 223, R. A. M., 1929, Lowville, NY, (CO) Lewis, (JD) Jun. 7, 1921
Shepheard, Edward W.: (F) Member Temple Lodge, No. 14, 1900, Albany, NY
Shepheard, John H.: (F) Member Temple Lodge, No. 14, 1900, Albany, NY
Sherman, General W. T.: (F) Member Sons of New England, New England Society of the City of Brooklyn, 1887, (CMTS)*"Brooklyn Eagle,"* Dec. 22, 1887, Annual Dinner, Attendees
Sherman, General William T.: (F) Member Sons of New England, New England Society of the City of Brooklyn, 1890, (CMTS)*"Brooklyn Eagle,"* Dec. 21, 1890, 11th Annual Dinner, Attendees
Sherman, John T.: (F) Member Sons of New England, New England Society of the City of Brooklyn, 1890, (CMTS)*"Brooklyn Eagle,"* Dec. 21, 1890, 11th Annual Dinner, Attendees
Sherman, John T.: (F) Member Sons of New England, New England Society of the City of Brooklyn, 1887, (CMTS)*"Brooklyn Eagle,"* Dec. 22, 1887, Annual Dinner, Attendees
Sherrill, Charles L.: (F) Member Temple Lodge, No. 14, 1900, Albany, NY
Sherwood, J.: (F) Member Long Island Lodge, No. 382, F. &. A. M., 1874, NY
Sherwood, John E.: (F) Member Temple Lodge, No. 14, 1900, Albany, NY
Sherwood, Miller G.: (F) Member Lowville Lodge No. 134, F. & A. M., 1929, Lowville, NY, (CO) Lewis, (JD) Feb. 18, 1898
Sherwood, Miller G.: (F) Member Lowville Chapter No. 223, R. A. M., 1929, Lowville, NY, (CO) Lewis, (JD) Mar. 29, 1908
Shevlin, James: (F) Member Friendly Sons of St. Patrick,1893, Brooklyn, (CMTS)*"Brooklyn Eagle,"* May 18,1893, Article regarding the election of Andrew T. Sullivan as postmaster. In the article it mentioned that there were only 50 members in this Society., Guest. It is unknown if a member of the Society.
Shilling, Mrs.: (F) Member Nativity Sewing Society, 1900, Brooklyn, (I) *"Brooklyn Eagle,"* Feb. 3, 1900. Article regarding raising money to buy clothing for the poor.
Shoemaker, A. McD.: (F) Member Mount Vernon Lodge, No. 3, 1900, Albany, NY
Shoemaker, James: (F) Member Temple Lodge, No. 14, 1900, Albany, NY
Shoemaker, William H : (F) Member Mount Vernon Lodge, No. 3, 1900, Albany, NY, (CMTS) Past Master 1873
Short, Brother: (F) Member Acanthus Lodge No. 719, F. A. M., (CMTS)

Meeting Notes, *"Brooklyn Eagle,"* Mar. 13, 1887, of Stella

Shreeve, H. Prescott: (F) Member Society of American Magicians, Apr., 1931, New York, (RES) Summitt, NJ

Shultz, Howard H.: (F) Member Mount Vernon Lodge, No. 3, 1900, Albany, NY

Shumway, Herman N.: (F) Member Lowville Chapter No. 223, R. A. M., 1929, Lowville, NY, (CO) Lewis, (JD) Feb. 17, 1908

Sidey, G.: (F) Member Long Island Lodge, No. 382, F. &. A. M., 1874, NY

Siebs, J.: (F) Member Herber Lodge, No. 698,1898, F. & A. M., New York, NY, Greenpoint area, (RES) New York City

Siegfried, Dora: (F) Member Hope Rebekah Lodge No. 10, 1949-1950, Brockport, NY, (CO) Monroe

Siems, Geo.: (F) Member Herber Lodge, No. 698,1898, F. & A. M., New York, NY, Greenpoint area, (RES) New York City

Silleck, W. Fred: (F) Member Long Island Lodge, No. 382, F. &. A. M., 1874, NY

Silliman, Benjamin D.: (F) Member Sons of New England, New England Society of the City of Brooklyn, 1890, (CMTS) *"Brooklyn Eagle,"* Dec. 21, 1890, 11th Annual Dinner, Attendees

Silliman, Benjamin D.: (F) Member Sons of New England, New England Society of the City of Brooklyn, 1887, (CMTS) *"Brooklyn Eagle,"* Dec. 22, 1887, Annual Dinner, Attendees

Simmons, Harry: (F) Member Temple Lodge, No. 14, 1900, Albany, NY

Simms, Wm. E.: (F) Member Society of American Magicians, Apr., 1931, New York, (RES) Yonkers, NJ

Simon, Lester C.: (F) Member Lowville Lodge No. 134, F. & A. M., 1929, Lowville, NY, (CO) Lewis, (JD) Mar. 20, 1908

Simonson, J. H.: (F) Member Washington Lodge, No. 85, 1900, Albany, NY, (CMTS) Past Members

Simpson, John: (F) Member Long Island Lodge, No. 382, F. &. A. M., 1874, NY

Simpson, Mrs. James E.: (F) Member Lenox Ladies Aid Society of Lenox Road M. E. Church, Brooklyn, 1900, (CMTS) *"Brooklyn Eagle,"* Mar. 13, 1900. Meeting Notice, Board of Managers

Simpson, Jr., J. E.: (F) Member Long Island Lodge, No. 382, F. &. A. M., 1874, NY

Sims, Edward C.: (F) Member Temple Lodge, No. 14, 1900, Albany, NY

Sims, Gardner C.: (F) Member Temple Lodge, No. 14, 1900, Albany, NY

Sinclair, M.D., Daniel A.: (F) Member Society of American Magicians, Apr., 1931, New York, (RES) New York City

Singer, Frderick J.: (F) Member Lowville Lodge No. 134, F. & A. M., 1929, Lowville, NY, (CO) Lewis, (JD) May 20, 1910

Singer, Frederick J.: (F) Member Lowville Lodge No. 134, F. & A. M., 1929, Lowville, NY, (CO) Lewis, (JD) May 20, 1910

Sinn, Walter L.: (I) *"Brooklyn Eagle,"* Dec. 7, 1896. 12th Annual

Memorial Services, Plymouth Church, Brooklyn Lodge No. 22, B. F. O. Elks, Roll Call of the dead. Address made by Maryland Senator George L. Wellington. , (CMTS) Name called.

Sivertsen, C. G.: (F) Member Long Island Lodge, No. 382, F. &. A. M., 1874, NY

Skelly, Mrs.: (F) Member Nativity Sewing Society, 1900, Brooklyn, (I) *"Brooklyn Eagle,"* Feb. 3, 1900. Article regarding raising money to buy clothing for the poor.

Skelly, Mrs. W. J.: (F) Member Nativity Sewing Society, 1900, Brooklyn, (I) *"Brooklyn Eagle,"* Feb. 3, 1900. Article regarding raising money to buy clothing for the poor.

Skinner, Dr. D. S.: (F) Member Brooklyn Dental Society, 1877, Brooklyn, NY, (CMTS) *"Brooklyn Eagle,"* Dec. 15, 1877. Celebration of 10th Anniversary. Society established Dec. 14, 1867, (CMTS) Present from Brooklyn

Skinner, Edgar: (F) Member Commonwealth Lodge No. 409, (CMTS) Meeting Notes, *"Brooklyn Eagle,"* Mar. 13, 1887

Skinner, M. E.: (F) Member Mount Vernon Lodge, No. 3, 1900, Albany, NY

Skinner, William A.: (F) Member Temple Lodge, No. 14, 1900, Albany, NY

Slack, G. M.: (F) Member Long Island Lodge, No. 382, F. &. A. M., 1874, NY

Slack, Henry W.: (F) Member Lowville Lodge No. 134, F. & A. M., 1929, Lowville, NY, (CO) Lewis, (JD) May 2, 1893

Slack, Henry W.: (F) Member Lowville Lodge No. 134, F. & A. M., 1929, Lowville, NY, (CO) Lewis, (JD) May 2, 1893

Slingerland, Corn. H.: (F) Member Masters Lodge, No. 5, 1900, Albany, NY

Slocum, General H. W.: (F) Member Sons of New England, New England Society of the City of Brooklyn, 1890, (CMTS) *"Brooklyn Eagle,"* Dec. 21, 1890, 11th Annual Dinner, Attendees

Slocum, Humphrey E.: (F) Member Lowville Lodge No. 134, F. & A. M., 1929, Lowville, NY, (CO) Lewis, (JD) Dec. 7, 1906

Slocum, Humphrey E.: (F) Member Lowville Lodge No. 134, F. & A. M., 1929, Lowville, NY, (CO) Lewis, (JD) Dec. 7, 1906

Slocum, I. H.: (F) Member Long Island Lodge, No. 382, F. &. A. M., 1874, NY

Sloss, Robert A.: (F) Member Temple Lodge, No. 14, 1900, Albany, NY, (B) Jan. 8, 1830, (D) Oct. 28, 1913, (C) Albany Rural Cemetery, Albany, NY

Slote, Alonzo: (F) Member Sons of New England, New England Society of the City of Brooklyn, 1887, (CMTS) *"Brooklyn Eagle,"* Dec. 22, 1887, Annual Dinner, Attendees

Smith, Albert H.: (F) Member Lowville Lodge No. 134, F. & A. M., 1929, Lowville, NY, (CO) Lewis, (JD) Oct. 4, 1918

Smith, Albert T.: (F) Member Temple Lodge, No. 14, 1900, Albany, NY

Smith, Augustus H.: (F) Member Temple Lodge, No. 14, 1900, Albany, NY

Smith, C. G.: (F) Member Independent Order of Good Templars, Westhampton Lodge No. 885, instituted Apr. 16, 1889, New Officers installed Feb. 16, 1900, (CMTS) Meeting Notes, *"Brooklyn Eagle,"* Feb. 18, 1900, Treasurer

Smith, Carroll F.: (F) Member Temple Lodge, No. 14, 1900, Albany, NY

Smith, Charles A.: (F) Member Lowville Lodge No. 134, F. & A. M., 1929, Lowville, NY, (CO) Lewis, (JD) Mar. 15, 1901

Smith, Charles A.: (F) Member Lowville Lodge No. 134, F. & A. M., 1929, Lowville, NY, (CO) Lewis, (JD) Mar. 15, 1901

Smith, Charles F.: (I) *"Brooklyn Eagle,"* Dec. 7, 1896. 12th Annual Memorial Services, Plymouth Church, Brooklyn Lodge No. 22, B. F. O. Elks, Roll Call of the dead. Address made by Maryland Senator George L. Wellington. , (CMTS) Name called.

Smith, Charles Robinson: (F) Member Sons of New England, New England Society of the City of Brooklyn, 1890, (CMTS)*"Brooklyn Eagle,"* Dec. 21, 1890, 11th Annual Dinner, Attendees

Smith, Elihu R.: (F) Member Temple Lodge, No. 14, 1900, Albany, NY

Smith, G. J.: (F) Member Long Island Lodge, No. 382, F. &. A. M., 1874, NY

Smith, George A.: (F) Member Mount Vernon Lodge, No. 3, 1900, Albany, NY

Smith, George W.: (F) Member Lowville Lodge No. 134, F. & A. M., 1929, Lowville, NY, (CO) Lewis, (JD) Nov. 16, 1920

Smith, Glenn W.: (F) Member Lowville Lodge No. 134, F. & A. M., 1929, Lowville, NY, (CO) Lewis, (JD) Jun. 19, 1920

Smith, Henry C.: (F) Member Grand Council of the Princes of Jerusalem, 1882, Albany, NY

Smith, Henry C.: (F) Member Ineffable and Sublime Grand Lodge of Perfection, 1882, Albany, NY

Smith, Henry J.: (F) Member Acanthus Lodge No. 719, F. A. M., (CMTS) Meeting Notes, *"Brooklyn Eagle,"* Mar. 13, 1887, of Brooklyn

Smith, Henry L.: (F) Member Mount Vernon Lodge, No. 3, 1900, Albany, NY

Smith, Henry Lewis: (F) Member Albany Conclave, No. 8, Red Cross of Constantine, 1882, Albany, NY

Smith, Henry Lyle: (F) Member Grand Council of the Princes of Jerusalem, 1882, Albany, NY

Smith, Henry Lyle: (F) Member Ineffable and Sublime Grand Lodge of Perfection, 1882, Albany, NY

Smith, Howard F.: (F) Member Lowville Lodge No. 134, F. & A. M., 1929, Lowville, NY, (CO) Lewis, (JD) Nov. 28, 1917

Smith, Howard F.: (F) Member Lowville Lodge No. 134, F. & A. M.,

1929, Lowville, NY, (CO) Lewis, (JD) Nov. 28, 1917
Smith, I. Ives: (F) Member Lowville Chapter No. 223, R. A. M., 1929, Lowville, NY, (CO) Lewis, (JD) Dec. 26, 1911
Smith, J. N.: (F) Member Long Island Lodge, No. 382, F. &. A. M., 1874, NY
Smith, J. W.: (F) Member Long Island Lodge, No. 382, F. &. A. M., 1874, NY
Smith, James P.: (F) Member Masters Lodge, No. 5, 1900, Albany, NY
Smith, James W.: (F) Member Sons of New England, New England Society of the City of Brooklyn, 1890, (CMTS) *"Brooklyn Eagle,"* Dec. 21, 1890, 11th Annual Dinner, Attendees
Smith, John P.: (I) *"Brooklyn Eagle,"* Jun. 2, 1879, Dedication of the burial plot of the Order of Elks in Evergreen Cemetery, (CMTS) Marshal
Smith, Leon H.: (F) Member Lowville Lodge No. 134, F. & A. M., 1929, Lowville, NY, (CO) Lewis, (JD) May 20, 1913
Smith, Leonard: (F) Member Lowville Lodge No. 134, F. & A. M., 1929, Lowville, NY, (CO) Lewis, (JD) Apr. 16, 1920
Smith, Leonard D.: (F) Member Lowville Lodge No. 134, F. & A. M., 1929, Lowville, NY, (CO) Lewis, (JD) Apr. 16, 1920
Smith, Millard F.: (F) Member Sons of New England, New England Society of the City of Brooklyn, 1890, (CMTS) *"Brooklyn Eagle,"* Dec. 21, 1890, 11th Annual Dinner, Attendees
Smith, Milton M.: (F) Member Society of American Magicians, Apr., 1931, New York, (RES) Teachers College, Columbia University, NY
Smith, Mrs. Helen L.: (F) Member First District Suffolk, Jepthah's Daughter, No. 187, 1923, Huntington, NY, (CMTS) Secretary, (RES) Huntington
Smith, Myron S.: (F) Member Temple Lodge, No. 14, 1900, Albany, NY
Smith, Oscar: (F) Member Temple Lodge, No. 14, 1900, Albany, NY
Smith, P.: (F) Member Long Island Lodge, No. 382, F. &. A. M., 1874, NY
Smith, Rensselaer J.: (F) Member Mount Vernon Lodge, No. 3, 1900, Albany, NY
Smith, Sherman D.: (F) Member Lowville Chapter No. 223, R. A. M., 1929, Lowville, NY, (CO) Lewis, (JD) Apr. 4, 1912
Smith, Theodore E.: (F) Member Sons of New England, New England Society of the City of Brooklyn, 1890, (CMTS) *"Brooklyn Eagle,"* Dec. 21, 1890, 11th Annual Dinner, Attendees
Smith, Walter D.: (F) Member Monticello Lodge, No. 532, F. & A. M., (CO) Sullivan Co., NY, (CMTS) Past Master 1908, 1909
Smith, William Henry: (F) Member Temple Lodge, No. 14, 1900, Albany, NY
Smith, Winford A.: (F) Member Lowville Lodge No. 134, F. & A. M., 1929, Lowville, NY, (CO) Lewis, (JD) Nov. 28, 1919

Smith, Winford A.: (F) Member Lowville Lodge No. 134, F. & A. M., 1929, Lowville, NY, (CO) Lewis, (JD) Nov. 28, 1919

Smith, Winford A.: (F) Member Lowville Chapter No. 223, R. A. M., 1929, Lowville, NY, (CO) Lewis, (JD) Nov. 13, 1923

Smyley, William: (F) Member Mount Vernon Lodge, No. 3, 1900, Albany, NY

Smythe, Charles G.: (F) Member Temple Lodge, No. 14, 1900, Albany, NY

Sneider, Tiny: (F) Member Mispah Circle, 1888, Brooklyn, (I) *"Brooklyn Eagle,"* Dec. 12, 1888. Mentioned in an article about a fair raising funds for a Home for the Blind

Sniper, Gustavus C.: (F) Member Temple Lodge, No. 14, 1900, Albany, NY

Snook, F. G.: (F) Member Monticello Lodge, No. 532, F. & A. M., (CO) Sullivan Co., NY, (CMTS) Past Master 1877, 1878, 1879

Snow, Whiting G.: (F) Member Masters Lodge, No. 5, 1900, Albany, NY

Snow, William: (I) *"Brooklyn Eagle,"* Dec. 7, 1896. 12th Annual Memorial Services, Plymouth Church, Brooklyn Lodge No. 22, B. F. O. Elks, Roll Call of the dead. Address made by Maryland Senator George L. Wellington. , (CMTS) Name called.

Snyder, Clarence E.: (F) Member Lowville Chapter No. 223, R. A. M., 1929, Lowville, NY, (CO) Lewis, (JD) Apr. 10, 1923

Snyder, Lamont C.: (F) Member Lowville Lodge No. 134, F. & A. M., 1929, Lowville, NY, (CO) Lewis, (JD) Nov. 2, 1923

Snyder, Louis G. A.: (F) Member Temple Lodge, No. 14, 1900, Albany, NY

Solcum, Jr., Henry W.: (F) Member Sons of New England, New England Society of the City of Brooklyn, 1890, (CMTS)*"Brooklyn Eagle,"* Dec. 21, 1890, 11th Annual Dinner, Attendees

Somers, Arthur : (F) Member Friendly Sons of St. Patrick,1893, Brooklyn, (CMTS)*"Brooklyn Eagle,"* May 18,1893, Article regarding the election of Andrew T. Sullivan as postmaster. In the article it mentioned that there were only 50 members in this Society., Guest. It is unknown if a member of the Society.

Somers, Arthur S.: (F) Member Friendly Sons of St. Patrick, 1899, Brooklyn, (CMTS)*"Brooklyn Eagle,"* Dec. 9, 1899, Article regarding the election of officers for 1900, (CMTS) Trustee

Somers, Daniel: (F) Member Sons of New England, New England Society of the City of Brooklyn, 1890, (CMTS)*"Brooklyn Eagle,"* Dec. 21, 1890, 11th Annual Dinner, Attendees

Somers, E. M.: (F) Member Sons of New England, New England Society of the City of Brooklyn, 1887, (CMTS)*"Brooklyn Eagle,"* Dec. 22, 1887, Annual Dinner, Attendees

Somerville, Robert: (F) Member Mount Vernon Lodge, No. 3, 1900, Albany, NY

Soulier, Henry P.: (F) Member Masters Lodge, No. 5, 1900, Albany, NY

Southard, George H.: (F) Member Sons of New England, New England Society of the City of Brooklyn, 1890, (CMTS)*"Brooklyn Eagle,"* Dec. 21, 1890, 11th Annual Dinner, Attendees

Southern, Samuel: (F) Member Temple Lodge, No. 14, 1900, Albany, NY

Southworth, A. G.: (F) Member Murray Lodge, No. 380, F. & A. M., 1906, Holley, Orleans, Co., NY

Sparrow, E.: (F) Member Long Island Lodge, No. 382, F. &. A. M., 1874, NY

Spawn, William H. A.: (F) Member Temple Lodge, No. 14, 1900, Albany, NY

Spedick, P.: (F) Member Long Island Lodge, No. 382, F. &. A. M., 1874, NY

Speir, Smith J.: (F) Member Masters Lodge, No. 5, 1900, Albany, NY

Speir, Stuart G.: (F) Member Masters Lodge, No. 5, 1900, Albany, NY, (CMTS) Past Master

Spelman, T. J.: (F) Member Sons of New England, New England Society of the City of Brooklyn, 1890, (CMTS)*"Brooklyn Eagle,"* Dec. 21, 1890, 11th Annual Dinner, Attendees

Spencer, James E.: (F) Member Sons of New England, New England Society of the City of Brooklyn, 1890, (CMTS)*"Brooklyn Eagle,"* Dec. 21, 1890, 11th Annual Dinner, Attendees

Sperry, Frank: (F) Member Sons of New England, New England Society of the City of Brooklyn, 1887, (CMTS)*"Brooklyn Eagle,"* Dec. 22, 1887, Annual Dinner, Attendees

Sperry, J. A.: (F) Member Friendly Sons of St. Patrick,1893, Brooklyn, (CMTS)*"Brooklyn Eagle,"* May 18,1893, Article regarding the election of Andrew T. Sullivan as postmaster. In the article it mentioned that there were only 50 members in this Society., Guest. It is unknown if a member of the Society.

Spicer, Elihu: (F) Member Sons of New England, New England Society of the City of Brooklyn, 1890, (CMTS)*"Brooklyn Eagle,"* Dec. 21, 1890, 11th Annual Dinner, Attendees

Spierre, Alexander H.: (F) Member Temple Lodge, No. 14, 1900, Albany, NY

Spiltz, Ervin S.: (F) Member Society of American Magicians, Apr., 1931, New York, (RES) Brooklyn, NY

Spoo, John: (F) Member Mount Vernon Lodge, No. 3, 1900, Albany, NY

Sprague, D. D.: (F) Member Murray Lodge, No. 380, F. & A. M., 1906, Holley, Orleans, Co., NY, (CMTS) Past Master

Sprague, J. D.: (F) Member Murray Lodge, No. 380, F. & A. M., 1906, Holley, Orleans, Co., NY

Sprague, N. T.: (F) Member Sons of New England, New England Society of the City of Brooklyn, 1887, (CMTS)*"Brooklyn Eagle,"* Dec. 22, 1887, Annual Dinner, Attendees

Sprague, W. R.: (F) Member Masters Lodge, No. 5, 1900, Albany, NY

Sprague, William B.: (F) Member Grand Council of the Princes of Jerusalem, 1882, Albany, NY

Springsteen, Eugene J.: (F) Member Lowville Lodge No. 134, F. & A. M., 1929, Lowville, NY, (CO) Lewis, (JD) Jan. 5, 1923

Squier, Frank: (F) Member Sons of New England, New England Society of the City of Brooklyn, 1890, (CMTS) *"Brooklyn Eagle,"* Dec. 21, 1890, 11th Annual Dinner, Attendees

Squire, A. J.: (F) Member Murray Lodge, No. 380, F. & A. M., 1906, Holley, Orleans, Co., NY

Squire, A. R.: (F) Member Murray Lodge, No. 380, F. & A. M., 1906, Holley, Orleans, Co., NY

Staats, Edward P.: (F) Member Mount Vernon Lodge, No. 3, 1900, Albany, NY

Stacpole, Horatio P.: (F) Member Grand Council of the Princes of Jerusalem, 1882, Albany, NY

Stacpole, Horatio P.: (F) Member Ineffable and Sublime Grand Lodge of Perfection, 1882, Albany, NY

Stacpole, Horatio P.: (F) Member Masters Lodge, No. 5, 1900, Albany, NY

Stadtler, G. A.: (F) Member Herber Lodge, No. 698, 1898, F. & A. M., New York, NY, Greenpoint area, (RES) New York City

Staechia, William: (F) Member Temple Lodge, No. 14, 1900, Albany, NY

Stafford, Brother: (F) Member Acanthus Lodge No. 719, F. A. M., (CMTS) Meeting Notes, *"Brooklyn Eagle,"* Mar. 13, 1887, of Brooklyn

Standford, Leland H: (F) Member Lowville Lodge No. 134, F. & A. M., 1929, Lowville, NY, (CO) Lewis, (JD) Oct. 17, 1913

Standford, Leland H.: (F) Member Lowville Chapter No. 223, R. A. M., 1929, Lowville, NY, (CO) Lewis, (JD) Dec. 2, 1913

Standish, Miles: (F) Member Sons of New England, New England Society of the City of Brooklyn, 1890, (CMTS) *"Brooklyn Eagle,"* Dec. 21, 1890, 11th Annual Dinner, Attendees

Stange, H.: (F) Member Herber Lodge, No. 698, 1898, F. & A. M., New York, NY, Greenpoint area, (RES) Brooklyn

Stanton, Harley N.: (F) Member Lowville Lodge No. 134, F. & A. M., 1929, Lowville, NY, (CO) Lewis, (JD) Jan. 18, 1929

Stanton, Lewis N.: (F) Member Monticello Lodge, No. 532, F. & A. M., (CO) Sullivan Co., NY, (CMTS) Past Master 1918

Staples, Cyrus E.: (F) Member Sons of New England, New England Society of the City of Brooklyn, 1890, (CMTS) *"Brooklyn Eagle,"* Dec. 21, 1890, 11th Annual Dinner, Attendees

Staples, Ernest W.: (F) Member Sons of New England, New England Society of the City of Brooklyn, 1890, (CMTS) *"Brooklyn Eagle,"* Dec. 21, 1890, 11th Annual Dinner, Attendees

Stark, Charles: (F) Member Mount Vernon Lodge, No. 3, 1900, Albany, NY

Starns, J. M.: (F) Member Mount Vernon Lodge, No. 3, 1900, Albany, NY

Starr, Charles S.: (F) Member Monticello Lodge, No. 532, F. & A. M., (CO) Sullivan Co., NY, (CMTS) Past Master 1880, Trustee 1897

Starr, Davis G.: (F) Member Monticello Lodge, No. 532, F. & A. M., (CO) Sullivan Co., NY, (CMTS) Past Master, 1862,1863, 1864, 1868, 1869

Starr, Ethel: (F) Member Hope Rebekah Lodge No. 10, 1949-1950, Brockport, NY, (CO) Monroe, (CMTS) Outside Guardian

Starr, Frederick W.: (F) Member Friendly Sons of St. Patrick,1893, Brooklyn, (CMTS)*"Brooklyn Eagle,"* May 18,1893, Article regarding the election of Andrew T. Sullivan as postmaster. In the article it mentioned that there were only 50 members in this Society., Guest. It is unknown if a member of the Society.

Starr, Mrs. Burton: (F) Member Hope Rebekah Lodge No. 10, 1949-1950, Brockport, NY, (CO) Monroe

Staton, Charles I.: (F) Member Lexington Lodge, 310, F. A. & M., 1900, Brooklyn, (I) *"Brooklyn Eagle,"* Feb. 3, 1900. Meeting Notice., (CMTS) Secretary

Stauderman, J.: (F) Member Herber Lodge, No. 698,1898, F. & A. M., New York, NY, Greenpoint area, (RES) New York City

Steele, Chas. R.: (F) Member Society of American Magicians, Apr., 1931, New York, (RES) E. Orange, NJ

Steele, Fannie: (F) Member Hope Rebekah Lodge No. 10, 1949-1950, Brockport, NY, (CO) Monroe, (CMTS) Finance Committee

Steele, Newell B.: (F) Member Lowville Lodge No. 134, F. & A. M., 1929, Lowville, NY, (CO) Lewis, (JD) Nov. 29, 1907

Steen, Andrew G.: (F) Member Society of American Magicians, Apr., 1931, New York, (RES) Laurelton, Long Island, NY

Steenburg, B. U.: (F) Member Mount Vernon Lodge, No. 3, 1900, Albany, NY

Steffany, F.: (F) Member Long Island Lodge, No. 382, F. &. A. M., 1874, NY

Stein, L. H.: (F) Member Long Island Lodge, No. 382, F. &. A. M., 1874, NY

Steinhilber, Charles H.: (F) Member Lowville Lodge No. 134, F. & A. M., 1929, Lowville, NY, (CO) Lewis, (JD) Jun. 4, 1926

Steinhilber, E. William: (F) Member Lowville Lodge No. 134, F. & A. M., 1929, Lowville, NY, (CO) Lewis, (JD) Feb. 19, 1926

Stephenson, Matthew: (F) Member Temple Lodge, No. 14, 1900, Albany, NY

Stephenson, Mrs. James: (F) Member Ladies' Willing Aid Society, 1888, Brooklyn, (I) *"Brooklyn Eagle,"* Dec. 12, 1888. Article regarding

Societies aiding churches., (CMTS) Helping Green Avenue Presbyterian Church, First Directress

Stephenson, Samuel T.: (F) Member Temple Lodge, No. 14, 1900, Albany, NY

Stern, Henry E.: (F) Member Washington Lodge, No. 85, 1900, Albany, NY, (CMTS) Past Members

Stetson, William M.: (F) Member Temple Lodge, No. 14, 1900, Albany, NY

Stetten, Jr., Dewitt: (F) Member Society of American Magicians, Apr., 1931, New York, (RES) New York City

Stevens, G. E.: (F) Member Long Island Lodge, No. 382, F. &. A. M., 1874, NY

Stevens, George E.: (F) Member Lowville Lodge No. 134, F. & A. M., 1929, Lowville, NY, (CO) Lewis, (JD) Feb. 6, 1925

Stevens, George T.: (F) Member Mount Vernon Lodge, No. 3, 1900, Albany, NY

Stevens, Harold B.: (F) Member Lowville Lodge No. 134, F. & A. M., 1929, Lowville, NY, (CO) Lewis, (JD) Feb. 19, 1926

Stevens, Harold B.: (F) Member Lowville Chapter No. 223, R. A. M., 1929, Lowville, NY, (CO) Lewis, (JD) Mar. 8, 1927

Stevens, Joseph B,: (F) Member Temple Lodge, No. 14, 1900, Albany, NY, (CMTS) Past Master 1894

Stevens, Richard V.: (F) Member Ineffable and Sublime Grand Lodge of Perfection, 1882, Albany, NY

Stevenson, Mrs.: (F) Member Ladies' Home and Foreign Mission Society, 1888, Brooklyn, (I) *"Brooklyn Eagle,"* Dec. 12, 1888. Article regarding Societies aiding churches., (CMTS) Helping Green Avenue Presbyterian Church, Secretary

Stewart, David A.: (F) Member Lowville Lodge No. 134, F. & A. M., 1929, Lowville, NY, (CO) Lewis, (CMTS) Past Master 1851, 1852

Stewart, David R.: (F) Member Mount Vernon Lodge, No. 3, 1900, Albany, NY

Stewart, John S.: (F) Member Lowville Lodge No. 134, F. & A. M., 1929, Lowville, NY, (CO) Lewis, (CMTS) Past Master 1872

Stickney, Milton W.: (F) Member Albany Conclave, No. 8, Red Cross of Constantine, 1882, Albany, NY

Stickney, Milton W.: (F) Member Grand Council of the Princes of Jerusalem, 1882, Albany, NY

Stiles, Alfred H.: (F) Member Lowville Lodge No. 134, F. & A. M., 1929, Lowville, NY, (CO) Lewis, (JD) Apr. 7, 1922

Stiles, Miss: (F) Member Nativity Sewing Society, 1900, Brooklyn, (I) *"Brooklyn Eagle,"* Feb. 3, 1900. Article regarding raising money to buy clothing for the poor.

Stillman, William O.: (F) Member Masters Lodge, No. 5, 1900, Albany, NY

Stine, Charles H.: (F) Member Lowville Lodge No. 134, F. & A. M.,

1929, Lowville, NY, (CO) Lewis, (JD) Feb. 6, 1925
Stine, John V.: (F) Member Temple Lodge, No. 14, 1900, Albany, NY
Stnickey, Milton W.: (F) Member Ineffable and Sublime Grand Lodge of Perfection, 1882, Albany, NY
Stock, Helen: (F) Member Hope Rebekah Lodge No. 10, 1949-1950, Brockport, NY, (CO) Monroe, (CMTS) Finance Committee
Stockford, G.: (F) Member Long Island Lodge, No. 382, F. &. A. M., 1874, NY
Stockwell, U. G.: (F) Member Temple Lodge, No. 14, 1900, Albany, NY
Stoddard, Earl W.: (F) Member Lowville Lodge No. 134, F. & A. M., 1929, Lowville, NY, (CO) Lewis, (JD) Dec. 6, 1918
Stoddard, H. Ferdinand: (F) Member Lowville Lodge No. 134, F. & A. M., 1929, Lowville, NY, (CO) Lewis, (JD) Nov. 30, 1900
Stoddard, Richard H.: (F) Member Lowville Lodge No. 134, F. & A. M., 1929, Lowville, NY, (CO) Lewis, (JD) May 14, 1928
Stoddard, Wait J.: (F) Member Lowville Lodge No. 134, F. & A. M., 1929, Lowville, NY, (CO) Lewis, (JD) Apr. 21, 1905
Stoddard, Wait J.: (F) Member Lowville Chapter No. 223, R. A. M., 1929, Lowville, NY, (CO) Lewis, (JD) Mar. 27, 1906
Stodoff, P. W.: (F) Member Long Island Lodge, No. 382, F. &. A. M., 1874, NY
Stoenman, George T.: (F) Member Temple Lodge, No. 14, 1900, Albany, NY, (CMTS) Life Member
Stoker, William H. : (F) Member Temple Lodge, No. 14, 1900, Albany, NY
Storer, S. L.: (F) Member Long Island Lodge, No. 382, F. &. A. M., 1874, NY
Storrs, Augustus: (F) Member Sons of New England, New England Society of the City of Brooklyn, 1890, (CMTS) *"Brooklyn Eagle,"* Dec. 21, 1890, 11th Annual Dinner, Attendees
Storrs, Augustus: (F) Member Sons of New England, New England Society of the City of Brooklyn, 1887, (CMTS) *"Brooklyn Eagle,"* Dec. 22, 1887, Annual Dinner, Attendees
Storrs, William H.: (F) Member Temple Lodge, No. 14, 1900, Albany, NY
Story, James T.: (F) Member Temple Lodge, No. 14, 1900, Albany, NY, (CMTS) Life Member
Story, William: (F) Member Grand Council of the Princes of Jerusalem, 1882, Albany, NY
Story, William: (F) Member Ineffable and Sublime Grand Lodge of Perfection, 1882, Albany, NY
Story, William: (F) Member Masters Lodge, No. 5, 1900, Albany, NY, (CMTS) Past Master
Stott, Hiram W.: (F) Member Temple Lodge, No. 14, 1900, Albany, NY

Stranahan, J. S. T.: (F) Member Friendly Sons of St. Patrick,1893, Brooklyn, (CMTS) *"Brooklyn Eagle,"* May 18,1893, Article regarding the election of Andrew T. Sullivan as postmaster. In the article it mentioned that there were only 50 members in this Society., Guest. It is unknown if a member of the Society.

Stranahan, J. S. T.: (F) Member Sons of New England, New England Society of the City of Brooklyn, 1890, (CMTS) *"Brooklyn Eagle,"* Dec. 21, 1890, 11th Annual Dinner, Attendees

Stranahan, J. S. T.: (F) Member Sons of New England, New England Society of the City of Brooklyn, 1887, (CMTS) *"Brooklyn Eagle,"* Dec. 22, 1887, Annual Dinner, Attendees

Strasser, Benjamin: (F) Member Mount Vernon Lodge, No. 3, 1900, Albany, NY, (CMTS) Past Master 1897

Strasser, Isaac M.: (F) Member Mount Vernon Lodge, No. 3, 1900, Albany, NY

Strasser, Solomon: (F) Member Mount Vernon Lodge, No. 3, 1900, Albany, NY, (CMTS) Past Master 1887

Straub, Philip: (F) Member Long Island Lodge, No. 382, F. &. A. M., 1874, NY

Street, Alfred W.: (F) Member Temple Lodge, No. 14, 1900, Albany, NY

Street, G. N.: (F) Member Long Island Lodge, No. 382, F. &. A. M., 1874, NY

Stremple, J. Edward: (F) Member Temple Lodge, No. 14, 1900, Albany, NY

Stretch, W. M.: (F) Member Anglo Saxon Lodge No. 137, F. A. M., (CMTS) Meeting Notes, *"Brooklyn Eagle,"* Mar. 23, 1887, Predestrian at the meeting

Strickland, Ralph: (F) Member Masters Lodge, No. 5, 1900, Albany, NY

Stroeber, A.: (F) Member Herber Lodge, No. 698,1898, F. & A. M., New York, NY, Greenpoint area, (RES) New York City

Strong, Frederick S.: (F) Member Masters Lodge, No. 5, 1900, Albany, NY

Stuart, Donald C.: (F) Member Lowville Chapter No. 223, R. A. M., 1929, Lowville, NY, (CO) Lewis, (JD) Dec. 18, 1922

Stubblebine, Daniel H.: (F) Member Temple Lodge, No. 14, 1900, Albany, NY

Stuckebury, Edward: (F) Member Long Island Lodge, No. 382, F. &. A. M., 1874, NY

Stuckert, Abner M.: (F) Member Masters Lodge, No. 5, 1900, Albany, NY

Sturges, S. Perry: (F) Member Brooklyn Revenue Reform Club, 1886, (I) *"Brooklyn Eagle,"* Jan. ,27 1886, Attendees at a dinner

Sturges, Thomas: (F) Member Long Island Lodge, No. 382, F. &. A. M., 1874, NY

Sturtze, LouisF.: (F) Member Lowville Lodge No. 134, F. & A. M., 1929, Lowville, NY, (CO) Lewis, (JD) Mar. 21, 1919

Suchy, F.: (F) Member Herber Lodge, No. 698,1898, F. & A. M., New

York, NY, Greenpoint area, (RES) Brooklyn

Sullivan, Andrew T.: (F) Member Friendly Sons of St. Patrick, 1899, Brooklyn, (CMTS)*"Brooklyn Eagle,"* Dec. 9, 1899, Article regarding the election of officers for 1900, (CMTS) Trustee

Sullivan, Andrew T.: (F) Member Friendly Sons of St. Patrick,1893, Brooklyn, (CMTS)*"Brooklyn Eagle,"* May 18,1893, Article regarding the election of Andrew T. Sullivan as postmaster. In the article it mentioned that there were only 50 members in this Society., New Brooklyn Postmaster, President of the Society, Graduated from St. Francis Xavier College.

Sullivan, John W.: (F) Member Friendly Sons of St. Patrick,1893, Brooklyn, (CMTS)*"Brooklyn Eagle,"* May 18,1893, Article regarding the election of Andrew T. Sullivan as postmaster. In the article it mentioned that there were only 50 members in this Society., Guest. It is unknown if a member of the Society.

Sullivan, Mamie: (F) Member Mispah Circle, 1888, Brooklyn, (I) *"Brooklyn Eagle,"* Dec. 12, 1888. Mentioned in an article about a fair raising funds for a Home for the Blind

Sullivan, Miss Fannie: (F) Member Mispah Circle, 1888, Brooklyn, (I) *"Brooklyn Eagle,"* Dec. 12, 1888. Mentioned in an article about a fair raising funds for a Home for the Blind

Sullivan, Mrs. J.: (F) Member Nativity Sewing Society, 1900, Brooklyn, (I) *"Brooklyn Eagle,"* Feb. 3, 1900. Article regarding raising money to buy clothing for the poor.

Sullivan , John J.: (F) Member Friendly Sons of St. Patrick,1893, Brooklyn, (CMTS)*"Brooklyn Eagle,"* May 18,1893, Article regarding the election of Andrew T. Sullivan as postmaster. In the article it mentioned that there were only 50 members in this Society., Guest. It is unknown if a member of the Society.

Sunderhaft, Charles F.: (F) Member Lowville Lodge No. 134, F. & A. M., 1929, Lowville, NY, (CO) Lewis, (JD) Mar. 15, 1907

Sunderhaft, Charles F.: (F) Member Lowville Chapter No. 223, R. A. M., 1929, Lowville, NY, (CO) Lewis, (JD) Mar. 8, 1921

Sunderhaft, John B.: (F) Member Lowville Lodge No. 134, F. & A. M., 1929, Lowville, NY, (CO) Lewis, (JD) Feb. 19, 1909

Sutherland, CharlesR.: (F) Member Mount Vernon Lodge, No. 3, 1900, Albany, NY

Sutherland, Williard J.: (F) Member Temple Lodge, No. 14, 1900, Albany, NY

Sutherlin, Miss Lizzie: (F) Member Mispah Circle, 1888, Brooklyn, (I) *"Brooklyn Eagle,"* Dec. 12, 1888. Mentioned in an article about a fair raising funds for a Home for the Blind

Sutter, D.: (F) Member Herber Lodge, No. 698,1898, F. & A. M., New York, NY, Greenpoint area, (RES) New York City

Suydam, G. G.: (F) Member Long Island Lodge, No. 382, F. &. A. M., 1874, NY

Swan, C. W.: (F) Member Long Island Lodge, No. 382, F. &. A. M., 1874, NY

Swanstrom, J. E.: (F) Member Friendly Sons of St. Patrick,1893, Brooklyn, (CMTS) *"Brooklyn Eagle,"* May 18,1893, Article regarding the election of Andrew T. Sullivan as postmaster. In the article it mentioned that there were only 50 members in this Society., Guest. It is unknown if a member of the Society.

Swartout, Mrs. Henrietta: (F) Member Lenox Ladies Aid Society of Lenox Road M. E. Church, Brooklyn, 1900, (CMTS) *"Brooklyn Eagle,"* Mar. 13, 1900. Meeting Notice, Board of Managers

Swartz, Charles L.: (F) Member Temple Lodge, No. 14, 1900, Albany, NY

Swartz, HenryS.: (F) Member Long Island Lodge, No. 382, F. &. A. M., 1874, NY

Sweeney, A.: (F) Member Long Island Lodge, No. 382, F. &. A. M., 1874, NY

Sweeney, Mrs. J. J.: (F) Member Nativity Sewing Society, 1900, Brooklyn, (I) *"Brooklyn Eagle,"* Feb. 3, 1900. Article regarding raising money to buy clothing for the poor.

Swift, Mrs. E. H.: (F) Member Nativity Sewing Society, 1900, Brooklyn, (I) *"Brooklyn Eagle,"* Feb. 3, 1900. Article regarding raising money to buy clothing for the poor.

Sylvester, Gershom: (F) Member Denmark Ecclesiastical Society, Sep. 21, 1810, (CO) Lewis, (CMTS) Trustee

Sylvester, N. B.: (F) Member Society for the Acquistion of Useful Knowledge, Apr. 26, 1843, (CO) Lewis

Sylvester, Sidney: (F) Member Educational Society of Lewis Co., NY, Nov. 14, 1845, (CMTS) First Vice President, (CEN) 1880, Martinsburg, Lewis Co., NY, 61, Retired Farmer, Mary B. 41, wife, Sidney W., 22, clerk, Gran. B., 16, Charles C. Davenport, Brother in Law, 63, Hardware Merchant, Eliza S. Davenport, 59, Sister

Taft, Gilbert T.: (F) Member Murray Lodge, No. 380, F. & A. M., 1906, Holley, Orleans, Co., NY, (CMTS) Past Master, Deceased as of 1906

Taft, Raymond L.: (F) Member Society of American Magicians, Apr., 1931, New York, (RES) Kew Gardens, Long Island, NY

Talbot, S. C. : (F) Member Brooklyn Revenue Reform Club, 1886, (I) *"Brooklyn Eagle,"* Jan. ,27 1886, Attendees at a dinner

Tallcott, Edwin S.: (F) Member Temple Lodge, No. 14, 1900, Albany, NY

Tanner, Marvin: (F) Member Temple Lodge, No. 14, 1900, Albany, NY

Tanzer, J.: (F) Member Herber Lodge, No. 698,1898, F. & A. M., New York, NY, Greenpoint area, (RES) New York City

Tapken, Th.: (F) Member Herber Lodge, No. 698,1898, F. & A. M., New York, NY, Greenpoint area, (RES) New York City

Tapley, C. S.: (F) Member Murray Lodge, No. 380, F. & A. M., 1906, Holley, Orleans, Co., NY

Taplin, J. C.: (F) Member Sons of New England, New England Society of the City of Brooklyn, 1890, (CMTS) *"Brooklyn Eagle,"* Dec. 21, 1890, 11th Annual Dinner, Attendees

Tartus, Brother: (F) Member Acanthus Lodge No. 719, F. A. M., (CMTS) Meeting Notes, *"Brooklyn Eagle,"* Mar. 13, 1887, of Corner Stone

Taylor, Ald. S.: (F) Member St. Nicholas Society of Nassau Island, 1861, (CMTS)"Brooklyn Eag;e," Dec. 11, 1861, Article regarding the Anniversary Dinner, Gave a toast

Taylor, Edwy L.: (F) Member Grand Council of the Princes of Jerusalem, 1882, Albany, NY

Taylor, Edwy L.: (F) Member Masters Lodge, No. 5, 1900, Albany, NY, (CMTS) Past Master

Taylor, Edwy. L.: (F) Member Ineffable and Sublime Grand Lodge of Perfection, 1882, Albany, NY

Taylor, J. H.: (F) Member Murray Lodge, No. 380, F. & A. M., 1906, Holley, Orleans, Co., NY

Taylor, James : (F) Member Mount Vernon Lodge, No. 3, 1900, Albany, NY, (CMTS) Past Master 1890

Taylor, Jas. H.: (F) Member Long Island Lodge, No. 382, F. &. A. M., 1874, NY

Taylor, John A.: (F) Member Sons of New England, New England Society of the City of Brooklyn, 1887, (CMTS) *"Brooklyn Eagle,"* Dec. 22, 1887, Annual Dinner, Attendees

Taylor, John A.: (F) Member Brooklyn Revenue Reform Club, 1886, (I) *"Brooklyn Eagle,"* Jan. ,27 1886, Attendees at a dinner

Taylor, John H.: (F) Member Murray Lodge, No. 380, F. & A. M., 1906, Holley, Orleans, Co., NY, (CMTS) Past Master

Taylor, Mrs. Grant B.: (F) Member Lenox Ladies Aid Society of Lenox Road M. E. Church, Brooklyn, 1900, (CMTS) *"Brooklyn Eagle,"* Mar. 13, 1900. Meeting Notice, Board of Managers

Taylor, Nicholas B.: (F) Member Masters Lodge, No. 5, 1900, Albany, NY

Taylor, Samuel F.: (F) Member Temple Lodge, No. 14, 1900, Albany, NY

Taylor, Theodore A.: (F) Member Anglo Saxon Lodge No. 137, F. A. M., (CMTS) Meeting Notes, *"Brooklyn Eagle,"* Mar. 13, 1887, D. D. G. M. Third District, Present at the meeting unoffically.

Taylor, William: (F) Member Lowville Lodge No. 134, F. & A. M., 1929, Lowville, NY, (CO) Lewis, (JD) Apr. 26, 1888

Taylor, William H.: (F) Member Sons of New England, New England Society of the City of Brooklyn, 1890, (CMTS) *"Brooklyn Eagle,"* Dec. 21, 1890, 11th Annual Dinner, Attendees

Taylor, William James: (F) Member Temple Lodge, No. 14, 1900, Albany, NY

Taylor, Z. S.: (F) Member Mount Vernon Lodge, No. 3, 1900,

Albany, NY
Teale, Oscar S.: (F) Member Society of American Magicians, Apr., 1931, New York, (RES) Bloomfield, NJ
Tebbetts, Noah: (F) Member Friendly Sons of St. Patrick,1893, Brooklyn, (CMTS) *"Brooklyn Eagle,"* May 18,1893, Article Regarding the election of Andrew T. Sullivan as postmaster. In the article it mentioned that there were only 50 members in this Society., Guest. It is unknown if a member of the Society.
Tebbutt, Harry K.: (F) Member Temple Lodge, No. 14, 1900, Albany, NY
Tebbutt, Marshall W.: (F) Member Temple Lodge, No. 14, 1900, Albany, NY, (CMTS) Life Member
Teeling, George W.: (F) Member Temple Lodge, No. 14, 1900, Albany, NY
Ten Eyck, Clinton: (F) Member Temple Lodge, No. 14, 1900, Albany, NY
Ten Eyck, James: (F) Member Grand Council of the Princes of Jerusalem, 1882, Albany, NY
Ten Eyck, James: (F) Member Ineffable and Sublime Grand Lodge of Perfection, 1882, Albany, NY
Ten Eyck, James: (F) Member Masters Lodge, No. 5, 1900, Albany, NY, (CMTS) Past Master
Ten Eyck, James: (F) Member Temple Lodge, No. 14, 1900, Albany, NY, (CMTS) Honorary Member
Terrell, N. L.: (F) Member Long Island Lodge, No. 382, F. &. A. M., 1874, NY
Terrell, William H.: (F) Member Temple Lodge, No. 14, 1900, Albany, NY
Terry, G. Terry: (F) Member Independent Order of Good Templars, Westhampton Lodge No. 885, instituted Apr. 16, 1889, New Officers installed Feb. 16, 1900, (CMTS) Meeting Notes, *"Brooklyn Eagle,"* Feb. 18, 1900, Fianancial Secretary
Terry, Harold B.: (F) Member Lowville Lodge No. 134, F. & A. M., 1929, Lowville, NY, (CO) Lewis, (JD) Apr. 16, 1920
Terry, Miss Elizabeth: (F) Member Independent Order of Good Templars, Westhampton Lodge No. 885, instituted Apr. 16, 1889, New Officers installed Feb. 16, 1900, (CMTS) Meeting Notes, *"Brooklyn Eagle,"* Feb. 18, 1900, Marshal
Thacher, George H.: (F) Member Masters Lodge, No. 5, 1900, Albany, NY
Thacher, John Boyd: (F) Member Albany Conclave, No. 8, Red Cross of Constantine, 1882, Albany, NY
Thacher, John Boyd: (F) Member Grand Council of the Princes of Jerusalem, 1882, Albany, NY
Thacher, John Boyd: (F) Member Ineffable and Sublime Grand Lodge of Perfection, 1882, Albany, NY
Thacher, John Boyd: (F) Member Masters Lodge, No. 5, 1900,

Albany, NY, (CMTS) Past Master
Thacher, Ralph W.: (F) Member Masters Lodge, No. 5, 1900, Albany, NY
Thacher, Jr., Geo. H.: (F) Member Ineffable and Sublime Grand Lodge of Perfection, 1882, Albany, NY
Thatcher, Charles A.: (F) Member Temple Lodge, No. 14, 1900, Albany, NY
Thatcher, George A.: (F) Member Grand Council of the Princes of Jerusalem, 1882, Albany, NY
Thatcher, George A.: (F) Member Ineffable and Sublime Grand Lodge of Perfection, 1882, Albany, NY
Thatcher, George A.: (F) Member Temple Lodge, No. 14, 1900, Albany, NY
Thatcher, Julian A.: (F) Member Temple Lodge, No. 14, 1900, Albany, NY
Thayer, W. W.: (F) Member Long Island Lodge, No. 382, F. &. A. M., 1874, NY
Thayer, Walter B.: (F) Member Temple Lodge, No. 14, 1900, Albany, NY
Thoman, T. R.: (F) Member Long Island Lodge, No. 382, F. &. A. M., 1874, NY
Thomas, Geo.: (F) Member Murray Lodge, No. 380, F. & A. M., 1906, Holley, Orleans, Co., NY
Thomas, George: (F) Member Long Island Lodge, No. 382, F. &. A. M., 1874, NY
Thomas, I. J.: (F) Member Long Island Lodge, No. 382, F. &. A. M., 1874, NY, (CMTS) Past Master
Thomas, II, George L.: (F) Member Temple Lodge, No. 14, 1900, Albany, NY
Thomason, John: (F) Member Society of American Magicians, Apr., 1931, New York, (RES) New York City
Thomason, Mrs. C. W.: (F) Member Lenox Ladies Aid Society of Lenox Road M. E. Church, Brooklyn, 1900, (I) *"Brooklyn Eagle,"* Mar. 13, 1900. Meeting Notice, Board of Managers
Thompson, Charles E.: (F) Member Lowville Chapter No. 223, R. A. M., 1929, Lowville, NY, (CO) Lewis, (JD) Feb. 22, 1884
Thompson, Charles W.: (F) Member Temple Lodge, No. 14, 1900, Albany, NY
Thompson, Curtiss E.: (F) Member Temple Lodge, No. 14, 1900, Albany, NY
Thompson, D.: (F) Member Long Island Lodge, No. 382, F. &. A. M., 1874, NY
Thompson, D. A.: (F) Member Knights of the Maccabees, Prospect Tent No. 209, 1900, Brooklyn, (I) *"Brooklyn Eagle,"* Feb. 3, 1900. Meeting Notice., (CMTS) Commander
Thompson, David A.: (F) Member Masters Lodge, No. 5, 1900, Albany, NY
Thompson, Fern: (F) Member Hope Rebekah Lodge No. 10, 1949-1950,

Brockport, NY, (CO) Monroe, (CMTS) Musician

Thompson, G.: (F) Member Long Island Lodge, No. 382, F. &. A. M., 1874, NY

Thompson, George C.: (F) Member Temple Lodge, No. 14, 1900, Albany, NY

Thompson, John: (F) Member Mount Vernon Lodge, No. 3, 1900, Albany, NY

Thompson, John R.: (F) Member Friendly Sons of St. Patrick,1893, Brooklyn, (CMTS) *"Brooklyn Eagle,"* May 18,1893, Article Regarding the election of Andrew T. Sullivan as postmaster. In the article it mentioned that there were only 50 members in this Society., Guest. It is unknown if a member of the Society.

Thompson , Kathryn: (F) Member Hope Rebekah Lodge No. 10, 1949-1950, Brockport, NY, (CO) Monroe, (CMTS) Noble Grand

Thompson, M.D., Samuel A.: (F) Member Society of American Magicians, Apr., 1931, New York, (RES) New York City

Thomsen, A. E.: (F) Member Herber Lodge, No. 698,1898, F. & A. M., New York, NY, Greenpoint area, (RES) New York City

Thorley, Charles: (I) *"Brooklyn Eagle,"* Feb. 19, 1902. Funeral Services at the Club House of the Brooklyn Lodge, No. 22, B. P. O. Elks for Wm. H. West. Elk services were first then masonic services by New York Lodge No. 330, F. A. & M., (CMTS) Made a floral gift.

Thornberg, A.: (F) Member Long Island Lodge, No. 382, F. &. A. M., 1874, NY

Thornton, Cleon D.: (F) Member Lowville Chapter No. 223, R. A. M., 1929, Lowville, NY, (CO) Lewis, (JD) Jan. 16, 1923

Thornton, Francis L.: (F) Member Temple Lodge, No. 14, 1900, Albany, NY

Thorp, James H.: (F) Member Sons of New England, New England Society of the City of Brooklyn, 1887, (CMTS)*"Brooklyn Eagle,"* Dec. 22, 1887, Annual Dinner, Attendees

Thorp, Thomas S.: (F) Member Sons of New England, New England Society of the City of Brooklyn, 1887, (CMTS)*"Brooklyn Eagle,"* Dec. 22, 1887, Annual Dinner, Attendees

Thowless, Arthur J.: (F) Member Society of American Magicians, Apr., 1931, New York, (RES) Newark, NJ

Thurston, E. N.: (F) Member Long Island Lodge, No. 382, F. &. A. M., 1874, NY

Thurston, Howard: (F) Member Society of American Magicians, Apr., 1931, New York, (RES) New York City

Tilton, Mrs. William C.: (F) Member Lenox Ladies Aid Society of Lenox Road M. E. Church, Brooklyn, 1900, (CMTS) *"Brooklyn Eagle,"* Mar. 13, 1900. Meeting Notice, Vice President

Tindale, John J.: (I) *"Brooklyn Eagle,"* Jun. 2, 1879, Dedication of the burial plot of the Order of Elks in Evergreen Cemetery, (CMTS) District Deputy of the Exalted Grande Ruler for the State of New

York
Tipton, J. Benton: (F) Member Masters Lodge, No. 5, 1900, Albany, NY
Tisse, Donald E.: (F) Member Lowville Lodge No. 134, F. & A. M., 1929, Lowville, NY, (CO) Lewis, (JS) Apr. 6, 1917
Toban, David: (I) *"Brooklyn Eagle,"* Feb. 19, 1902. Funeral Services at the Club House of the Brooklyn Lodge, No. 22, B. P. O. Elks for Wm. H. West. Elk services were first then masonic services by New York Lodge No. 330, F. A. & M., (CMTS) Pallbearer
Toch, Maximillan: (F) Member Society of American Magicians, Apr., 1931, New York, (RES) New York City
Toedt, E. B.: (F) Member Masters Lodge, No. 5, 1900, Albany, NY
Tolle, Otto A.: (F) Member Masters Lodge, No. 5, 1900, Albany, NY
Tompkins, Almet: (F) Member Mount Vernon Lodge, No. 3, 1900, Albany, NY
Tonjes, August H.: (F) Member Society of American Magicians, Apr., 1931, New York, (RES) New York City
Topp, Charles: (F) Member Herber Lodge, No. 698,1898, F. & A. M., New York, NY, Greenpoint area, (RES) New York City
Topping, Robert R.: (F) Member Temple Lodge, No. 14, 1900, Albany, NY
Topping, Washington: (F) Member Temple Lodge, No. 14, 1900, Albany, NY
Toren, Augustus H.: (F) Member Temple Lodge, No. 14, 1900, Albany, NY
Towneer, S. B.: (F) Member Masters Lodge, No. 5, 1900, Albany, NY
Towner, Samuel B.: (F) Member Grand Council of the Princes of Jerusalem, 1882, Albany, NY
Towner, Samuel H.: (F) Member Ineffable and Sublime Grand Lodge of Perfection, 1882, Albany, NY
Townsend, Henry E.: (F) Member Sons of New England, New England Society of the City of Brooklyn, 1887, (CMTS)*"Brooklyn Eagle,"* Dec. 22, 1887, Annual Dinner, Attendees
Townsend, John DeP.: (F) Member Grand Council of the Princes of Jerusalem, 1882, Albany, NY
Townsend, John DeP.: (F) Member Ineffable and Sublime Grand Lodge of Perfection, 1882, Albany, NY
Townsend, John DeP.: (F) Member Masters Lodge, No. 5, 1900, Albany, NY, (CMTS) Past Master
Townsend, Rex,: (F) Member Society of American Magicians, Apr., 1931, New York, (RES) New York City
Tracy, Benjamin F.: (F) Member Sons of New England, New England Society of the City of Brooklyn, 1887, (CMTS)*"Brooklyn Eagle,"* Dec. 22, 1887, Annual Dinner, Attendees
Tracy, Henry P.: (F) Member Mount Vernon Lodge, No. 3, 1900, Albany, NY
Train, Frederick C.: (F) Member Sons of New England, New England

Society of the City of Brooklyn, 1890, (CMTS) *"Brooklyn Eagle,"*
Dec. 21, 1890, 11th Annual Dinner, Attendees

Treadwell, George H.: (F) Member Grand Council of the Princes of
Jerusalem, 1882, Albany, NY

Treadwell, George H.: (F) Member Ineffable and Sublime Grand Lodge of
Perfection, 1882, Albany, NY

Treadwell, George H.: (F) Member Temple Lodge, No. 14, 1900,
Albany, NY

Treber, Chr.: (F) Member Herber Lodge, No. 698, 1898, F. & A. M., New
York, NY, Greenpoint area, (RES) New York City

Treearton, E. H.: (F) Member Sons of New England, New England
Society of the City of Brooklyn, 1890, (CMTS) *"Brooklyn Eagle,"*
Dec. 21, 1890, 11th Annual Dinner, Attendees

Treflio, Frank: (F) Member Society of American Magicians, Apr., 1931,
New York, (RES) Brooklyn, NY

Treiss, Jr., G. P.: (F) Member Lessing Lodge No. 608, (CMTS) Meeting
Notes, *"Brooklyn Eagle,"* Mar. 23, 1887, Master at the meeting

Trepel, Jack: (F) Member Society of American Magicians, Apr., 1931,
New York, (RES) Brooklyn, NY

Tripp, E. B.: (F) Member Long Island Lodge, No. 382, F. &. A. M.,
1874, NY

Trowbridge, C. F.: (F) Member Long Island Lodge, No. 382, F. &. A. M.,
1874, NY

Troy, Thomas H.: (F) Member Sons of New England, New England
Society of the City of Brooklyn, 1890, (CMTS) *"Brooklyn Eagle,"*
Dec. 21, 1890, 11th Annual Dinner, Attendees

Tryon, Williard F.: (F) Member Temple Lodge, No. 14, 1900,
Albany, NY

Tucker, Frederick G.: (F) Member Albany Conclave, No. 8, Red Cross of
Constantine, 1882, Albany, NY

Tucker, Frederick G.: (F) Member Grand Council of the Princes of
Jerusalem, 1882, Albany, NY

Tucker, H. V. W.: (F) Member Long Island Lodge, No. 382, F. &. A. M.,
1874, NY

Tucker, Miss Ida: (F) Member Mispah Circle, 1888, Brooklyn, (I)
*"Brooklyn Eagle,"* Dec. 12, 1888. Mentioned in an article about a
fair raising funds for a Home for the Blind

Tucker, Willis G.: (F) Member Masters Lodge, No. 5, 1900, Albany, NY

Tucker, Jr., M.D., H. A.: (F) Member Sons of New England, New England
Society of the City of Brooklyn, 1890, (CMTS) *"Brooklyn Eagle,"*
Dec. 21, 1890, 11th Annual Dinner, Attendees

Tucker, M.D., H. A.: (F) Member Sons of New England, New England
Society of the City of Brooklyn, 1890, (CMTS) *"Brooklyn Eagle,"*
Dec. 21, 1890, 11th Annual Dinner, Attendees

Tuffts, Miss Ella: (F) Member Young People's Association, 1888,
Brooklyn, (I) *"Brooklyn Eagle,"* Dec. 12, 1888. Article regarding

Societies aiding churches., (CMTS) Helping St. John's Methodist Episcopal Church, Secretary

Tully, James H.: (F) Member Friendly Sons of St. Patrick,1893, Brooklyn, (CMTS)*"Brooklyn Eagle,"* May 18,1893, Article regarding the election of Andrew T. Sullivan as postmaster. In the article it mentioned that there were only 50 members in this Society., Guest. It is unknown if a member of the Society.

Tunison, W. H.: (F) Member Long Island Lodge, No. 382, F. &. A. M., 1874, NY

Turnbull, George R.: (F) Member Sons of New England, New England Society of the City of Brooklyn, 1890, (CMTS)*"Brooklyn Eagle,"* Dec. 21, 1890, 11th Annual Dinner, Attendees

Turner, George: (F) Member Brooklyn Revenue Reform Club, 1886, (I)*"Brooklyn Eagle,"* Jan. ,27 1886, Attendees at a dinner

Turner, H. E.: (F) Member Murray Lodge, No. 380, F. & A. M., 1906, Holley, Orleans, Co., NY

Turner, J. Spencer: (F) Member Sons of New England, New England Society of the City of Brooklyn, 1890, (CMTS)*"Brooklyn Eagle,"* Dec. 21, 1890, 11th Annual Dinner, Attendees

Turner, S W.: (F) Member Herber Lodge, No. 698,1898, F. & A. M., New York, NY, Greenpoint area, (RES) New York City

Tutchings, Everett: (F) Member Society of American Magicians, Apr., 1931, New York, (RES) New York City

Tuthill, I. S.: (F) Member Long Island Lodge, No. 382, F. &. A. M., 1874, NY

Tuthill, Mrs. M. B.: (F) Member First Suffolk District, Stirling Chapter, No. 216, 1923, Greenport, NY, (CMTS) Secretary, (RES) Greenport

Tuttle, Derwood B.: (F) Member Monticello Lodge, No. 532, F. & A. M., (CO) Sullivan Co., NY, (CMTS) Past Master 1914, 1915

Tuttle, George E.: (F) Member Murray Lodge, No. 380, F. & A. M., 1906, Holley, Orleans, Co., NY, (CMTS) Past Master, Deceased as of 1906

Tuttle, Nellie: (F) Member Hope Rebekah Lodge No. 10, 1949-1950, Brockport, NY, (CO) Monroe

Tweedy, John: (F) Member Sons of New England, New England Society of the City of Brooklyn, 1890, (CMTS)*"Brooklyn Eagle,"* Dec. 21, 1890, 11th Annual Dinner, Attendees

Twitchell, George A.: (F) Member Lowville Lodge No. 134, F. & A. M., 1929, Lowville, NY, (CO) Lewis, (JD) Apr. 3, 1908

Twitchell, Henry E.: (F) Member Lowville Lodge No. 134, F. & A. M., 1929, Lowville, NY, (CO) Lewis, (JD) Jun. 4, 1915

Twitchells, Henry E.: (F) Member Lowville Chapter No. 223, R. A. M., 1929, Lowville, NY, (CO) Lewis, (JD) Jan. 23, 1917

Uffner, Frank N.: (I) *"Brooklyn Eagle,"* Dec. 7, 1896. 12th Annual Memorial Services, Plymouth Church, Brooklyn Lodge No. 22,

B. F. O. Elks, Roll Call of the dead. Address made by Maryland Senator George L. Wellington. , (CMTS) Name called.

Uline, Andrew B.: (F) Member Albany Conclave, No. 8, Red Cross of Constantine, 1882, Albany, NY

Uline, Andrew B.: (F) Member Grand Council of the Princes of Jerusalem, 1882, Albany, NY

Uline, Andrew B.: (F) Member Ineffable and Sublime Grand Lodge of Perfection, 1882, Albany, NY

Ulrich, Peter J.: (F) Member Lowville Lodge No. 134, F. & A. M., 1929, Lowville, NY, (CO) Lewis, (JD) Apr. 2, 1926

Underhill, Daniel: (F) Member Temple Lodge, No. 14, 1900, Albany, NY, (CMTS) Past Master 1874

Underhill, Edward H.: (F) Member Temple Lodge, No. 14, 1900, Albany, NY

Underhill, Frank : (F) Member Sons of New England, New England Society of the City of Brooklyn, 1890, (CMTS) *"Brooklyn Eagle,"* Dec. 21, 1890, 11th Annual Dinner, Attendees

Underhill, George R.: (F) Member Temple Lodge, No. 14, 1900, Albany, NY

Urban, H.: (F) Member Long Island Lodge, No. 382, F. &. A. M., 1874, NY

Utley, Samuel W.: (F) Member Temple Lodge, No. 14, 1900, Albany, NY

Utter, Samuel S.: (F) Member Sons of New England, New England Society of the City of Brooklyn, 1890, (CMTS) *"Brooklyn Eagle,"* Dec. 21, 1890, 11th Annual Dinner, Attendees

Vadney, Albertus: (F) Member Temple Lodge, No. 14, 1900, Albany, NY

Vail, J. J.: (F) Member Brooklyn Revenue Reform Club, 1886, (I) *"Brooklyn Eagle,"* Jan. ,27 1886, Attendees at a dinner

Van Aernam, C. H.: (F) Member Mount Vernon Lodge, No. 3, 1900, Albany, NY

Van Allen, Adam: (F) Member Masters Lodge, No. 5, 1900, Albany, NY

Van Allen, Charles H.: (F) Member Masters Lodge, No. 5, 1900, Albany, NY

Van Allen, Garret A.: (F) Member Masters Lodge, No. 5, 1900, Albany, NY

Van Allen, William: (F) Member Mount Vernon Lodge, No. 3, 1900, Albany, NY

Van Allen, William H.: (F) Member Grand Council of the Princes of Jerusalem, 1882, Albany, NY

Van Allen, Wm. H.: (F) Member Ineffable and Sublime Grand Lodge of Perfection, 1882, Albany, NY

Van Alstyne, Frank P.: (F) Member Temple Lodge, No. 14, 1900, Albany, NY

Van Alstyne, Thos. J.: (F) Member Mount Vernon Lodge, No. 3, 1900, Albany, NY, (CMTS) Past Master 1858
Van Alstyne, William: (F) Member Masters Lodge, No. 5, 1900, Albany, NY
Van Alstyne, Wm. C.: (F) Member Masters Lodge, No. 5, 1900, Albany, NY
Van Amber, M. Wilbur: (F) Member Lowville Lodge No. 134, F. & A. M., 1929, Lowville, NY, (CO) Lewis, (JD) Jun. 4, 1924
Van Amber, M. Wilbur: (F) Member Lowville Chapter No. 223, R. A. M., 1929, Lowville, NY, (CO) Lewis, (JD) May 5, 1908
Van Atta, Leon O.: (F) Member Lowville Lodge No. 134, F. & A. M., 1929, Lowville, NY, (CO) Lewis, (JD) May 12, 1928
Van Calkenburg, J. L.: (F) Member Temple Lodge, No. 14, 1900, Albany, NY
Van Cott, Brother: (F) Member Acanthus Lodge No. 719, F. A. M., (CMTS) Meeting Notes, *"Brooklyn Eagle,"* Mar. 13, 1887, of Ridgewood
Van De Carr, Charles: (F) Member Temple Lodge, No. 14, 1900, Albany, NY
Van Denburgh, R. L.: (F) Member Albany Conclave, No. 8, Red Cross of Constantine, 1882, Albany, NY
Van Dereef, A. F.: (F) Member Anglo Saxon Lodge No. 137, F. A. M., (CMTS) Meeting Notes, *"Brooklyn Eagle,"* Mar. 23, 1887, Predestrian at the meeting
Van Dien, Richard: (F) Member Society of American Magicians, Apr., 1931, New York, (RES) Jersey City, NJ
Van Eps, Alexander: (F) Member Grand Council of the Princes of Jerusalem, 1882, Albany, NY
Van Eps, Alexander: (F) Member Ineffable and Sublime Grand Lodge of Perfection, 1882, Albany, NY
Van Heusen, John M.: (F) Member Masters Lodge, No. 5, 1900, Albany, NY
Van Hoesen, Henry: (F) Member Washington Lodge, No. 85, 1900, Albany, NY, (CMTS) Past Members
Van Iderstine, Mrs. Addie: (F) Member The Ladies Sewing Society, 1888, Brooklyn, (I) *"Brooklyn Eagle,"* Dec. 12, 1888. Article regarding Societies aiding churches., (CMTS) Helping Plymouth Church, Secretary
Van Loon, Charles: (F) Member Mount Vernon Lodge, No. 3, 1900, Albany, NY
Van Loon, William H.: (F) Member Mount Vernon Lodge, No. 3, 1900, Albany, NY
Van Mater, Mrs.: (F) Member Lenox Ladies Aid Society of Lenox Road M. E. Church, Brooklyn, 1900, (CMTS) *"Brooklyn Eagle,"* Mar. 13, 1900. Meeting Notice, Board of Managers
Van Nordstron, Miss Lizzie: (F) Member Mispah Circle, 1888, Brooklyn,

(I) *"Brooklyn Eagle,"* Dec. 12, 1888. Mentioned in an article about a fair raising funds for a Home for the Blind

Van Santford, H. S.: (F) Member Masters Lodge, No. 5, 1900, Albany, NY

Van Wagoner, C. S.: (F) Member Sons of New England, New England Society of the City of Brooklyn, 1890, (CMTS)*"Brooklyn Eagle,"* Dec. 21, 1890, 11th Annual Dinner, Attendees

Van Wie, Claude: (F) Member Lowville Lodge No. 134, F. & A. M., 1929, Lowville, NY, (CO) Lewis, (JD) May 16, 1924

Van Wie, William: (F) Member Temple Lodge, No. 14, 1900, Albany, NY

Van Wie, William W.: (F) Member Temple Lodge, No. 14, 1900, Albany, NY

Van Wyck, Judge August C.: (F) Member Sons of New England, New England Society of the City of Brooklyn, 1890, (CMTS)*"Brooklyn Eagle,"* Dec. 21, 1890, 11th Annual Dinner, Attendees

Vandenberg, Jno.: (F) Member Clyde Lodge No. 341, F. A. M., 1905, Clyde, NY, (CO) Wayne, (CMTS) Past Master 1871, 1872, 1873

Vandenburggh, R. L.: (F) Member Grand Council of the Princes of Jerusalem, 1882, Albany, NY

Vandenburgh, R. L.: (F) Member Ineffable and Sublime Grand Lodge of Perfection, 1882, Albany, NY

Vanderbilt, Judge: (F) Member St. Nicholas Society of Nassau Island, 1861, (CMTS)"Brooklyn Eag;e," Dec. 11, 1861, Article regarding the Anniversary Dinner, Marshalled the members to the banquet hall.

Vanderbilt, Richard: (F) Member Mount Vernon Lodge, No. 3, 1900, Albany, NY

Vanderpool, Samuel D.: (F) Member Grand Council of the Princes of Jerusalem, 1882, Albany, NY

Vandervoort, W. L.: (F) Member Sons of New England, New England Society of the City of Brooklyn, 1890, (CMTS)*"Brooklyn Eagle,"* Dec. 21, 1890, 11th Annual Dinner, Attendees

Vanderzee, Newton B.: (F) Member Masters Lodge, No. 5, 1900, Albany, NY

VanRiper, J. S.: (F) Member Long Island Lodge, No. 382, F. &. A. M., 1874, NY

VanVechten, A. C.: (F) Member Long Island Lodge, No. 382, F. &. A. M., 1874, NY

Varney, Amasa L.: (F) Member Temple Lodge, No. 14, 1900, Albany, NY

Vary, George M.: (F) Member Lowville Lodge No. 134, F. & A. M., 1929, Lowville, NY, (CO) Lewis, (JD) Mar. 21, 1919

Vary, Mason W.: (F) Member Lowville Lodge No. 134, F. & A. M.; 1929, Lowville, NY, (CO) Lewis, (JD) May 31, 1918

Vary, Willette A.: (F) Member Lowville Lodge No. 134, F. & A. M., 1929, Lowville, NY, (CO) Lewis, (JD) Apr. 26, 1923

Vaupel, William: (F) Member Temple Lodge, No. 14, 1900,

Albany, NY

Veach, Stewart J.: (F) Member Lowville Lodge No. 134, F. & A. M., 1929, Lowville, NY, (CO) Lewis, (JD) Apr. 4, 1924

Venter, Jr., Peter: (F) Member Temple Lodge, No. 14, 1900, Albany, NY

Vermilye, Joseph W.: (F) Member Society of American Magicians, Apr., 1931, New York, (RES) New York City

Veza, Miss: (F) Member Nativity Sewing Society, 1900, Brooklyn, (I) *"Brooklyn Eagle,"* Feb. 3, 1900. Article regarding raising money to buy clothing for the poor.

Vineberg, Archibald: (F) Member Temple Lodge, No. 14, 1900, Albany, NY

Virkler, Arthur N.: (F) Member Lowville Lodge No. 134, F. & A. M., 1929, Lowville, NY, (CO) Lewis, (JD) Apr. 21, 1922

Virkler, Chester K.: (F) Member Lowville Lodge No. 134, F. & A. M., 1929, Lowville, NY, (CO) Lewis, (JD) Apr. 21, 1922

Virkler, Chester K.: (F) Member Lowville Chapter No. 223, R. A. M., 1929, Lowville, NY, (CO) Lewis, (JD) Apr. 17, 1923

Virkler, Leonard K.: (F) Member Lowville Lodge No. 134, F. & A. M., 1929, Lowville, NY, (CO) Lewis, (JD) Sep. 21, 1928

Virkler, M. Caarlton: (F) Member Lowville Chapter No. 223, R. A. M., 1929, Lowville, NY, (CO) Lewis

Virkler, M. Carlton: (F) Member Lowville Lodge No. 134, F. & A. M., 1929, Lowville, NY, (CO) Lewis, (JD) Mar. 30, 1928

Virkler, Maurice N.: (F) Member Lowville Lodge No. 134, F. & A. M., 1929, Lowville, NY, (CO) Lewis, (JD) Jul. 2, 1920

Virkler, Sidney F.: (F) Member Lowville Lodge No. 134, F. & A. M., 1929, Lowville, NY, (CO) Lewis, (JD) Apr. 4, 1924

Voelkner, A.: (F) Member Long Island Lodge, No. 382, F. &. A. M., 1874, NY

Vogel, Miss: (F) Member Mispah Circle, 1888, Brooklyn, (I) *"Brooklyn Eagle,"* Dec. 12, 1888. Mentioned in an article about a fair raising funds for a Home for the Blind

Vogt, Chas.: (F) Member Herber Lodge, No. 698,1898, F. & A. M., New York, NY, Greenpoint area, (RES) New York City

Vogt, Wm.: (F) Member Herber Lodge, No. 698,1898, F. & A. M., New York, NY, Greenpoint area, (RES) New York City

Von Zierolshofen, Paul H.: (F) Member Lowville Lodge No. 134, F. & A. M., 1929, Lowville, NY, (CO) Lewis, (JD) Mar. 28, 1890

Von Zierolshofen, Paul H.: (F) Member Lowville Chapter No. 223, R. A. M., 1929, Lowville, NY, (CO) Lewis, (JD) Mar. 3, 1891

Vosburgh, Andrew J.: (F) Member Temple Lodge, No. 14, 1900, Albany NY

Voss, William C. F. H.: (F) Member Lexington Lodge, 310, F. A. & M., 1900, Brooklyn, (I) *"Brooklyn Eagle,"* Feb. 3, 1900. Meeting Notice., (CMTS) Treasurer

Vreman, V. C.: (F) Member Brooklyn Revenue Reform Club,

1886, (I)*"Brooklyn Eagle,"* Jan. ,27 1886, Attendees at a dinner
Vriman, John F.: (F) Member Temple Lodge, No. 14, 1900, Albany, NY
Wadhams, Frederick K.: (F) Member Masters Lodge, No. 5, 1900, Albany, NY
Wadton, Harriet: (F) Member Mispah Circle, 1888, Brooklyn, (I) *"Brooklyn Eagle,"* Dec. 12, 1888. Mentioned in an article about a fair raising funds for a Home for the Blind
Wagner, Robert C.: (F) Member Mount Vernon Lodge, No. 3, 1900, Albany, NY
Wagoner, Martin V. E.: (F) Member Temple Lodge, No. 14, 1900, Albany, NY
Wagoner, Richard B.: (F) Member Temple Lodge, No. 14, 1900, Albany NY
Waite, Dennison: (F) Member Murray Lodge, No. 380, F. & A. M., 1906, Holley, Orleans, Co., NY
Waldecker, Max: (F) Member Mount Vernon Lodge, No. 3, 1900, Albany, NY
Walden, Schuyler: (F) Member Sons of New England, New England Society of the City of Brooklyn, 1890, (CMTS)*"Brooklyn Eagle,"* Dec. 21, 1890, 11th Annual Dinner, Attendees
Waldron, Abram L.: (F) Member Lowville Lodge No. 134, F. & A. M., 1929, Lowville, NY, (CO) Lewis, (JD) Mar. 16, 1920
Waldron, Abram L.: (F) Member Lowville Chapter No. 223, R. A. M., 1929, Lowville, NY, (CO) Lewis, (JD) May 23, 1922
Waldron, Bert: (F) Member Lowville Lodge No. 134, F. & A. M., 1929, Lowville, NY, (CO) Lewis, (JD) Feb. 6, 1925
Wale, William D.: (F) Member Sons of New England, New England Society of the City of Brooklyn, 1890, (CMTS)*"Brooklyn Eagle,"* Dec. 21, 1890, 11th Annual Dinner, Attendees
Walker, H. B.: (I) *"Brooklyn Eagle,"* Dec. 7, 1896. 12th Annual Memorial Services, Plymouth Church, Brooklyn Lodge No. 22, B. F. O. Elks, Roll Call of the dead. Address made by Maryland Senator George L. Wellington. , (CMTS) Name called.
Walker, Harriet: (F) Member Hope Rebekah Lodge No. 10, 1949-1950, Brockport, NY, (CO) Monroe
Wallace, Charles B.: (F) Member Lowville Lodge No. 134, F. & A. M., 1929, Lowville, NY, (CO) Lewis, (JD) Dec. 6, 1907
Wallace, Robert A.: (F) Member Temple Lodge, No. 14, 1900, Albany, NY, (CMTS) Life Member
Wallace, Warren L.: (F) Member Temple Lodge, No. 14, 1900, Albany, NY
Wallace, William A.: (F) Member Temple Lodge, No. 14, 1900, Albany, NY
Waller, George E.: (F) Member Monticello Lodge, No. 532, F. & A. M., (CO) Sullivan Co., NY, (CMTS) Past Master 1900
Walsh, John D.: (F) Member Friendly Sons of St. Patrick,1893,

Brooklyn, (CMTS)*"Brooklyn Eagle,"* May 18,1893,
Article regarding the election of Andrew T. Sullivan as postmaster. In the article it mentioned that there were only 50 members in this Society., Guest. It is unknown if a member of the Society.

Walsh, Mrs. R. L.: (F) Member Nativity Sewing Society, 1900, Brooklyn, (I) *"Brooklyn Eagle,"* Feb. 3, 1900. Article regarding raising money to buy clothing for the poor.

Walter, Louis: (F) Member Society of American Magicians, Apr., 1931, New York, (RES) New York City

Wands, Robert J.: (F) Member Temple Lodge, No. 14, 1900, Albany, NY

Wantz, Gilbert M.: (F) Member Lowville Lodge No. 134, F. & A. M., 1929, Lowville, NY, (CO) Lewis, (JD) Apr. 20, 1906

Ward, Frederick A.: (F) Member Sons of New England, New England Society of the City of Brooklyn, 1890, (CMTS)*"Brooklyn Eagle,"* Dec. 21, 1890, 11th Annual Dinner, Attendees

Ward, Friend K.: (F) Member Lowville Chapter No. 223, R. A. M., 1929, Lowville, NY, (CO) Lewis, (JD) May 8, 1923

Ward, R.: (F) Member Sons of New England, New England Society of the City of Brooklyn, 1890, (CMTS)*"Brooklyn Eagle,"* Dec. 21, 1890, 11th Annual Dinner, Attendees

Ward, Walter E.: (F) Member Temple Lodge, No. 14, 1900, Albany, NY

Ward, William J.: (F) Member Mount Vernon Lodge, No. 3, 1900, Albany, NY

Ware, M.D., Charles: (F) Member Sons of New England, New England Society of the City of Brooklyn, 1890, (CMTS)*"Brooklyn Eagle,"* Dec. 21, 1890, 11th Annual Dinner, Attendees

Wareing, Jr., Thomas : (F) Member Mount Vernon Lodge, No. 3, 1900, Albany, NY, (CMTS) Past Master 1899

Warner, Edward N.: (F) Member Lowville Lodge No. 134, F. & A. M., 1929, Lowville, NY, (CO) Lewis, (JD) Jan. 16, 1920

Warner, Harmon W.: (F) Member Temple Lodge, No. 14, 1900, Albany, NY

Warner, Luther C.: (F) Member Mount Vernon Lodge, No. 3, 1900, Albany, NY

Warren, C. H.: (F) Member Murray Lodge, No. 380, F. & A. M., 1906, Holley, Orleans, Co., NY

Warren, Clement H,: (F) Member Albany Conclave, No. 8, Red Cross of Constantine, 1882, Albany, NY

Warren, Clement H.: (F) Member Grand Council of the Princes of Jerusalem, 1882, Albany, NY

Warren, Clement H.: (F) Member Ineffable and Sublime Grand Lodge of Perfection, 1882, Albany, NY

Warwick, J. H.: (F) Member Anglo Saxon Lodge No. 137, F. A. M., (CMTS) Meeting Notes, *"Brooklyn Eagle,"* Mar. 23, 1887, Stood guard at the meeting, of Lexington Lodge No. 310

Washburn, H. L.: (F) Member Masters Lodge, No. 5, 1900,

Albany, NY
Waterbury, H.A.: (F) Member Clyde Lodge No. 341, F. A. M., 1905,
   Clyde, NY, (CO) Wayne, (CMTS) Past Master 1894, 1895, 1896
Waterhouse, Fred A.: (F) Member Temple Lodge, No. 14, 1900,
   Albany, NY
Waterman, Robert H.: (F) Member Albany Conclave, No. 8, Red Cross of
   Constantine, 1882, Albany, NY
Waterman, Robert H.: (F) Member Grand Council of the Princes of
   Jerusalem, 1882, Albany, NY
Waterman, Robert H.: (F) Member Ineffable and Sublime Grand Lodge of
   Perfection, 1882, Albany, NY
Waters, George H.: (F) Member Lowville Chapter No. 223, R. A. M.,
   1929, Lowville, NY, (CO) Lewis, (JD) Sep. 14, 1920
Waters, Herbert N.: (F) Member Lowville Lodge No. 134, F. & A. M.,
   1929, Lowville, NY, (CO) Lewis, (JD) Apr. 30, 1920
Waterson, G.: (F) Member Long Island Lodge, No. 382, F. &. A. M.,
   1874, NY
Wath, Brother: (F) Member Acanthus Lodge No. 719, F. A. M., (CMTS)
   Meeting Notes, *"Brooklyn Eagle,"* Mar. 13, 1887, of Manhattan
Watson, James H.: (F) Member Masters Lodge, No. 5, 1900, Albany, NY
Watson, James H.: (F) Member Temple Lodge, No. 14, 1900,
   Albany, NY
Watson, Jos.: (F) Member Clyde Lodge No. 341, F. A. M., 1905, Clyde,
   NY, (CO) Wayne, (CMTS) Past Master 1856
Watson, T. B.: (F) Member Long Island Lodge, No. 382, F. &. A. M.,
   1874, NY
Waugh, D. S.: (F) Member Long Island Lodge, No. 382, F. &. A. M.,
   1874, NY
Way, John Lewis: (F) Member Temple Lodge, No. 14, 1900, Albany, NY
Way, Thomas P.: (F) Member Albany Conclave, No. 8, Red Cross of
   Constantine, 1882, Albany, NY
Way, Thomas P.: (F) Member Grand Council of the Princes of Jerusalem,
   1882, Albany, NY
Way, Thomas P.: (F) Member Ineffable and Sublime Grand Lodge of
   Perfection, 1882, Albany, NY
Wayne, Benjamin P.: (F) Member Temple Lodge, No. 14, 1900, Albany,
   NY
Weatherwax, Charles: (F) Member Temple Lodge, No. 14, 1900, Albany,
   NY, (B) Dec., 1836, (D) Jul. 5, 1900, (MD) Nov. 18, 1863,
   (Spouse) Sarah Godfrey, (PRTS) Henry Weatherwax and Malinda
   Soule
Weatherwax, Frank H.: (F) Member Temple Lodge, No. 14, 1900,
   Albany, NY
Weaver, Abram H.: (F) Member Temple Lodge, No. 14, 1900, Albany,
   NY
Weaver, William H.: (F) Member Temple Lodge, No. 14, 1900,

Albany, NY, (CMTS) Life Member
Webb, J. W.: (F) Member Long Island Lodge, No. 382, F. &. A. M., 1874, NY
Webb, Robert J.: (I) *"Brooklyn Eagle,"* Feb. 19, 1902. Funeral Services at the Club House of the Brooklyn Lodge, No. 22, B. P. O. Elks for Wm. H. West. Elk services were first then masonic services by New York Lodge No. 330, F. A. & M., (CMTS) Member of Metropolitian Male Quartet. Member of the Elks
Webber, L.: (F) Member Long Island Lodge, No. 382, F. &. A. M., 1874, NY
Weber, Joe: (I) *"Brooklyn Eagle,"* Feb. 19, 1902. Funeral Services at the Club House of the Brooklyn Lodge, No. 22, B. P. O. Elks for Wm. H. West. Elk services were first then masonic services by New York Lodge No. 330, F. A. & M., (CMTS) Pallbearer
Weber, W. T.: (F) Member Long Island Lodge, No. 382, F. &. A. M., 1874, NY
Webster, Clark W.: (F) Member Murray Lodge, No. 380, F. & A. M., 1906, Holley, Orleans, Co., NY
Webster, D. S.: (F) Member Murray Lodge, No. 380, F. & A. M., 1906, Holley, Orleans, Co., NY
Webster, Mason L.: (F) Member Lowville Lodge No. 134, F. & A. M., 1929, Lowville, NY, (CO) Lewis, (JD) Mar. 15, 1907
Weed, Samuel: (F) Member Clyde Lodge No. 341, F. A. M., 1905, Clyde, NY, (CO) Wayne, (CMTS) Past Master 1861, 1864
Weed, William E.: (F) Member Lowville Chapter No. 223, R. A. M., 1929, Lowville, NY, (CO) Lewis, (JD) Feb. 15, 1887
Weibezahl, R.: (F) Member Herber Lodge, No. 698,1898, F. & A. M., New York, NY, Greenpoint area, (RES) New York City
Weidman, John A.: (F) Member Temple Lodge, No. 14, 1900, Albany, NY
Weidman, Reuben L.: (F) Member Mount Vernon Lodge, No. 3, 1900, Albany, NY
Weir, Alex.: (F) Member Long Island Lodge, No. 382, F. &. A. M., 1874, NY
Weir, Myron L.: (F) Member Lowville Lodge No. 134, F. & A. M., 1929, Lowville, NY, (CO) Lewis, (JD) Feb. 6, 1925
Welch, James G.: (F) Member Lowville Chapter No. 223, R. A. M., 1929, Lowville, NY, (CO) Lewis, (JD) Jan. 28, 1925
Weller, Alson P.: (F) Member Lowville Lodge No. 134, F. & A. M., 1929, Lowville, NY, (CO) Lewis, (JD) May 19, 1916
Wells, Charles H.: (F) Member Society of American Magicians, Apr., 1931, New York, (RES) Brooklyn, NY
Wells, Edw. B.: (F) Member Clyde Lodge No. 341, F. A. M., 1905, Clyde, NY, (CO) Wayne, (CMTS) Past Master 1867, 1868, 1869, 1870, 1874, 1875, 1880, 1882
Wells, George A.: (F) Member Masters Lodge, No. 5, 1900,

Albany, NY

Wemple, Benj. V. Z.: (F) Member Grand Council of the Princes of Jerusalem, 1882, Albany, NY, (CEN) 1880, 14th Ward, Albany, Albany Co., NY, Listed with D. W. Wemple, 47, NY, Cashier State Bank, Hester A., 48, Jessie C., 18, daughter, Benj. V. Z., 47, brother, banker

Wemple, Benj.V. Z.: (F) Member Ineffable and Sublime Grand Lodge of Perfection, 1882, Albany, NY, (CEN) 1880, 14th Ward, Albany, Albany Co., NY, Listed with D. W. Wemple, 47, NY, Cashier State Bank, Hester A., 48, Jessie C., 18, daughter, Benj. V. Z., 47, brother, banker

Werner, Helen: (F) Member Hope Rebekah Lodge No. 10, 1949-1950, Brockport, NY, (CO) Monroe

Werner, Mrs. Nettie: (F) Member Society of American Magicians, Apr., 1931, New York, (RES) Brooklyn, NY

Werner, Otto P.: (F) Member Lowville Lodge No. 134, F. & A. M., 1929, Lowville, NY, (CO) Lewis, (JD) Jan. 18, 1929

West, C. L.: (F) Member Long Island Lodge, No. 382, F. &. A. M., 1874, NY

West, Mrs. William H.: (I) *"Brooklyn Eagle,"* Feb. 19, 1902. Funeral Services at the Club House of the Brooklyn Lodge, No. 22, B. P. O. Elks for Wm. H. West. Elk services were first then masonic services by New York Lodge No. 330, F. A. & M., (CMTS) Made a floral gift., (CEN) 1880 3rd Ward, Brooklyn, Kings Co., NY, 26, NY, Broker, Emma A., 22, Grace E., 1, Ada J. Traver, 20 neice

West, William H.: (I) *"Brooklyn Eagle,"* Feb. 19, 1902. Funeral Services at the Club House of the Brooklyn Lodge, No. 22, B. P. O. Elks for Wm. H. West. Elk services were first then masonic services by New York Lodge No. 330, F. A. & M., (CMTS) Deceased Funeral Service, (CEN) 1880 3rd Ward, Brooklyn, Kings Co., NY, 26, NY, Broker, Emma A., 22, Grace E., 1, Ada J. Traver, 20 neice

Westcott, Henry R.: (F) Member Mount Vernon Lodge, No. 3, 1900, Albany, NY, (CMTS) Past Master1893,
(CEN) 1880 North Greenbush, Rensselaer Co., NY, 35, NY, Auctioneer, Pauline, 33, Cornelia, 14, Robert, 11, Harry, 2

Western, Benjamin R.: (F) Member Brooklyn Revenue Reform Club, 1886, (I)*"Brooklyn Eagle,"* Jan. ,27 1886, Attendees at a dinner

Weston, Jas. A.: (F) Member Long Island Lodge, No. 382, F. &. A. M., 1874, NY

Wetherbee, Albert C.: (F) Member Temple Lodge, No. 14, 1900, Albany, NY

Wetmore, Roscoe F.: (F) Member Lowville Lodge No. 134, F. & A. M., 1929, Lowville, NY, (CO) Lewis, (JD) Jun. 20, 1924

Whalen, Edmund A.: (F) Member Catholic Benevolent Legion, New York State Council District No. 1, 1900, Brooklyn, (I) *"Brooklyn*

*Eagle,"* Feb. 3, 1900. Meeting Notice., (CMTS) Secretary

Wheat, F. S.: (F) Member Long Island Lodge, No. 382, F. &. A. M., 1874, NY

Wheeler, Alfred A.: (F) Member Long Island Lodge, No. 382, F. &. A. M., 1874, NY

Wheeler, Dr. C. F.: (F) Member Brooklyn Dental Society, 1877, Brooklyn, NY, (CMTS) *"Brooklyn Eagle,"* Dec. 15, 1877. Celebration of 10th Anniversary. Society established Dec. 14, 1867, (CMTS) Present from Albany, NY

Wheeler, Edward J.: (F) Member Masters Lodge, No. 5, 1900, Albany, NY

Wheeler, George E.: (F) Member Long Island Lodge, No. 382, F. &. A. M., 1874, NY

Wheeler, H. W.: (F) Member Sons of New England, New England Society of the City of Brooklyn, 1890, (CMTS)*"Brooklyn Eagle,"* Dec. 21, 1890, 11th Annual Dinner, Attendees

Wheeler, Hassan H.: (F) Member Sons of New England, New England Society of the City of Brooklyn, 1890, (CMTS)*"Brooklyn Eagle,"* Dec. 21, 1890, 11th Annual Dinner, Attendees

Wheeler, Hassem H.: (I) *"Brooklyn Eagle,"* Dec. 7, 1896. 12th Annual Memorial Services, Plymouth Church, Brooklyn Lodge No. 22, B. F. O. Elks, Roll Call of the dead. Address made by Maryland Senator George L. Wellington. , (CMTS) Name called.

Wheeler, Seth: (F) Member Temple Lodge, No. 14, 1900, Albany, NY

Wheeler , F. L.: (F) Member Sons of New England, New England Society of the City of Brooklyn, 1887, (CMTS)*"Brooklyn Eagle,"* Dec. 22, 1887, Annual Dinner, Attendees

Wheeler , H. H.: (F) Member Sons of New England, New England Society of the City of Brooklyn, 1887, (CMTS)*"Brooklyn Eagle,"* Dec. 22, 1887, Annual Dinner, Attendees

Whintey, Mayor: (F) Member Sons of New England, New England Society of the City of Brooklyn, 1887, (CMTS)*"Brooklyn Eagle,"* Dec. 22, 1887, Annual Dinner, Attendees

Whish, Charles F.: (F) Member Mount Vernon Lodge, No. 3, 1900, Albany, NY, (CEN) 1880 17th Ward, Albany, Albany Co., NY Listed with Charles Whish, 44, NY, Coppersmith, Catherine, 39, George W., 12, Frank S., 5, Charles, 2

Whish, George W.: (F) Member Mount Vernon Lodge, No. 3, 1900, Albany, NY, (CEN) 1880 17th Ward, Albany, Albany Co., NY Listed with Charles Whish, 44, NY, Coppersmith, Catherine, 39, George W., 12, Frank S., 5, Charles, 2

Whish, John: (F) Member Mount Vernon Lodge, No. 3, 1900, Albany, NY

Whish, William C.: (F) Member Mount Vernon Lodge, No. 3, 1900,

Albany, NY, (CEN) 1880 11th Ward, Albany, Albany Co., NY Listed with William Whish, 50, NY, Engineer, Anna, 48, Wm. C., 18, Boatman

Whish, William H.: (F) Member Mount Vernon Lodge, No. 3, 1900, Albany, NY, (CMTS) Past Master 1871

Whitbeck, Theodore H.: (F) Member Temple Lodge, No. 14, 1900, Albany, NY

Whitbeck, William H.: (F) Member Temple Lodge, No. 14, 1900, Albany, NY

White, A. M.: (F) Member Sons of New England, New England Society of the City of Brooklyn, 1887, (CMTS)*"Brooklyn Eagle,"* Dec. 22, 1887, Annual Dinner, Attendees

White, A. T.: (F) Member Sons of New England, New England Society of the City of Brooklyn, 1890, (CMTS)*"Brooklyn Eagle,"* Dec. 21, 1890, 11th Annual Dinner, Attendees

White, A. T.: (F) Member Sons of New England, New England Society of the City of Brooklyn, 1887, (CMTS)*"Brooklyn Eagle,"* Dec. 22, 1887, Annual Dinner, Attendees

White, Addison: (F) Member Temple Lodge, No. 14, 1900, Albany, NY

White, Andrew G.: (F) Member Grand Council of the Princes of Jerusalem, 1882, Albany, NY

White, Andrew G.: (F) Member Ineffable and Sublime Grand Lodge of Perfection, 1882, Albany, NY

White, Andrew G.: (F) Member Masters Lodge, No. 5, 1900, Albany, NY

White, Charles M.: (F) Member Long Island Lodge, No. 382, F. &. A. M., 1874, NY

White, Charles T.: (I) *"Brooklyn Eagle,"* Jun. 2, 1879, Dedication of the burial plot of the Order of Elks in Evergreen Cemetery, (CMTS) Unveiled the Bronze Elk

White, Dr. S. S.: (F) Member Brooklyn Dental Society, 1877, Brooklyn, NY, (CMTS) *"Brooklyn Eagle,"* Dec. 15, 1877. Celebration of 10th Anniversary. Society established Dec. 14, 1867, (CMTS) Present from Philadelphia

White, Frederick W.: (F) Member Masters Lodge, No. 5, 1900, Albany, NY

White, G. Willis: (F) Member Long Island Lodge, No. 382, F. &. A. M., 1874, NY

White, George A.: (F) Member Masters Lodge, No. 5, 1900, Albany, NY

White, H. D.: (F) Member Long Island Lodge, No. 382, F. &. A. M., 1874, NY

White, James: (F) Member Temple Lodge, No. 14, 1900, Albany, NY

White, John R.: (F) Member Temple Lodge, No. 14, 1900, Albany, NY

White, Thomas: (F) Member Sons of New England, New England Society of the City of Brooklyn, 1890, (CMTS)*"Brooklyn Eagle,"* Dec. 21, 1890, 11th Annual Dinner, Attendees

Whitefield, Robert P.: (F) Member Temple Lodge, No. 14, 1900, Albany, NY

Whitman, Henry B.: (F) Member Grand Council of the Princes of Jerusalem, 1882, Albany, NY

Whitman, Henry B.: (F) Member Ineffable and Sublime Grand Lodge of Perfection, 1882, Albany, NY

Whitmore, Adelbert: (F) Member Temple Lodge, No. 14, 1900, Albany, NY

Whitney, Charles L. A.: (F) Member Temple Lodge, No. 14, 1900, Albany, NY

Whitney, Stephen W.: (F) Member Masters Lodge, No. 5, 1900, Albany, NY

Whitney, W. D.: (F) Member Murray Lodge, No. 380, F. & A. M., 1906, Holley, Orleans, Co., NY

Whittet, Joseph L.: (F) Member Grand Council of the Princes of Jerusalem, 1882, Albany, NY

Whittet, Joseph L.: (F) Member Ineffable and Sublime Grand Lodge of Perfection, 1882, Albany, NY

Whittle, Daniel: (F) Member Masters Lodge, No. 5, 1900, Albany, NY

Wicken, C.: (F) Member Long Island Lodge, No. 382, F. &. A. M., 1874, NY

Wiederhold, E.: (F) Member Herber Lodge, No. 698,1898, F. & A. M., New York, NY, Greenpoint area, (RES) New York City

Wiederholt, G.: (F) Member Long Island Lodge, No. 382, F. &. A. M., 1874, NY

Wiederick, Henry: (F) Member Long Island Lodge, No. 382, F. &. A. M., 1874, NY

Wieken, John H.: (F) Member Star of Bethlem No. 322, F. A. M., 1900, Brooklyn, (I) *"Brooklyn Eagle,"* Feb. 3, 1900. Meeting Notice., (CMTS) Treasurer

Wiemann, Fred J.: (F) Member Society of American Magicians, Apr., 1931, New York, (RES) Little Neck, Long Island, NY

Wiencke, G.: (F) Member Herber Lodge, No. 698,1898, F. & A. M., New York, NY, Greenpoint area, (RES) New York City

Wieter, F. L.: (F) Member Herber Lodge, No. 698,1898, F. & A. M., New York, NY, Greenpoint area, (RES) New York City

Wilcox, A. Ray: (F) Member Lowville Chapter No. 223, R. A. M., 1929, Lowville, NY, (CO) Lewis, (JD) May 8, 1922

Wilcox, George B.: (F) Member Masters Lodge, No. 5, 1900, Albany, NY

Wilcox, William H.: (F) Member Lowville Lodge No. 134, F. & A. M., 1929, Lowville, NY, (CO) Lewis, (JD) Jun. 29, 1906

Wild, W. P.: (F) Member Long Island Lodge, No. 382, F. &. A. M., 1874, NY

Wilder, Leroy C.: (F) Member Lowville Lodge No. 134, F. & A. M., 1929, Lowville, NY, (CO) Lewis, (JD) Mar. 5, 1920

Wilkins, H.: (F) Member Long Island Lodge, No. 382, F. &. A. M.,

1874, NY
Wilkinson, Miss J.: (F) Member Ladies Aid Society of Flatbush, Brooklyn, 1888, (CMTS) *"Brooklyn Eagle,"* Oct. 7, 1888, Meeting Notice, Treasurer
Wilkinson, Jr., George: (F) Member Temple Lodge, No. 14, 1900, Albany, NY
Willaims, Daviel D.: (F) Member Temple Lodge, No. 14, 1900, Albany, NY
Willaims, George M. B.: (F) Member Lowville Chapter No. 223, R. A. M., 1929, Lowville, NY, (CO) Lewis, (JD) Bov. 18, 1902
Willaims, Perey G.: (I) *"Brooklyn Eagle,"* Feb. 19, 1902. Funeral Services at the Club House of the Brooklyn Lodge, No. 22, B. P. O. Elks for Wm. H. West. Elk services were first then masonic services by New York Lodge No. 330, F. A. & M., (CMTS) Pallbearer
Willard, James N.: (F) Member Temple Lodge, No. 14, 1900, Albany, NY
Willers, Jr., Diedrich: (F) Member Masters Lodge, No. 5, 1900, Albany, NY
Willey, J. F.: (F) Member Long Island Lodge, No. 382, F. &. A. M., 1874, NY
William, Robert D.: (F) Member Grand Council of the Princes of Jerusalem, 1882, Albany, NY
Williams, Charles: (F) Member Lowville Lodge No. 134, F. & A. M., 1929, Lowville, NY, (CO) Lewis, (JD) Feb. 20, 1897
Williams, D.: (F) Member Long Island Lodge, No. 382, F. &. A. M., 1874, NY
Williams, Edward P.: (F) Member Temple Lodge, No. 14, 1900, Albany, NY
Williams, Everett: (F) Member Lowville Chapter No. 223, R. A. M., 1929, Lowville, NY, (CO) Lewis, (JD) Dec. 18, 1899
Williams, George: (F) Member Long Island Lodge, No. 382, F. &. A. M., 1874, NY
Williams, George A.: (F) Member Temple Lodge, No. 14, 1900, Albany, NY
Williams, Howard F.: (F) Member Lowville Lodge No. 134, F. & A. M., 1929, Lowville, NY, (CO) Lewis, (JD) Dec. 23, 1912
Williams, Howard F.: (F) Member Lowville Chapter No. 223, R. A. M., 1929, Lowville, NY, (CO) Lewis, (JD) Mar. 18, 1913
Williams, Perry G.: (F) Member Lowville Lodge No. 134, F. & A. M., 1929, Lowville, NY, (CO) Lewis, (JD) May 31, 1907
Williams, Robert D.: (F) Member Ineffable and Sublime Grand Lodge of Perfection, 1882, Albany, NY
Williams, Robert D.: (F) Member Masters Lodge, No. 5, 1900, Albany, NY, (CMTS) Past Master
Williams, Stephen: (F) Member Ineffable and Sublime Grand Lodge of Perfection, 1882, Albany, NY
Williams, Thomas J.: (F) Member Temple Lodge, No. 14, 1900,

Albany, NY
Williams, William A.: (F) Member Lowville Chapter No. 223, R. A. M., 1929, Lowville, NY, (CO) Lewis, (JD) Feb. 11, 1908
Williams, William H.: (F) Member Grand Council of the Princes of Jerusalem, 1882, Albany, NY
Williams, William H.: (F) Member Sons of New England, New England Society of the City of Brooklyn, 1890, (CMTS)*"Brooklyn Eagle,"* Dec. 21, 1890, 11th Annual Dinner, Attendees
Williams, William H.: (F) Member Sons of New England, New England Society of the City of Brooklyn, 1887, (CMTS)*"Brooklyn Eagle,"* Dec. 22, 1887, Annual Dinner, Attendees
Williams, Wm. H.: (F) Member Ineffable and Sublime Grand Lodge of Perfection, 1882, Albany, NY
Williams , James H.: (F) Member Sons of New England, New England Society of the City of Brooklyn, 1890, (CMTS)*"Brooklyn Eagle,"* Dec. 21, 1890, 11th Annual Dinner, Attendees
Williams , William A.: (F) Member Lowville Lodge No. 134, F. & A. M., 1929, Lowville, NY, (CO) Lewis, (JD) Jun. 21, 1907
Williamson, Charles H.: (I) *"Brooklyn Eagle,"* Feb. 19, 1902. Funeral Services at the Club House of the Brooklyn Lodge, No. 22, B. P. O. Elks for Wm. H. West. Elk services were first then masonic services by New York Lodge No. 330, F. A. & M., (CMTS) Reading Knight
Williamson, G.: (F) Member Long Island Lodge, No. 382, F. &. A. M., 1874, NY
Williamson, Mrs. Abraham P.: (F) Member Lenox Ladies Aid Society of Lenox Road M. E. Church, Brooklyn, 1900, (CMTS) *"Brooklyn Eagle,"* Mar. 13, 1900. Meeting Notice, Secretary
Willinin, Mrs. J.: (F) Member Nativity Sewing Society, 1900, Brooklyn, (I) *"Brooklyn Eagle,"* Feb. 3, 1900. Article regarding raising money to buy clothing for the poor.
Willsey, E. M.: (F) Member Temple Lodge, No. 14, 1900, Albany, NY
Willstatter, Alfred: (F) Member Society of American Magicians, Apr., 1931, New York, (RES) New York City
Wilmarth, J. R.: (F) Member Sons of New England, New England Society of the City of Brooklyn, 1890, (CMTS)*"Brooklyn Eagle,"* Dec. 21, 1890, 11th Annual Dinner, Attendees
Wilson, C. W.: (F) Member Friendly Sons of St. Patrick,1893, Brooklyn, (CMTS)*"Brooklyn Eagle,"* May 18,1893, Article regarding the election of Andrew T. Sullivan as postmaster. In the article it mentioned that there were only 50 members in this Society., Guest. It is unknown if a member of the Society.
Wilson, Geo. O.: (F) Member Murray Lodge, No. 380, F. & A. M., 1906, Holley, Orleans, Co., NY
Wilson, George: (I) *"Brooklyn Eagle,"* Feb. 19, 1902. Funeral Services

at the Club House of the Brooklyn Lodge, No. 22, B. P. O. Elks for Wm. H. West. Elk services were first then masonic services by New York Lodge No. 330, F. A. & M., (CMTS) Made a floral gift.

Wilson, H. C.: (F) Member Long Island Lodge, No. 382, F. &. A. M., 1874, NY

Wilson, John: (F) Member Long Island Lodge, No. 382, F. &. A. M., 1874, NY

Wilson, Mathew F.: (F) Member Friendly Sons of St. Patrick,1893, Brooklyn, (CMTS)*"Brooklyn Eagle,"* May 18,1893, Article regarding the election of Andrew T. Sullivan as postmaster. In the article it mentioned that there were only 50 members in this Society., Guest. It is unknown if a member of the Society.

Wilson, Mr.: (F) Member St. Nicholas Society of Nassau Island, 1861, (CMTS)"Brooklyn Eag;e," Dec. 11, 1861, Article regarding the Anniversary Dinner, Sang "All's Well," in duet

Wilson, Mrs. George: (I) *"Brooklyn Eagle,"* Feb. 19, 1902. Funeral Services at the Club House of the Brooklyn Lodge, No. 22, B. P. O. Elks for Wm. H. West. Elk services were first then masonic services by New York Lodge No. 330, F. A. & M., (CMTS) Made a floral gift.

Wilson, Mrs. J.: (F) Member Nativity Sewing Society, 1900, Brooklyn, (I) *"Brooklyn Eagle,"* Feb. 3, 1900. Article regarding raising money to buy clothing for the poor.

Wilson, Oren E.: (F) Member Temple Lodge, No. 14, 1900, Albany, NY

Wilson, S. H.: (F) Member Long Island Lodge, No. 382, F. &. A. M., 1874, NY

Wilson, W. W.: (F) Member Murray Lodge, No. 380, F. & A. M., 1906, Holley, Orleans, Co., NY

Wilton, Alf. T.: (F) Member Society of American Magicians, Apr., 1931, New York, (RES) New York City

Wiltse, James W.: (F) Member Temple Lodge, No. 14, 1900, Albany, NY

Wing, Chas. S.: (F) Member Murray Lodge, No. 380, F. & A. M., 1906, Holley, Orleans, Co., NY

Wingate, General George: (F) Member Sons of New England , New England Society of the City of Brooklyn, 1890, CMTS)*"Brooklyn Eagle,"* Dec. 21, 1890, 11th Annual Dinner, Attendees

Winhold, Louis C.: (F) Member Temple Lodge, No. 14, 1900, Albany, NY

Winne, Charles: (F) Member Temple Lodge, No. 14, 1900, Albany, NY

Winne, Charles H.: (F) Member Temple Lodge, No. 14, 1900, Albany, NY

Winne, Charles V.: (F) Member Temple Lodge, No. 14, 1900, Albany, NY

WInne, John: (F) Member Temple Lodge, No. 14, 1900, Albany, NY

Winne, Lansing B..: (F) Member Temple Lodge, No. 14, 1900, Albany, NY

Winne, Walter M.: (F) Member Temple Lodge, No. 14, 1900,
Albany, NY
Winslow, E.: (F) Member Sons of New England, New England
Society of the City of Brooklyn, 1890, (CMTS) *"Brooklyn Eagle,"*
Dec. 21, 1890, 11th Annual Dinner, Attendees
Winslow, J.: (F) Member Long Island Lodge, No. 382, F. &. A. M.,
1874, NY
Winslow, John: (F) Member Sons of New England, New England
Society of the City of Brooklyn, 1887, (CMTS) *"Brooklyn Eagle,"*
Dec. 22, 1887, Annual Dinner, Attendees, President
Winslow, John : (F) Member Sons of New England, New England
Society of the City of Brooklyn, 1890, (CMTS) *"Brooklyn Eagle,"*
Dec. 21, 1890, 11th Annual Dinner, Attendees
Wise, G. Walter: (F) Member Lowville Lodge No. 134, F. & A. M., 1929,
Lowville, NY, (CO) Lewis, (JD) Nov. 28, 1911
Wise, John S.: (F) Member Sons of New England, New England
Society of the City of Brooklyn, 1890, (CMTS) *"Brooklyn Eagle,"*
Dec. 21, 1890, 11th Annual Dinner, Attendees, Ex Congressman
Wiske, C. Mortimer: (F) Member Brooklyn Choral Society, 1889,
(CMTS) *"Brooklyn Eagle,"* Oct. 2, 1889, (CMTS) Musical
Director
Wisner, Henry P.: (F) Member Lowville Lodge No. 134, F. & A. M.,
1929, Lowville, NY, (CO) Lewis, (JD) Dec. 18, 1885
Wisner, Henry P.: (F) Member Lowville Chapter No. 223, R. A. M., 1929,
Lowville, NY, (CO) Lewis, (JD) Mar. 6, 1888
Wittich, H.: (F) Member Herber Lodge, No. 698, 1898, F. & A. M., New
York, NY, Greenpoint area, (RES) New York City
Woddhall, David M.: (F) Member Ineffable and Sublime Grand Lodge of
Perfection, 1882, Albany, NY
Wolcott, George : (F) Member Sons of New England, New England
Society of the City of Brooklyn, 1890, (CMTS) *"Brooklyn Eagle,"*
Dec. 21, 1890, 11th Annual Dinner, Attendees
Wolf, Frank: (F) Member Society of American Magicians,
Apr., 1931, New York, (RES) New York City
Wolf, H.: (F) Member Long Island Lodge, No. 382, F. &. A. M.,
1874, NY
Wolferman, Horace D.: (F) Member Society of American Magicians,
Apr., 1931, New York, (RES) New York City
Wolfgang, F. A.: (F) Member Mount Vernon Lodge, No. 3, 1900,
Albany, NY
Woltz, Frederick : (F) Member Friendly Sons of St. Patrick, 1893,
Brooklyn, (CMTS) *"Brooklyn Eagle,"* May 18, 1893,
Article regarding the election of Andrew T. Sullivan as postmaster.
In the article it mentioned that there were only 50 members in this
Society., Guest. It is unknown if a member of the Society.
Wolz, V.: (F) Member Herber Lodge, No. 698, 1898, F. & A. M., New

York, NY, Greenpoint area, (RES) New York City
Wood, A. J.: (F) Member Mount Vernon Lodge, No. 3, 1900, Albany, NY
Wood, E. N.: (F) Member Long Island Lodge, No. 382, F. &. A. M., 1874, NY
Wood, John B.: (F) Member Mount Vernon Lodge, No. 3, 1900, Albany, NY
Wood, Levi: (F) Member Temple Lodge, No. 14, 1900, Albany, NY
Wood, Miss Mildred: (F) Member First Suffolk District, Stirling Chapter, No. 216, 1923, Greenport, NY, (CMTS) Associate Matron, (RES) Greenport
Woodford, General Stewart L.: (F) Member Sons of New England, New England Society of the City of Brooklyn, 1890, (CMTS) *"Brooklyn Eagle,"* Dec. 21, 1890, 11th Annual Dinner, Attendees
Woodford, Stewart J.: (F) Member Sons of New England, New England Society of the City of Brooklyn, 1887, (CMTS) *"Brooklyn Eagle,"* Dec. 22, 1887, Annual Dinner, Attendees
Woodhall, David M.: (F) Member Grand Council of the Princes of Jerusalem, 1882, Albany, NY
Woodruff, A. C.: (F) Member Sons of New England, New England Society of the City of Brooklyn, 1887, (CMTS) *"Brooklyn Eagle,"* Dec. 22, 1887, Annual Dinner, Attendees
Woodruff, Halsey: (F) Member Temple Lodge, No. 14, 1900, Albany, NY
Woodruff, T. L.: (F) Member Sons of New England, New England Society of the City of Brooklyn, 1890, (CMTS) *"Brooklyn Eagle,"* Dec. 21, 1890, 11th Annual Dinner, Attendees
Woods, Gerald K.: (F) Member Lowville Chapter No. 223, R. A. M., 1929, Lowville, NY, (CO) Lewis, (JD) May 10, 1927
Woods, S.: (F) Member Long Island Lodge, No. 382, F. &. A. M., 1874, NY
Woodward, Dr. C. A.: (F) Member Brooklyn Dental Society, 1877, Brooklyn, NY, (CMTS) *"Brooklyn Eagle,"* Dec. 15, 1877. Celebration of 10th Anniversary. Society established Dec. 14, 1867, (CMTS) Present from New York
Woodward, Edwin F.: (F) Member Lowville Lodge No. 134, F. & A. M., 1929, Lowville, NY, (CO) Lewis, (JD) Mar. 21, 1888
Woodward, Edwin F.: (F) Member Lowville Chapter No. 223, R. A. M., 1929, Lowville, NY, (CO) Lewis, (JD) Mar. 17m, 1891
Woodward, General J. B.: (F) Member Sons of New England, New England Society of the City of Brooklyn, 1890, (CMTS) *"Brooklyn Eagle,"* Dec. 21, 1890, 11th Annual Dinner, Attendees
Woodward, James O.: (F) Member Masters Lodge, No. 5, 1900, Albany, NY
Woodward, John: (F) Member Grand Council of the Princes of Jerusalem, 1882, Albany, NY

Woodward, John: (F) Member Ineffable and Sublime Grand Lodge of Perfection, 1882, Albany, NY
Woodward, John B.: (F) Member Sons of New England, New England Society of the City of Brooklyn, 1887, (CMTS)*"Brooklyn Eagle,"* Dec. 22, 1887, Annual Dinner, Attendees
Woodward, Walter M.: (F) Member Masters Lodge, No. 5, 1900, Albany, NY
Wooley, Jesse B.: (F) Member Mount Vernon Lodge, No. 3, 1900, Albany, NY
Woolschkager, Theodore P.: (F) Member Lowville Lodge No. 134, F. & A. M., 1929, Lowville, NY, (CO) Lewis, (JD) Jan. 21, 1921
Woolschlager, Fred H.: (F) Member Lowville Lodge No. 134, F. & A. M., 1929, Lowville, NY, (CO) Lewis, (JD) Jan. 21, 1921
Woolschlager, Fred W.: (F) Member Lowville Chapter No. 223, R. A. M., 1929, Lowville, NY, (CO) Lewis, (JD) Apr. 10, 1923
Woolschlager, John F.: (F) Member Lowville Chapter No. 223, R. A. M., 1929, Lowville, NY, (CO) Lewis, (JD) Dec. 29, 1914
Woolschlager, Jr., Jacob W.: (F) Member Lowville Lodge No. 134, F. & A. M., 1929, Lowville, NY, (CO) Lewis, (JD) Dec. 15, 1811
Wooseter, Benj. W.: (F) Member Ineffable and Sublime Grand Lodge of Perfection, 1882, Albany, NY
Wooster, Benjamin W.: (F) Member Grand Council of the Princes of Jerusalem, 1882, Albany, NY
Wooster, Samuel C.: (F) Member Temple Lodge, No. 14, 1900, Albany, NY
Worcester, Edwin D.: (F) Member Grand Council of the Princes of Jerusalem, 1882, Albany, NY
Worchester, Edwin D.: (F) Member Ineffable and Sublime Grand Lodge of Perfection, 1882, Albany, NY
Worchester, Edwin D.: (F) Member Masters Lodge, No. 5, 1900, Albany, NY
Wormwood, Almon F.: (F) Member Lowville Lodge No. 134, F. & A. M., 1929, Lowville, NY, (CO) Lewis, (JD) Apr. 12, 1889, (B) Dec. 21, 1860, (BP) Watson, Lewis Co., NY, (D) 1942, (PRTS) John Wormwood and Salina Wakefield
Wrege, F.: (F) Member Herber Lodge, No. 698,1898, F. & A. M., New York, NY, Greenpoint area, (RES) Jersey City
Wright, Alfred W.: (F) Member Temple Lodge, No. 14, 1900, Albany, NY
Wright, Chester: (F) Member Denmark Ecclesiastical Society, Sep. 21, 1810, (CO) Lewis, (CMTS) Trustee, (B) Nov. 10, 1789, (D) Jun. 25, 1835, (PRTS) Lucis F. Wright
Wright, Frank L.: (F) Member Temple Lodge, No. 14, 1900, Albany, NY
Wright, Freedom: (F) Member Denmark Ecclesiastical Society, Sep. 21, 1810, (CO) Lewis, (CMTS) Trustee
Wright, Mrs. F. H.: (F) Member Ladies' Relief Society, 1888, Brooklyn,

(I) *"Brooklyn Eagle,"* Dec. 12, 1888. Article regarding Societies aiding churches., (CMTS) Helping All Souls Universalist Church, President

Wright, Jr., Charles: (F) Member Harrisburgh Ecclesiastical Society, Jul. 9, 1805, (CO) Lewis

Yadah, Joseph W.: (F) Member Society of American Magicians, Apr., 1931, New York, (RES) Brooklyn, NY

Yale, Barnabas: (F) Member Lewis County Bible Society, 1812, Charter Officers, (CMTS) Secretary

Yale, Walter D.: (F) Member Society for the Acquistion of Useful Knowledge, Apr. 26, 1843, (CO) Lewis , (B) Jan. 16, 1826, (PRTS) Paul Yale and A. Dewey

Yandeau, George A.: (F) Member Lowville Lodge No. 134, F. & A. M., 1929, Lowville, NY, (CO) Lewis, (JD) Apr. 4, 1924

York, Milton W.: (F) Member Lowville Lodge No. 134, F. & A. M., 1929, Lowville, NY, (CO) Lewis

Yorke, Joseph W.: (F) Member Mount Vernon Lodge, No. 3, 1900, Albany, NY

Young, Carl D.: (F) Member Murray Lodge, No. 380, F. & A. M., 1906, Holley, Orleans, Co., NY

Young, Gladys: (F) Member Hope Rebekah Lodge No. 10, 1949-1950, Brockport, NY, (CO) Monroe, (CMTS) Flag Bearer

Young, Harlow C.: (F) Member Lowville Lodge No. 134, F. & A. M., 1929, Lowville, NY, (CO) Lewis, (JD) Jul. 5, 1918

Young, Harlow C.: (F) Member Lowville Chapter No. 223, R. A. M., 1929, Lowville, NY, (CO) Lewis, (JD) Mar. 25, 1919

Young, Hays: (F) Member Temple Lodge, No. 14, 1900, Albany, NY

Young, James: (F) Member Temple Lodge, No. 14, 1900, Albany, NY, (CMTS) Past Master 1870

Young, John H.: (F) Member Temple Lodge, No. 14, 1900, Albany, NY

Young, Mrs. Dewey: (F) Member Hope Rebekah Lodge No. 10, 1949-1950, Brockport, NY, (CO) Monroe

Young, Philip B.: (F) Member Temple Lodge, No. 14, 1900, Albany, NY

Young, Robert: (F) Member Mount Vernon Lodge, No. 3, 1900, Albany, NY

Yousey, Jule S.: (F) Member Lowville Lodge No. 134, F. & A. M., 1929, Lowville, NY, (CO) Lewis, (JD) Jun. 11, 1926

Yousey, Reuben C.: (F) Member Lowville Lodge No. 134, F. & A. M., 1929, Lowville, NY, (CO) Lewis, (JD) Feb. 17, 1922

Zahn, George W.: (F) Member Lowville Lodge No. 134, F. & A. M., 1929, Lowville, NY, (CO) Lewis, (JD) May 14, 1928

Zaiss, Miss Tessie: (F) Member Mispah Circle, 1888, Brooklyn, (I) *"Brooklyn Eagle,"* Dec. 12, 1888. Mentioned in an article about a fair raising funds for a Home for the Blind

Zaiss, Mr.: (F) Member Mispah Circle, 1888, Brooklyn, (I) *"Brooklyn Eagle,"* Dec. 12, 1888. Mentioned in an article about a fair raising funds for a Home for the Blind

Zander, S. J.: (F) Member Knights of the Maccabees, Prospect Tent No. 209, 1900, Brooklyn, (I) *"Brooklyn Eagle,"* Feb. 3, 1900. Meeting Notice, (CMTS) Record Keeper

Zautner, George: (F) Member Mount Vernon Lodge, No. 3, 1900, Albany, NY

Zeh, Charles: (F) Member Temple Lodge, No. 14, 1900, Albany, NY

Zehr, Elmer A.: (F) Member Lowville Lodge No. 134, F. & A. M., 1929, Lowville, NY, (CO) Lewis, (JD) Apr. 2, 1926

Zimmer, F.: (F) Member Herber Lodge, No. 698,1898, F. & A. M., New York, NY, Greenpoint area, (RES) Brooklyn

Zingone, Louis G.: (F) Member Society of American Magicians, Apr., 1931, New York, (RES) East Elmhurst, Long Island, NY

Zinke, H.: (F) Member Herber Lodge, No. 698,1898, F. & A. M., New York, NY, Greenpoint area, (RES) New York City

Zipp, John: (I) *"Brooklyn Eagle,"* Dec. 7, 1896. 12th Annual Memorial Services, Plymouth Church, Brooklyn Lodge No. 22, B. F. O. Elks, Roll Call of the dead. Address made by Maryland Senator George L. Wellington. , (CMTS) Name called.

Zorn, F.: (F) Member Herber Lodge, No. 698,1898, F. & A. M., New York, NY, Greenpoint area, (RES) New York City

# INDEX

ADAMS, 28 Flora 9
ALLEN, Mrs Charles E 91
AMADIO, Laura 2 Louis 2
ARGENS, Wm R 2
ARMSTEAD, Mervin 6
ARMSTRONG, E B 3
ARTHUR, Kate 32
AUDELSON, Sarah 6
AUSTIN, Fannie 28
AVERY, Jerusha Lydia 54
BABB, Elizabeth Betty 11
BABCOCK, Carmen 32 Cecil 32 Martha 32
BARKER, Mary 31
BARRETT, Electa 16
BENTO, Vienna 28
BERRUS, Emily 35
BERRY, D W 28 Mary S 28
BIRCH, John G 34
BISHOPP, Edwin 21
BLISS, Rosina 57 William 23 William C 23
BLOCK, Sara 86
BOLDEN, Annie 6
BOOTH, Hannah 56
BRADLEY, Mary Agnes 115
BRANDT, Robert R 105
BROCKMAN, Fannie 6
BROSH, John 31
BROWN, Delaphina 35 Sarah Jane 130
BUCK, Linda 138
BUDINGTON, Dr 185
BURKLEY, David 1 Ella 1
BURLEY, Ella 1
BURTON, Mary Ann 185
CALLAHAN, Elaine 76
CANTINI, Edward Byron 39
CARATHANASIS, Audrey 11
CAREY, Jacqueline 44 William 44
CARLSON, R 13
CARTER, Oliver 9
CHAPIN, Joseph 23 Levi 23 Phebe 23 Phobe 23
CHILD, Lurainda 131
CLARK, Geo 10

CLEMENTS, 27
COBB, Elizabeth H 35
COLE Anna 54
COLLINS, Amanda 57 Glen 11 Jennifer 57 John 11 Katherine Rettig 11 Kathryn 57 Shawn 57
COMBS, Wilbur M 27
COOK, George C 185 Marion Josina 39
CORD, A E 75
COVERT, Cornelia 7 Thomas 7
DARING, Sarah 54
DAVENPORT, Charles C 204 Eliza S 204
DAVIDSON, Mary 6
DAVIES, William H 4
DAVIS, Eliza 94 Ella 71 George T 87 John Keyes 94 Justus D 94 Lorelei 44 Morris A 71 Sophia L 94 Steven 44
DAYAN, S C 159
DEFREITAS, Anthony 2 D Nick 2 Frances 2 Joseph 2
DELAHANTY, Louise 11
DELANO, Calista 1
DEMING, Bathsheba 26
DENSE, John 58
DEWANDERLEAR, Margaret 58
DEWEY, A 230 Fanny 163
DOIG, Betsey 11
DOLE, Betty 138
DOUGLAS, Mrs John 75
DOWNING, Isaac 22
DRAKE, Augusta 106
DWYER, Cathe 77
EARLE, Harriet A 163 Thomas 163
EGAR, Rev Dr 4
EPSTEIN, Bella 78
EVANS, Margaret Ann 73
FELT, Elizabeth 23
FISH, Edward 28 Mary Emma 28 Rebecca M 16
FLINT, Emogene 17
FONDAY, Isaac 72
FOOT, Ellis C 73
FOWLER, Julia 131

FRANCIS, Sally Ann 75
GADIS, Margaret 1
GAGLIARDI, Florence 2 Jerry 2
GANTZ, Charles A 78
GARDNER, Mary E 76
GARLICK, 4
GATES, Dr 75
GIBBS, 101
GILBERT, Jody 76
GIROUX, June 114
GLADSTONE, Mrs John O 75
GOETZ, Clara 78 79
GOODRICH, Dr 75
GRAVES, Jerome 4
GRAY, 23 Abgail 131 Clarinda J 115
   Elijah 115
GREENWOOD, Sophronia 31
GROUNDS, Mary 51
GROVES, John 4
HAMMOND, Jerusha 77
HARDING, Andrew 4 Jasmine 4
   Raima 4 Robin 4 Sonja 4
HARRIS, 139
HEATH, Giles 159 Mrs Giles 159
HEGENAUER, Anna Wissman 114
   Charles 114 Shirley 114
HEIMHILGER, Hannah 14
HELLMAN, 4
HENNESSEY, Ellen 11
HOFFMAN, Theo Lynne 139
HOLCOMB, Albert 90 Anna M 91
   Charles A 91 Grace F 91 Hamilton
   Renwick 90
HOOKS, Terry 6
HOTALING, Agness 47
IRELAND, Lillian 25
JACKSON, Cheryl 6 Henry 32 Jane
   71 Jennie 70
JONES, Kate 60 Mattie 32
JOSLIN, Amos 109 110 Caroline 109
   David 109 Francis 109 Frank 109
KAUFMAN, Mary 4
KERN, Viola 44
KERR, Harold 32
KIDDER, Lidya 115
KINNE, Bessie 138
KNOX, Maria Augusta 60
KUHN, Meg 57 Stephanie 57 Ted 57
   Teddy 57

LAPPEN, Alfred 32 Mrs T B 32
LIVINGSTON, Philip H 100
LOOMIS, Ada 66
LOTHROP, Deborah 115
LOUCKS, Edith C 67
LUITWIELER, Mrs C S Jr 91
MAHLER, Julia 135
MAIN, Phildelia 17
MANN, Bernice 138
MANNING, Lizzie 1 Rockwell
   Edward 1
MASON, Annie 16
MAURER, Rose C 14
MCCOY, Annie 6
MCCULLACH, Peter 23
MCEVOY, Dorothy 11
MCGRATH, Bridget 78
MCMILLAN, Lizzie 1
MCMORAN, Minnie 68
MERCHANT, Harriet 34
MESSITER, 27
MILLER, Mary 130 Matilda 68 Nancy
   163 Susan 163
MILLINGTON, S 4
MILLS, Amelia 68
MILLSBAUGH, Samuel W 28
MITCHELL, Julia 60
MITTERWAGER, Beverly 76 Jason
   76 Kenneth 76 Morgan 76
MOORE, Anthony 23 Frances Louise
   21 Mrs W D 159
MORSE, Jerome E 44 74 77 108 167
MURPHY, 76
ORMISTON, Dr 75
PELTON, 60
PFLANTZ, Anna H 86
PHALON, Mollie 58
PLUMB, Eleazer 68 Emma Maria 67
   68
PONTO, Sarah 11
POOLE, Harriet 58
POTTER, Amanda 131
POWELL, Jackie 6
PUTNAM, Gertrude Anna 35
QUAKENBUSH, Jane 25
RASMUSSEN, 23
RAYMOND, Sarah 115
REITSCH, Louis 7
RICE, Helen 129

RICHARDSON, Sarah 23
SCELLER, Mary 139
SCHUMANN, Dr 75
SCOTT, Martha J 21
SEARLE, Catherine 9
SEARS, Margaret Cameron 38
SEVERSON, Melissa 100 Nicholas 100
SEYMOUR, Eri 3 Mary 23
SHAUGHNESSEY, Alice 2
SHAW, Susannah 132
SHOEMAKER, Emma 73
SIFFERT, Andrew 38 Sean 38
SILVER, Elizabeth 6
SLATER, Louisa 9
SMITH, Calista 1 Elijah 1 Elmira 1 Margaret Gertrude 96 Virginia 6
SNYDER, Mrs William H 91
SOULE, Malinda 218
SOULES, Mildred 138
SPERRY, Theodosia 32
SPITZER, Frank 25
STACKHOUSE, Jack 77
STAR, Ella 9
STEPHENS, Charles 35 Sarah M 35
STEWART, 76 Jay 32 Polly 149
STILLMAN, Mary L 35
STILLWELL, Dewitt 159 Mrs Dewitt 159
STORMS, Rupert 32
STURGIS, Edna 32
SULLIVAN, Andrew T 25 30 36 38 42 46 49 51-53 60 61 63 65 68 70-72 74 77 78 88 89 95 97 103 104 108 113 116 129 132 134 135 141-144 153-159 162 165 170-173 178 181 183 190 191 196 197 199 202-204 206 208 211 217 225-227
TAYLOR, Eliza M 67 68 Elizabeth 54 Elizabeth Mae 68

THOMPSON, Elizabeth 78
TIFFANY, Maud 129
TITCOMB, Elizabeth 1
TOMKINS, Ann 76
TRAVER, Ada J 220
TREAT, Abbie H 24
TROWBRIDGE, Laura 58
TRYAL, Sarah 43
UNDERHILL, Elizabeth 132
VANDE MARK, Miriam Fulton 38
VANE, Frank 4
VANSICLEN, Peg 76
VIRRILL, Gloria 2
WAKEFIELD, Salina 229
WARRINER, Eleanor 51
WELLER, Alice M 9
WELLES, Charit 43
WELLINGTON, George L 15 18 32 39 69 81 115 122 133 143 144 146 150 152 154 156 172 173 175 176 178 184 186 190 193 194 196 212 216 221 231
WEST, Wm H 28 48 53 56 59-63 70 92 95 113 136 139 143 158 161 162 166 169 175 178-181 208 209 219 220 224-226
WHIPPLE, Cyrus C 16 Ellen M 16
WHITE, Abigail 42
WIDEMAN, Julie 149
WILCOX, Alma Edith 67
WILLARD, Sara Jane 106
WILLIAMS, Sophia 47 W W 4
WILLIARD, Anna 115
WILLS, Mary Ann 8
WINANS, Emily 41
WISSMAN, Anna 114
WOOD, Josiah 3
WOODHOUSE, Levi 32 Lillias S 32
ZEHR, Emma 68

Other Heritage Books by Sherida K. Eddlemon:

*Missouri Genealogical Records and Abstracts:*
  *Volume 1: 1766-1839*
  *Volume 2: 1752-1839*
  *Volume 3: 1787-1839*
  *Volume 4: 1741-1839*
  *Volume 5: 1755-1839*
  *Volume 6: 1621-1839*
  *Volume 7: 1535-1839*

*Missouri Genealogical Gleanings 1840 and Beyond, Volumes 1-9*

*1890 Genealogical Census Reconstruction: Mississippi, Volumes 1 and 2*

*1890 Genealogical Census Reconstruction: Missouri, Volumes 1-3*

*1890 Genealogical Census Reconstruction: Ohio, Volume 1*
(with Patricia P. Nelson)

*1890 Genealogical Census Reconstruction: Tennessee, Volume 1*

*A Genealogical Collection of Kentucky Birth and Death Records*

*Callaway County, Missouri, Marriage Records: 1821 to 1871*

*Cumberland Presbyterian Church, Volume One: 1836 and Beyond*

*Dickson County, Tennessee Marriage Records, 1817-1879*

*Genealogical Abstracts from Missouri Church Records and Other Religious Sources, Volume 1*

*Genealogical Abstracts from Tennessee Newspapers, 1791-1808*

*Genealogical Abstracts from Tennessee Newspapers, 1803-1812*

*Genealogical Abstracts from Tennessee Newspapers, 1821-1828*

*Tennessee Genealogical Records and Abstracts, Volume 1: 1787-1839*

*Genealogical Gleanings from New York Fraternal Organizations Volumes 1 and 2*

*Index to the Arkansas General Land Office, 1820-1907 Volumes 1-10*

*Kentucky Genealogical Records and Abstracts, Volume 1: 1781-1839*

*Kentucky Genealogical Records and Abstracts, Volume 2: 1796-1839*

*Lewis County, Missouri Index to Circuit Court Records, Volume 1, 1833-1841*

*Missouri Birth and Death Records, Volumes 1-4*

*Morgan County, Missouri Marriage Records, 1833-1893*

*Our Ancestors of Albany County, New York, Volumes 1 and 2*

*Our Ancestors of Cuyahoga County, Ohio, Volume 1*
(with Patricia P. Nelson)

*Ralls County, Missouri Settlement Records, 1832-1853*

*Records of Randolph County, Missouri, 1833-1964*

*Ten Thousand Missouri Taxpayers*

*7KH³ 6KRZ-0 H \* XIGH\R 0 IVRXU 6RXUHV\IRU
Genealogical and Historical Research*

CD: Dickson County, Tennessee Marriage Records, 1817-1879

CD: Index to the Arkansas General Land Office, 1820-1907 Volumes 1-10

CD: Missouri, Volume 3

CD: Tennessee Genealogical Records

CD: Tennessee Genealogical Records, Volumes 1-3

www.ingramcontent.com/pod-product-compliance
Lightning Source LLC
Chambersburg PA
CBHW070733160426
43192CB00009B/1420